FAIRY TAIL 100 YEARS QUEST

7

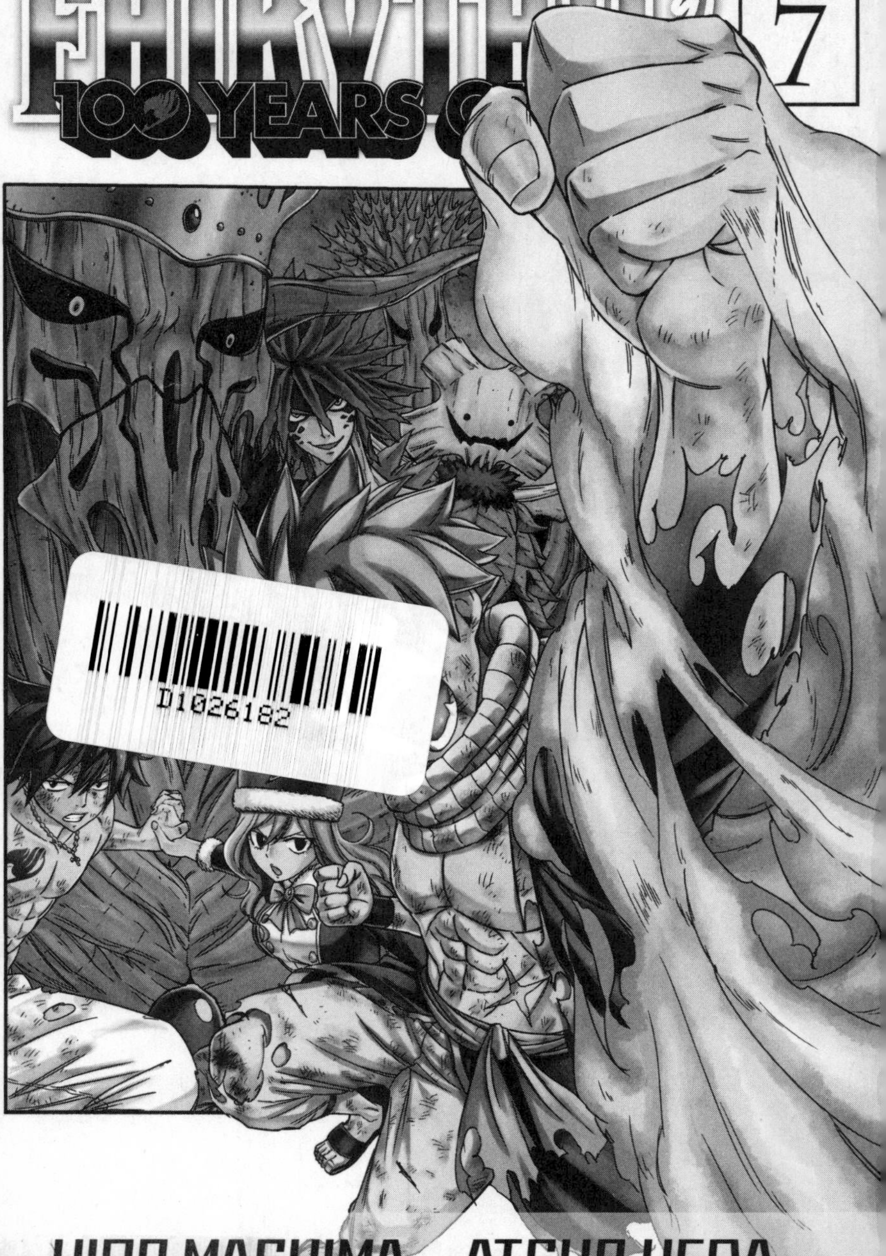

HIRO MASHIMA ATSUO UEDA

FAIRY TAIL 100 YEARS QUEST 7 CONTENTS

Chapter 55: A Destiny of Death

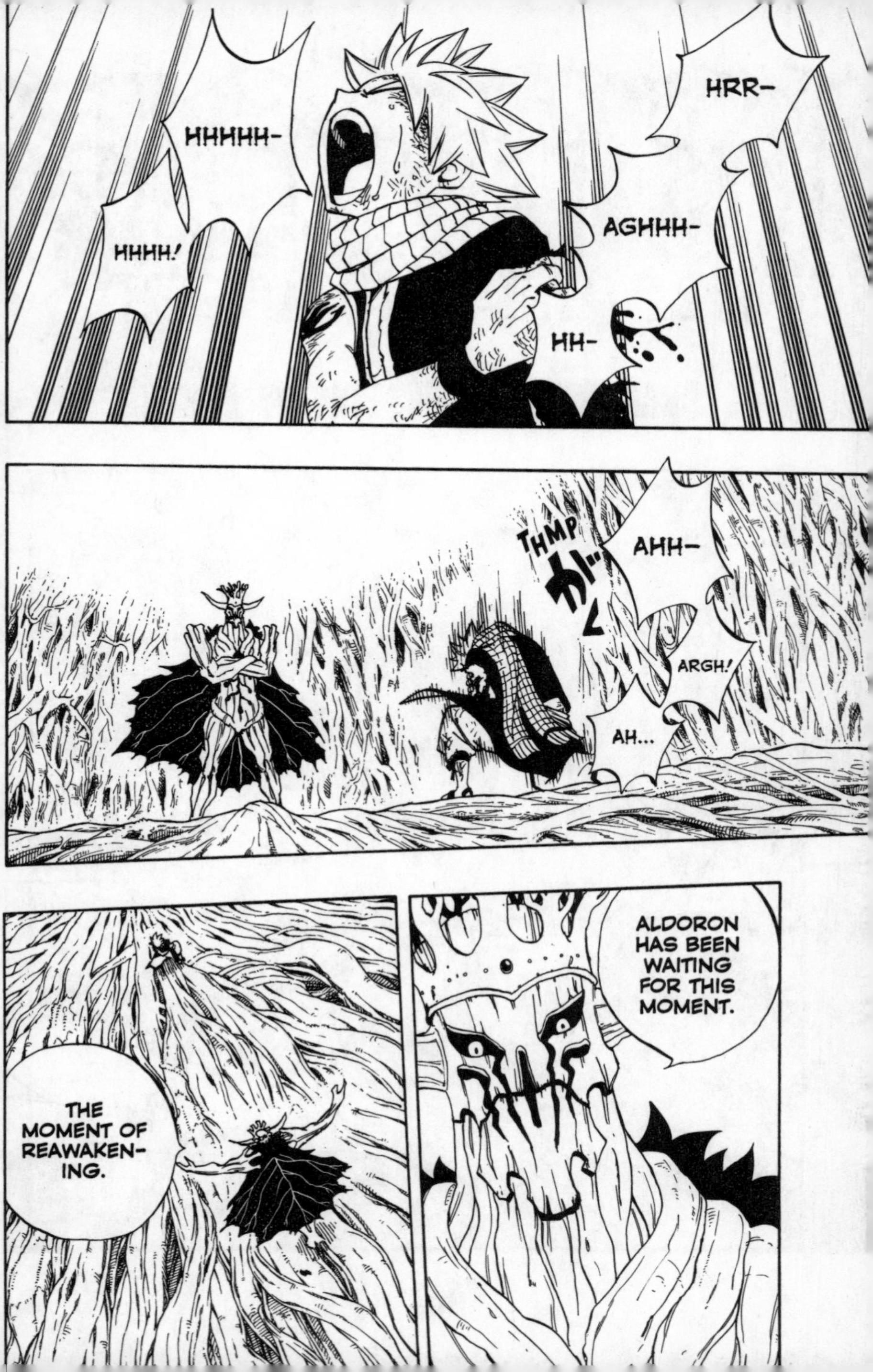
HRR-
HHHHH-
AGHHH-
HHHH!
HH-
THMP
AHH-
ARGH!
AH...
ALDORON HAS BEEN WAITING FOR THIS MOMENT.
THE MOMENT OF REAWAKEN-ING.

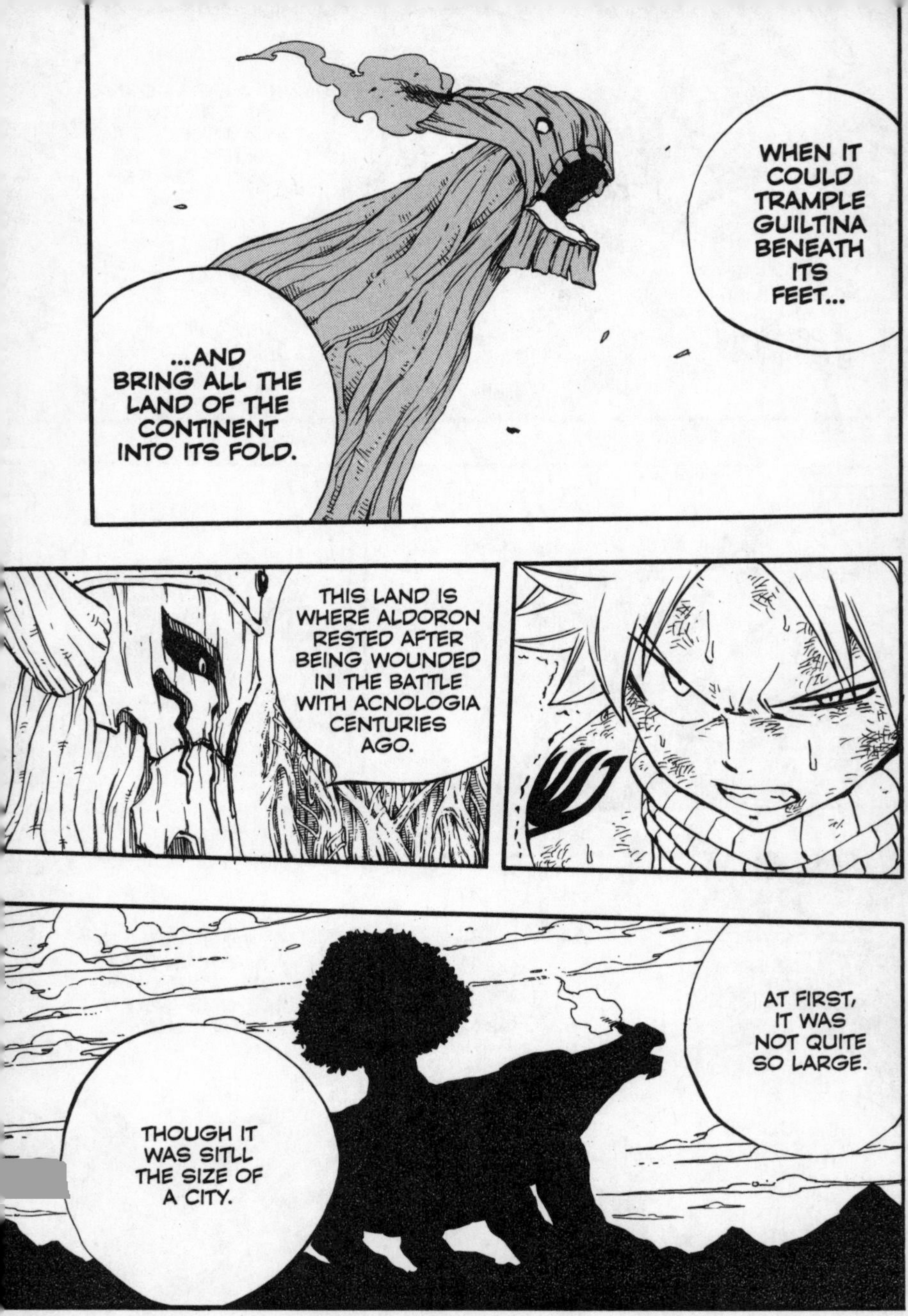
WHEN IT COULD TRAMPLE GUILTINA BENEATH ITS FEET...
...AND BRING ALL THE LAND OF THE CONTINENT INTO ITS FOLD.
THIS LAND IS WHERE ALDORON RESTED AFTER BEING WOUNDED IN THE BATTLE WITH ACNOLOGIA CENTURIES AGO.
AT FIRST, IT WAS NOT QUITE SO LARGE.
THOUGH IT WAS SITLL THE SIZE OF A CITY.

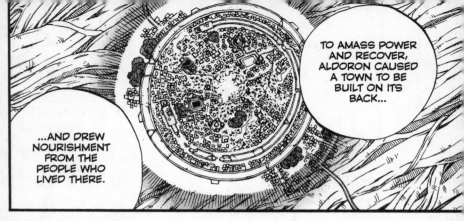

TO AMASS POWER AND RECOVER, ALDORON CAUSED A TOWN TO BE BUILT ON ITS BACK...

...AND DREW NOURISHMENT FROM THE PEOPLE WHO LIVED THERE.

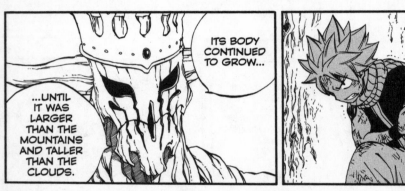

ITS BODY CONTINUED TO GROW...

...UNTIL IT WAS LARGER THAN THE MOUNTAINS AND TALLER THAN THE CLOUDS.

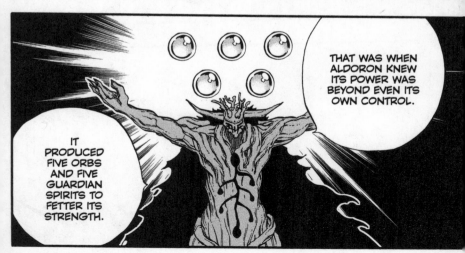

THAT WAS WHEN ALDORON KNEW ITS POWER WAS BEYOND EVEN ITS OWN CONTROL.

IT PRODUCED FIVE ORBS AND FIVE GUARDIAN SPIRITS TO FETTER ITS STRENGTH.

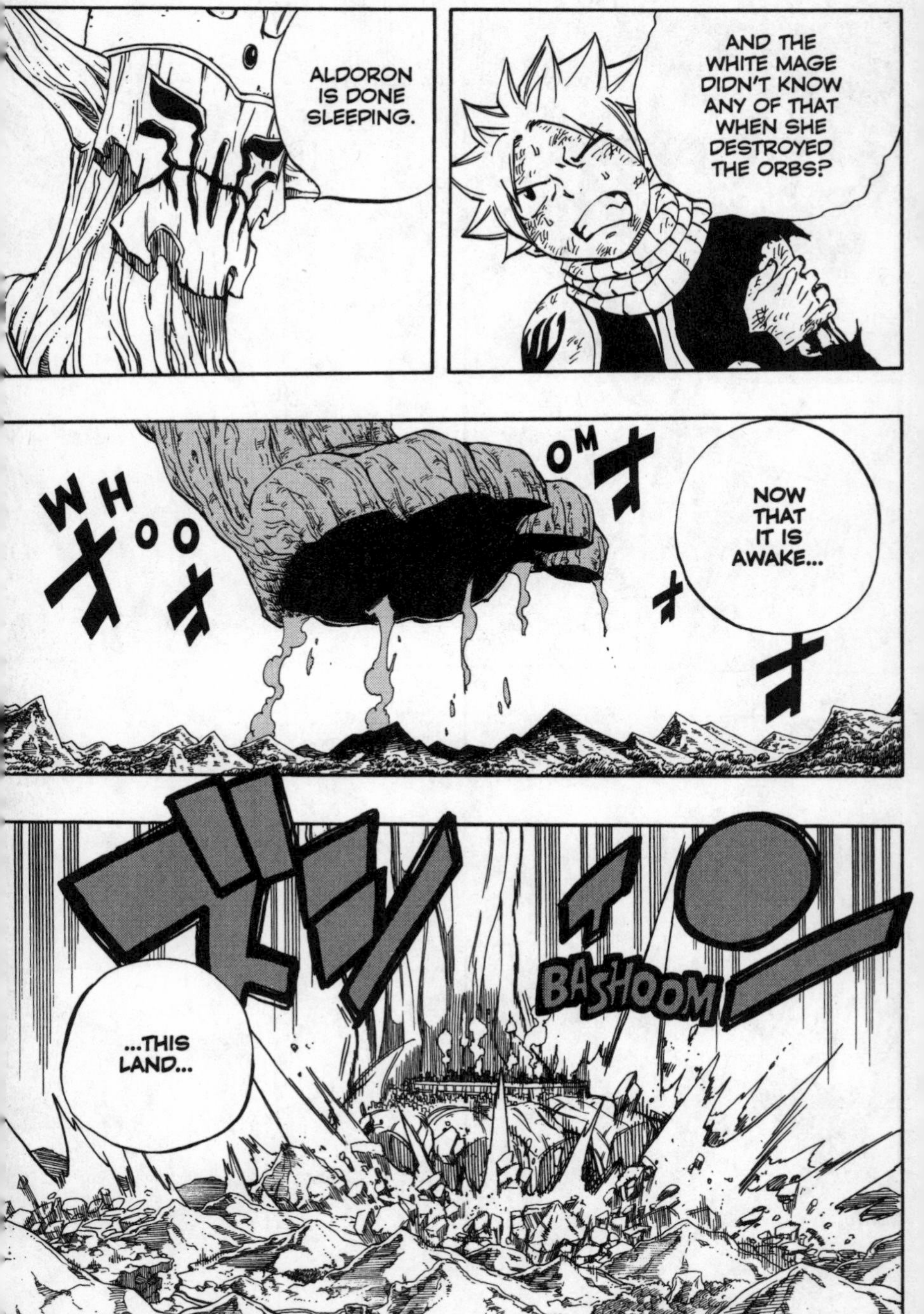
AND THE WHITE MAGE DIDN'T KNOW ANY OF THAT WHEN SHE DESTROYED THE ORBS?
ALDORON IS DONE SLEEPING.
NOW THAT IT IS AWAKE...
WHOOOM
BASHOOM
...THIS LAND...

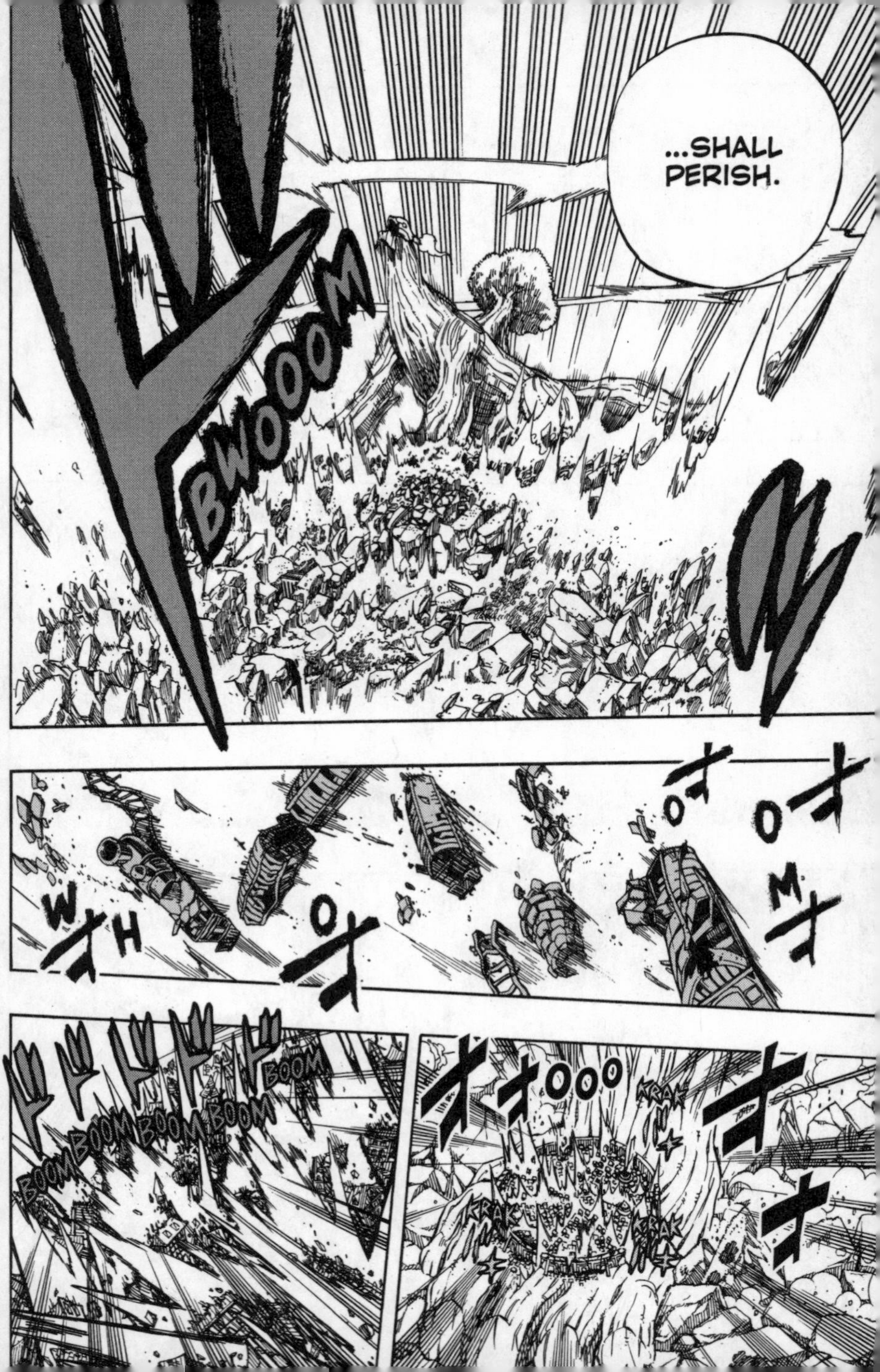
...SHALL PERISH.
BWOOOM
WHOOOM
OOO
KRAK
KRAK
KRAK
BOOM BOOM BOOM BOOM BOOM

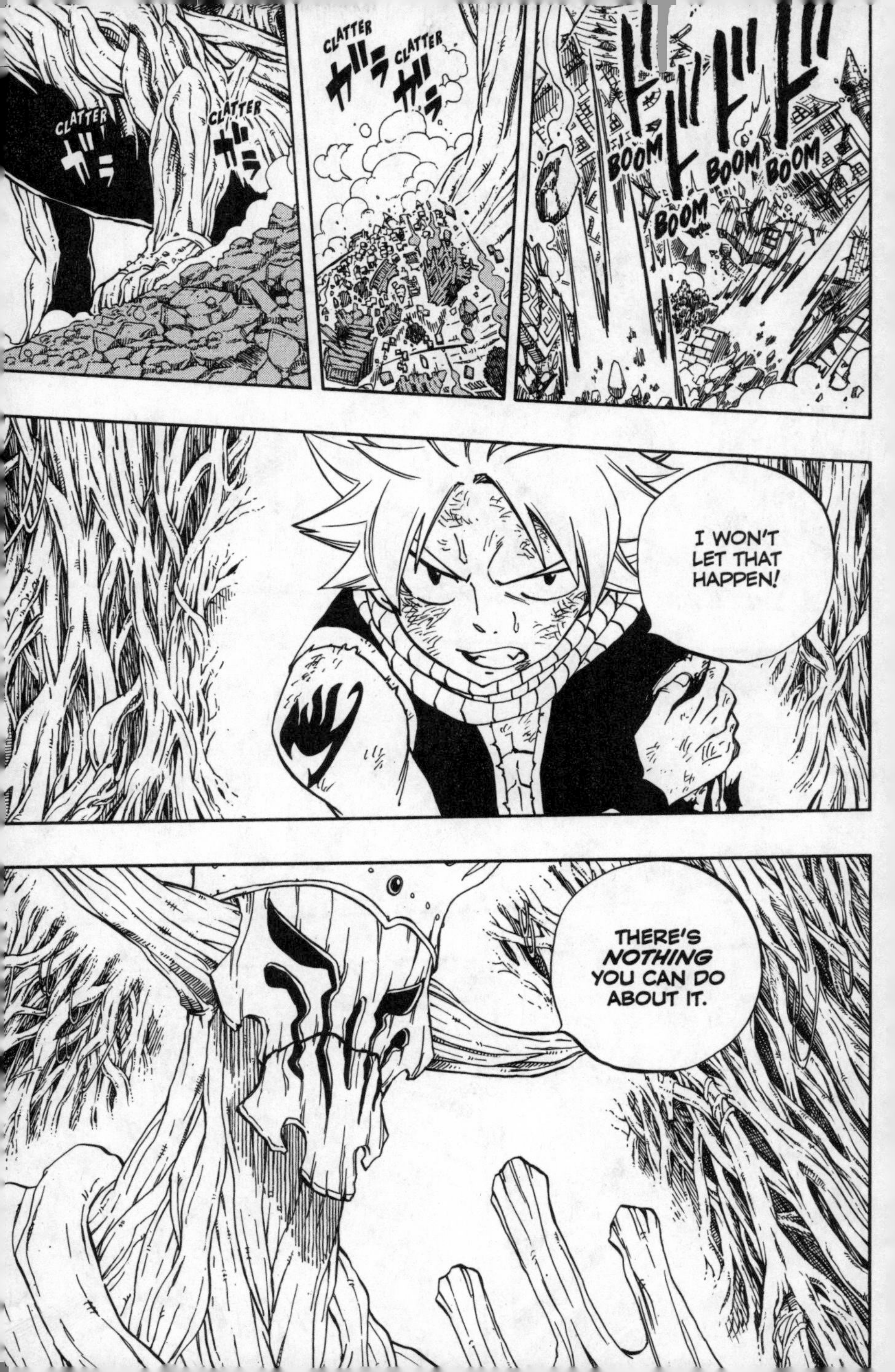
ドドドド
BOOM
BOOM
BOOM
BOOM
CLATTER ガラ
CLATTER ガラ
CLATTER ガラ
CLATTER ガラ
I WON'T LET THAT HAPPEN!
THERE'S *NOTHING* YOU CAN DO ABOUT IT.

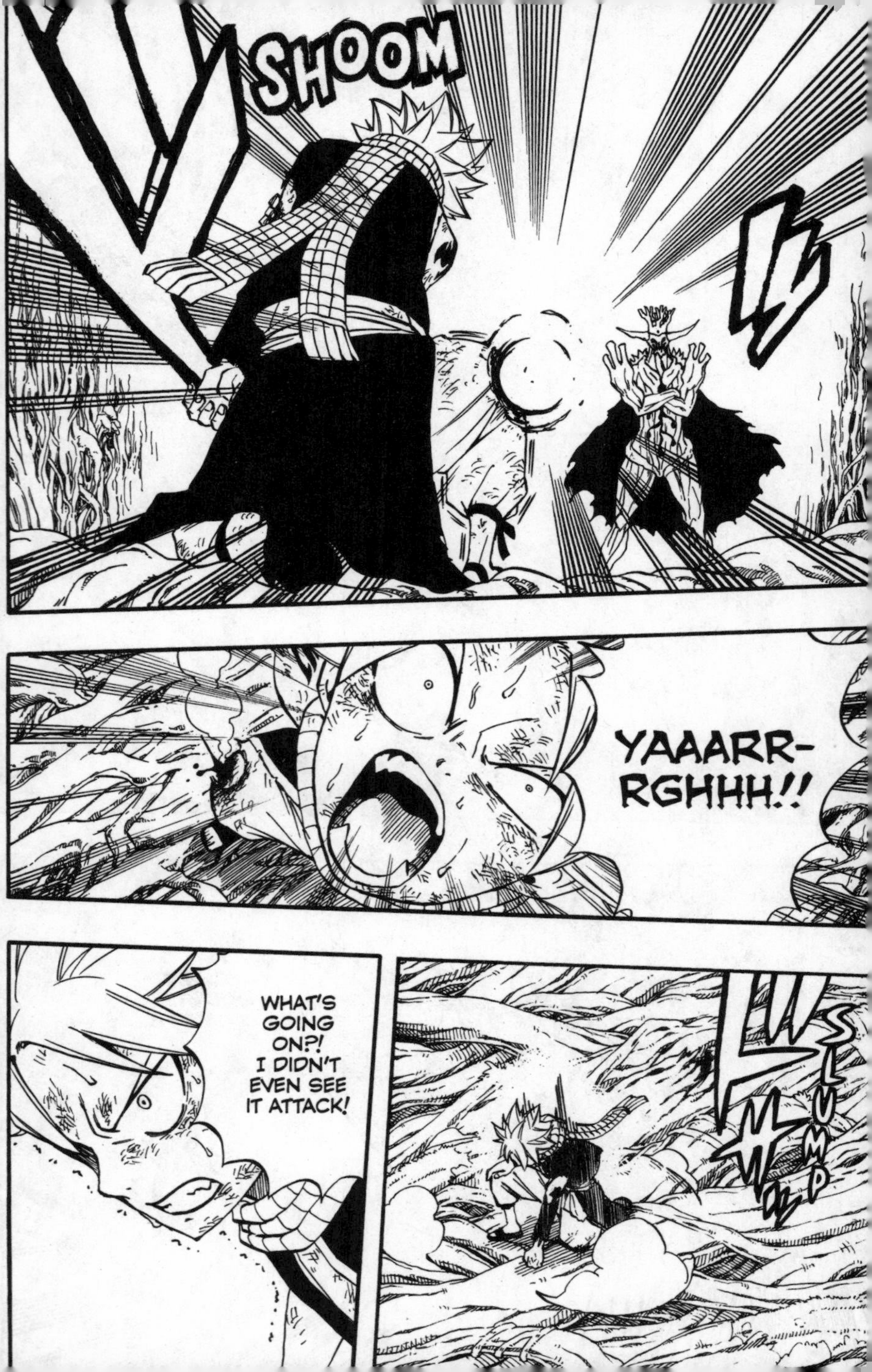
SHOOM
YAAARR-RGHHH!!
SLUMP
WHAT'S GOING ON?! I DIDN'T EVEN SEE IT ATTACK!

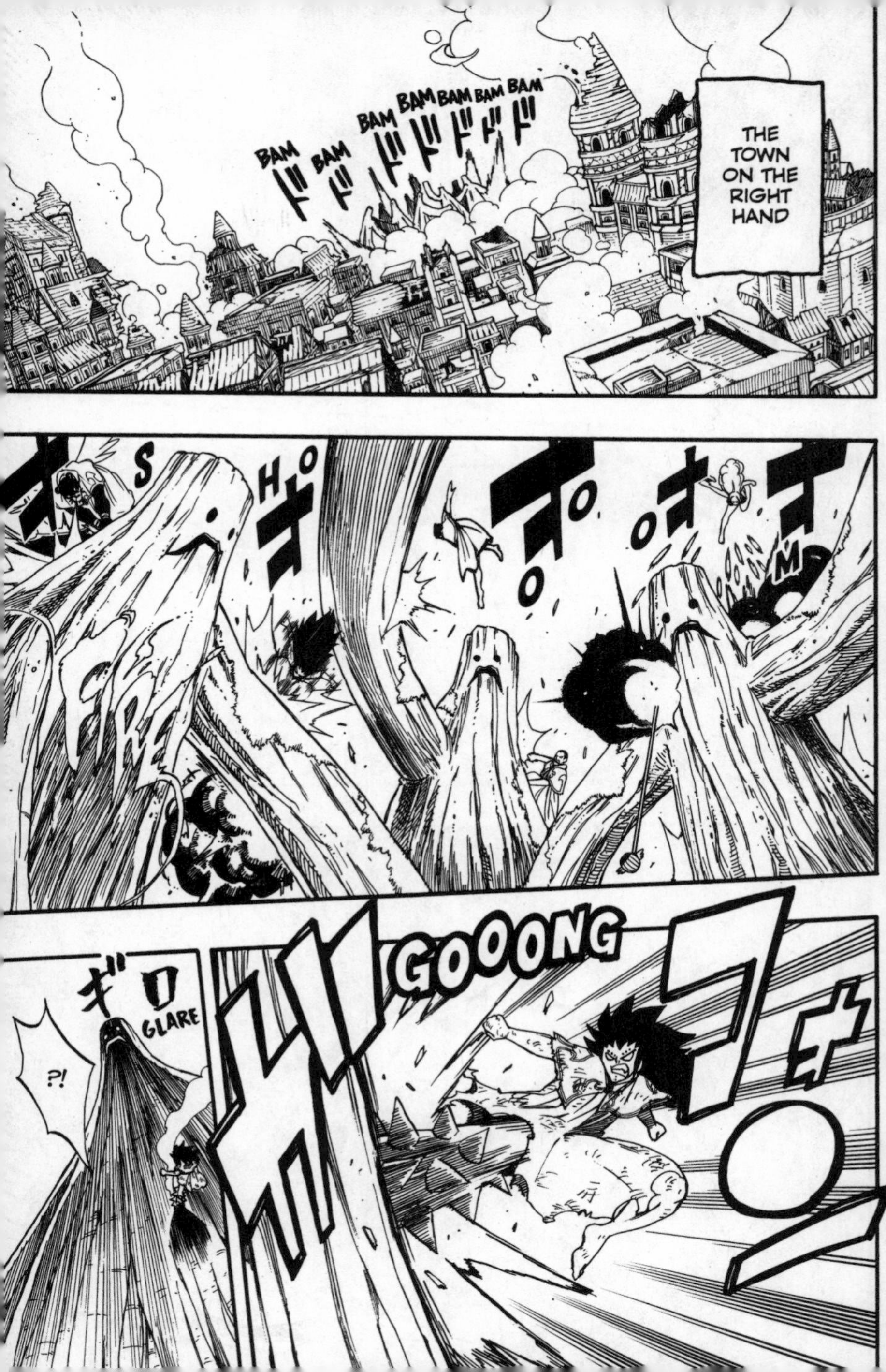

THE TOWN ON THE RIGHT HAND
BAM BAM BAM BAM BAM BAM BAM
GOOONG
GLARE
?!

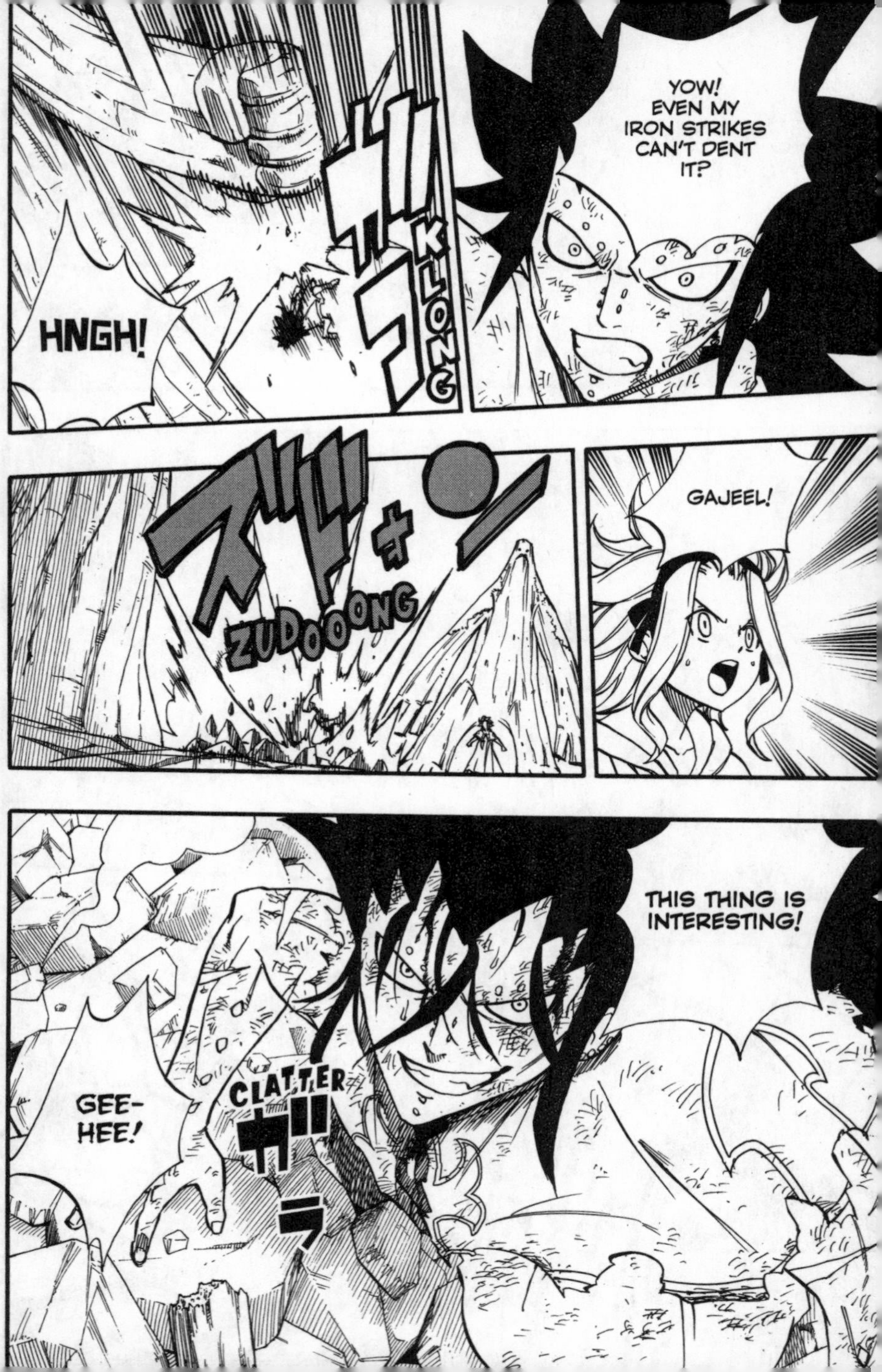
YOW! EVEN MY IRON STRIKES CAN'T DENT IT?
KLONG
HNGH!
GAJEEL!
ZUDOOONG
THIS THING IS INTERESTING!
CLATTER
GEE-HEE!

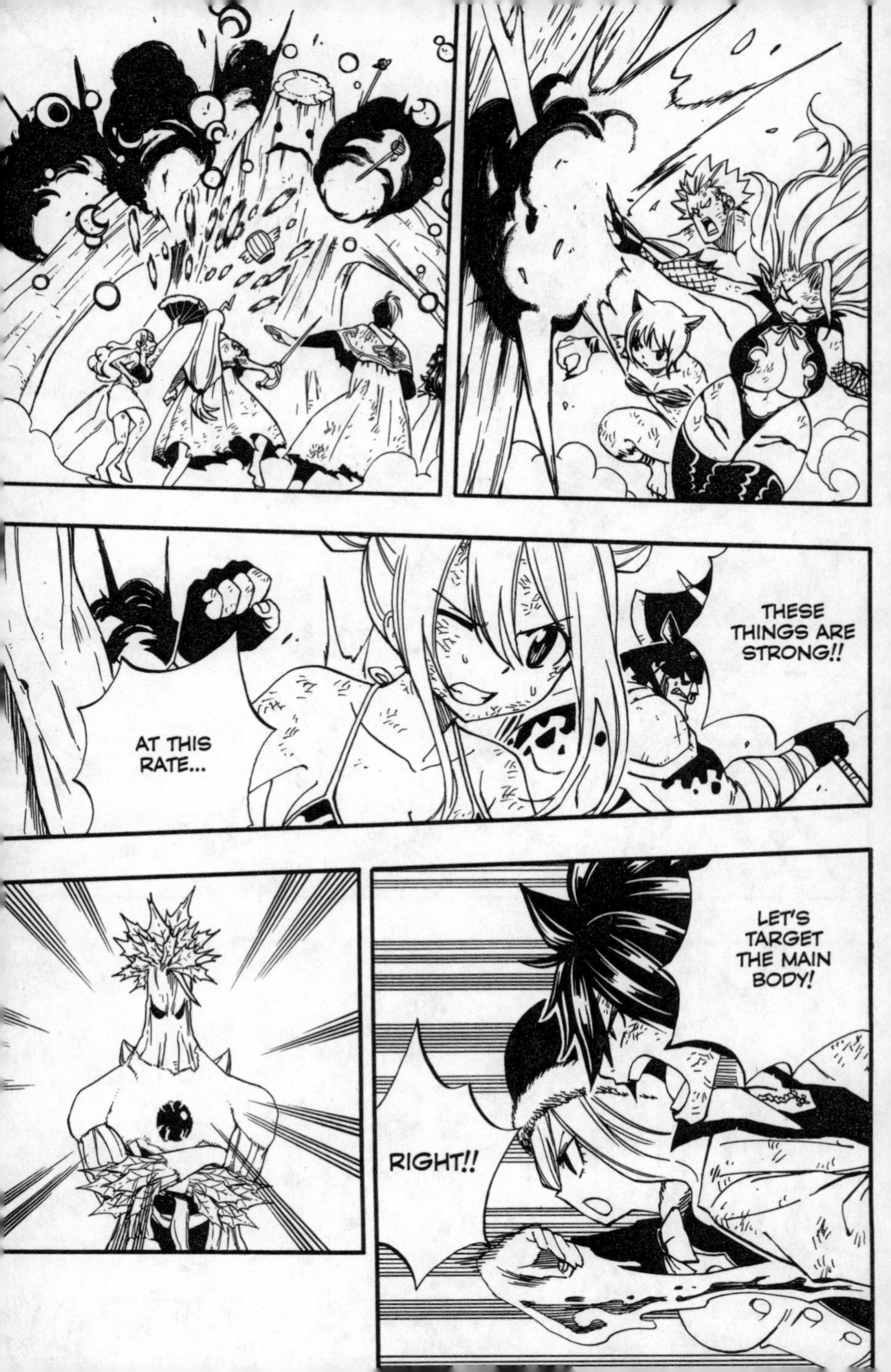
THESE THINGS ARE STRONG!!
AT THIS RATE...
LET'S TARGET THE MAIN BODY!
RIGHT!!

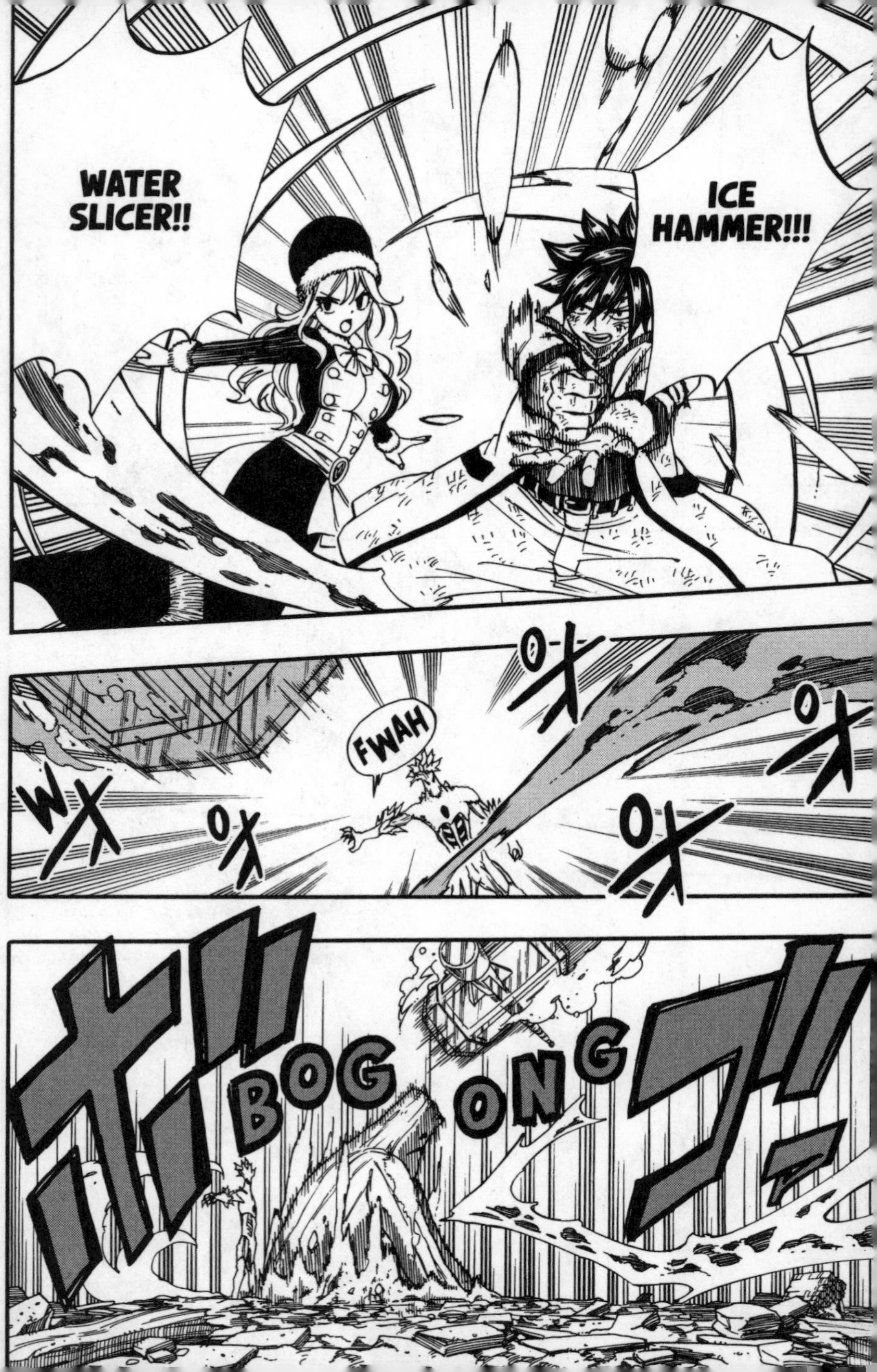
ICE HAMMER!!!
WATER SLICER!!
FWAH
BOG ONG

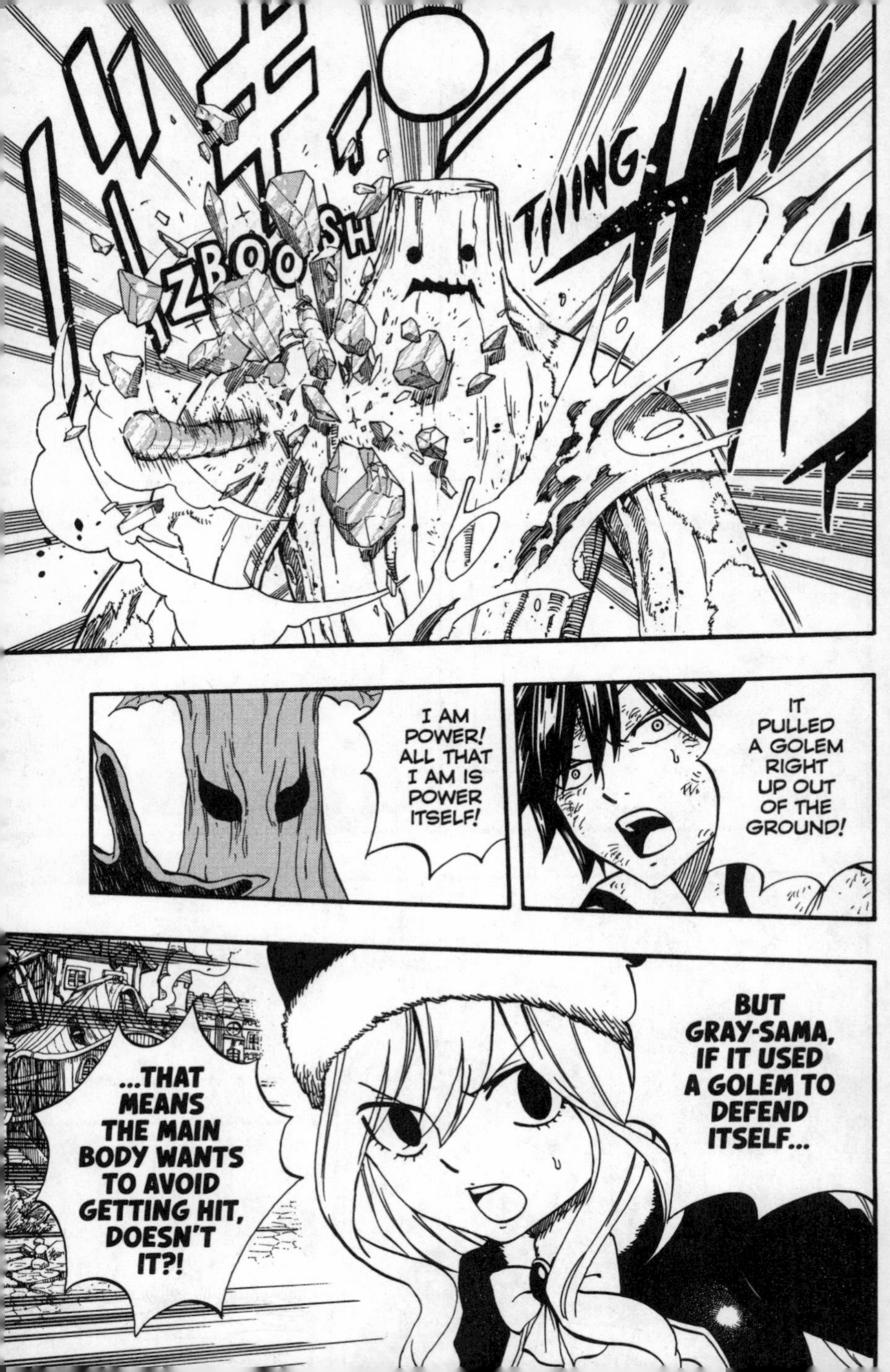
TIIING
ZBOOSH
IT PULLED A GOLEM RIGHT UP OUT OF THE GROUND!
I AM POWER! ALL THAT I AM IS POWER ITSELF!
BUT GRAY-SAMA, IF IT USED A GOLEM TO DEFEND ITSELF...
...THAT MEANS THE MAIN BODY WANTS TO AVOID GETTING HIT, DOESN'T IT?!

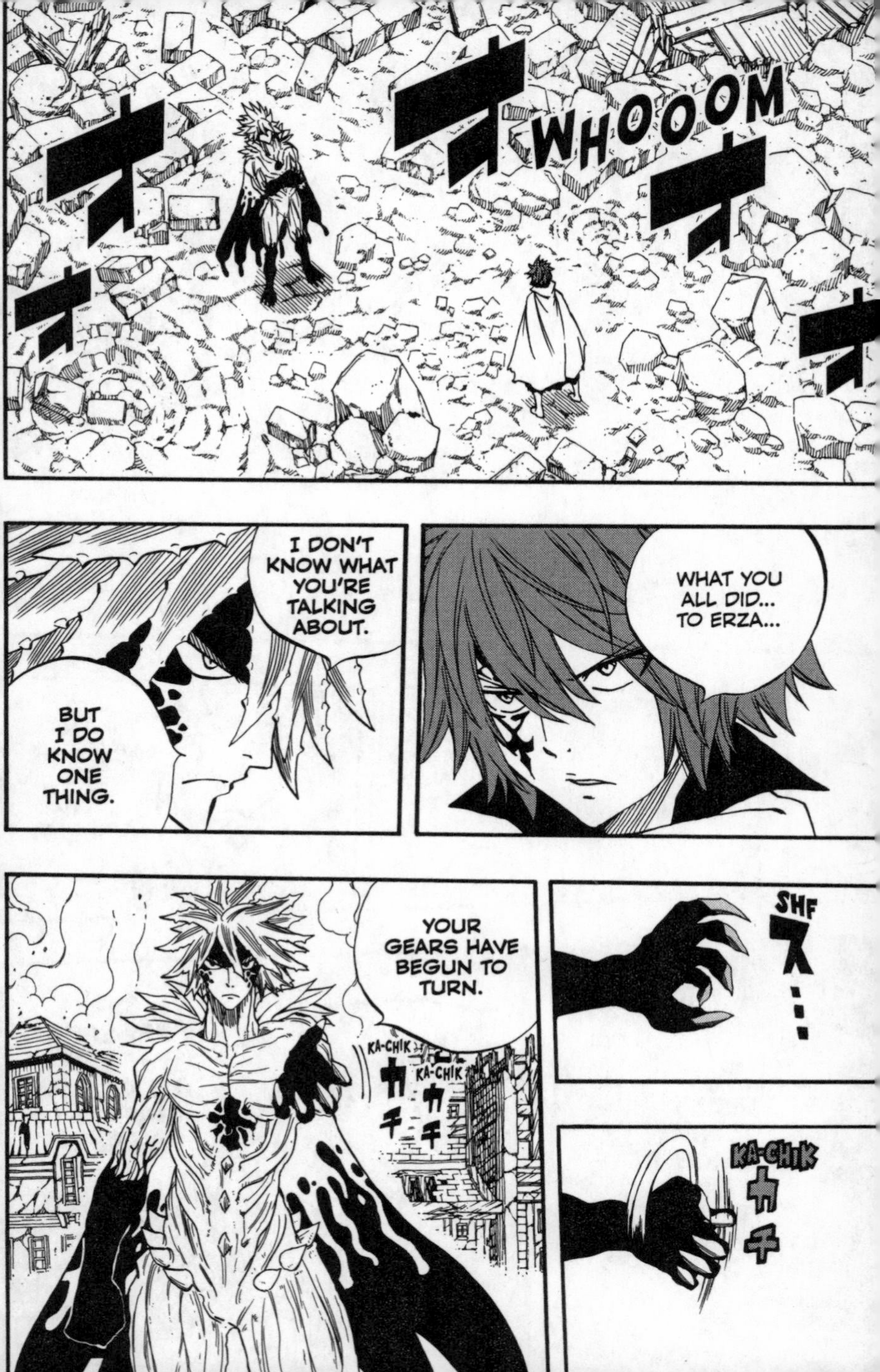
WHOOOM
WHAT YOU ALL DID... TO ERZA...
I DON'T KNOW WHAT YOU'RE TALKING ABOUT.
BUT I DO KNOW ONE THING.
SHF
ス...
KA-CHIK
カチ
YOUR GEARS HAVE BEGUN TO TURN.
KA-CHIK
カチ
KA-CHIK
カチ

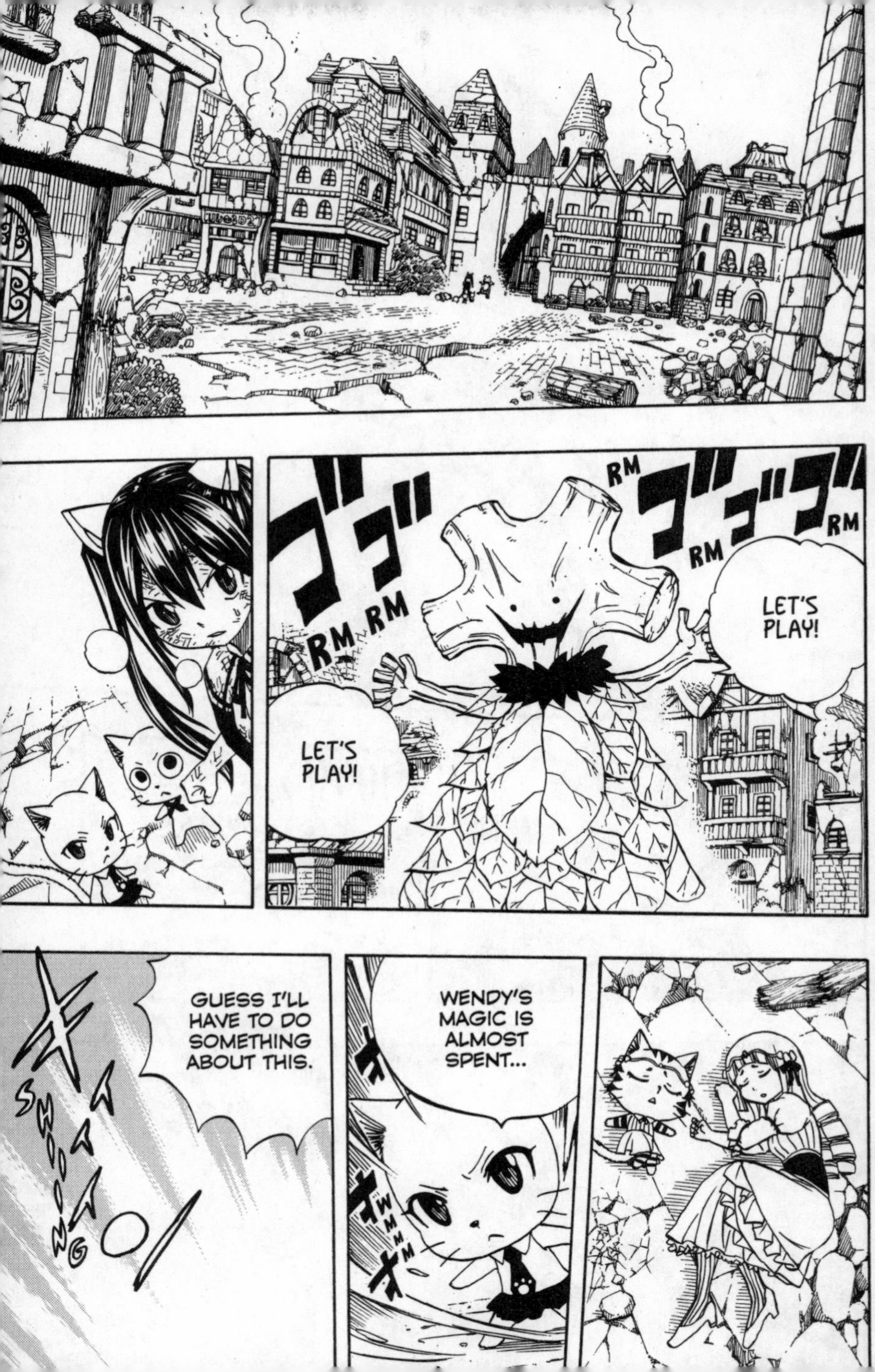
RM RM
RM RM
RM RM
LET'S PLAY!
LET'S PLAY!
WENDY'S MAGIC IS ALMOST SPENT...
WMMM
GUESS I'LL HAVE TO DO SOMETHING ABOUT THIS.
SHWOOONG

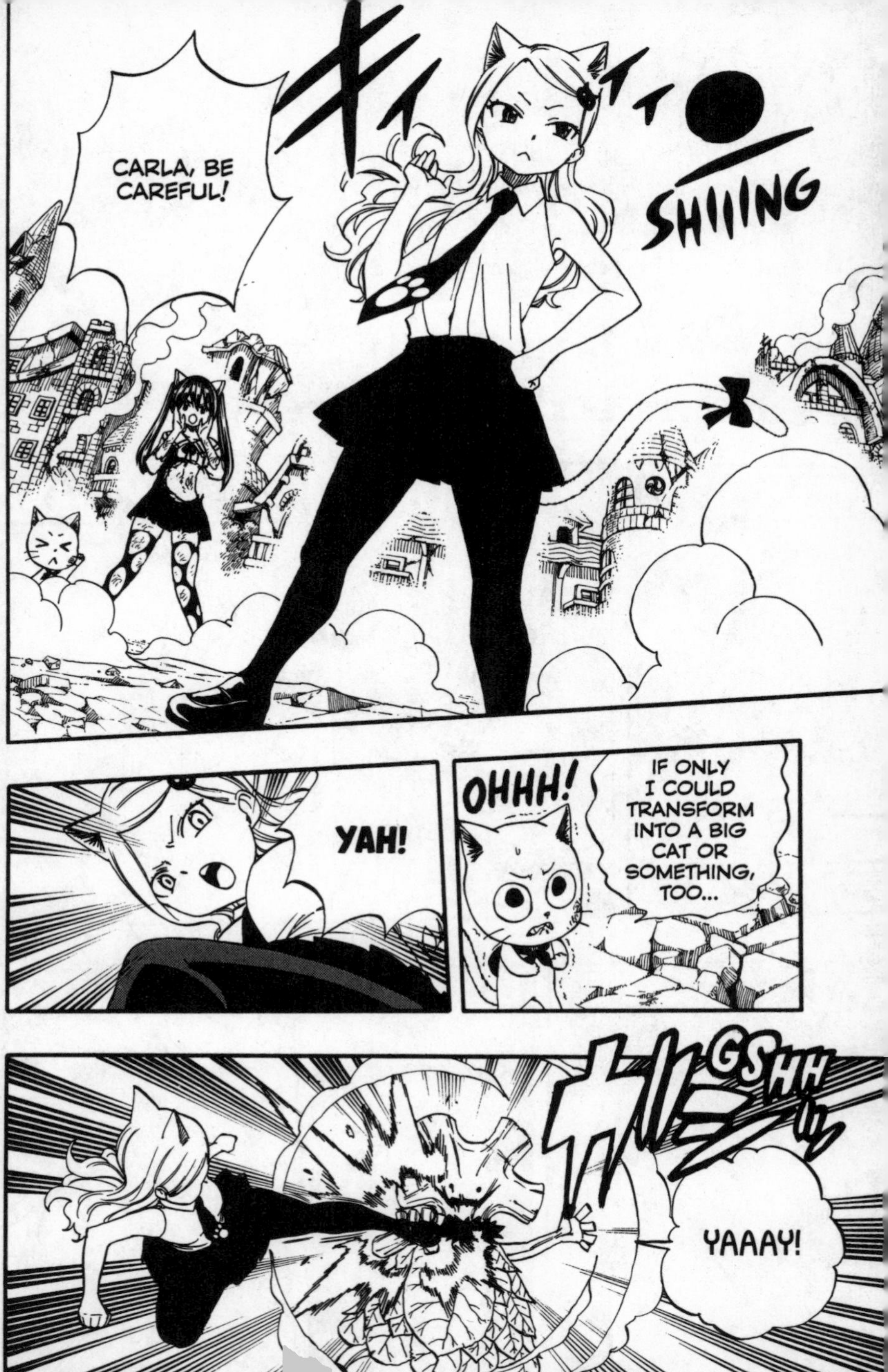
SHIIING
CARLA, BE CAREFUL!
IF ONLY I COULD TRANSFORM INTO A BIG CAT OR SOMETHING, TOO...
OHHH!
YAH!
GSHH
YAAAY!

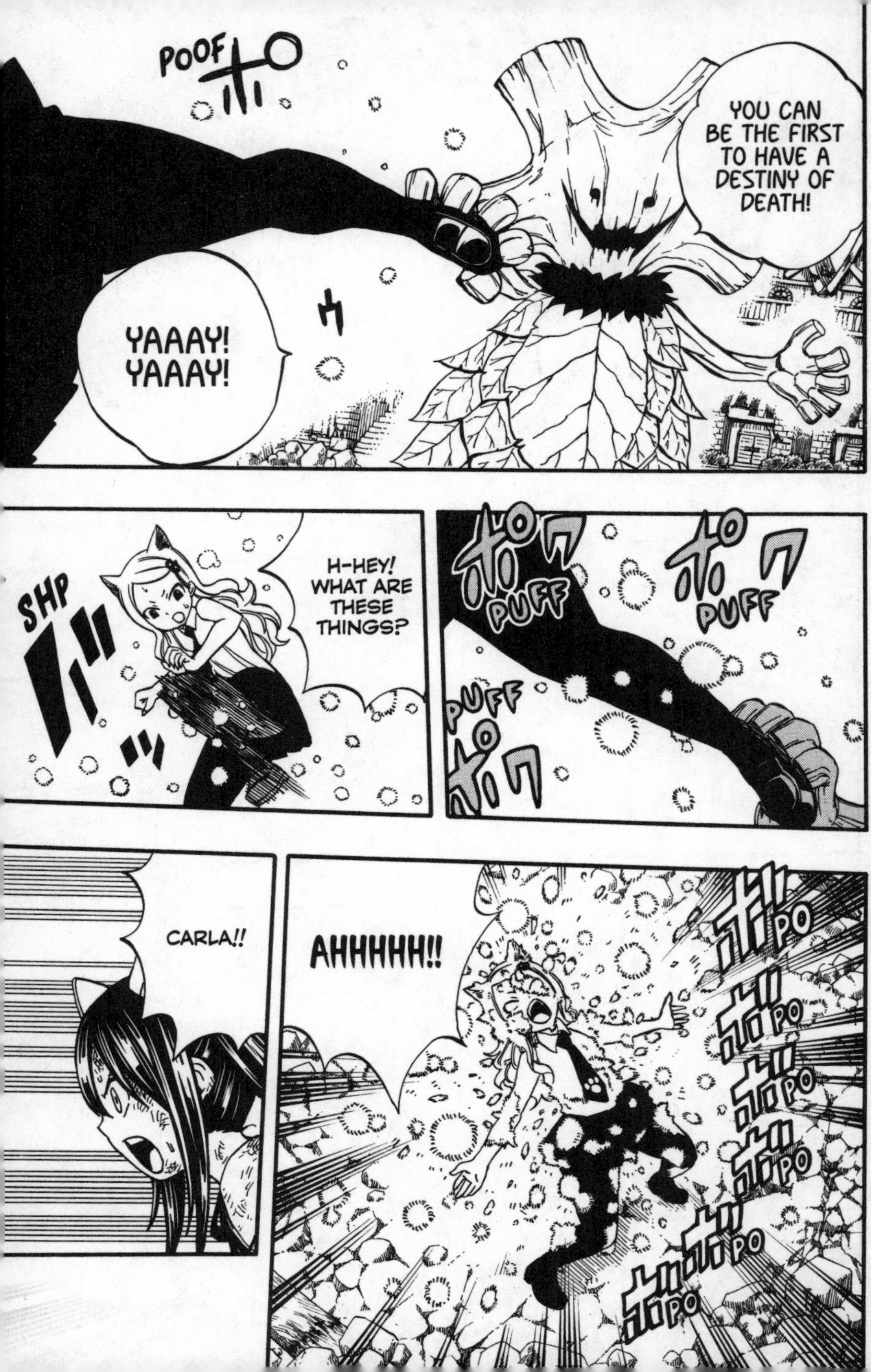
YOU CAN BE THE FIRST TO HAVE A DESTINY OF DEATH!
POOF
YAAAY! YAAAY!
PUFF
PUFF
PUFF
H-HEY! WHAT ARE THESE THINGS?
SHP
PO
PO
PO
PO
PO
PO
AHHHHH!!
CARLA!!

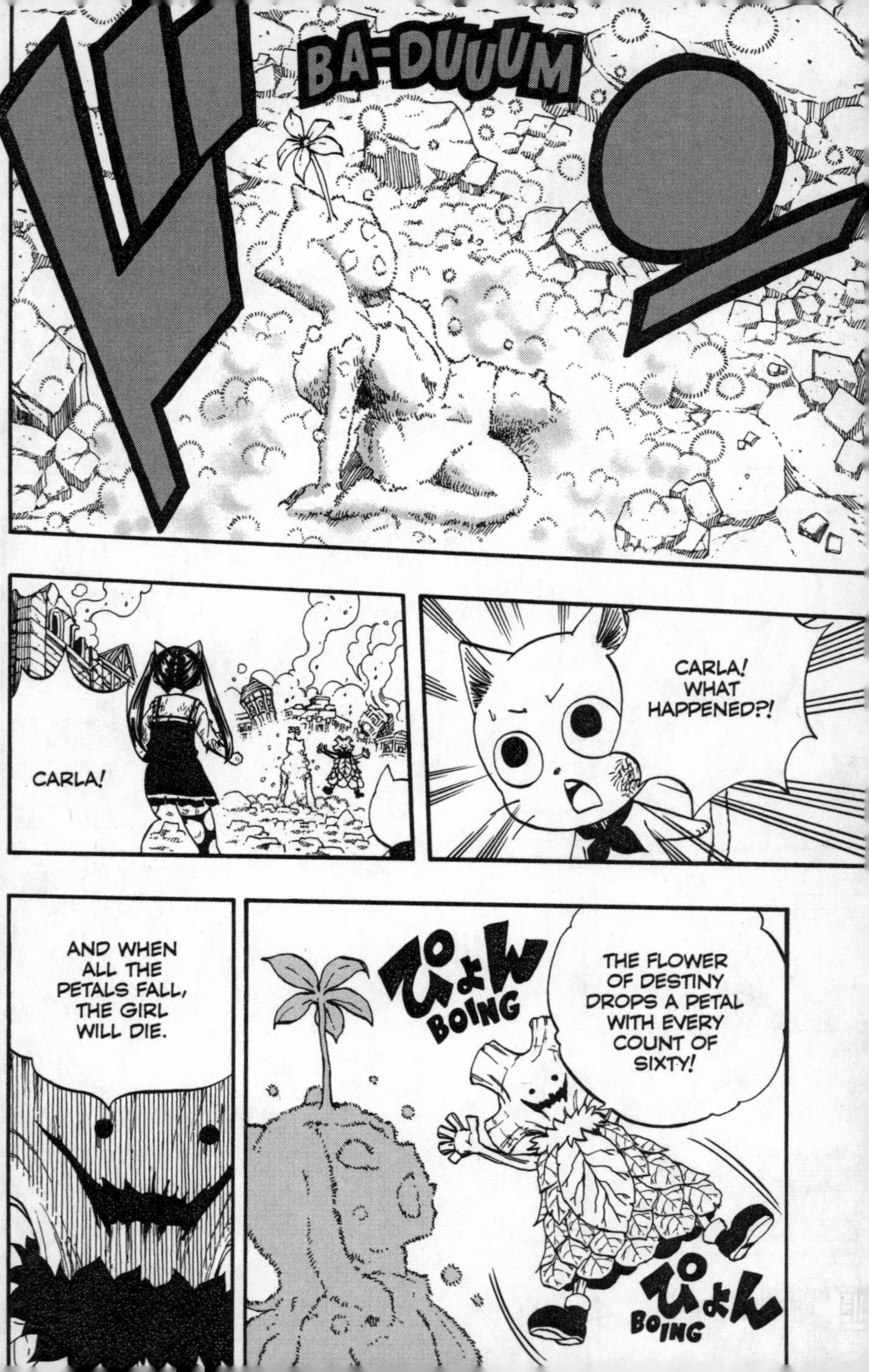
BA-DUUUM
CARLA! WHAT HAPPENED?!
CARLA!
ぴょん
BOING
THE FLOWER OF DESTINY DROPS A PETAL WITH EVERY COUNT OF SIXTY!
ぴょん
BOING
AND WHEN ALL THE PETALS FALL, THE GIRL WILL DIE.

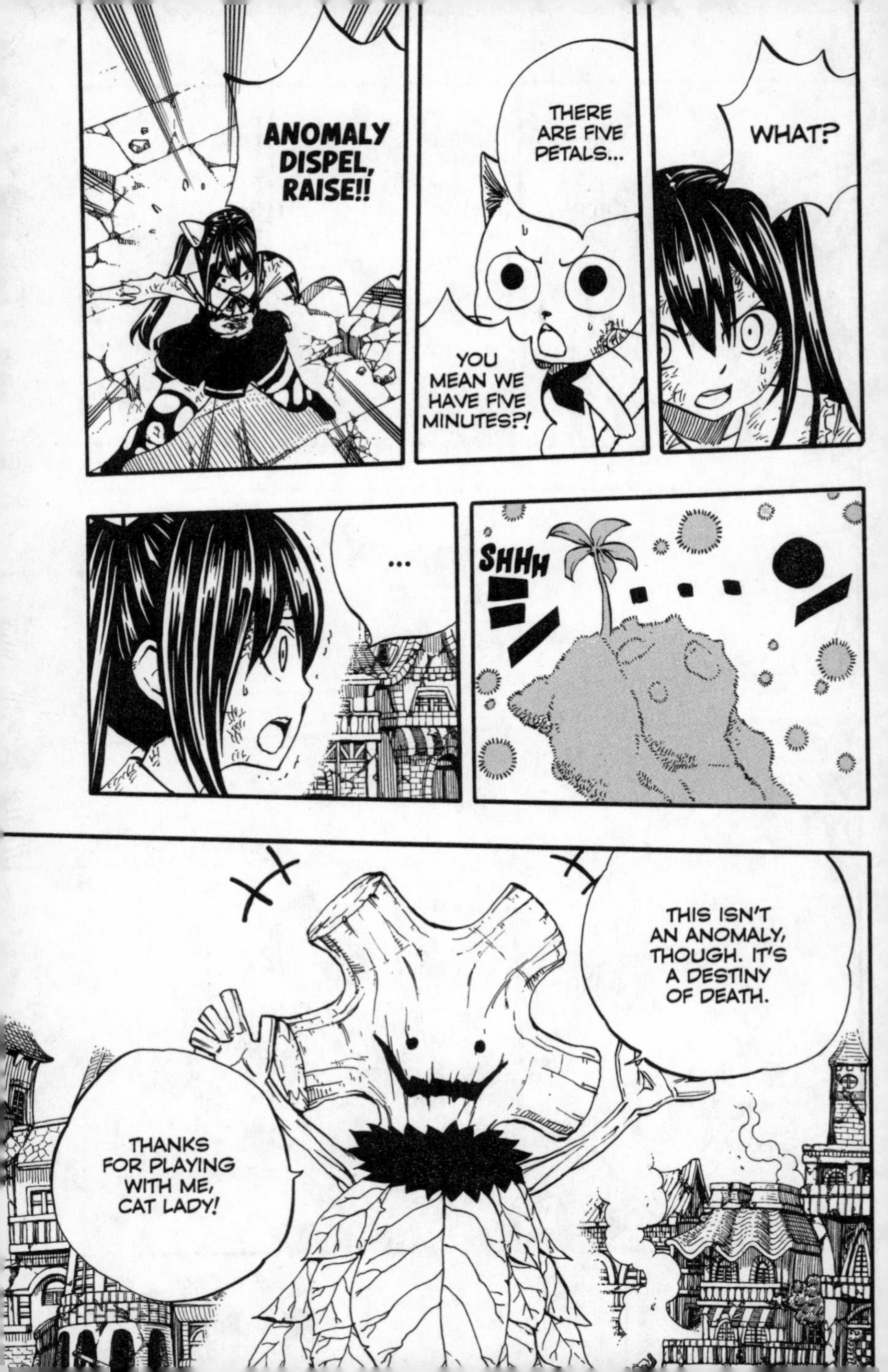
WHAT?
THERE ARE FIVE PETALS...
YOU MEAN WE HAVE FIVE MINUTES?!
ANOMALY DISPEL, RAISE!!
SHHH
...
THIS ISN'T AN ANOMALY, THOUGH. IT'S A DESTINY OF DEATH.
THANKS FOR PLAYING WITH ME, CAT LADY!

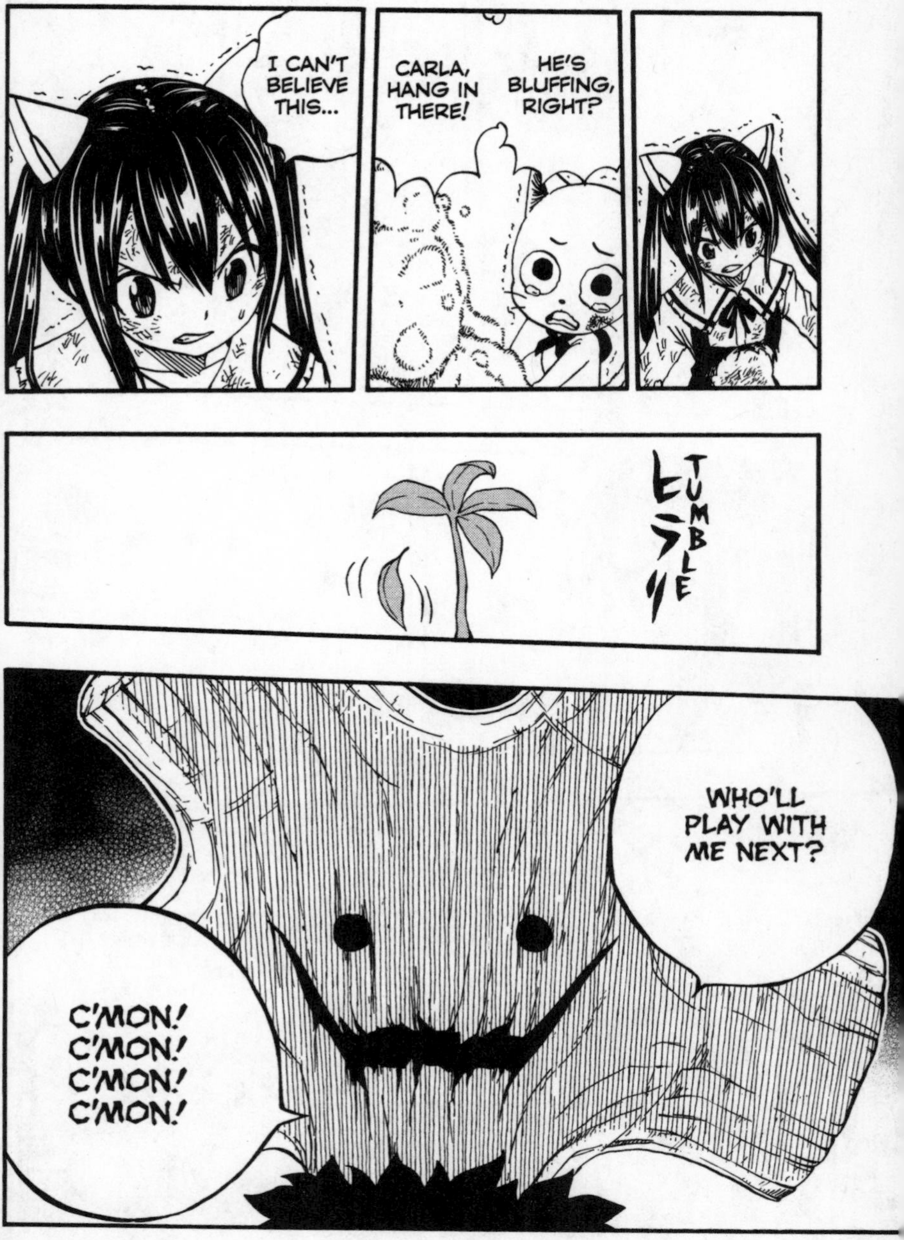
HE'S BLUFFING, RIGHT?
CARLA, HANG IN THERE!
I CAN'T BELIEVE THIS...
ヒラリ
TUMBLE
WHO'LL PLAY WITH ME NEXT?
C'MON! C'MON! C'MON! C'MON!

FAIRY TAIL 100 YEARS QUEST

Chapter 56: Friends You Can Count On

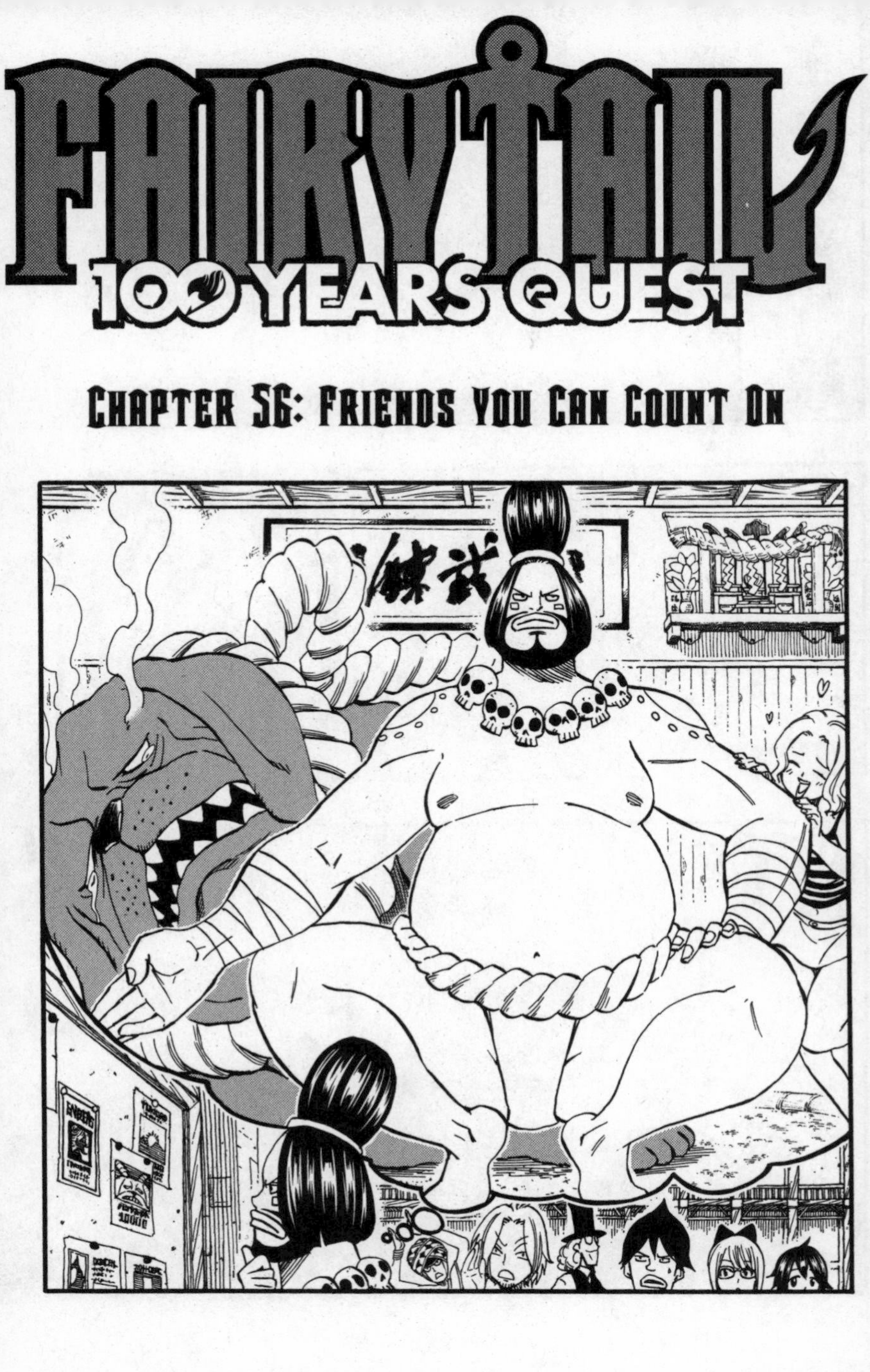

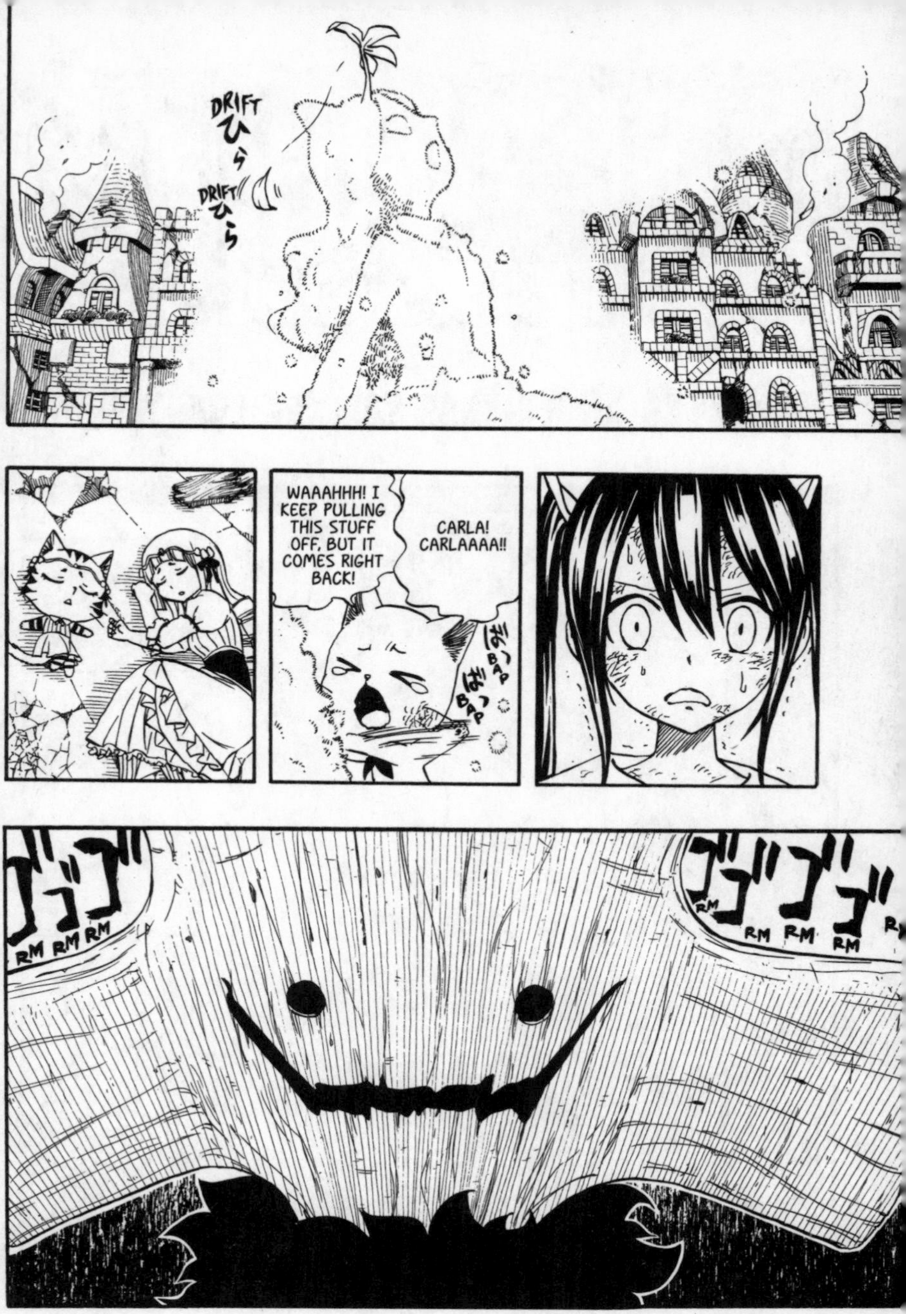
DRIFT
ひら
DRIFT
ひら
CARLA! CARLAAAA!!
WAAAHHH! I KEEP PULLING THIS STUFF OFF, BUT IT COMES RIGHT BACK!
ぱっ BAP
ぱっ BAP
RM RM RM RM
RM RM RM

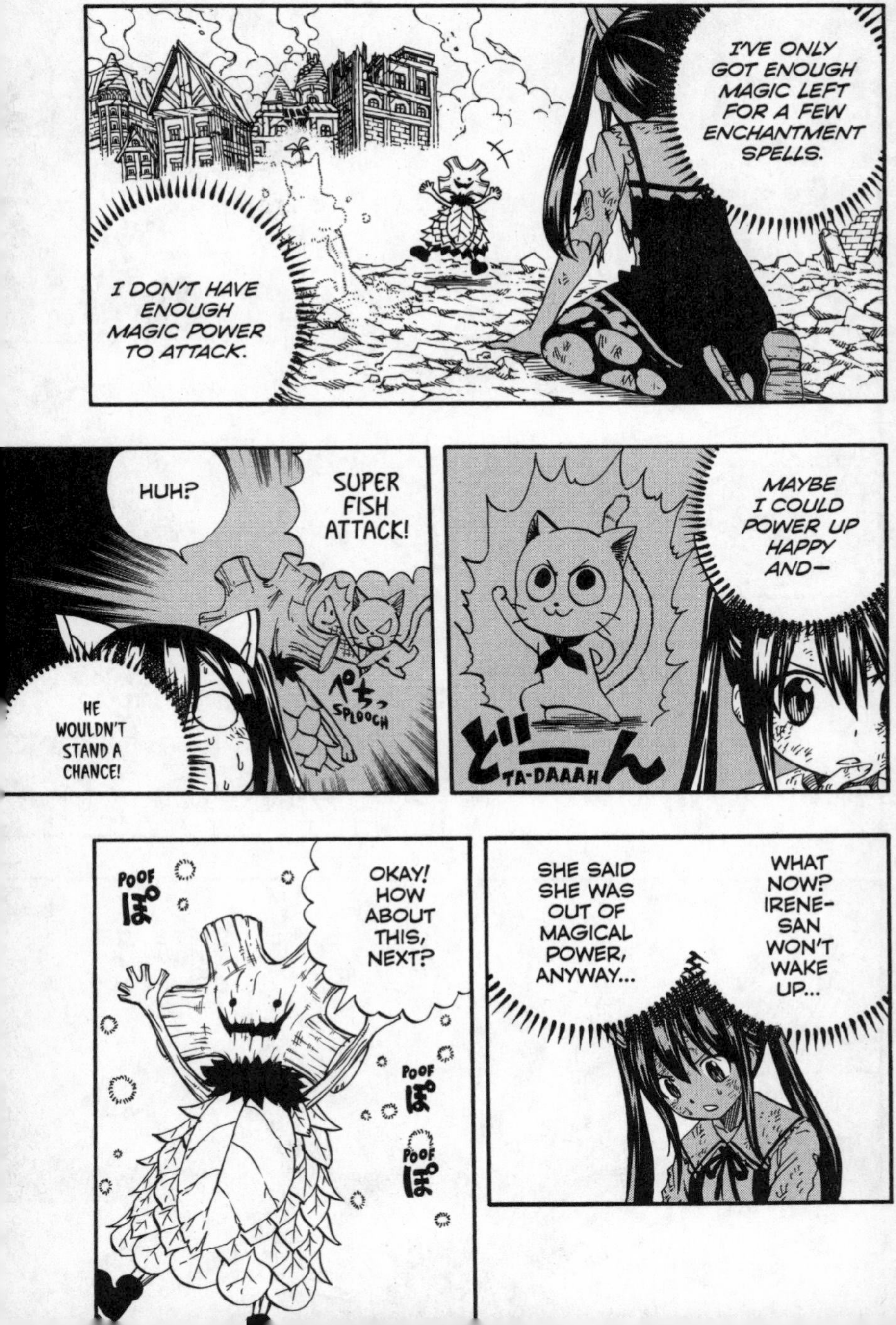
I'VE ONLY GOT ENOUGH MAGIC LEFT FOR A FEW ENCHANTMENT SPELLS.
I DON'T HAVE ENOUGH MAGIC POWER TO ATTACK.
MAYBE I COULD POWER UP HAPPY AND—
どーん
TA-DAAAH
SUPER FISH ATTACK!
HUH?
ぺちっ
SPLOOCH
HE WOULDN'T STAND A CHANCE!
WHAT NOW? IRENE-SAN WON'T WAKE UP...
SHE SAID SHE WAS OUT OF MAGICAL POWER, ANYWAY...
OKAY! HOW ABOUT THIS, NEXT?
POOF
ぽ
POOF
ぽ
POOF
ぽ

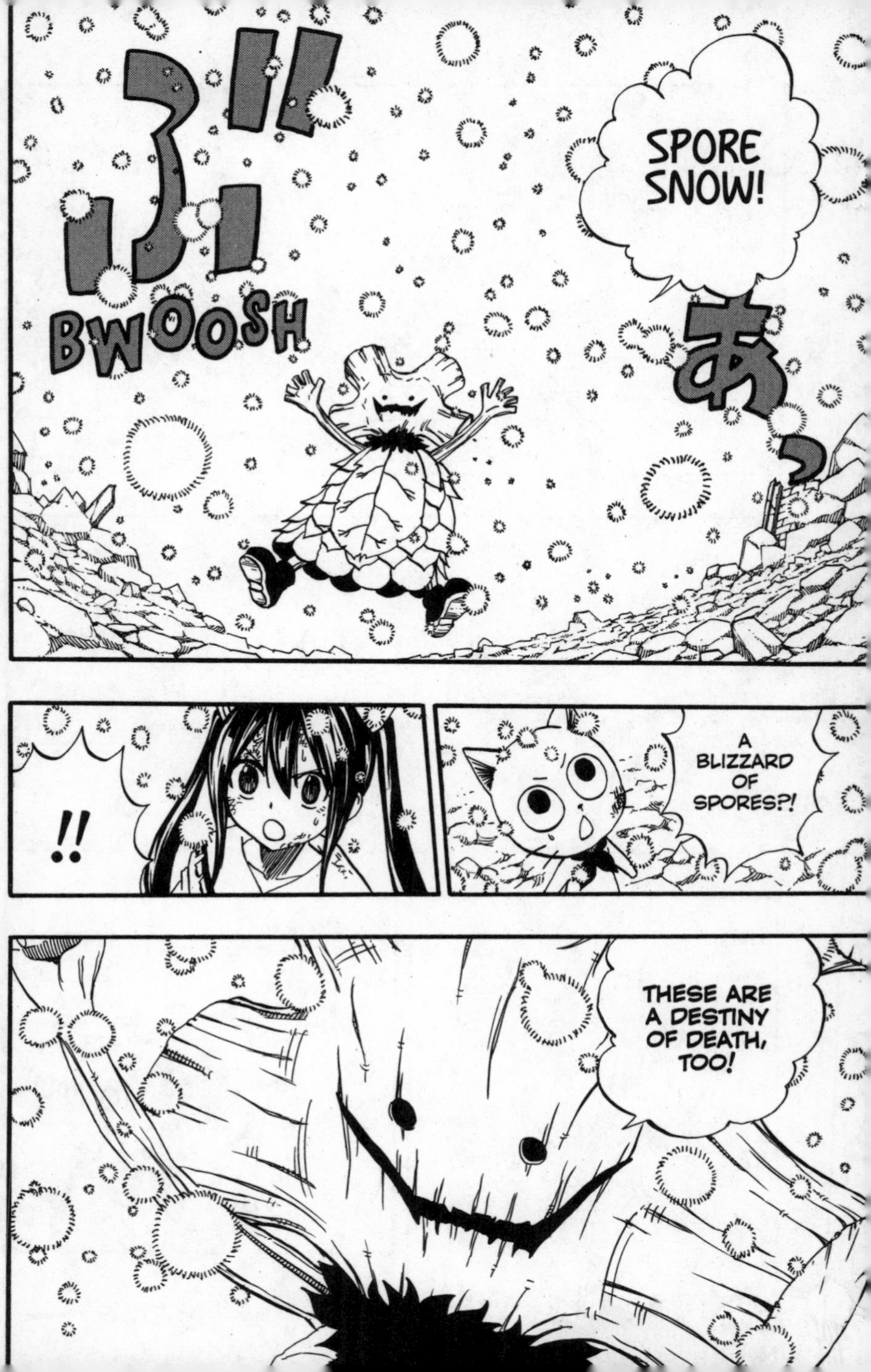
SPORE SNOW!
あっ
ぶ
BWOOSH
A BLIZZARD OF SPORES?!
!!
THESE ARE A DESTINY OF DEATH, TOO!

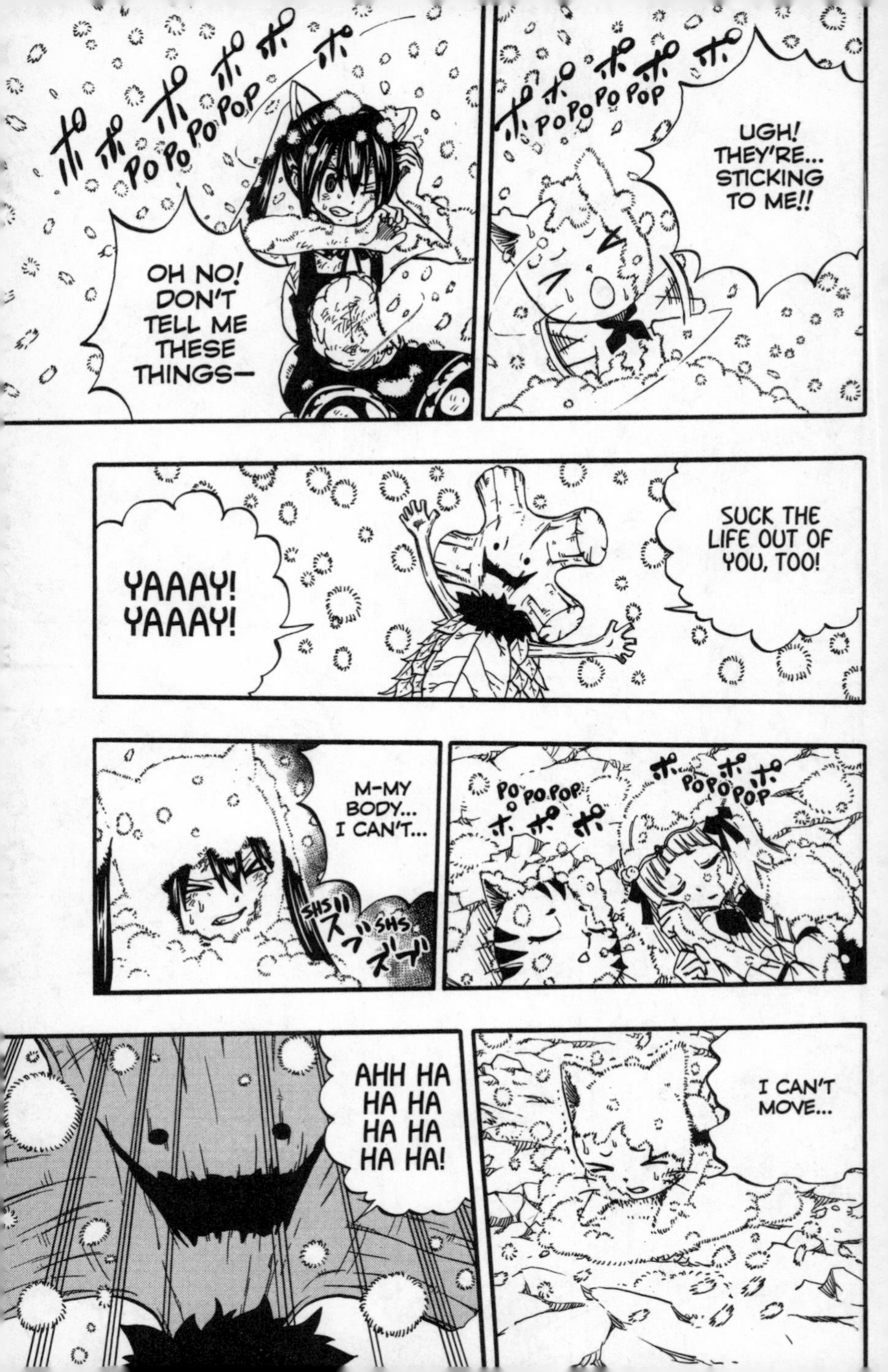
ポポポポポ
POPOPOPOP
UGH! THEY'RE... STICKING TO ME!!
ポポポポポ
POPOPOPOP
OH NO! DON'T TELL ME THESE THINGS—
SUCK THE LIFE OUT OF YOU, TOO!
YAAAY! YAAAY!
ポポポポ
POPOPOP
POPOPOP
ポポポ
M-MY BODY... I CAN'T...
SHS
SHS
I CAN'T MOVE...
AHH HA HA HA HA HA HA HA!

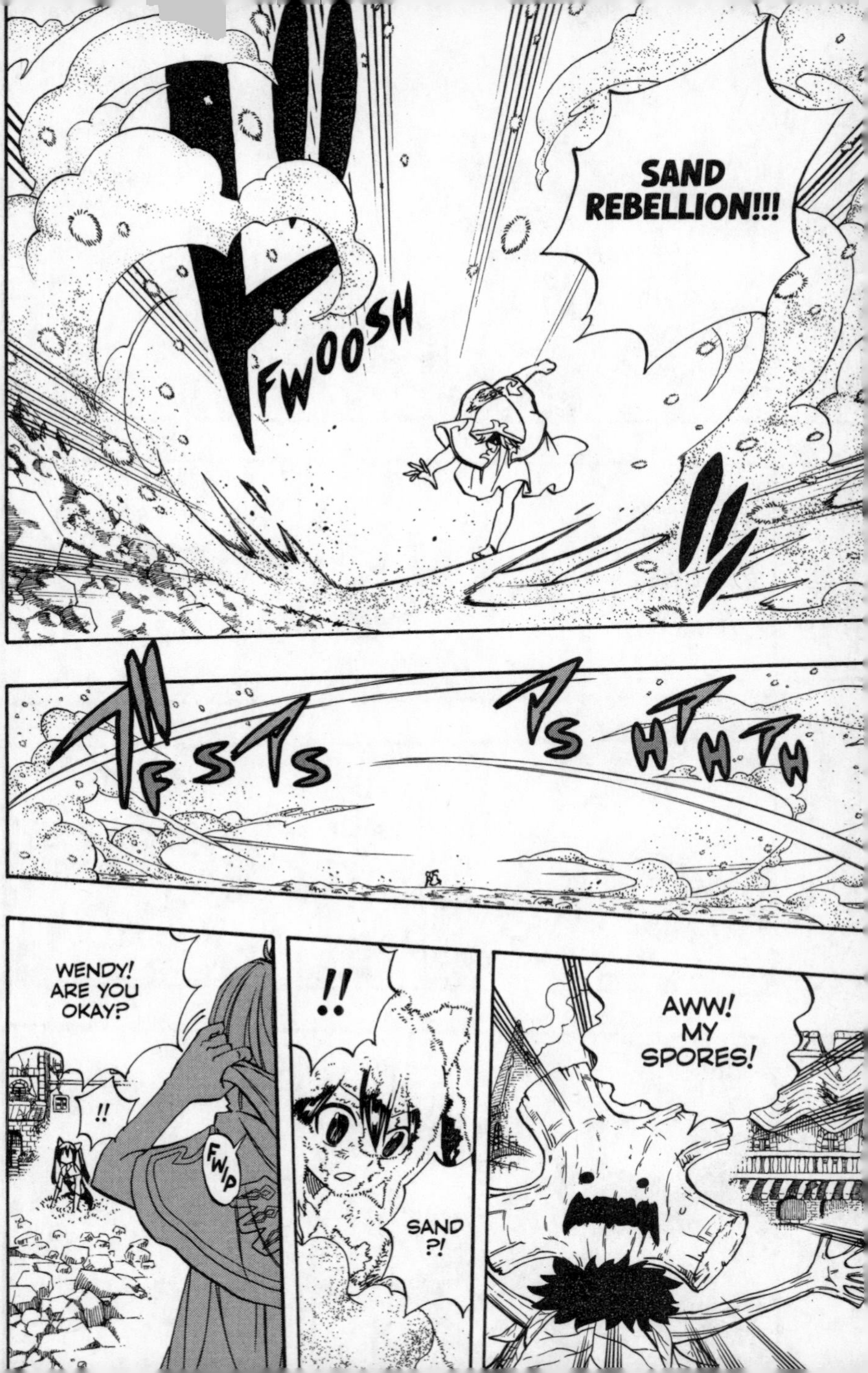
SAND REBELLION!!!
FWOOSH
FSSSHHHH
AWW! MY SPORES!
!!
SAND ?!
WENDY! ARE YOU OKAY?
!!
FWIP

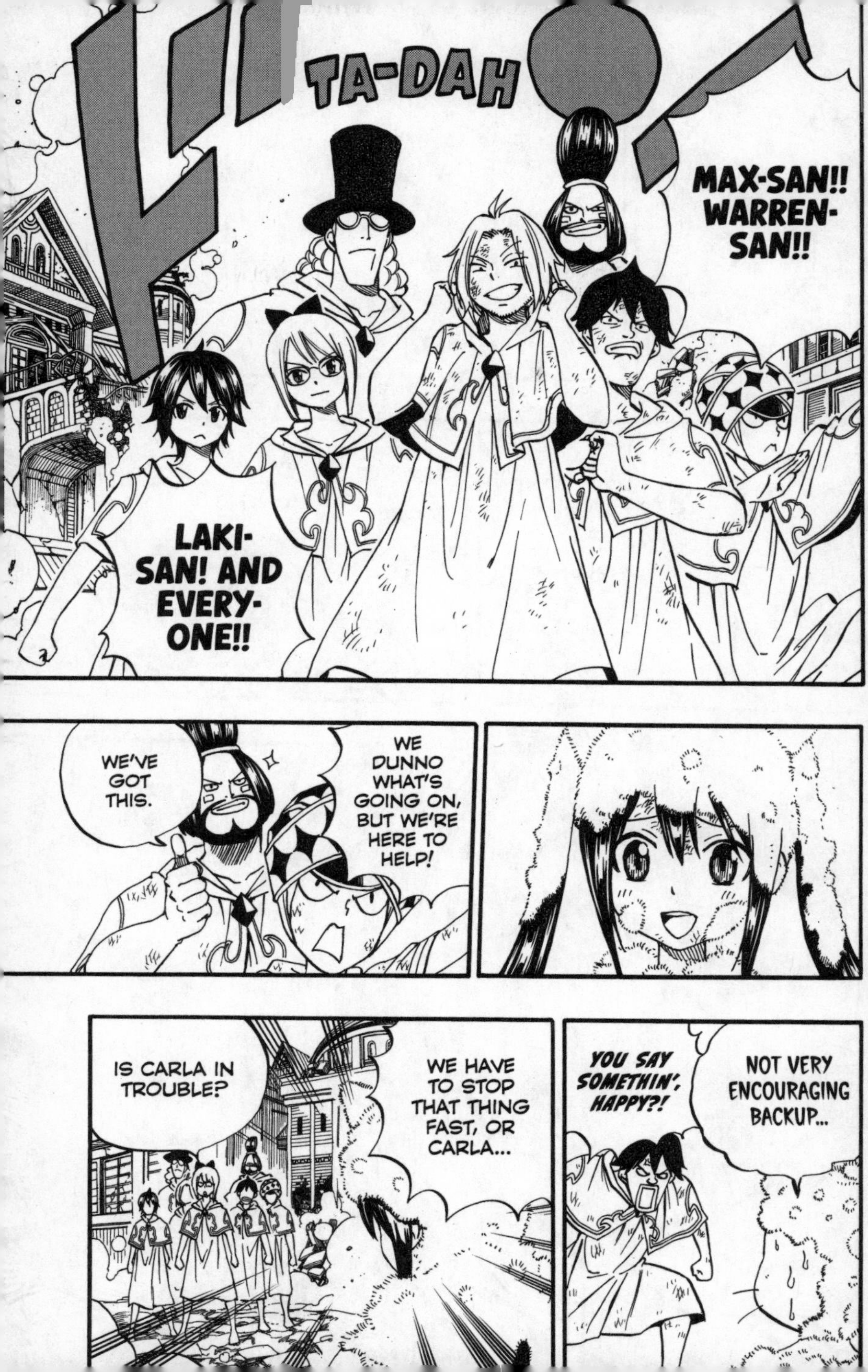
TA-DAH
MAX-SAN!! WARREN-SAN!!
LAKI-SAN! AND EVERY-ONE!!
WE DUNNO WHAT'S GOING ON, BUT WE'RE HERE TO HELP!
WE'VE GOT THIS.
NOT VERY ENCOURAGING BACKUP...
YOU SAY SOMETHIN', HAPPY?!
WE HAVE TO STOP THAT THING FAST, OR CARLA...
IS CARLA IN TROUBLE?

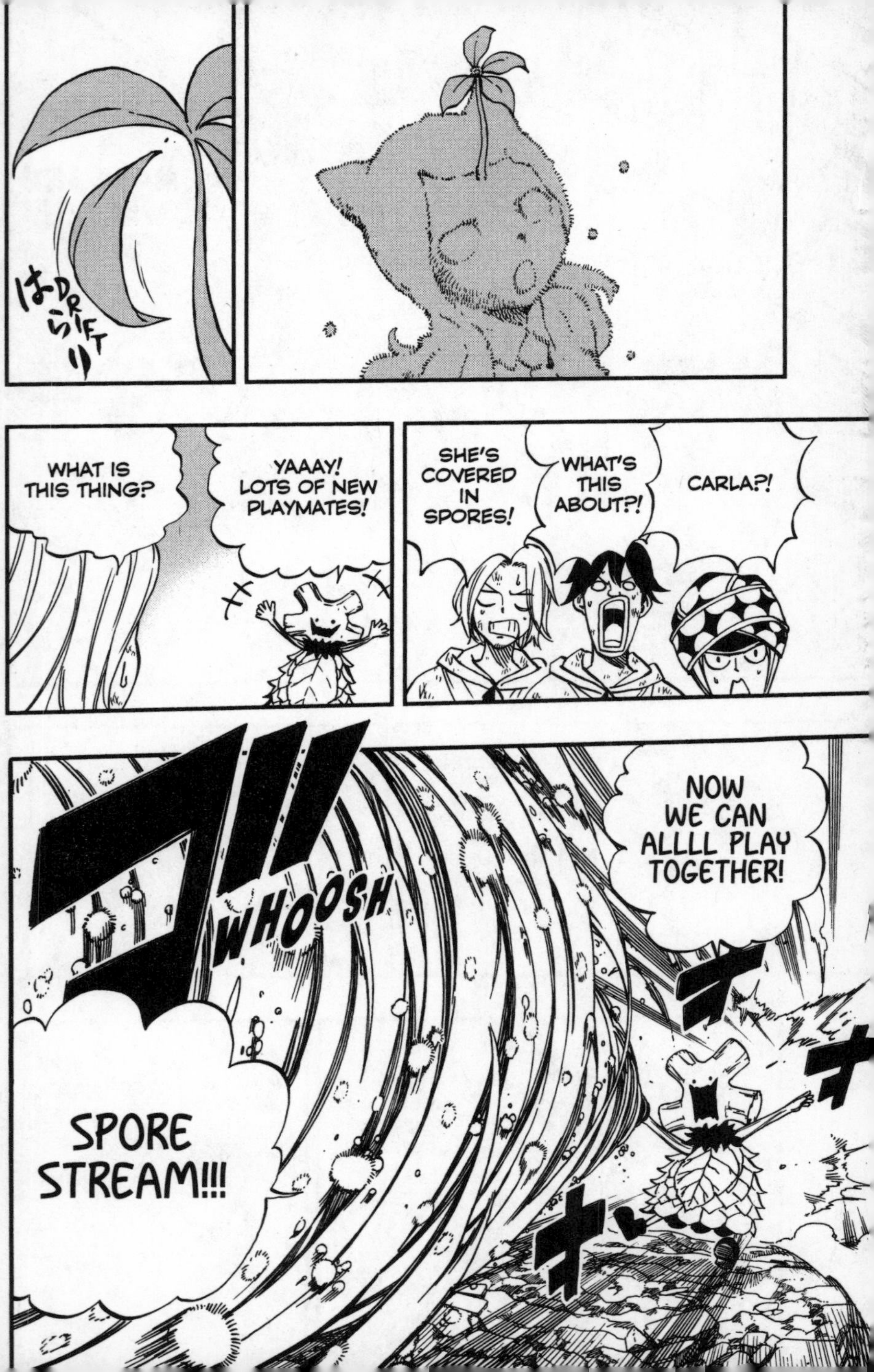
はらり
DRIFT
CARLA?!
WHAT'S THIS ABOUT?!
SHE'S COVERED IN SPORES!
YAAAY! LOTS OF NEW PLAYMATES!
WHAT IS THIS THING?
NOW WE CAN ALLLL PLAY TOGETHER!
WHOOSH
SPORE STREAM!!!

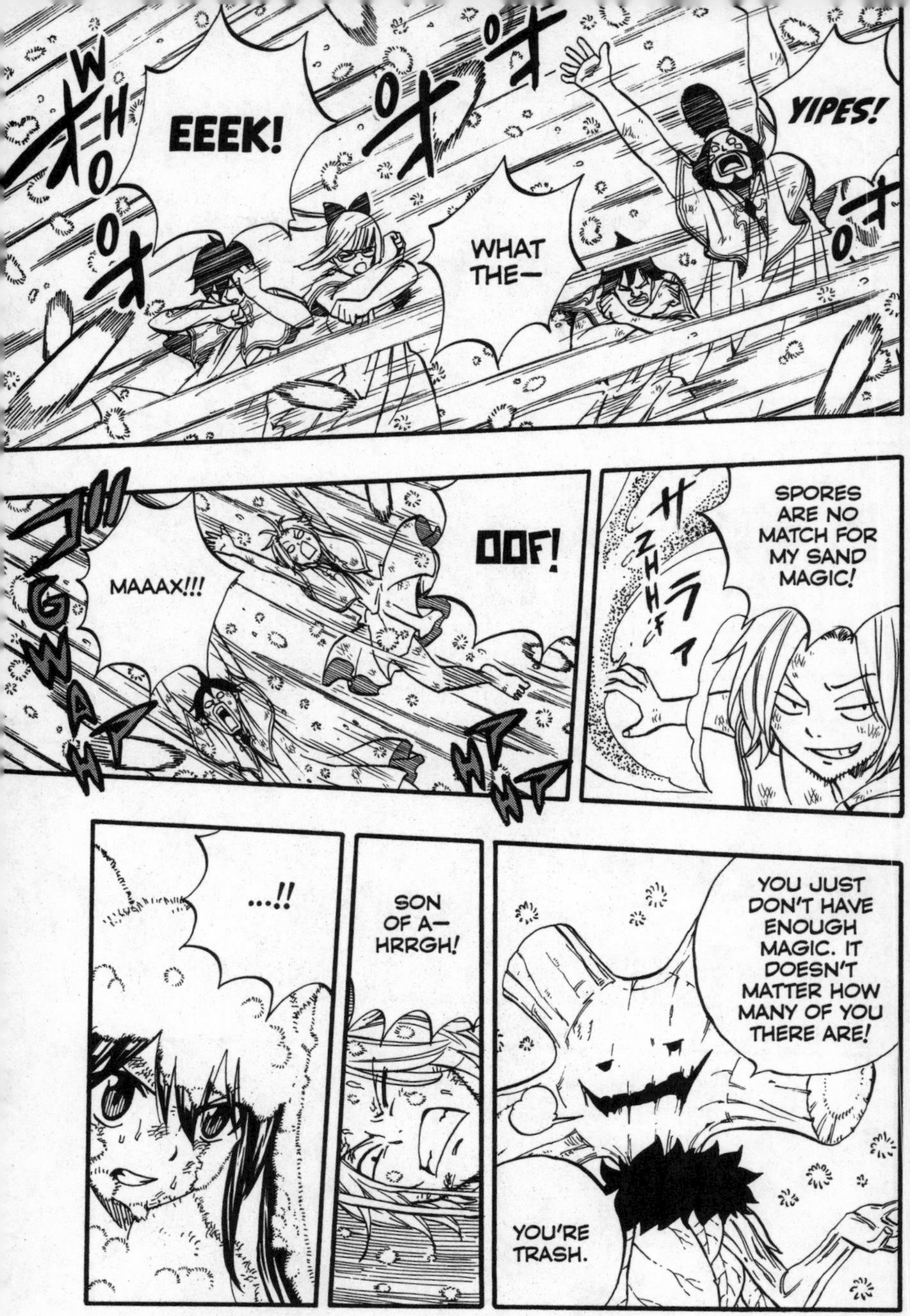
YIPES!
WHAT THE—
EEEK!
WHOOO
SPORES ARE NO MATCH FOR MY SAND MAGIC!
ZHHF
OOF!
MAAAX!!!
YOU JUST DON'T HAVE ENOUGH MAGIC. IT DOESN'T MATTER HOW MANY OF YOU THERE ARE!
YOU'RE TRASH.
SON OF A— HRRGH!
...!!

SHIIIING

I BELIEVE IN YOU ALL!!

I GRANT YOU AN ENCHANTMENT WITH ALL THE POWER I HAVE!

IT'S STRENGTH-ENING OUR MAGIC!

I CAN FEEL IT!

THIS— THIS POWER...

WHOA!

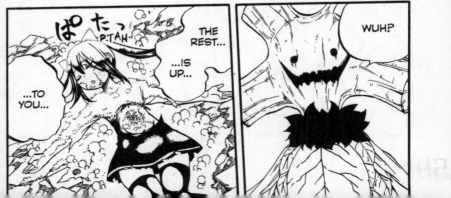

P-TAH

THE REST...

...IS UP...

...TO YOU...

WUH?

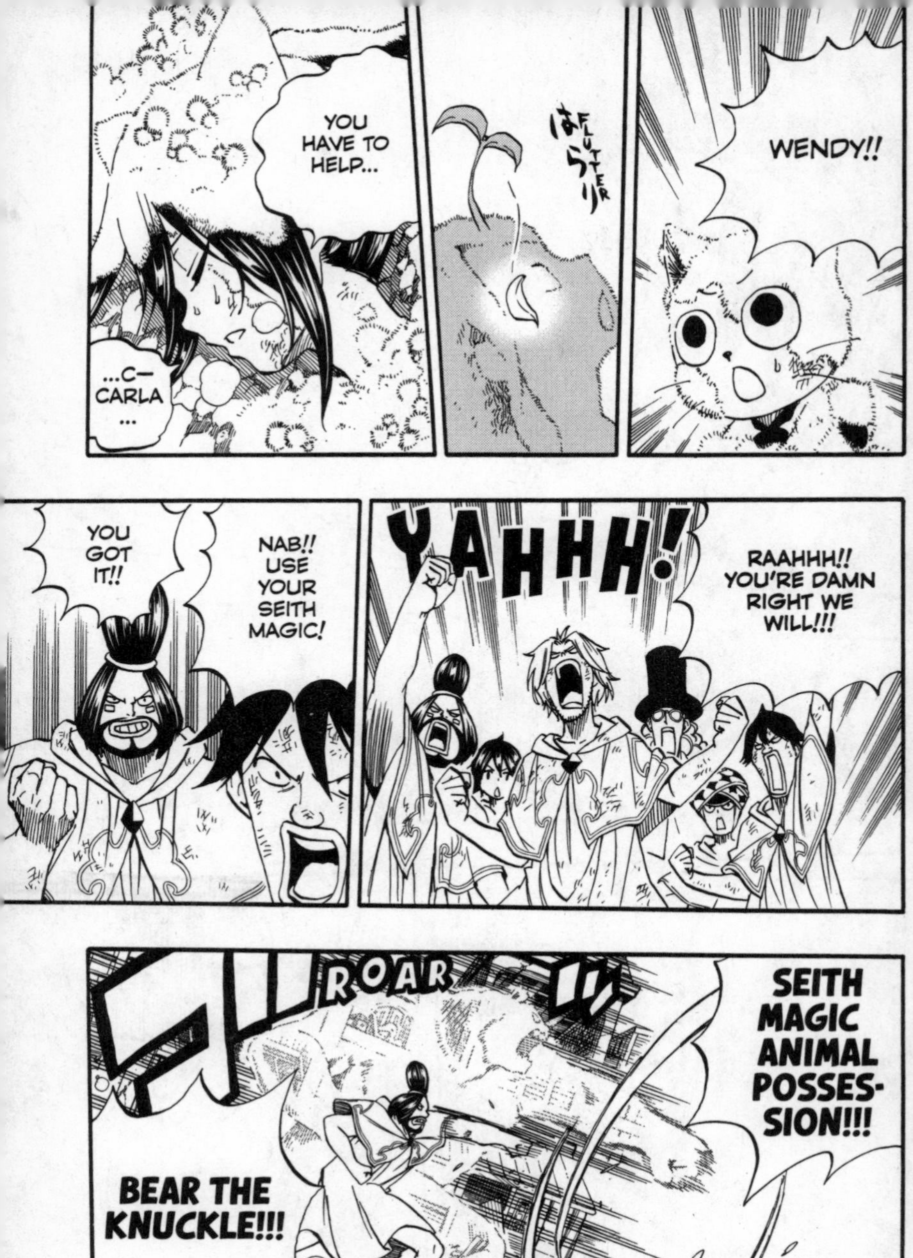
WENDY!!
はらり
FLUTTER
YOU HAVE TO HELP...
...C— CARLA ...
RAAHHH!! YOU'RE DAMN RIGHT WE WILL!!!
YAHHH!
NAB!! USE YOUR SEITH MAGIC!
YOU GOT IT!!
ROAR
SEITH MAGIC ANIMAL POSSES-SION!!!
BEAR THE KNUCKLE!!!

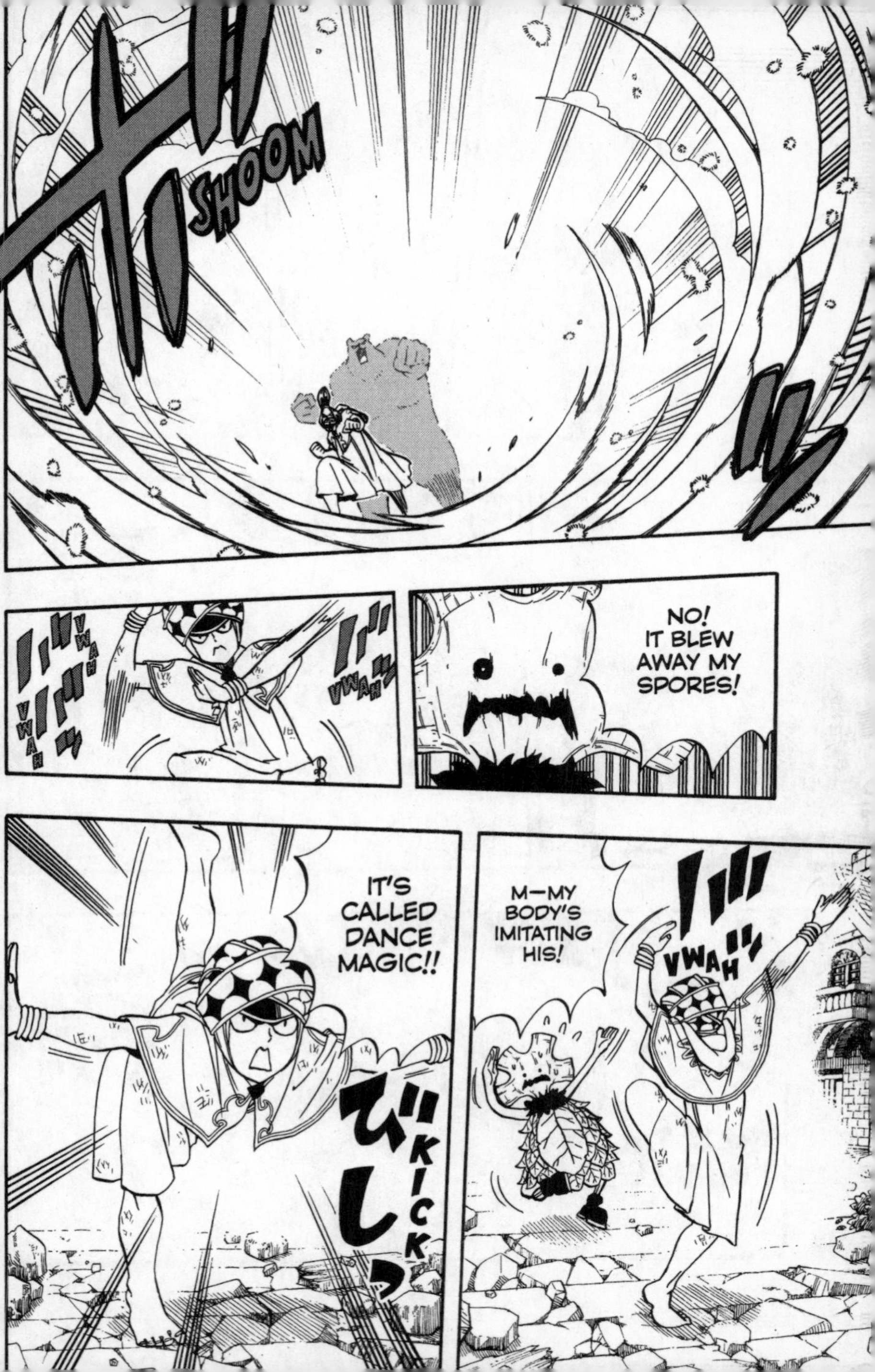
SHOOM
NO! IT BLEW AWAY MY SPORES!
VWAH
VWAH
VWAH
M—MY BODY'S IMITATING HIS!
VWAH
IT'S CALLED DANCE MAGIC!!
KICK

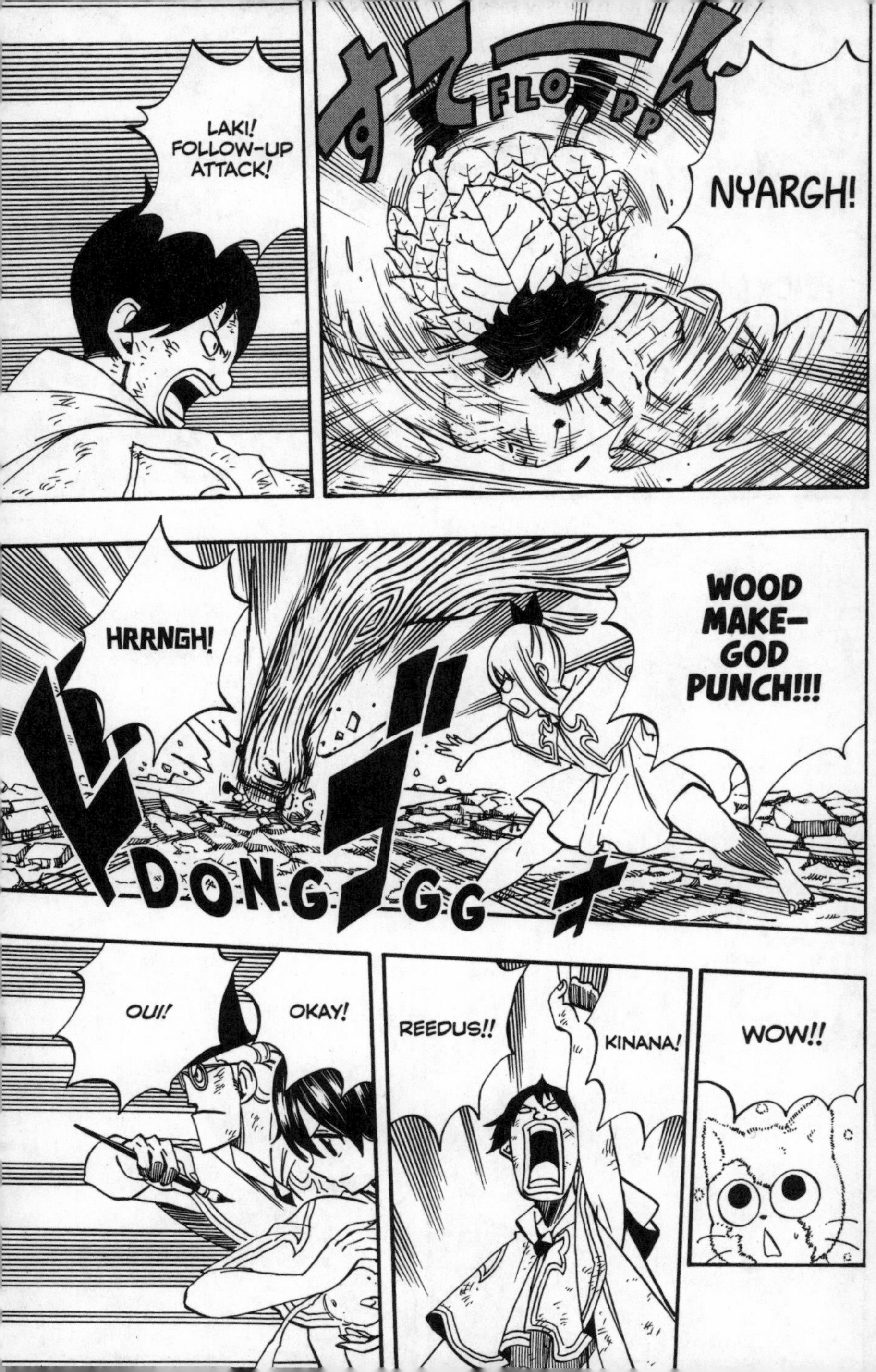
FLOPP
NYARGH!
LAKI! FOLLOW-UP ATTACK!
WOOD MAKE-GOD PUNCH!!!
HRRNGH!
DONGGG
WOW!!
KINANA!
REEDUS!!
OKAY!
OUI!

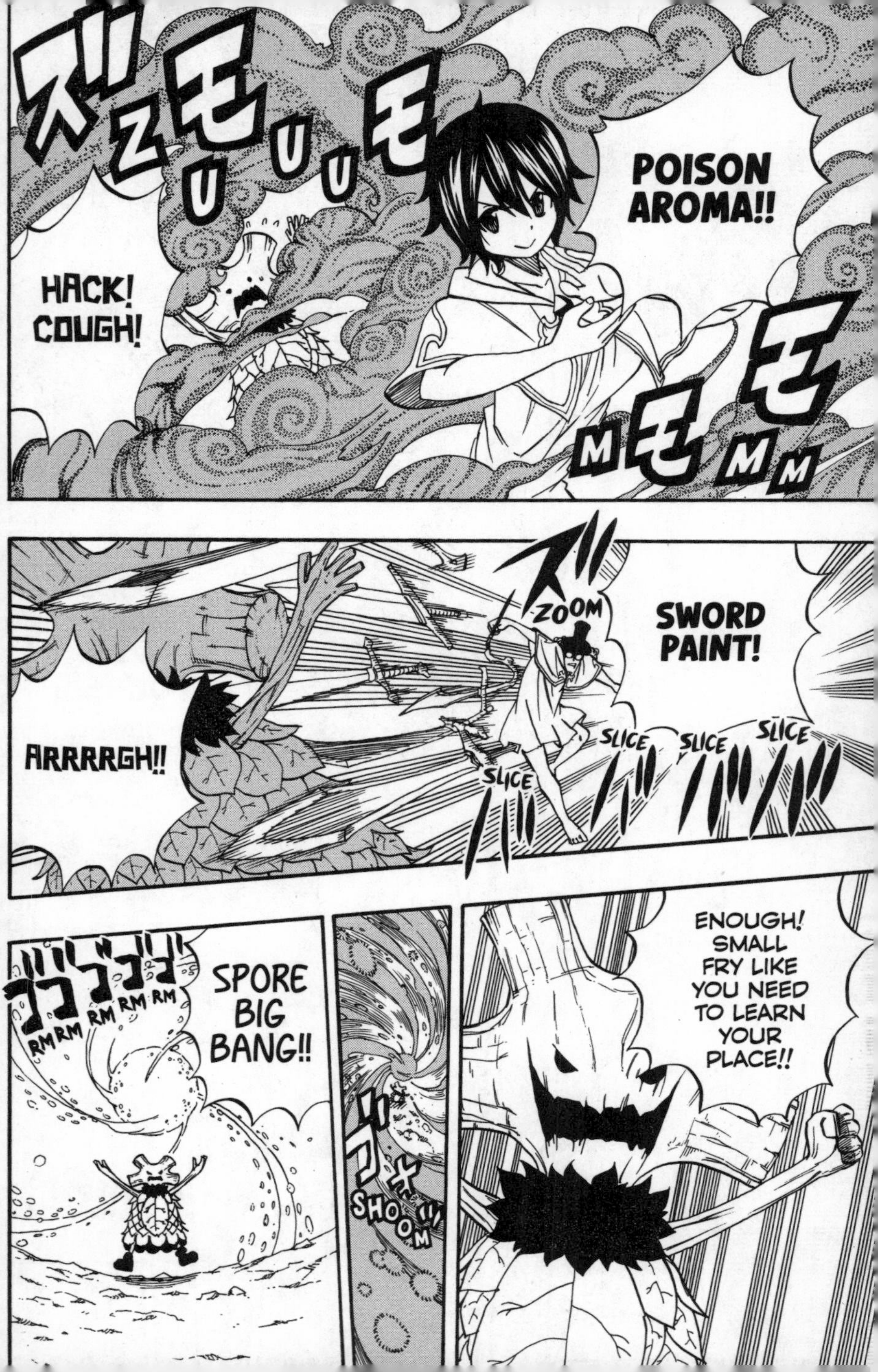
POISON AROMA!!
HACK! COUGH!
ZOOM
SWORD PAINT!
SLICE
SLICE
SLICE
SLICE
ARRRRGH!!
ENOUGH! SMALL FRY LIKE YOU NEED TO LEARN YOUR PLACE!!
SHOOOM
SPORE BIG BANG!!
RM RM RM RM RM

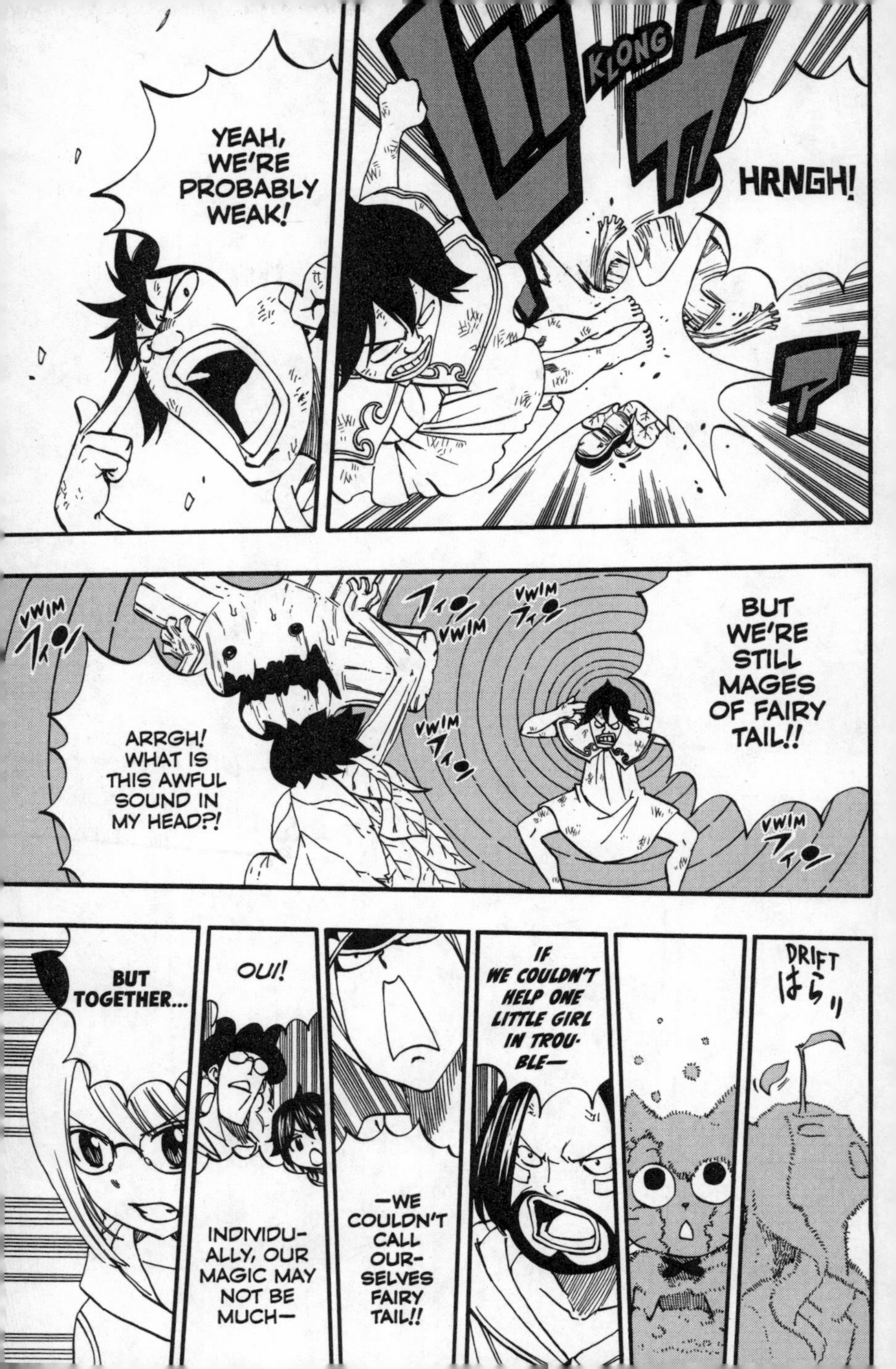
KLONG
HRNGH!
YEAH, WE'RE PROBABLY WEAK!
BUT WE'RE STILL MAGES OF FAIRY TAIL!!
VWIM
VWIM
VWIM
VWIM
VWIM
VWIM
ARRGH! WHAT IS THIS AWFUL SOUND IN MY HEAD?!
DRIFT
はらり
IF WE COULDN'T HELP ONE LITTLE GIRL IN TROUBLE—
—WE COULDN'T CALL OURSELVES FAIRY TAIL!!
OUI!
INDIVIDUALLY, OUR MAGIC MAY NOT BE MUCH—
BUT TOGETHER...

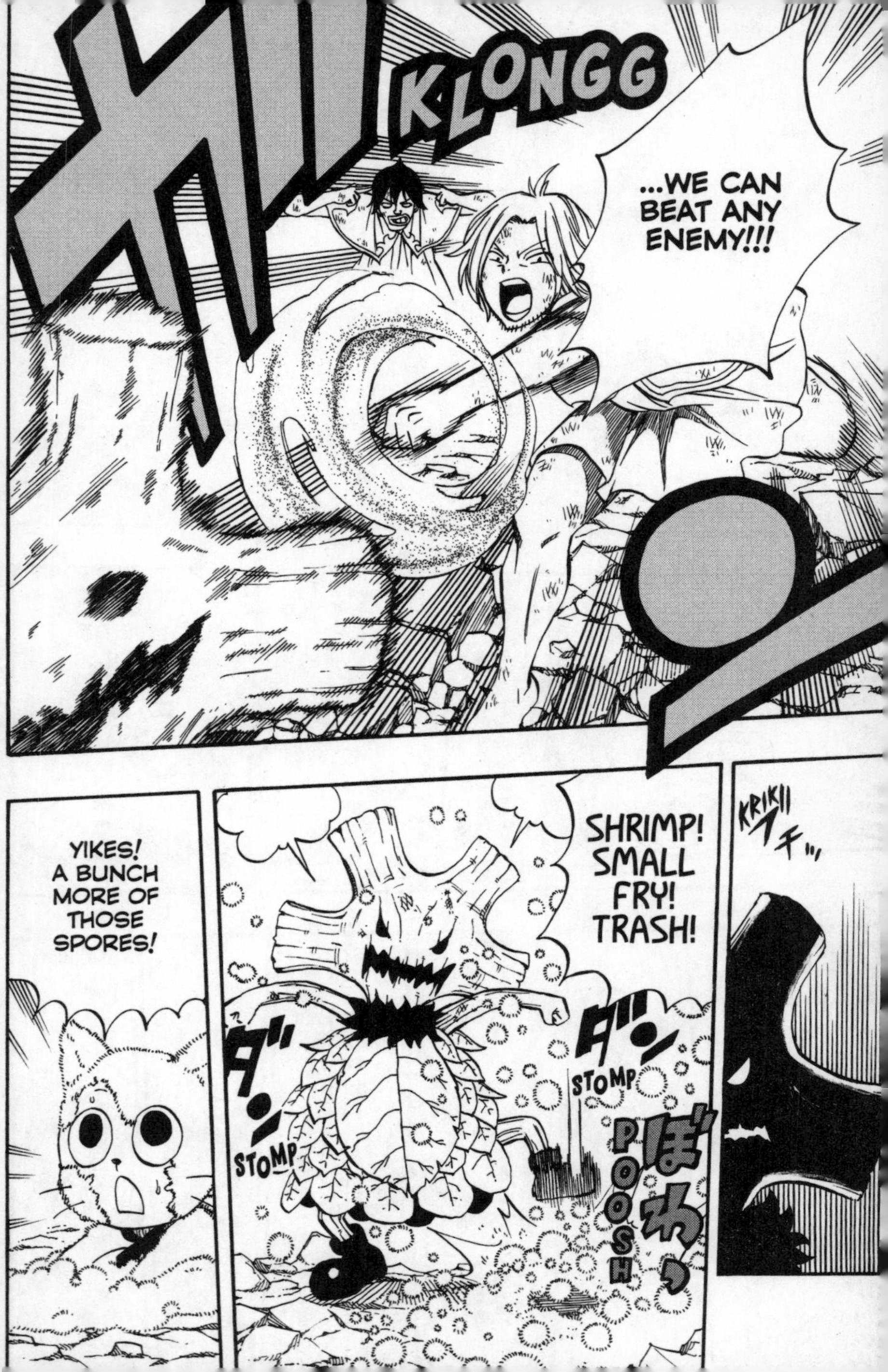
KLONGG
...WE CAN BEAT ANY ENEMY!!!
KRIK
SHRIMP! SMALL FRY! TRASH!
STOMP
STOMP
POOSH
YIKES! A BUNCH MORE OF THOSE SPORES!

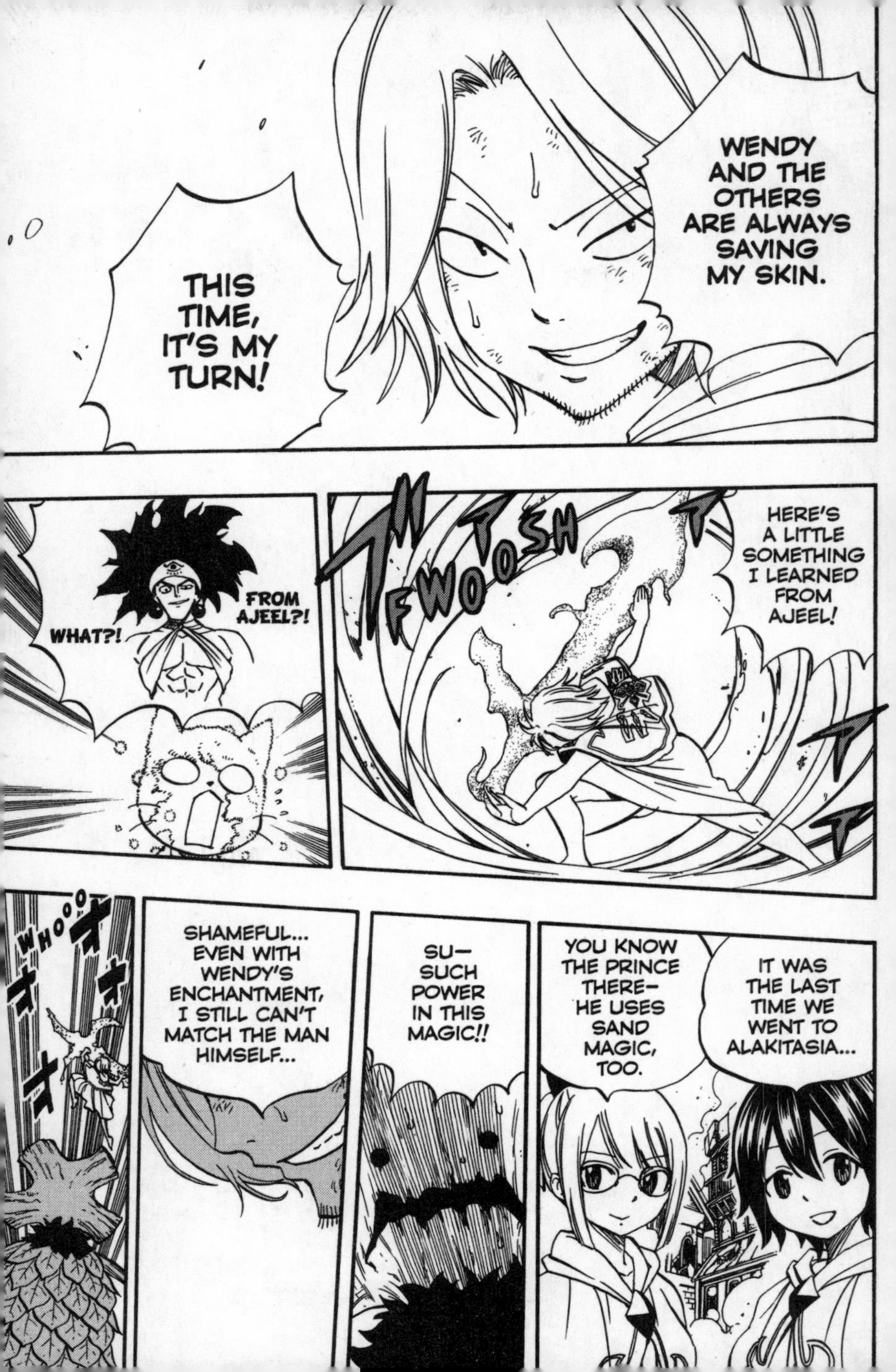
WENDY AND THE OTHERS ARE ALWAYS SAVING MY SKIN.
THIS TIME, IT'S MY TURN!
HERE'S A LITTLE SOMETHING I LEARNED FROM AJEEL!
FWOOSH
FROM AJEEL?!
WHAT?!
IT WAS THE LAST TIME WE WENT TO ALAKITASIA...
YOU KNOW THE PRINCE THERE— HE USES SAND MAGIC, TOO.
SU— SUCH POWER IN THIS MAGIC!!
SHAMEFUL... EVEN WITH WENDY'S ENCHANTMENT, I STILL CAN'T MATCH THE MAN HIMSELF...
WHOOO

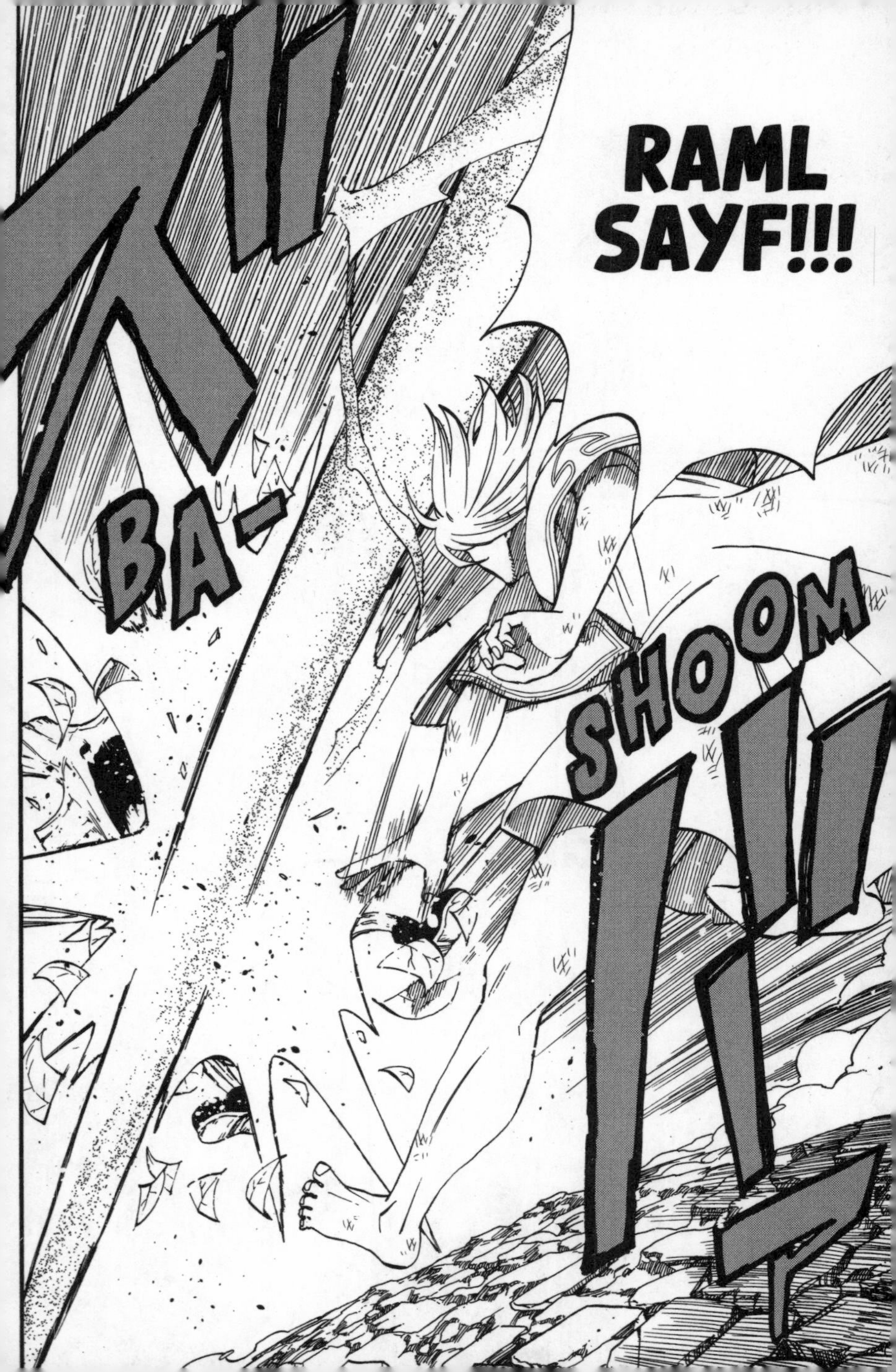
RAML SAYF!!!
SHOOM!!
BA-

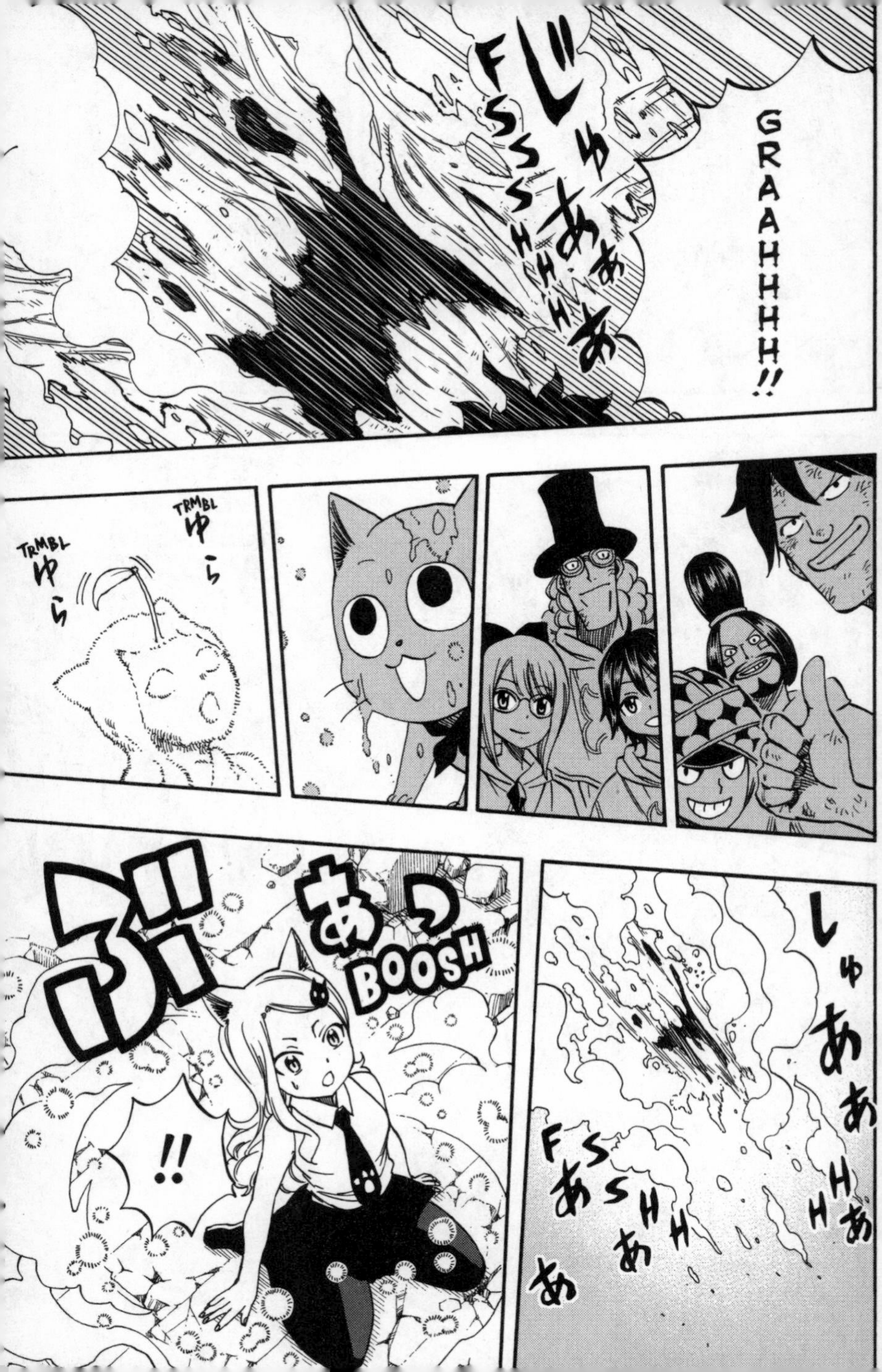

GRAAHHHH!!
じゅあああ
FSSSHHHH
TRMBL
ゆら
TRMBL
ゆら
しゅああああ
FSSHHH
ぶあっ
BOOSH
!!

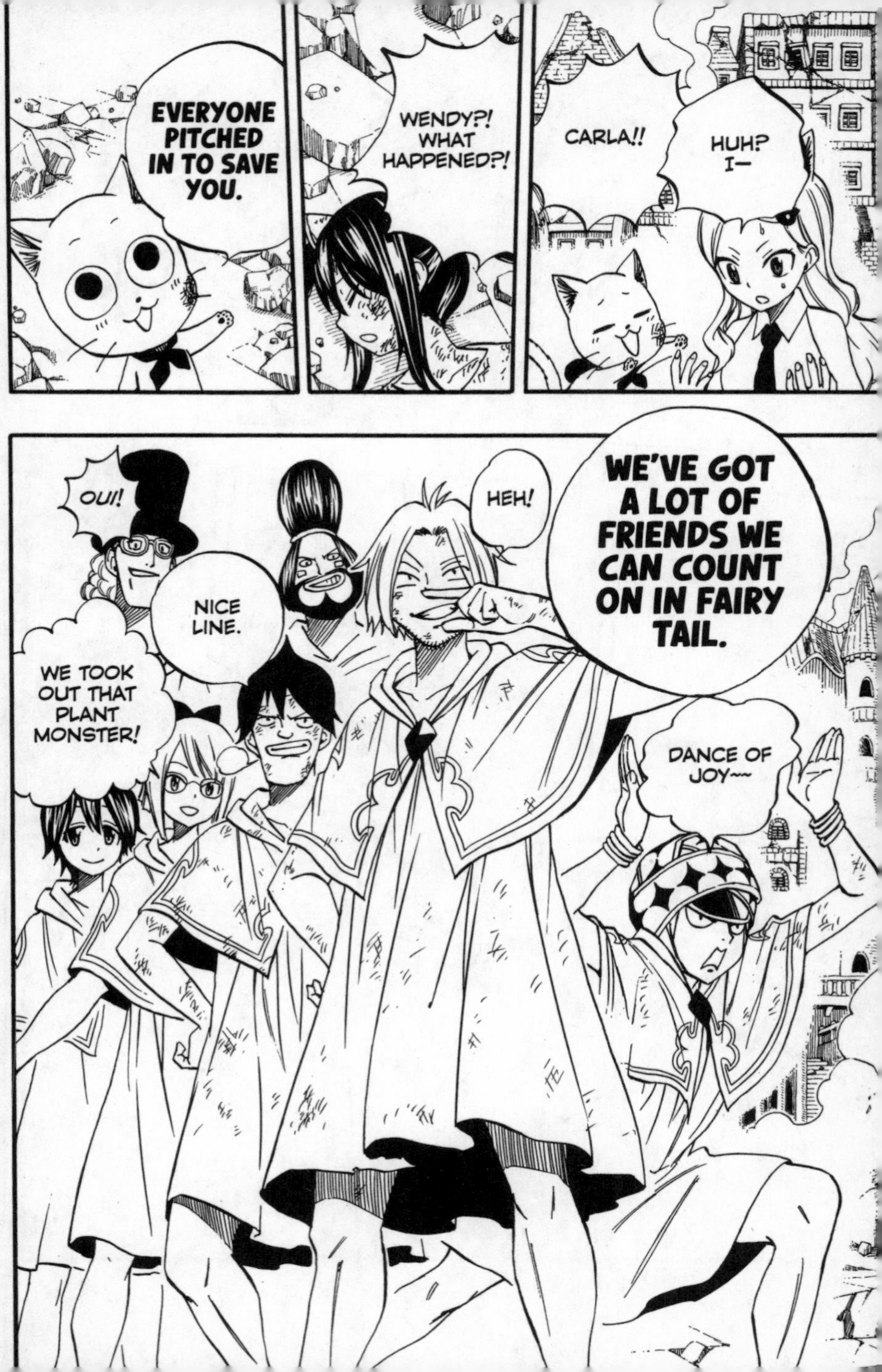
HUH? I—
CARLA!!
WENDY?! WHAT HAPPENED?!
EVERYONE PITCHED IN TO SAVE YOU.
WE'VE GOT A LOT OF FRIENDS WE CAN COUNT ON IN FAIRY TAIL.
HEH!
OUI!
NICE LINE.
DANCE OF JOY~~
WE TOOK OUT THAT PLANT MONSTER!

FAIRY TAIL 100 YEARS QUEST

Chapter 57: Strength to Live

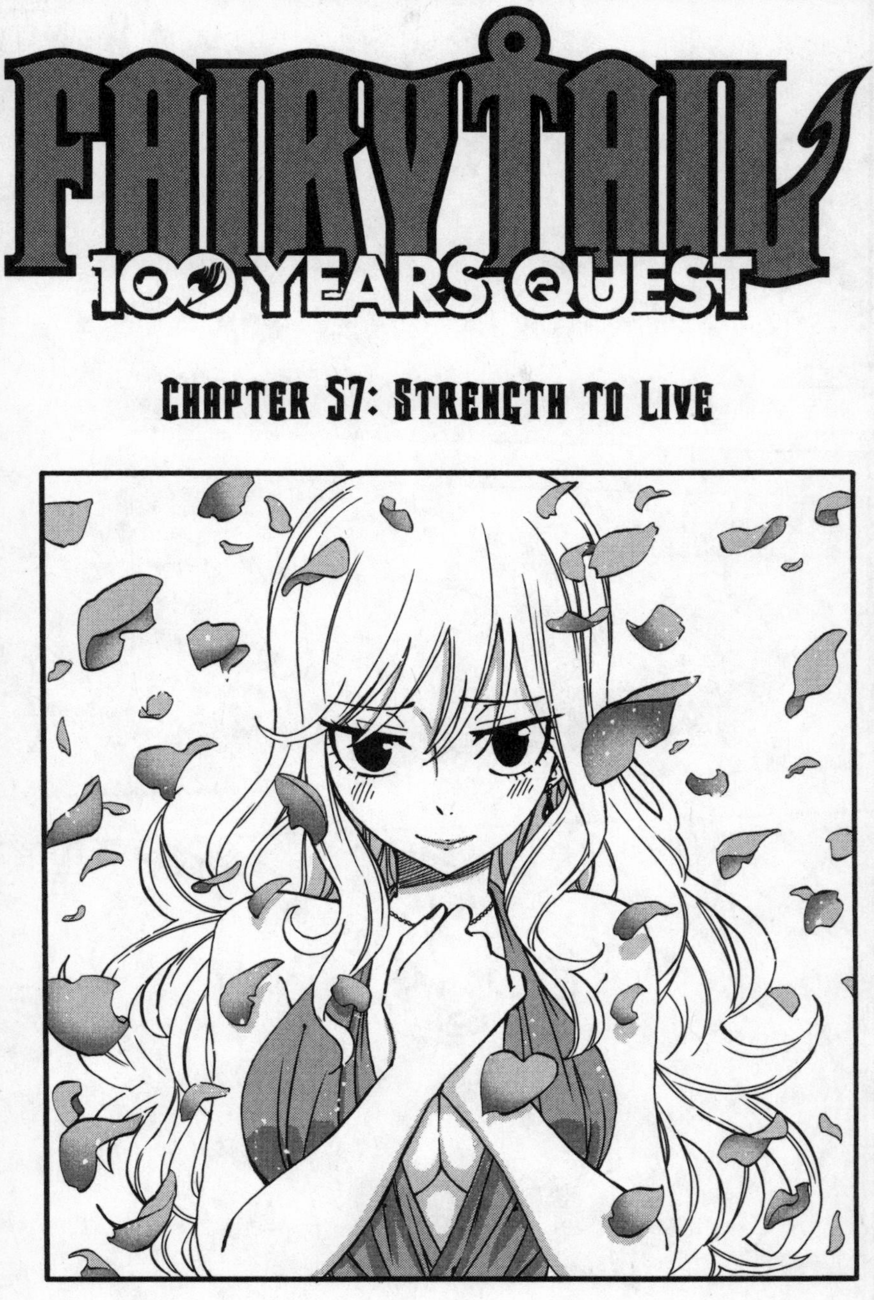

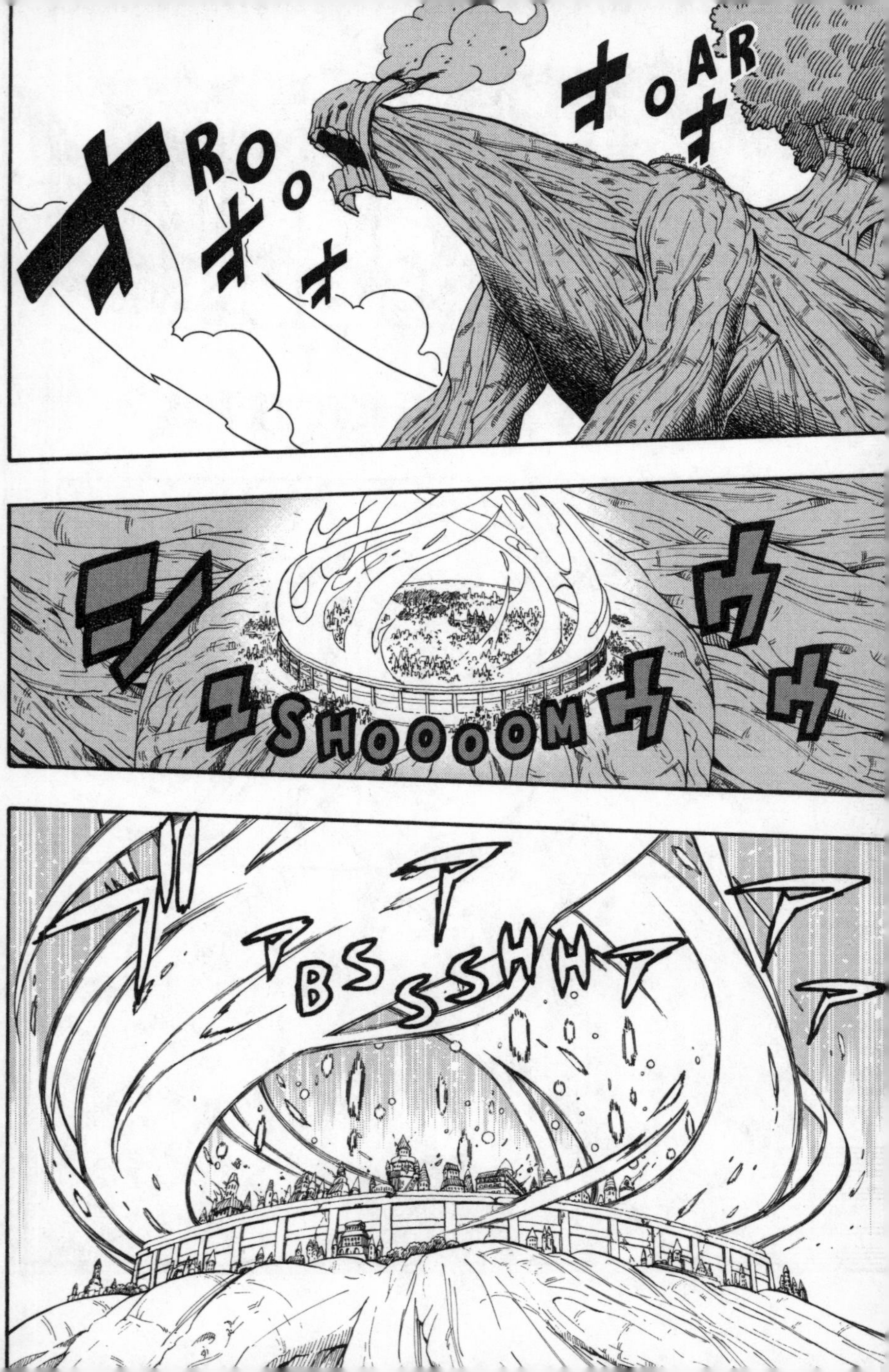

RO
O
OAR
SHOOOOM
BS
SSHH

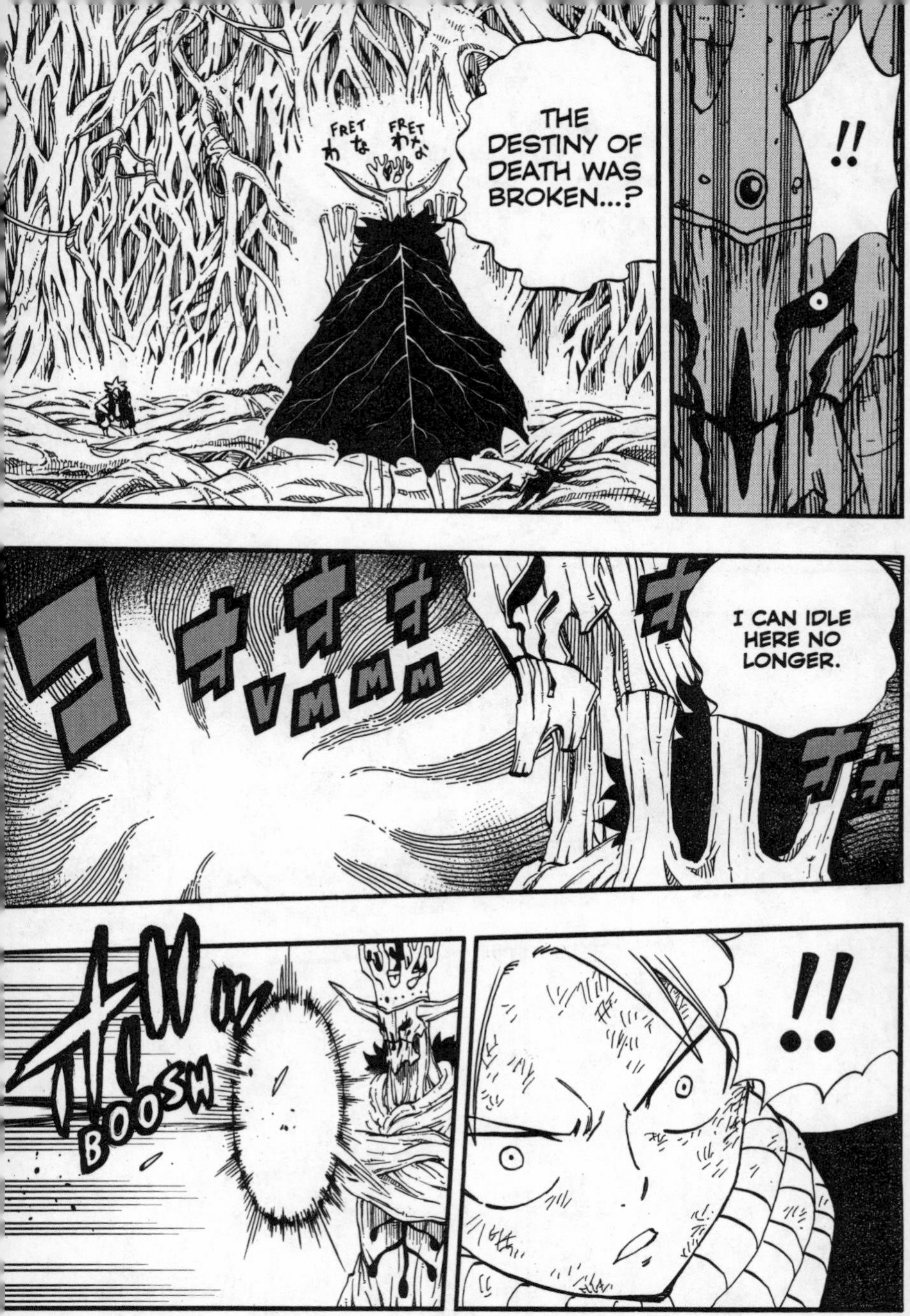
!!
THE DESTINY OF DEATH WAS BROKEN...?
FRET FRET
わなわな
I CAN IDLE HERE NO LONGER.
VMMM
!!
BOOSH

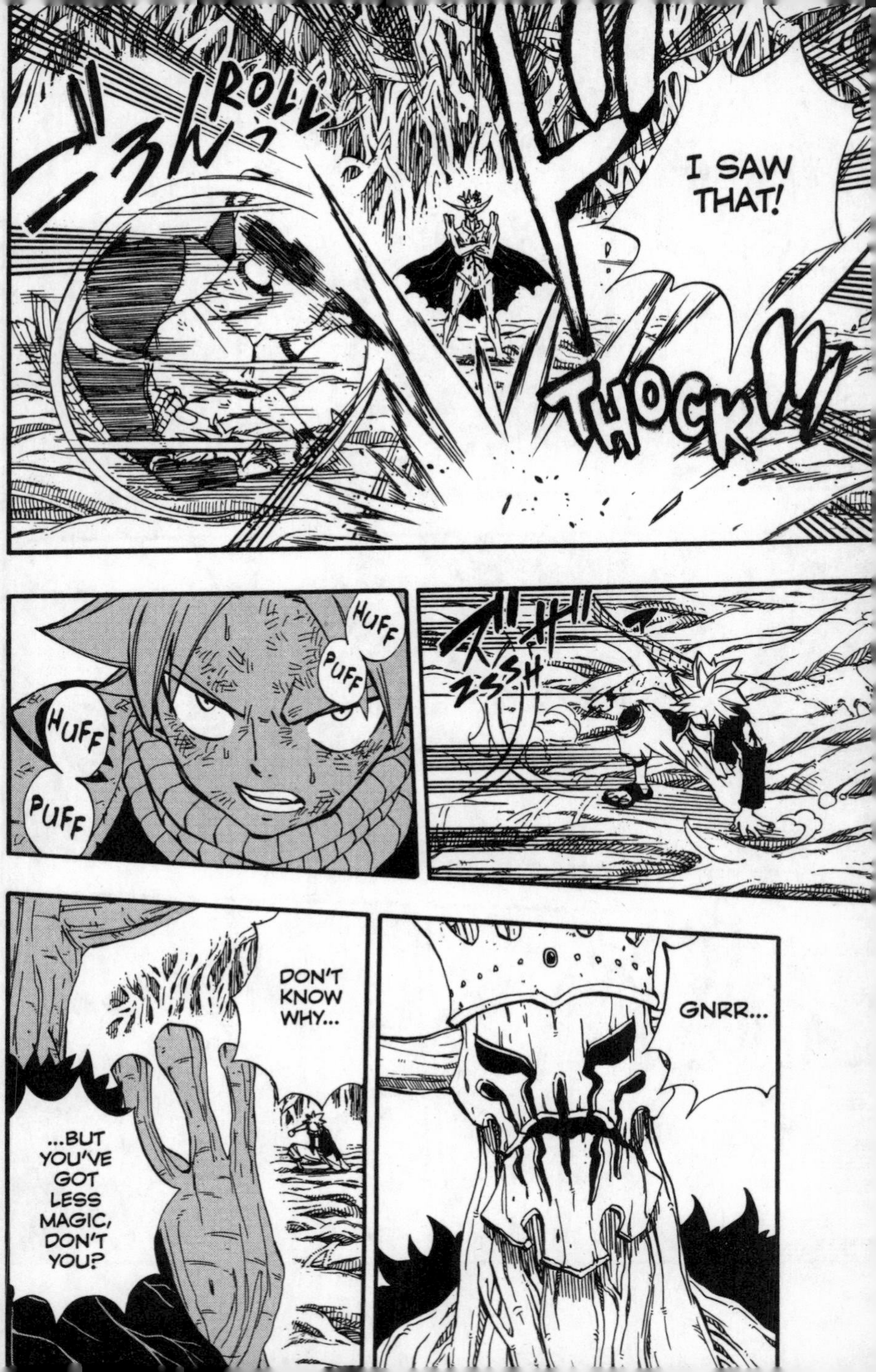
I SAW THAT!
ROLL
THOCK!!
ZSSH
HUFF
PUFF
HUFF
PUFF
GNRR...
DON'T KNOW WHY...
...BUT YOU'VE GOT LESS MAGIC, DON'T YOU?

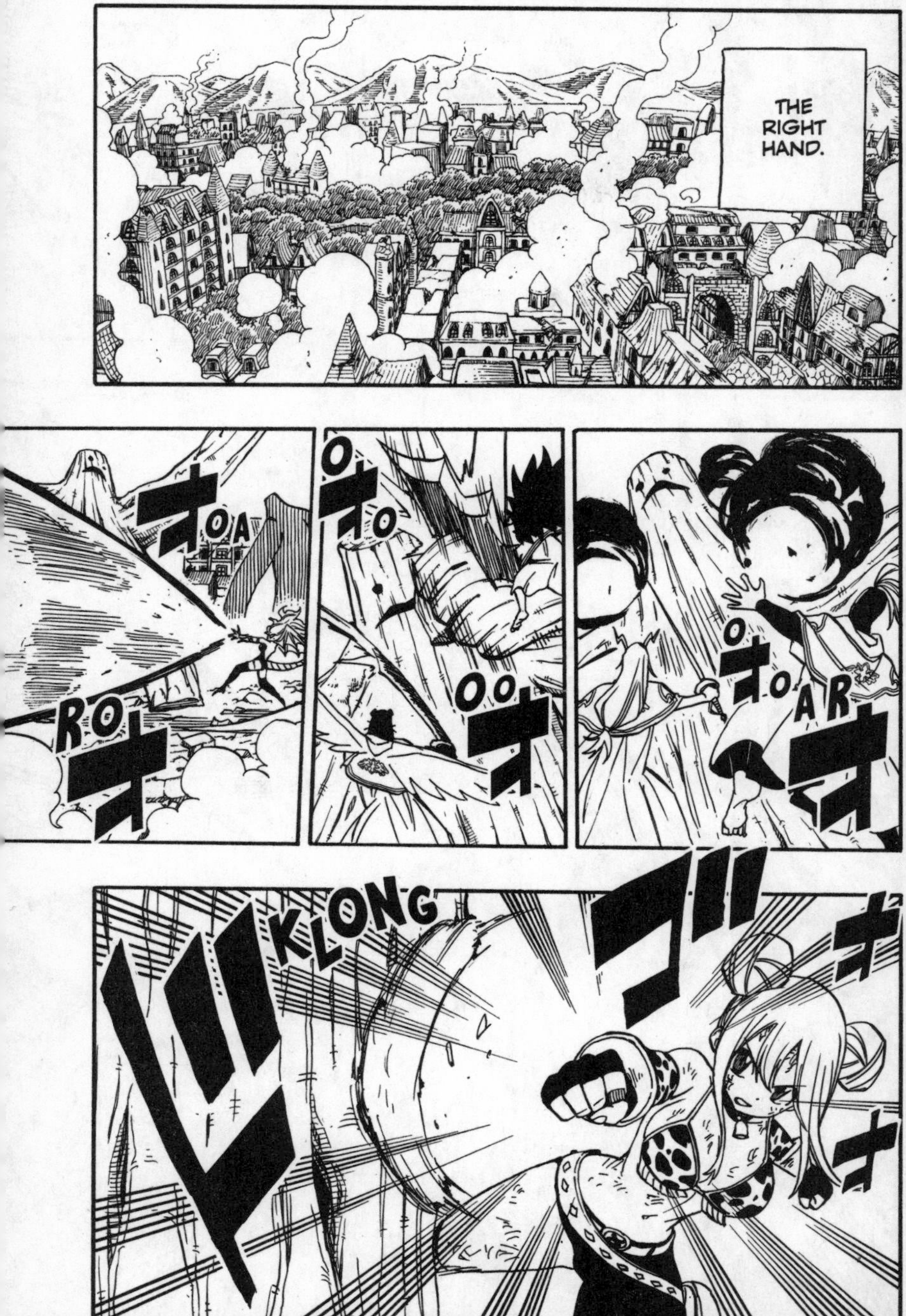
THE RIGHT HAND.
OOAR
OOOO
ROOA
KLONG

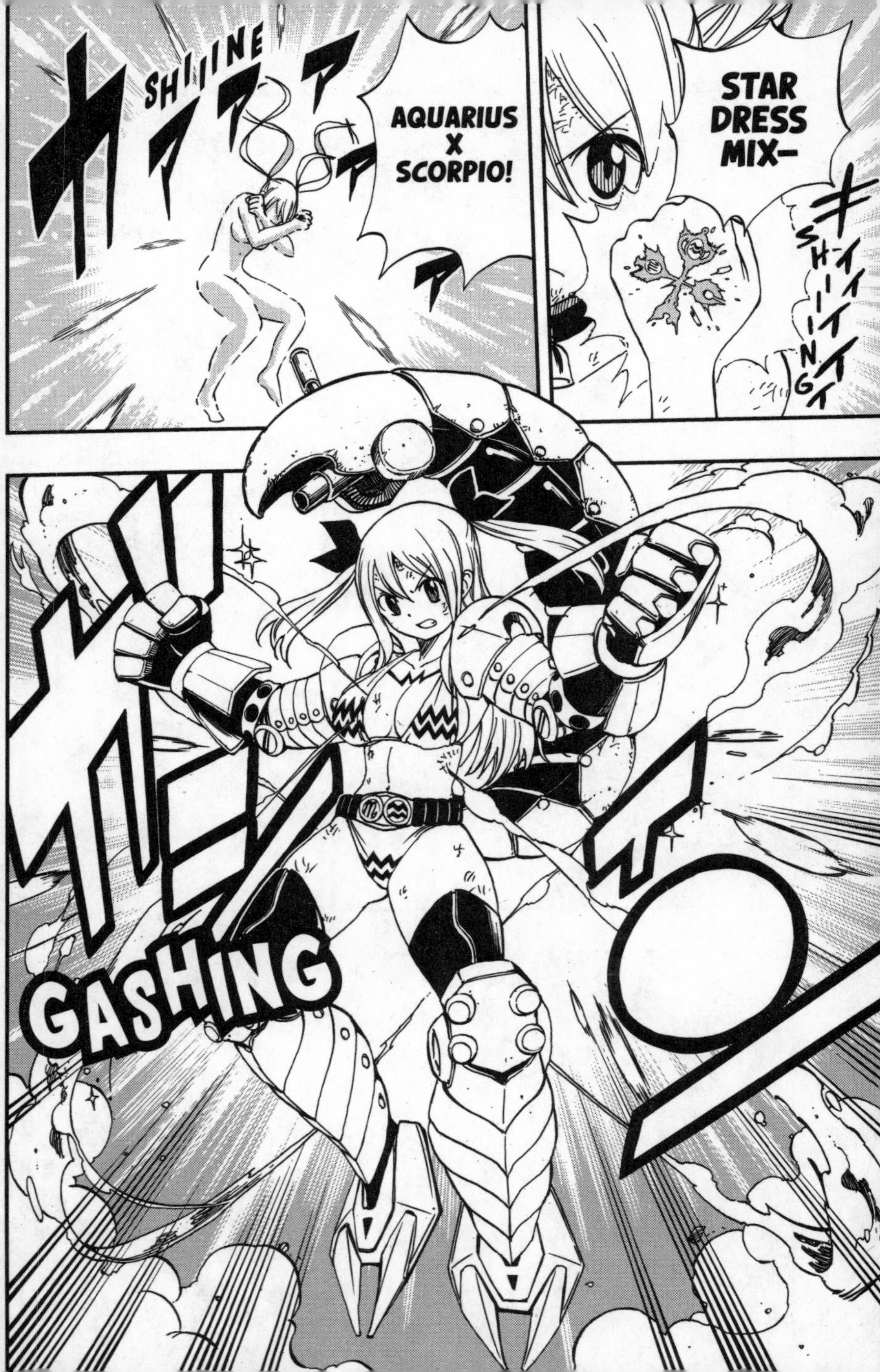
STAR DRESS MIX—
SHIIING
AQUARIUS X SCORPIO!
SHIIINE
GASHING

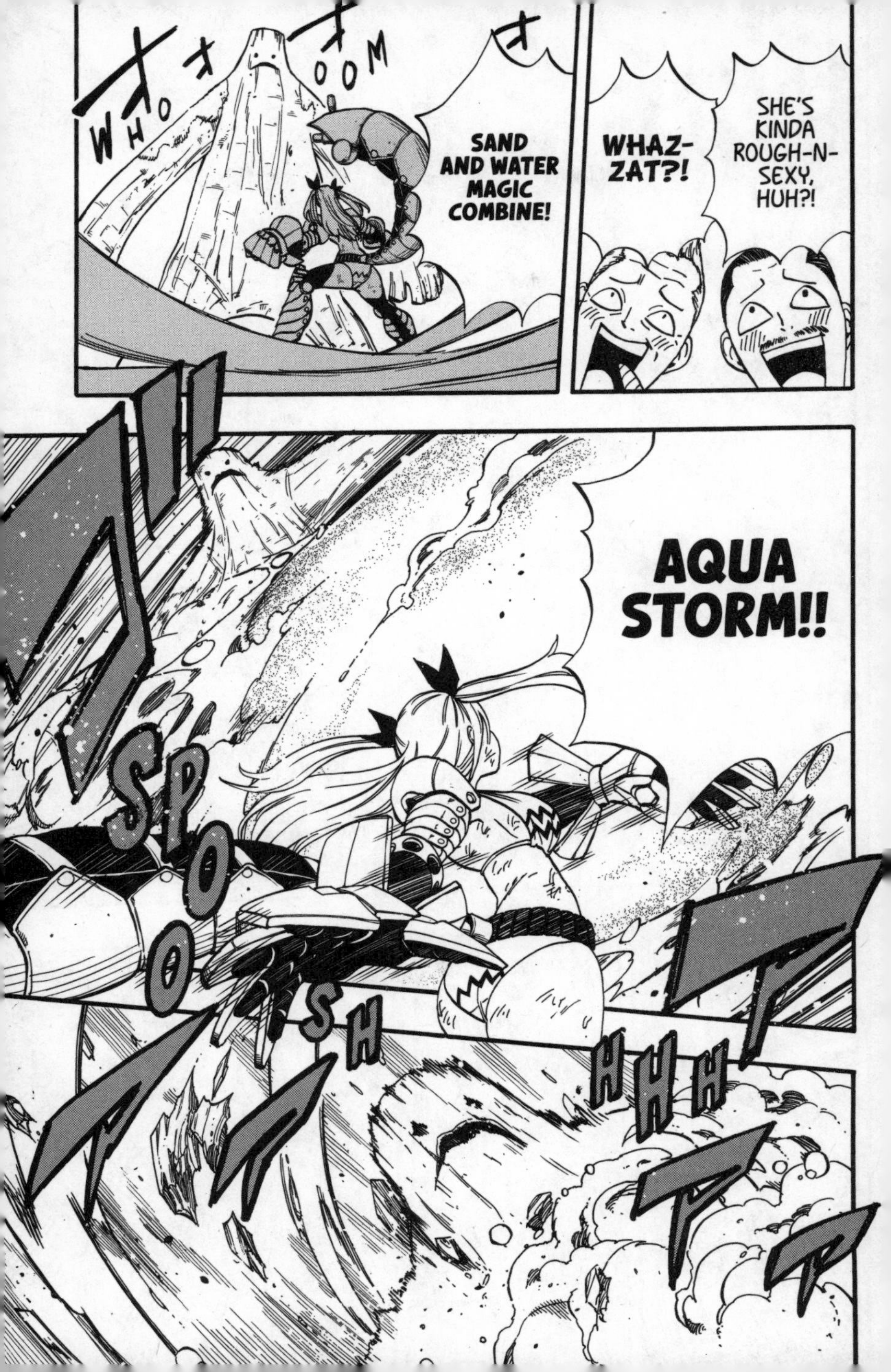
SHE'S KINDA ROUGH-N-SEXY, HUH?!
WHAZ-ZAT?!
WHOOOM
SAND AND WATER MAGIC COMBINE!
AQUA STORM!!
SPOOSH
HHHH

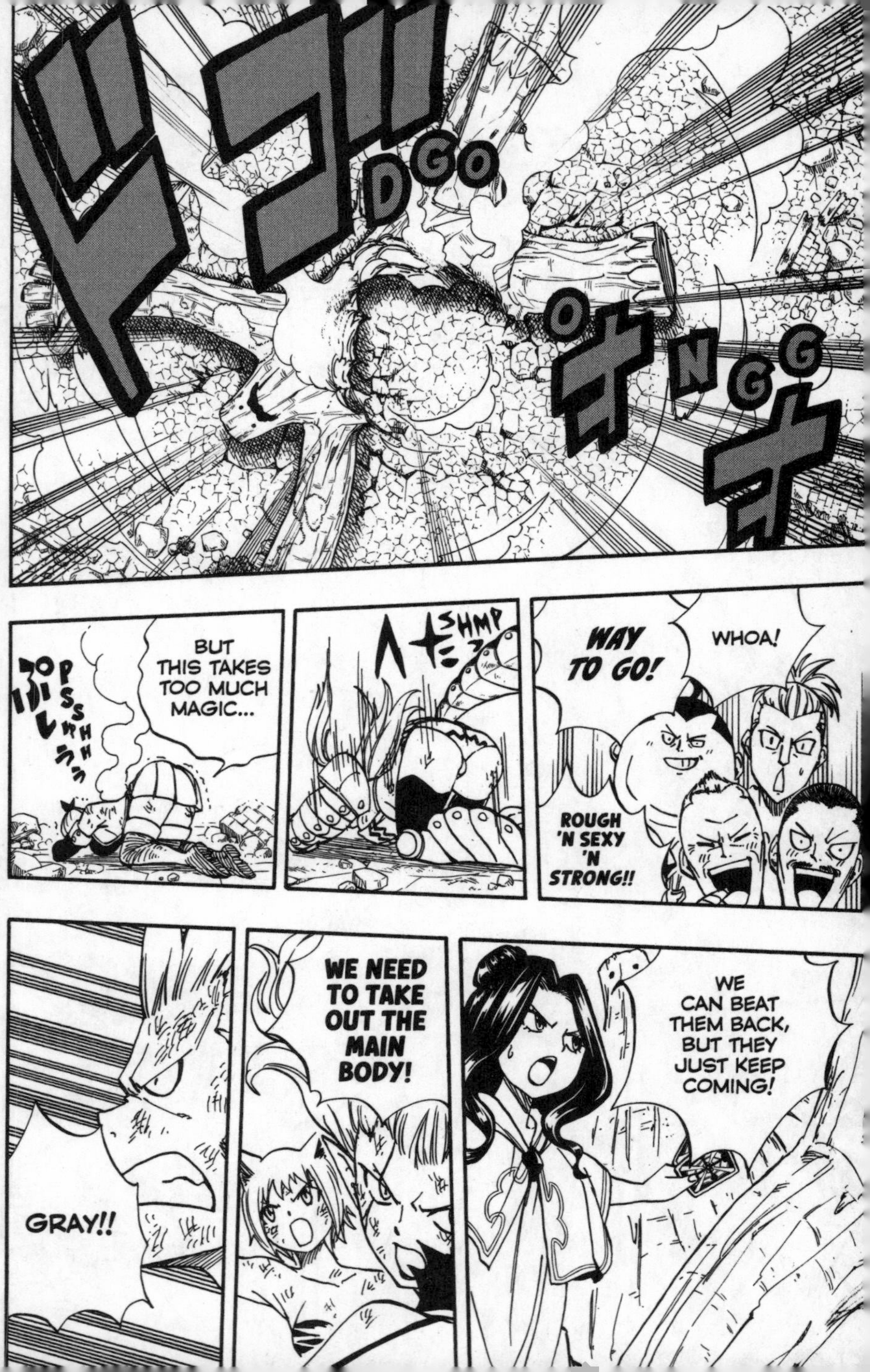
DGO
ONGG
WHOA!
WAY TO GO!
ROUGH 'N SEXY 'N STRONG!!
SHMP
BUT THIS TAKES TOO MUCH MAGIC...
PSSHH
WE CAN BEAT THEM BACK, BUT THEY JUST KEEP COMING!
WE NEED TO TAKE OUT THE MAIN BODY!
GRAY!!

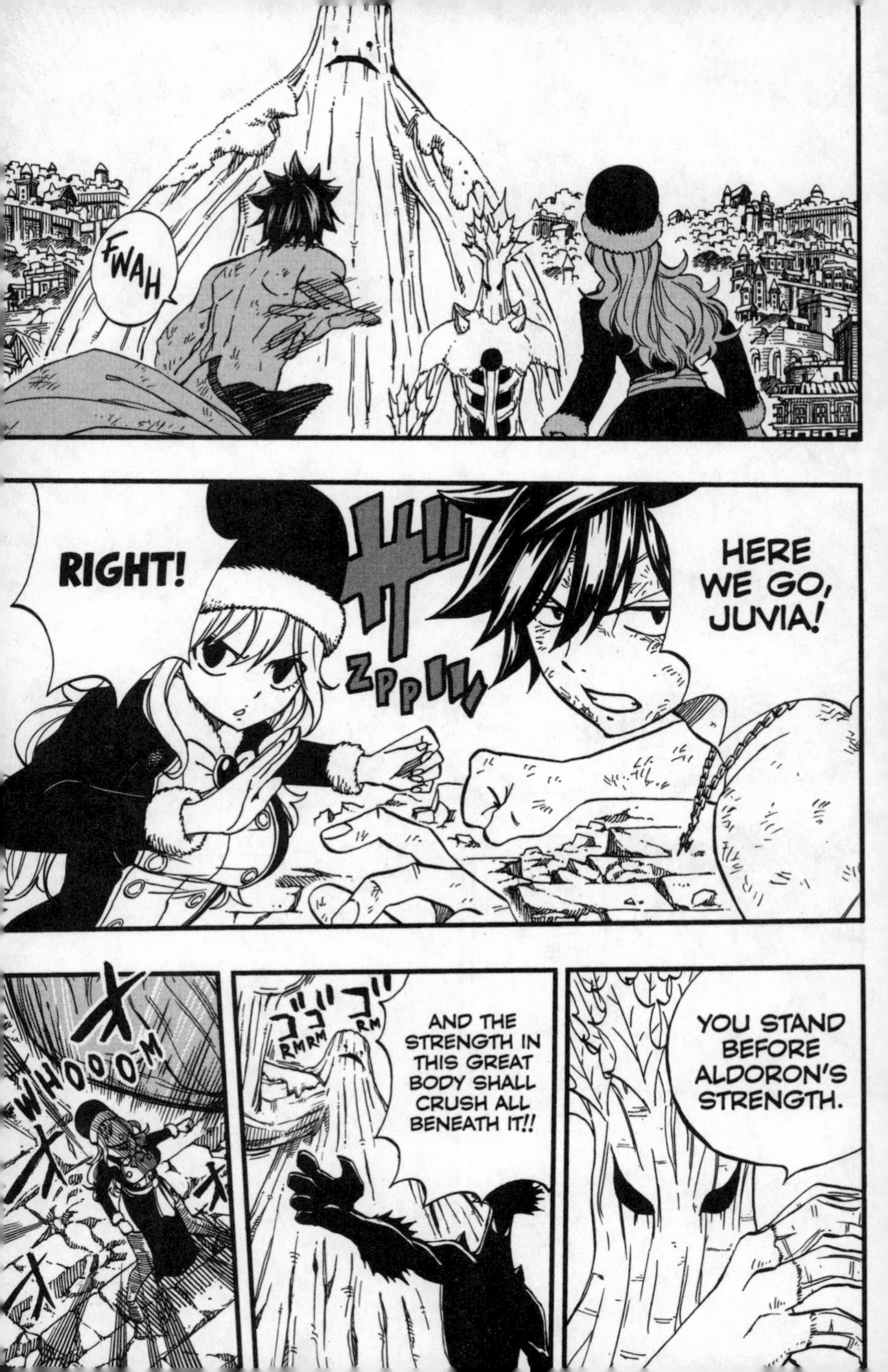
FWAH
HERE WE GO, JUVIA!
RIGHT!
ZPPIN
YOU STAND BEFORE ALDORON'S STRENGTH.
RMRM
RM
AND THE STRENGTH IN THIS GREAT BODY SHALL CRUSH ALL BENEATH IT!!
WHOOOM

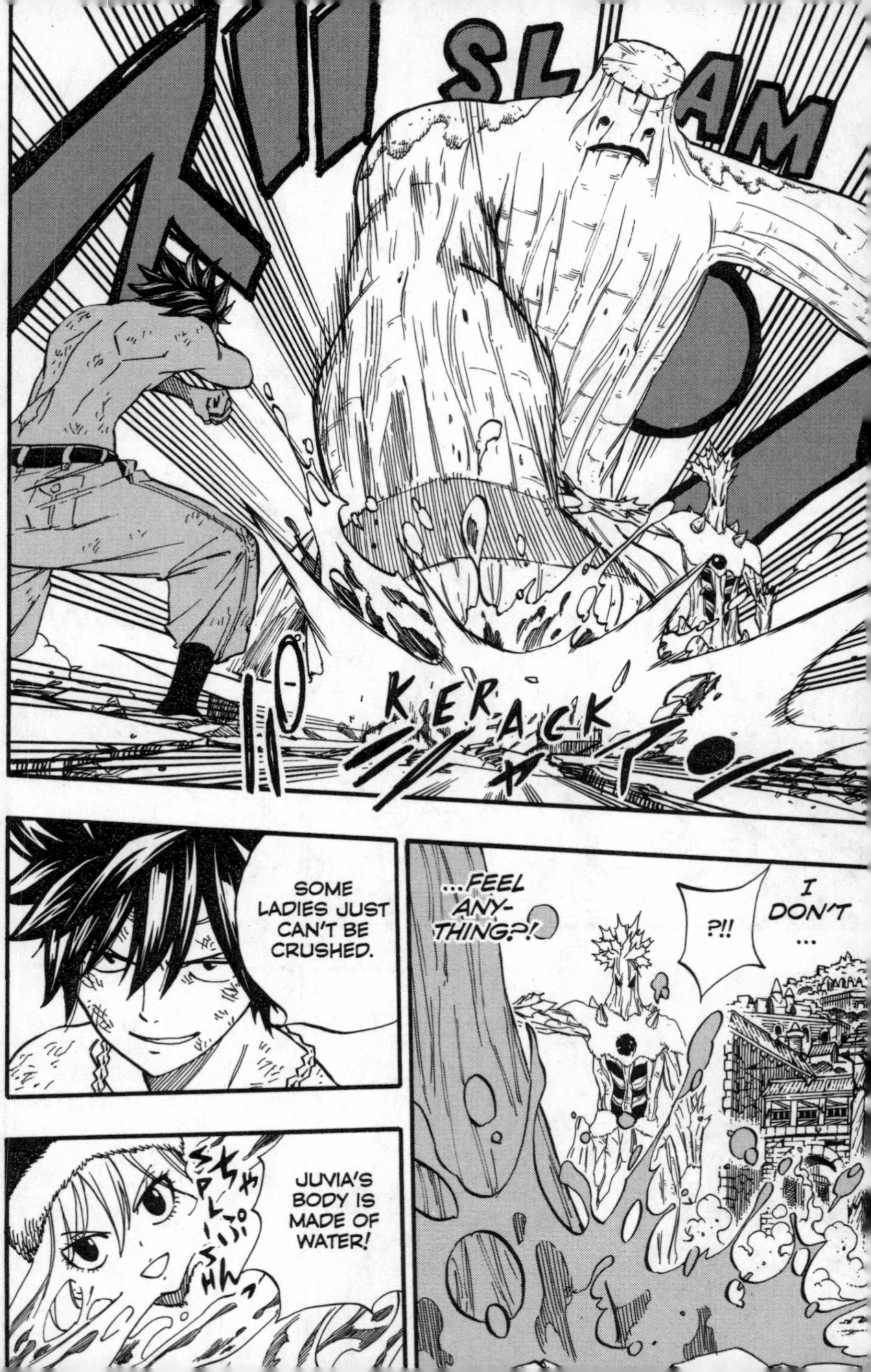
SLAM
KERACK
I DON'T ...
?!!
...FEEL ANY-THING?!
SOME LADIES JUST CAN'T BE CRUSHED.
JUVIA'S BODY IS MADE OF WATER!

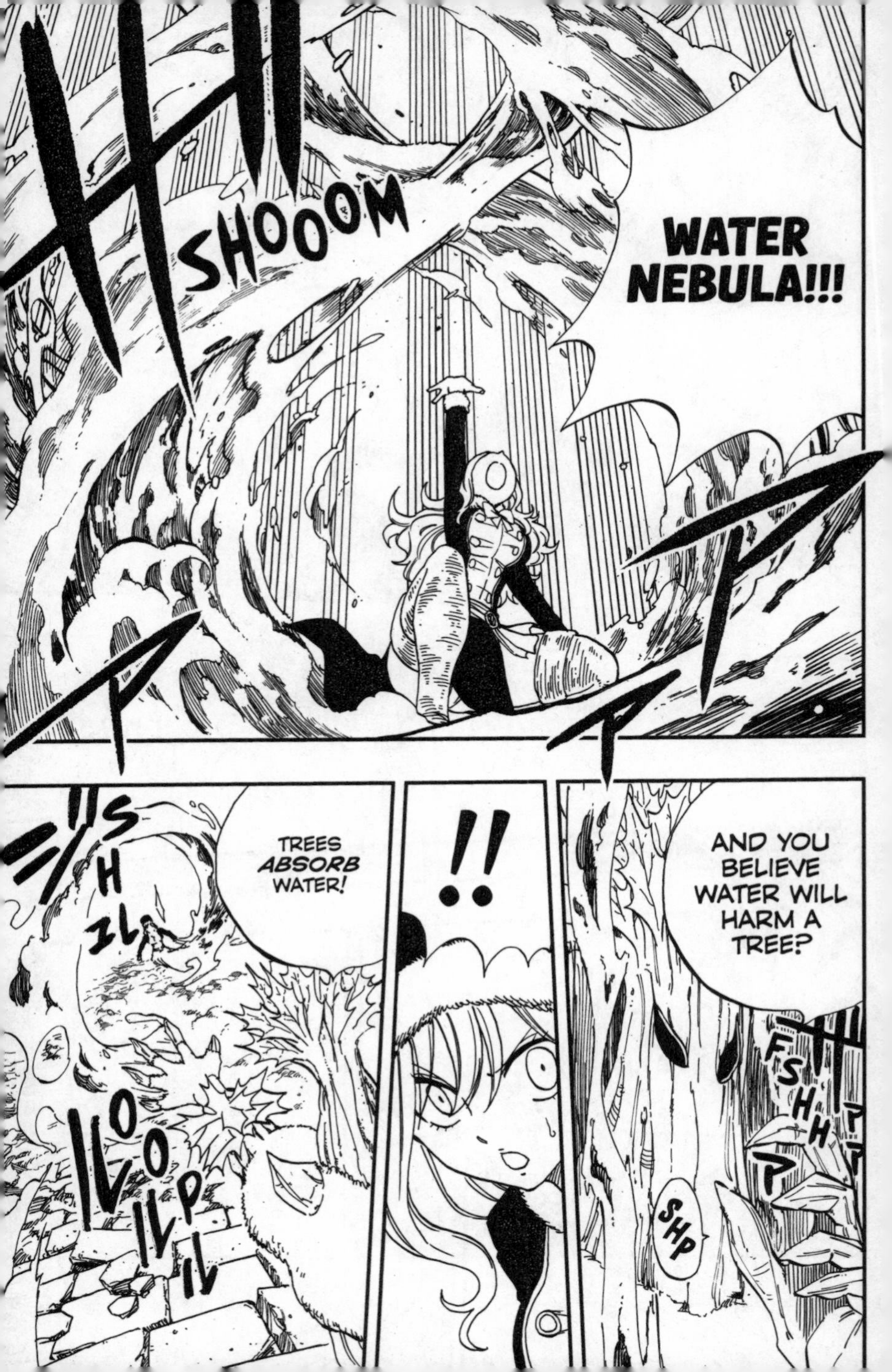
WATER NEBULA!!!
SHOOOM
AND YOU BELIEVE WATER WILL HARM A TREE?
FSHHP
SHP
!!
TREES ABSORB WATER!

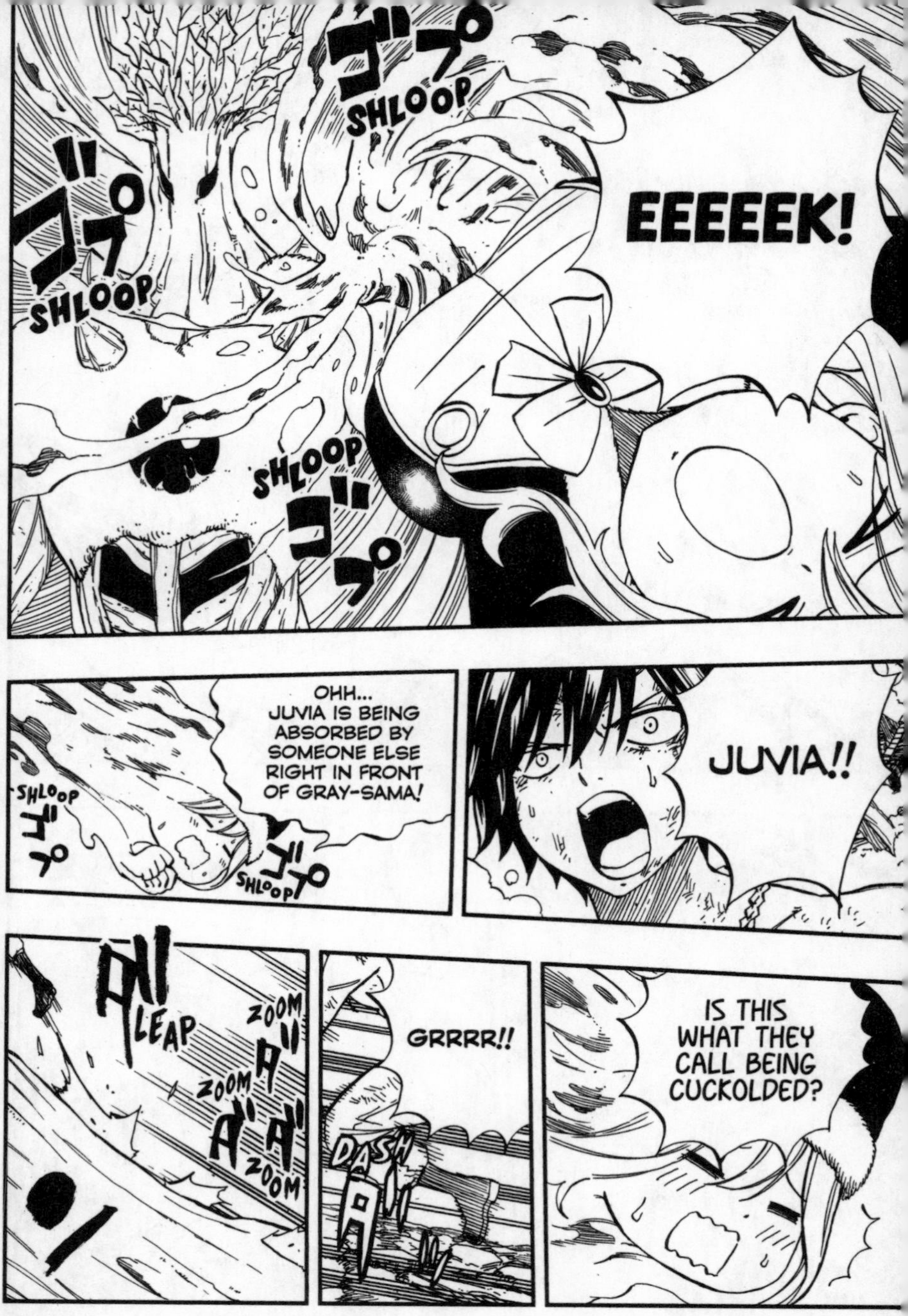
EEEEEK!
SHLOOP
SHLOOP
SHLOOP
JUVIA!!
OHH... JUVIA IS BEING ABSORBED BY SOMEONE ELSE RIGHT IN FRONT OF GRAY-SAMA!
SHLOOP
SHLOOP
IS THIS WHAT THEY CALL BEING CUCKOLDED?
GRRRR!!
DASH
LEAP
ZOOM
ZOOM
ZOOM

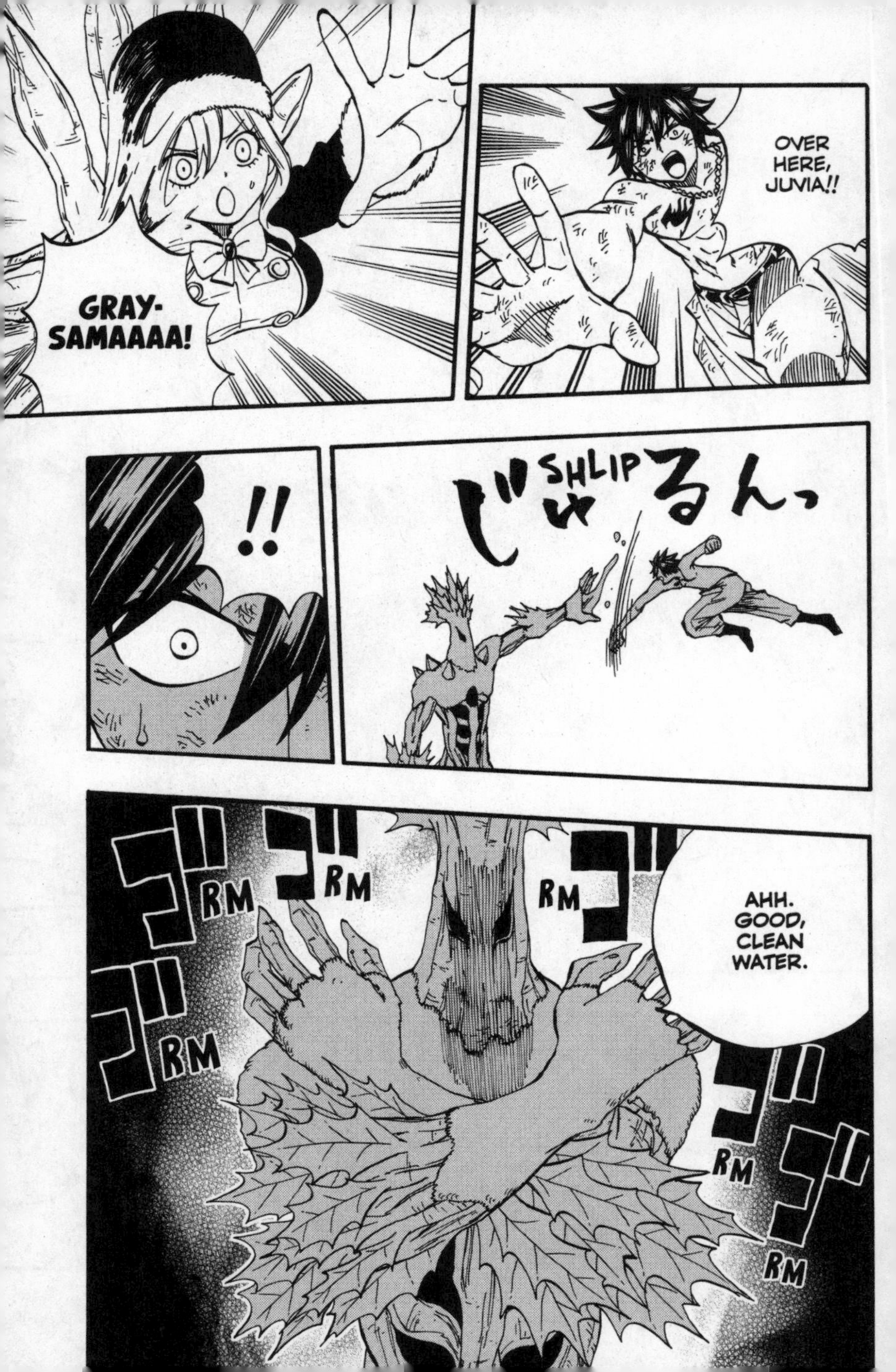
OVER HERE, JUVIA!!
GRAY-SAMAAAAA!
SHLIP
じゅるんっ
!!
AHH. GOOD, CLEAN WATER.
RM
RM
RM
RM
RM
RM

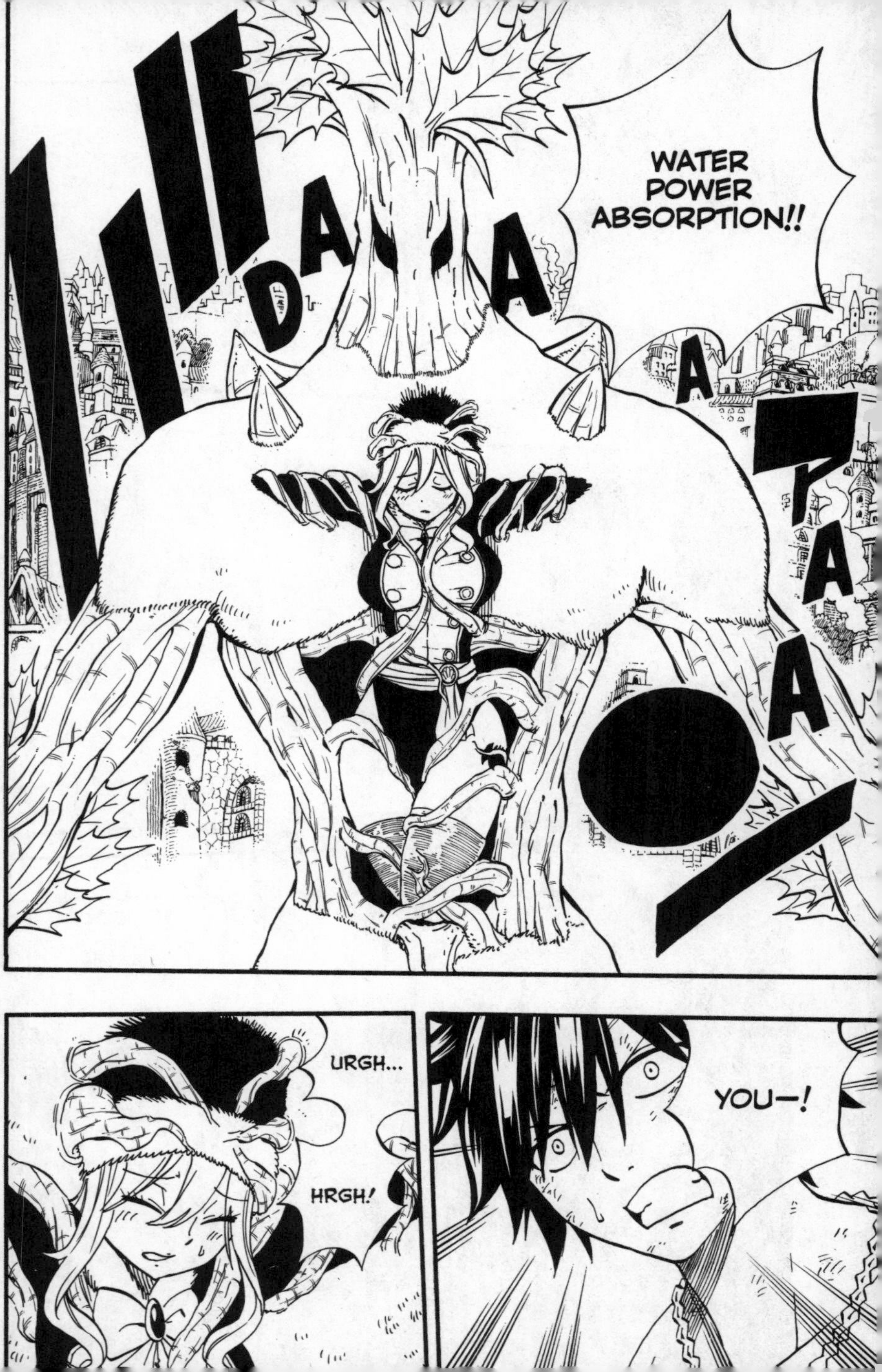
WATER POWER ABSORPTION!!
YOU—!
URGH...
HRGH!

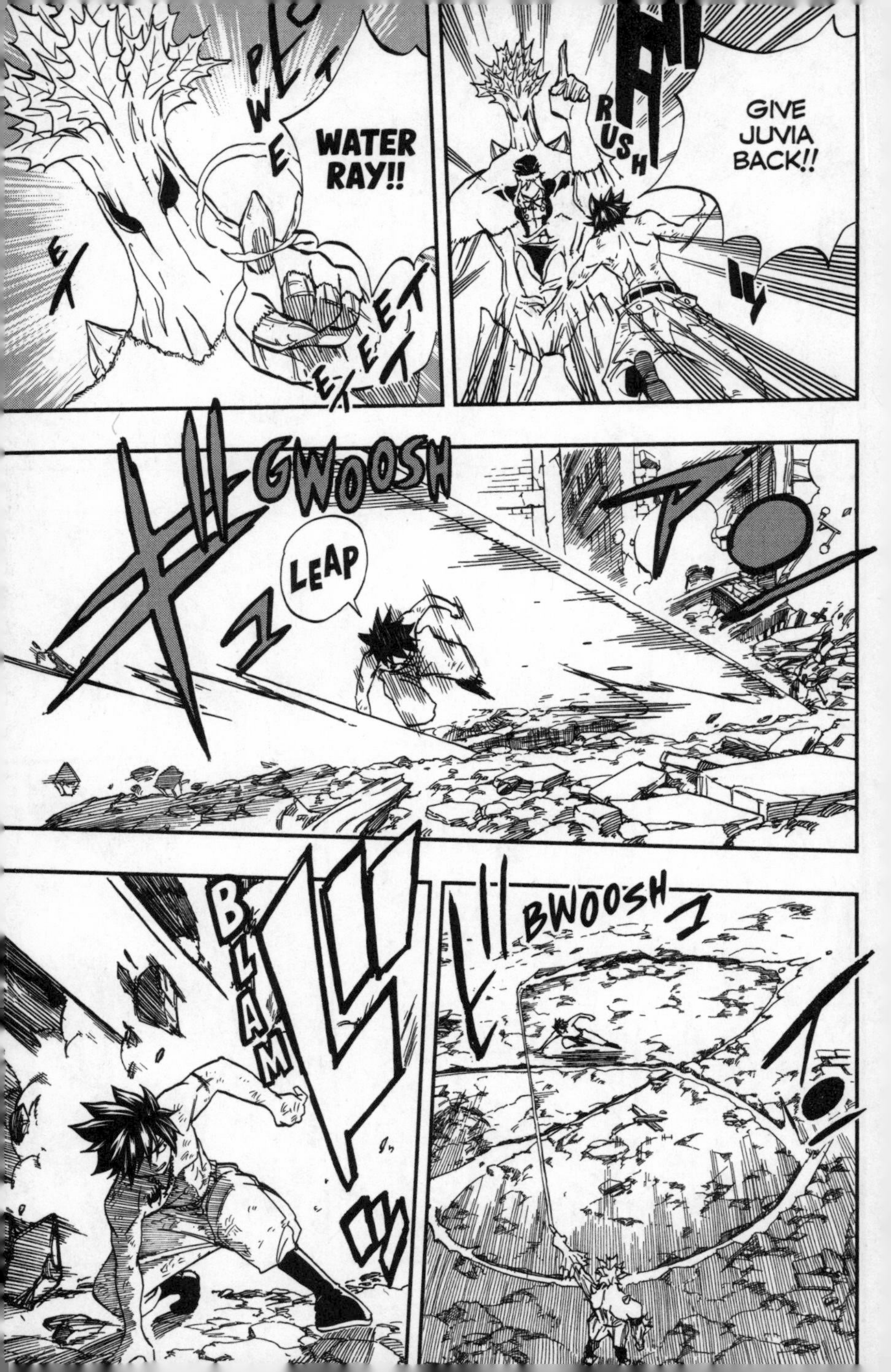
RUSH
GIVE JUVIA BACK!!
WATER RAY!!
GWOOSH
LEAP
BWOOSH
BLAM

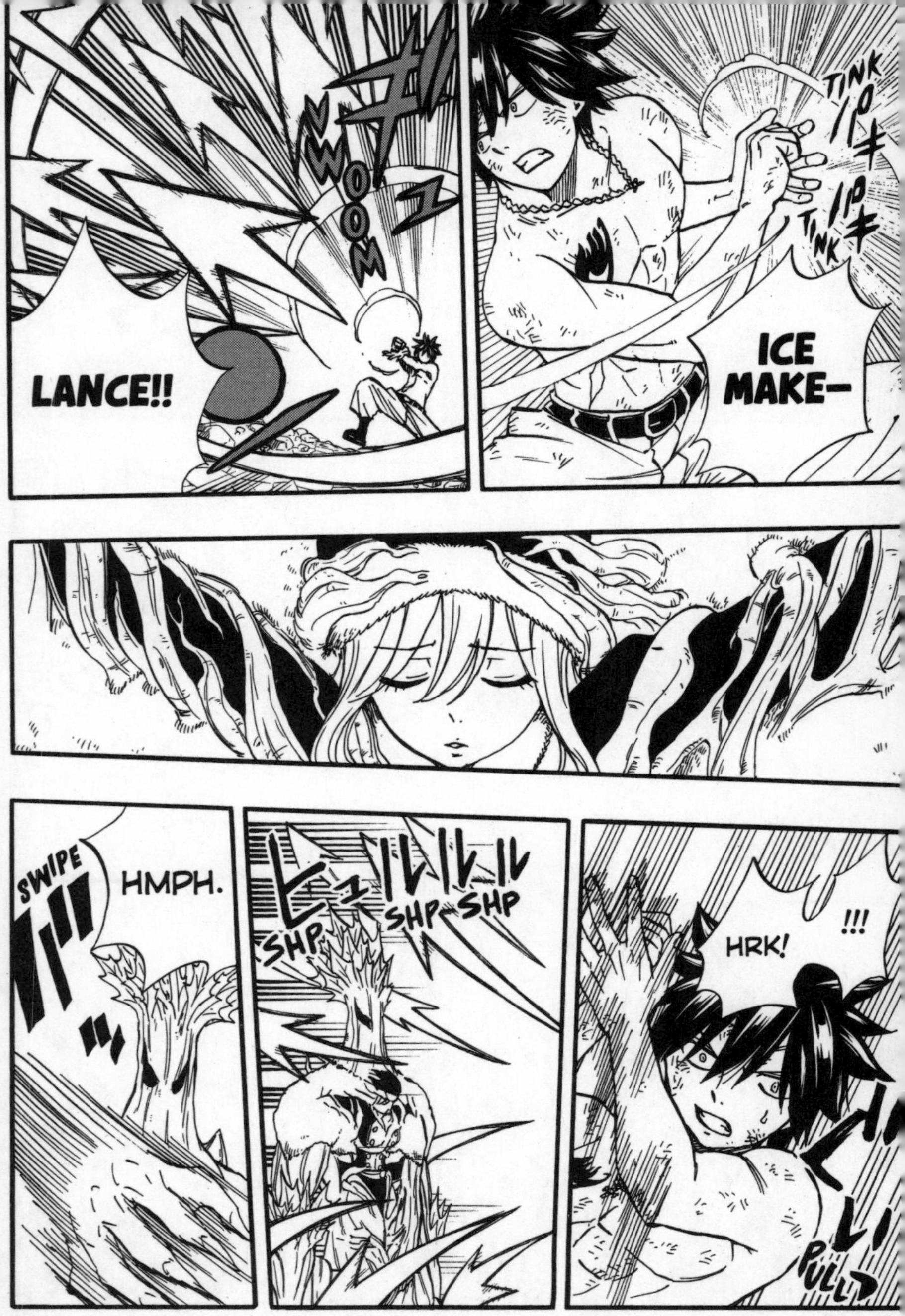
TINK
パキ
TINK
パキ
ICE MAKE—
VWOOOM
LANCE!!
!!!
HRK!
PULL
SHP SHP SHP
HMPH.
SWIPE

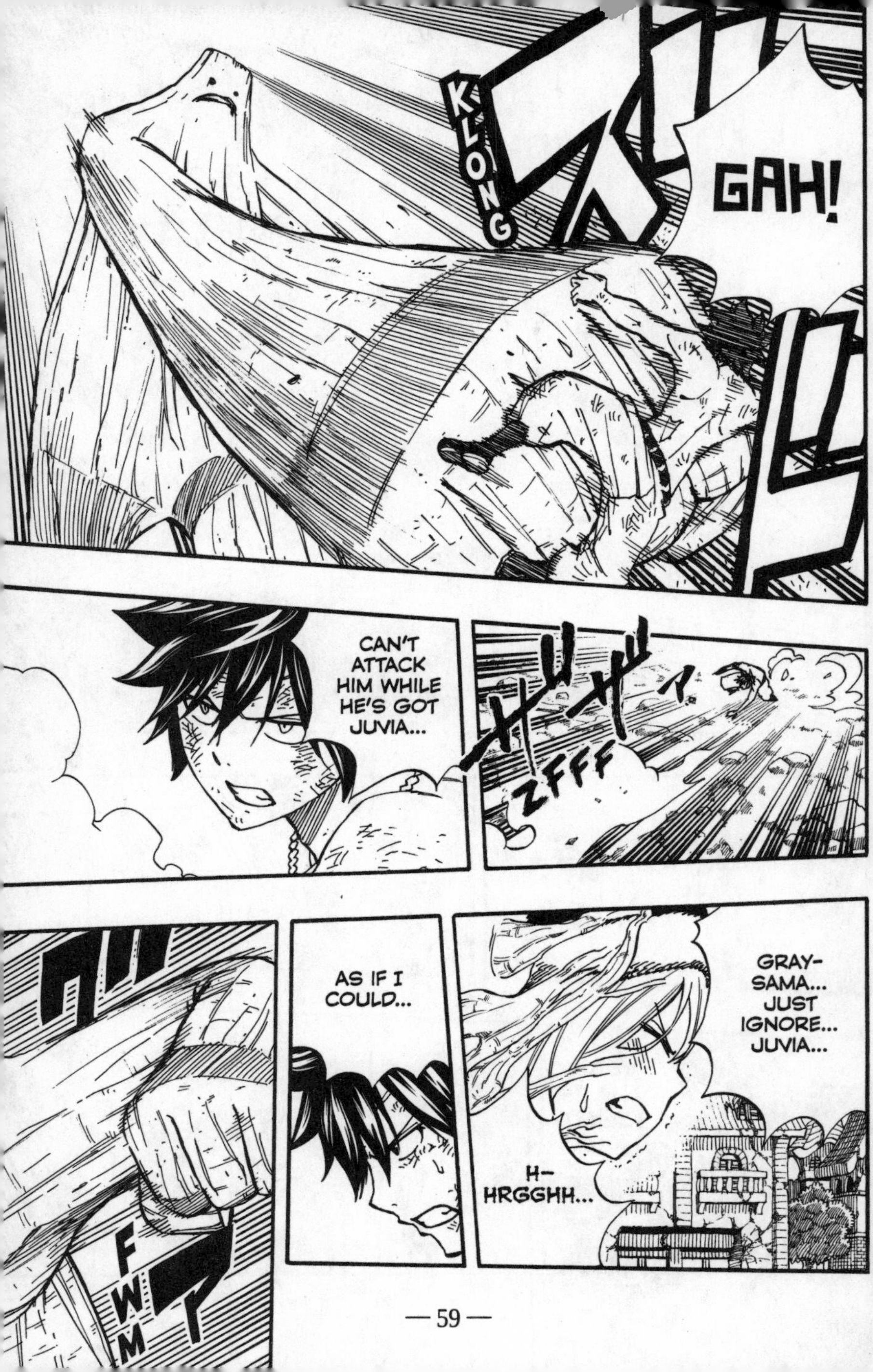
KLONG
GAH!
ZFFF
CAN'T ATTACK HIM WHILE HE'S GOT JUVIA...
GRAY-SAMA... JUST IGNORE... JUVIA...
H-HRGGHH...
AS IF I COULD...
FWM

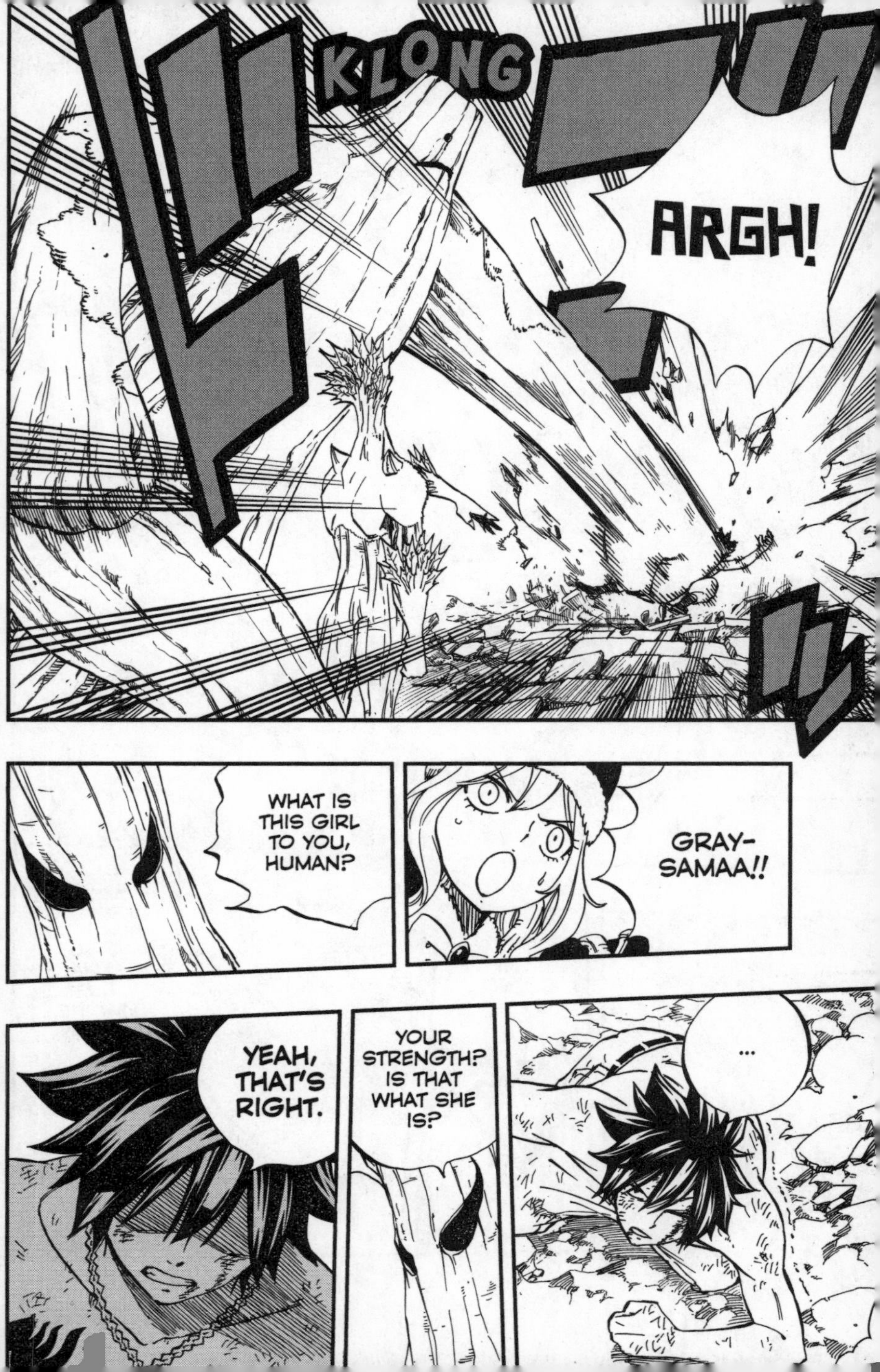
KLONG
ARGH!
GRAY-SAMAA!!
WHAT IS THIS GIRL TO YOU, HUMAN?
...
YOUR STRENGTH? IS THAT WHAT SHE IS?
YEAH, THAT'S RIGHT.

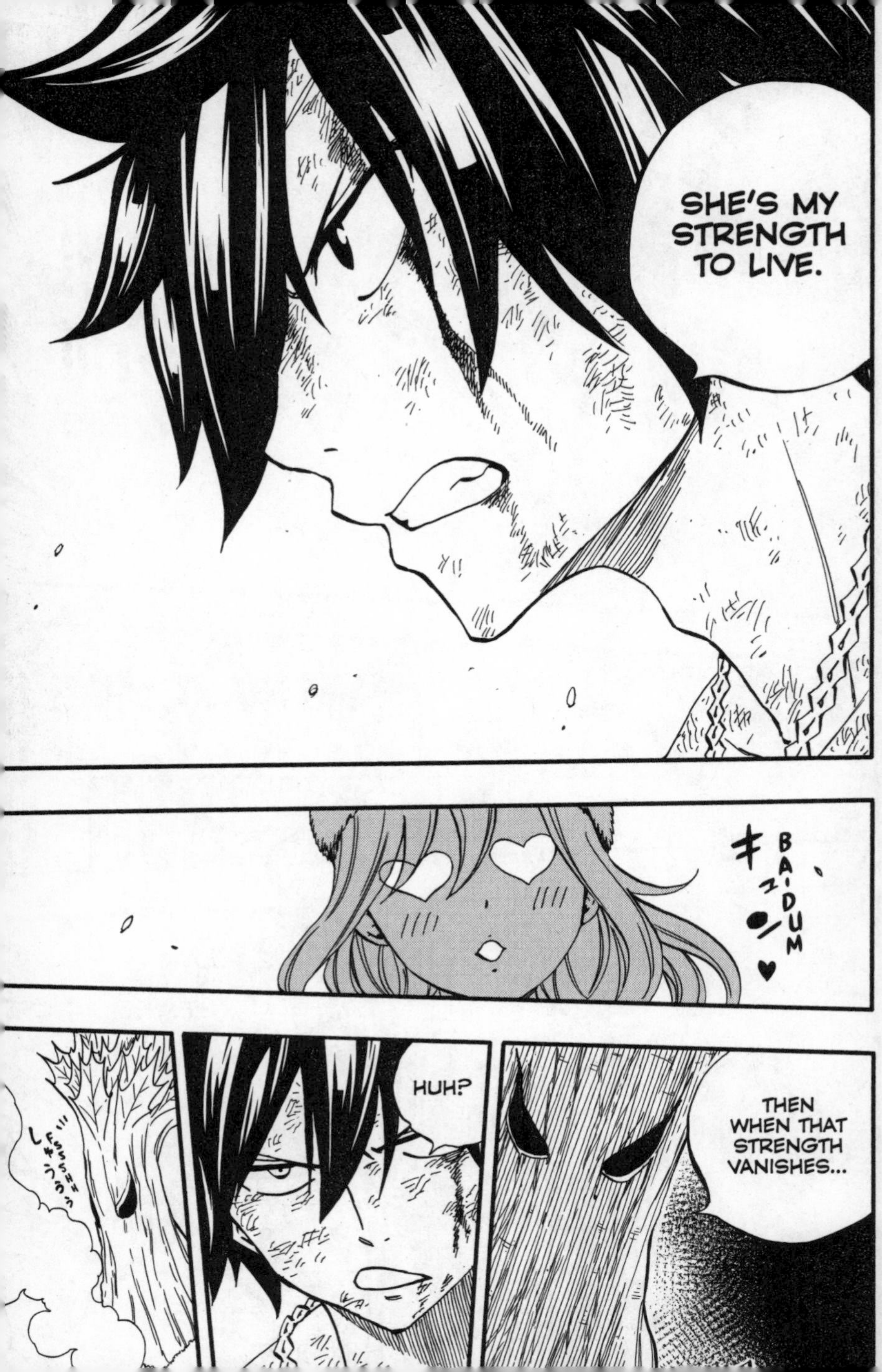
SHE'S MY STRENGTH TO LIVE.
BADUM
THEN WHEN THAT STRENGTH VANISHES...
HUH?
FSSSHH

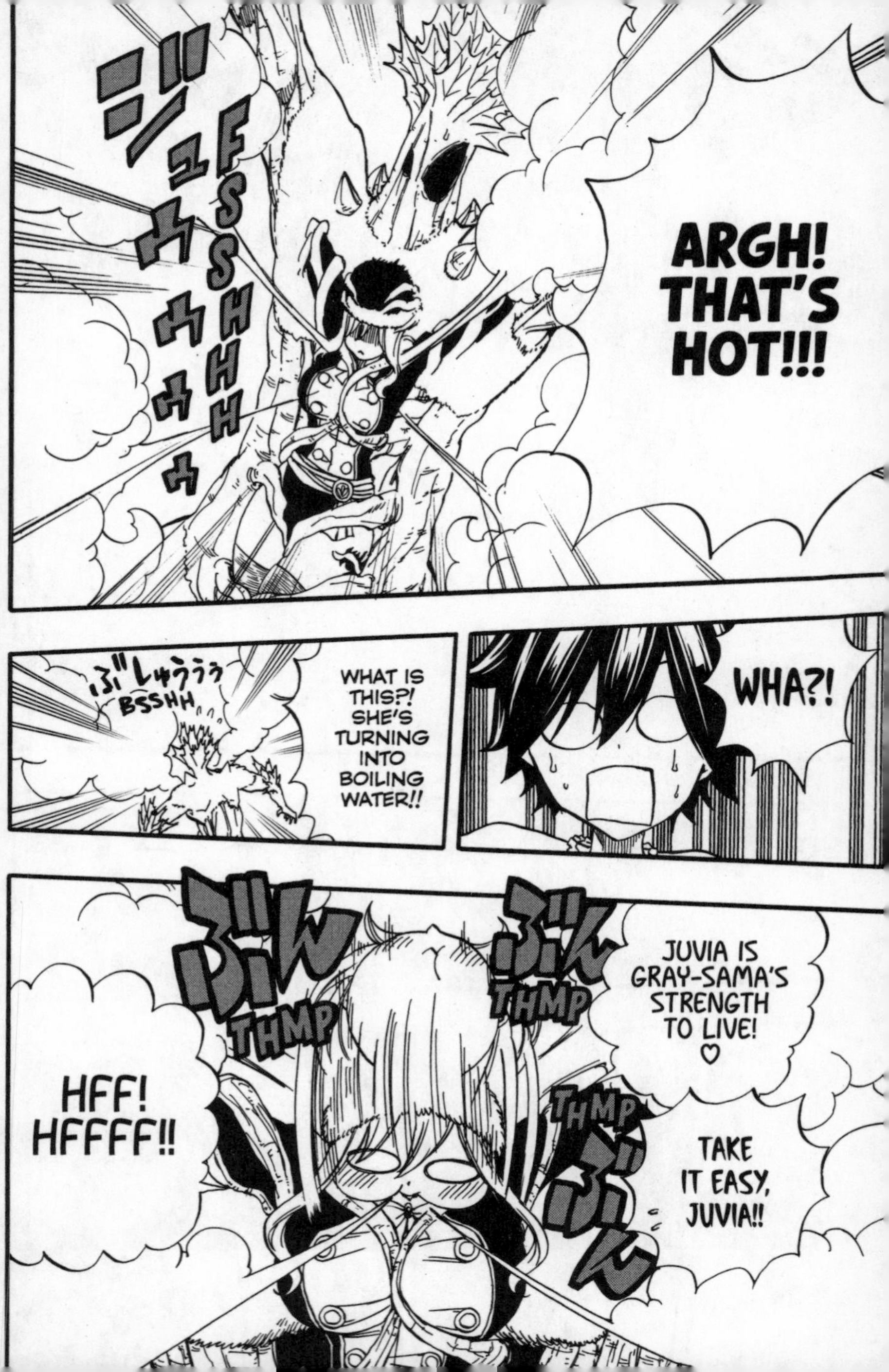
FSSHHHH
ARGH! THAT'S HOT!!!
WHA?!
BSSHH
WHAT IS THIS?! SHE'S TURNING INTO BOILING WATER!!
JUVIA IS GRAY-SAMA'S STRENGTH TO LIVE! ♡
THMP
THMP
THMP
TAKE IT EASY, JUVIA!!
HFF! HFFFF!!

FAIRY TAIL 100 YEARS QUEST

Chapter 58: Ice and Water

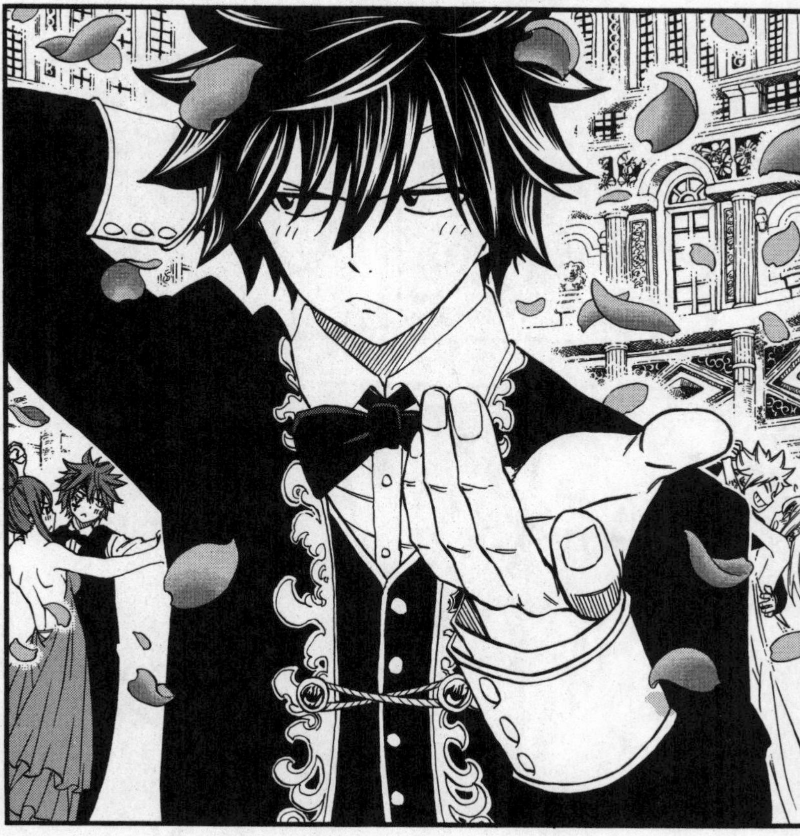

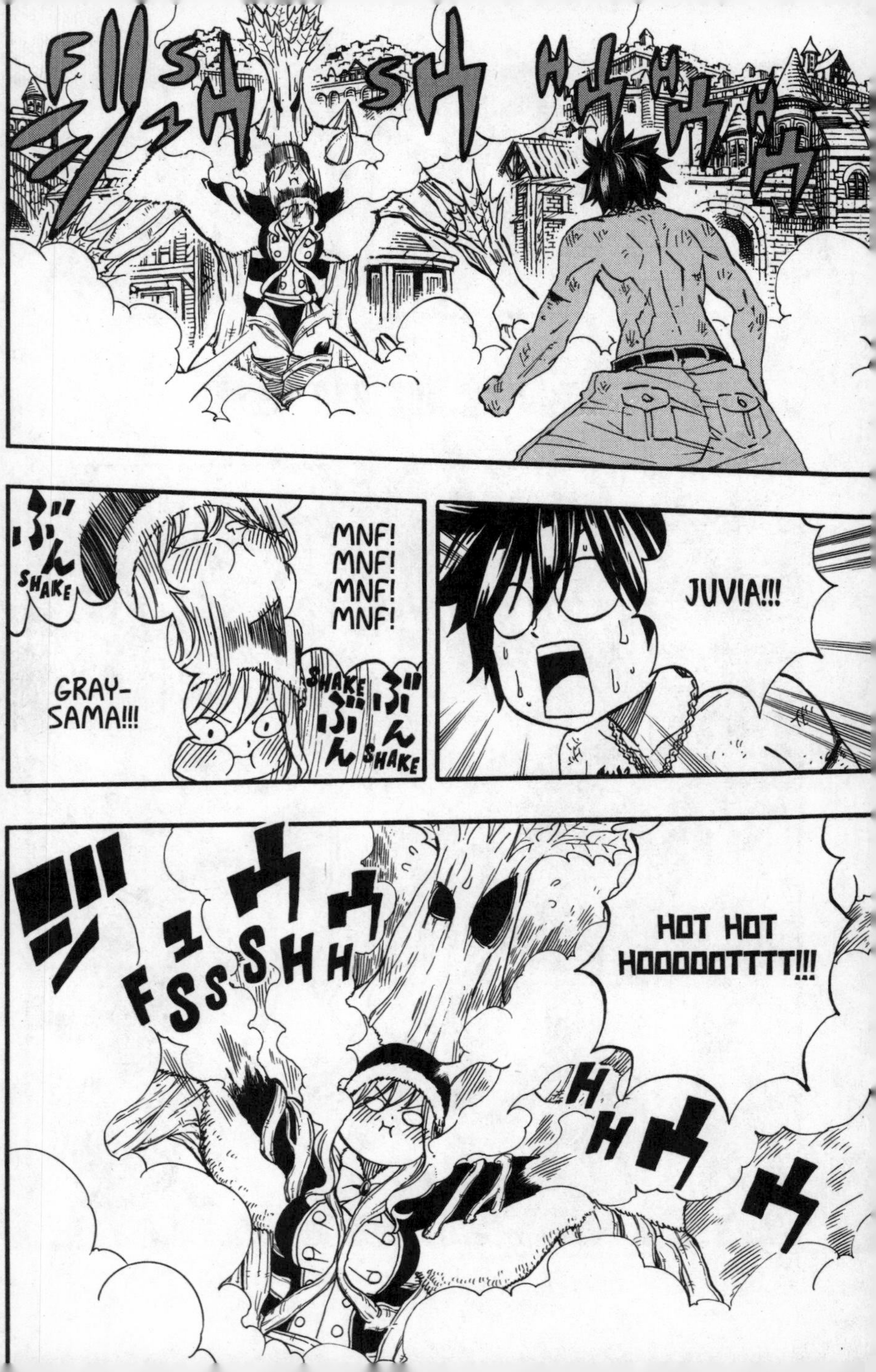

F
S
SH
JUVIA!!!
MNF!
MNF!
MNF!
MNF!
SHAKE
GRAY-
SAMA!!!
SHAKE
SHAKE
FSSSHH
HOT HOT
HOOOOOTTTTT!!!

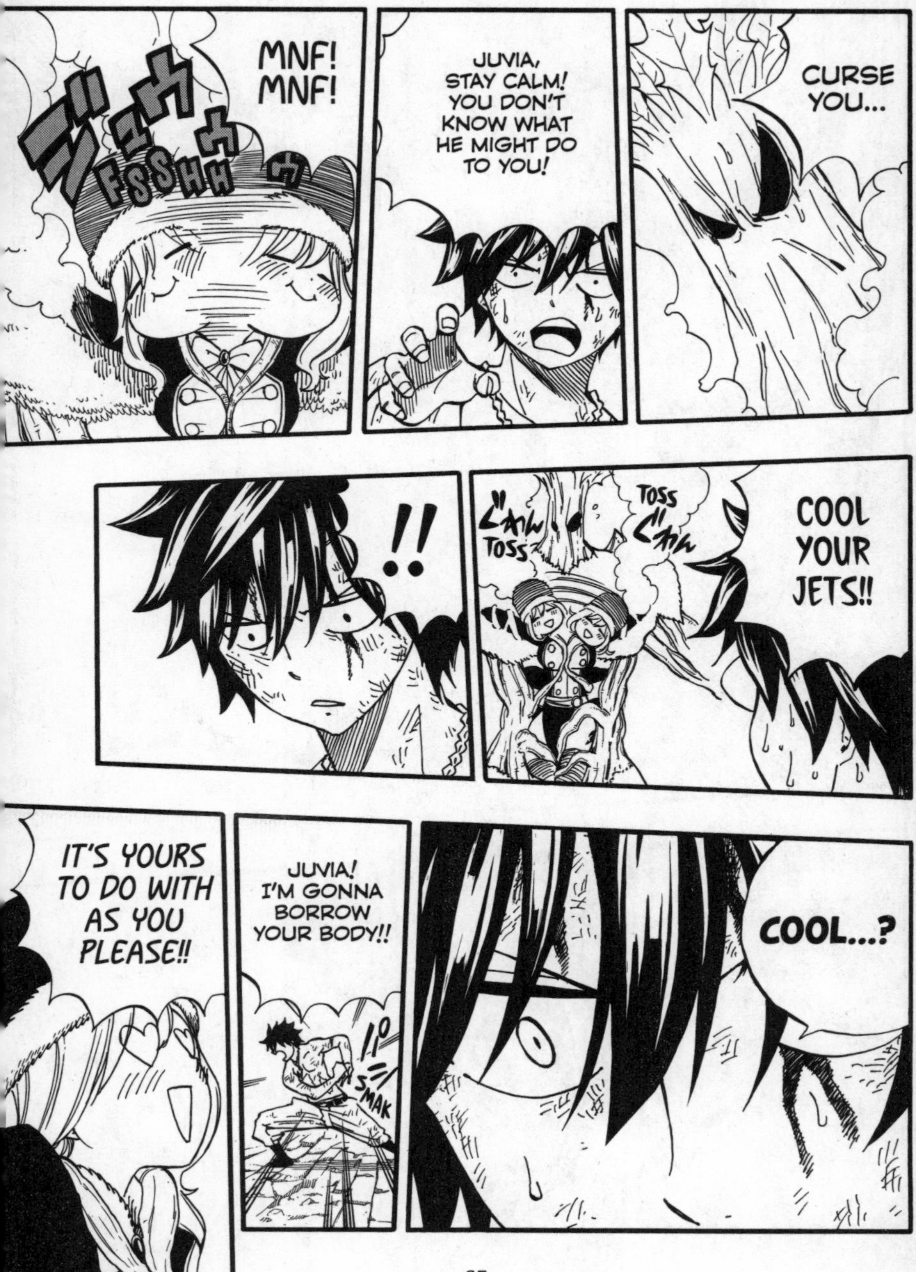
CURSE YOU...
JUVIA, STAY CALM! YOU DON'T KNOW WHAT HE MIGHT DO TO YOU!
MNF! MNF!
FSSHHH
COOL YOUR JETS!!
TOSS
TOSS
!!
COOL...?
JUVIA! I'M GONNA BORROW YOUR BODY!!
SMAK
IT'S YOURS TO DO WITH AS YOU PLEASE!!

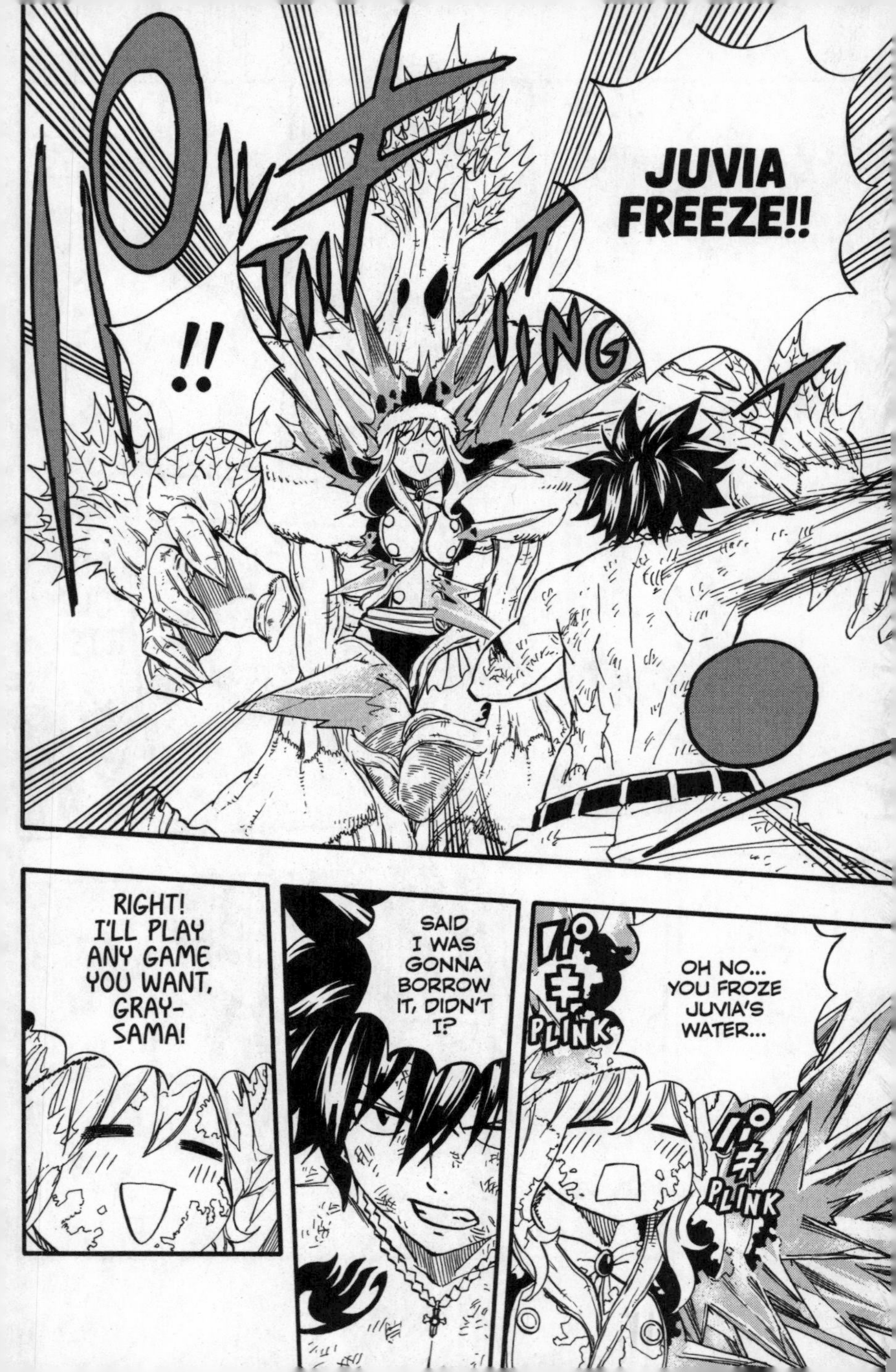
JUVIA FREEZE!!
!!
PLINK
OH NO... YOU FROZE JUVIA'S WATER...
PLINK
SAID I WAS GONNA BORROW IT, DIDN'T I?
RIGHT! I'LL PLAY ANY GAME YOU WANT, GRAY-SAMA!

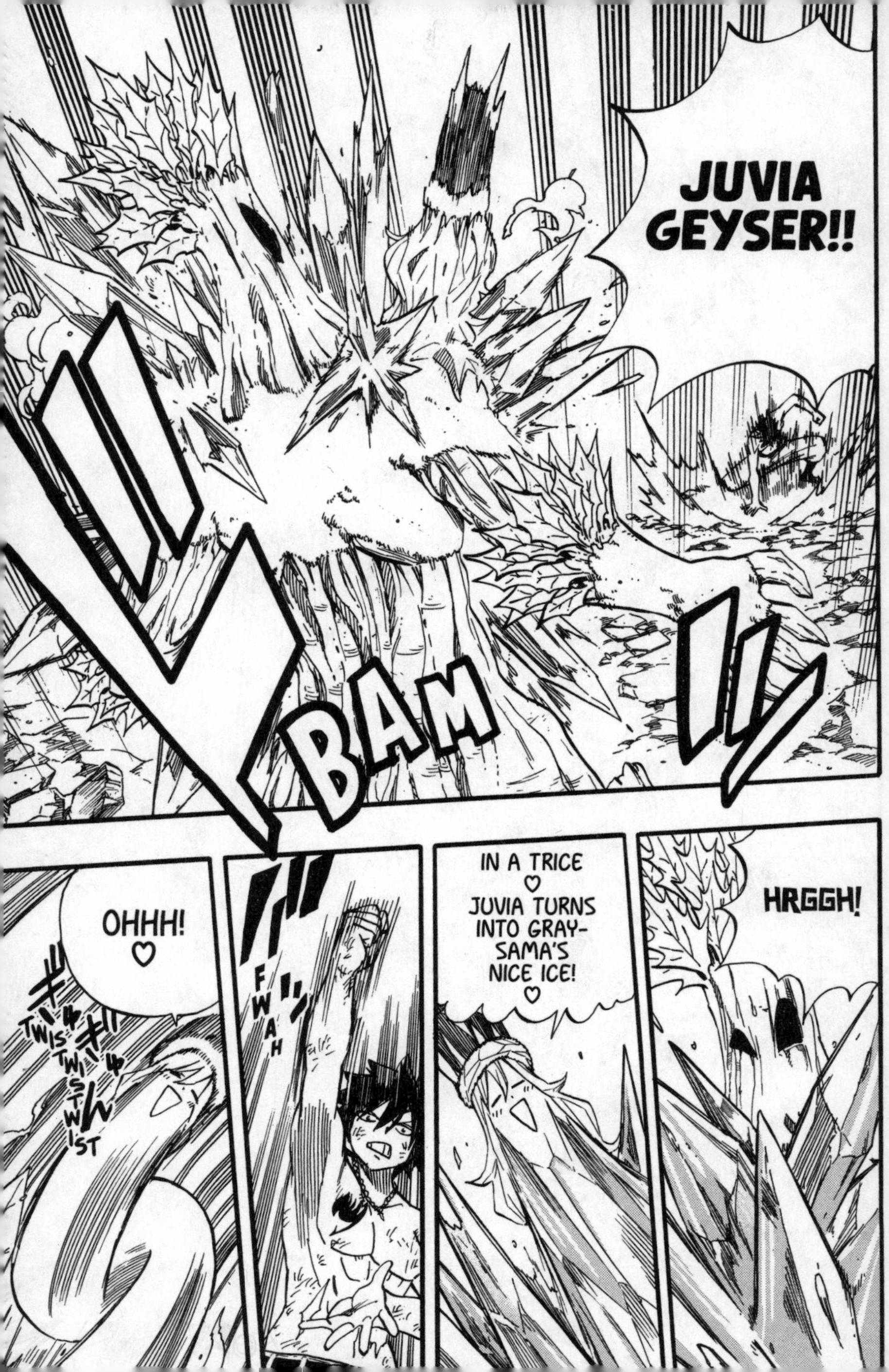
JUVIA GEYSER!!
BAM
HRGGH!
IN A TRICE ♡ JUVIA TURNS INTO GRAY-SAMA'S NICE ICE! ♡
FWAH
OHHH! ♡
TWIST TWIST TWIST

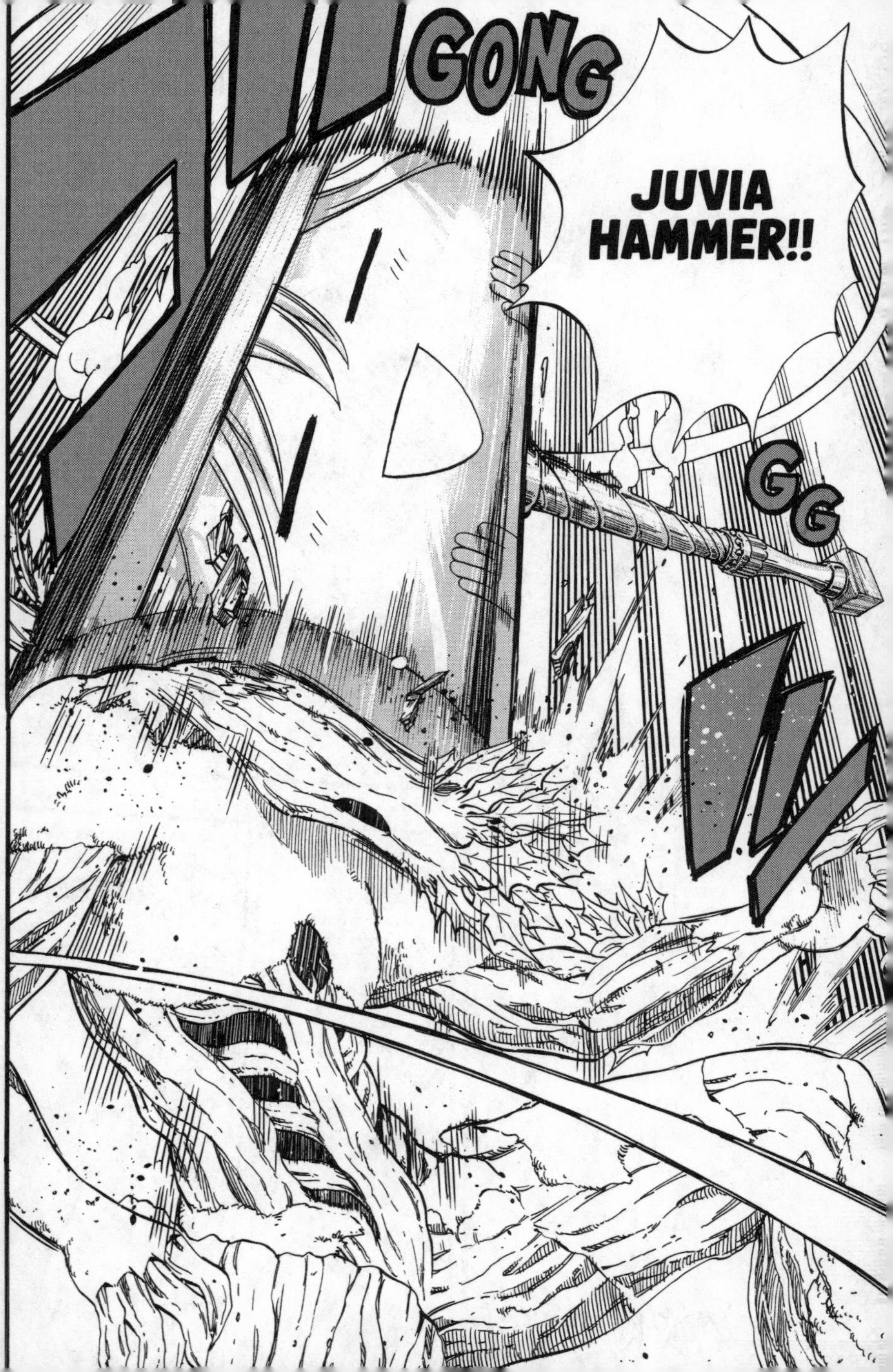
GONG
JUVIA HAMMER!!
GG

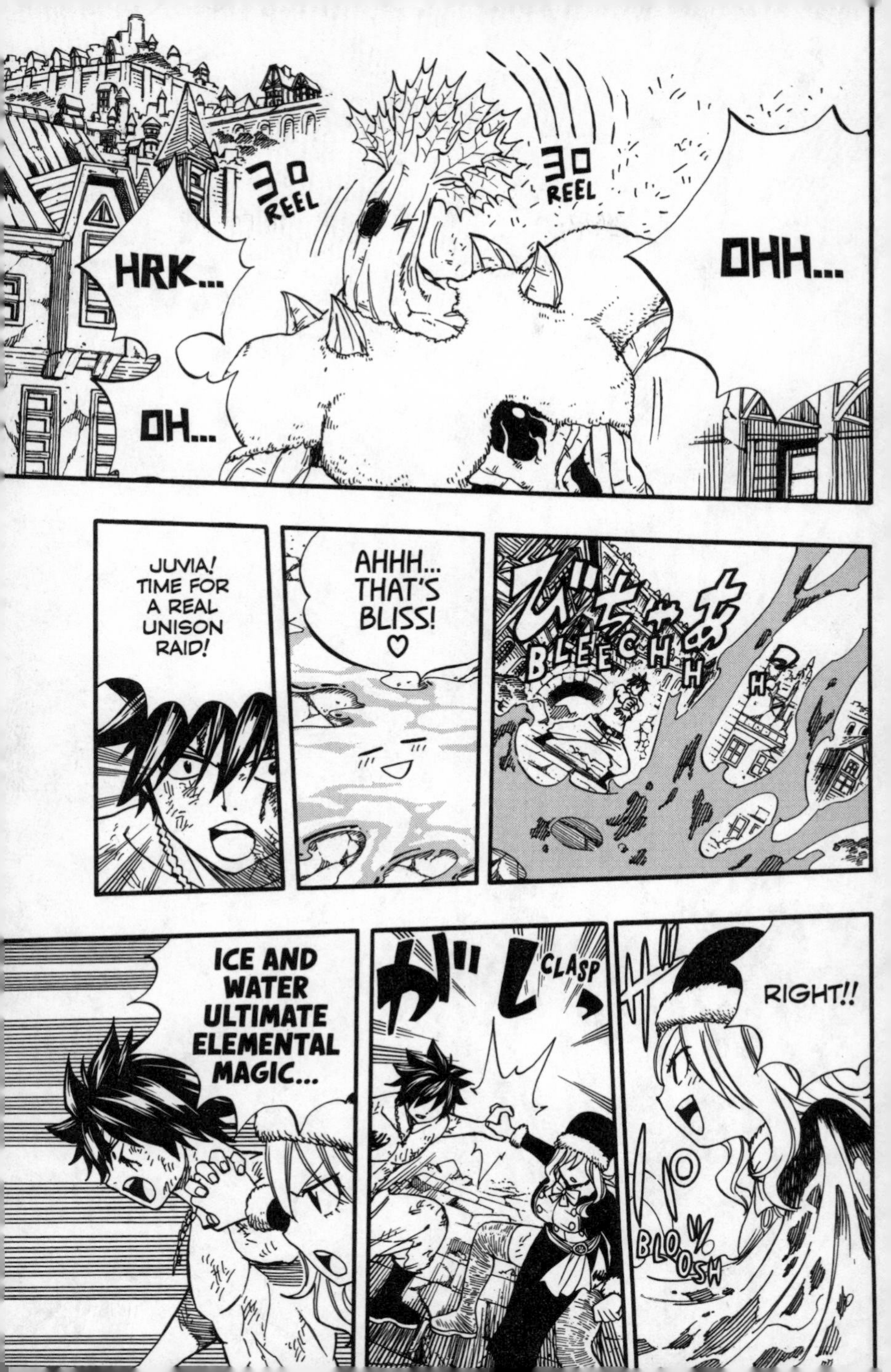
OHH...
ヨロ REEL
ヨロ REEL
HRK...
OH...
BLEECHHH
AHHH... THAT'S BLISS! ♡
JUVIA! TIME FOR A REAL UNISON RAID!
RIGHT!!
BLOOSH
CLASP
ICE AND WATER ULTIMATE ELEMENTAL MAGIC...

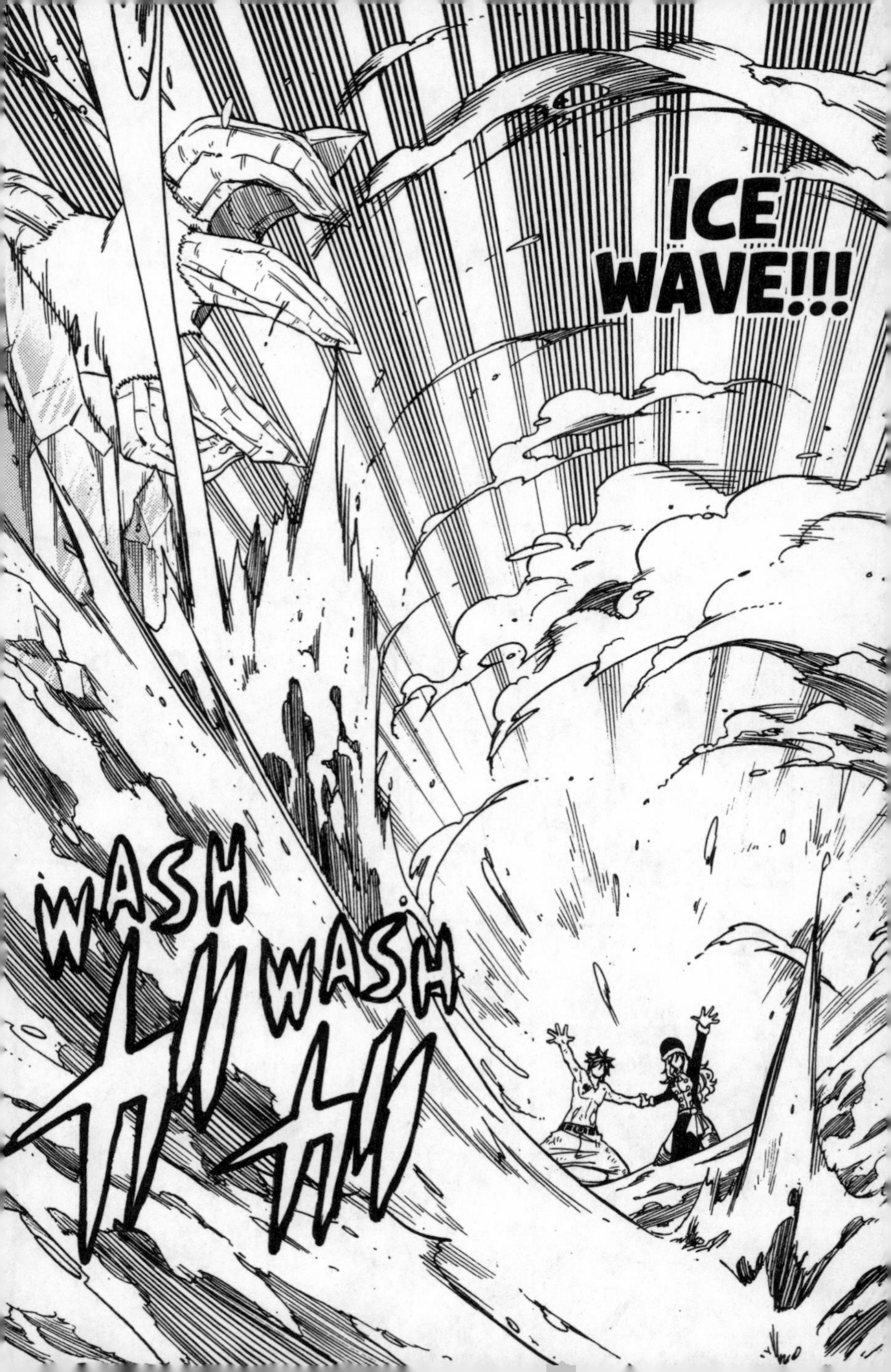
ICE WAVE!!!
WASH WASH

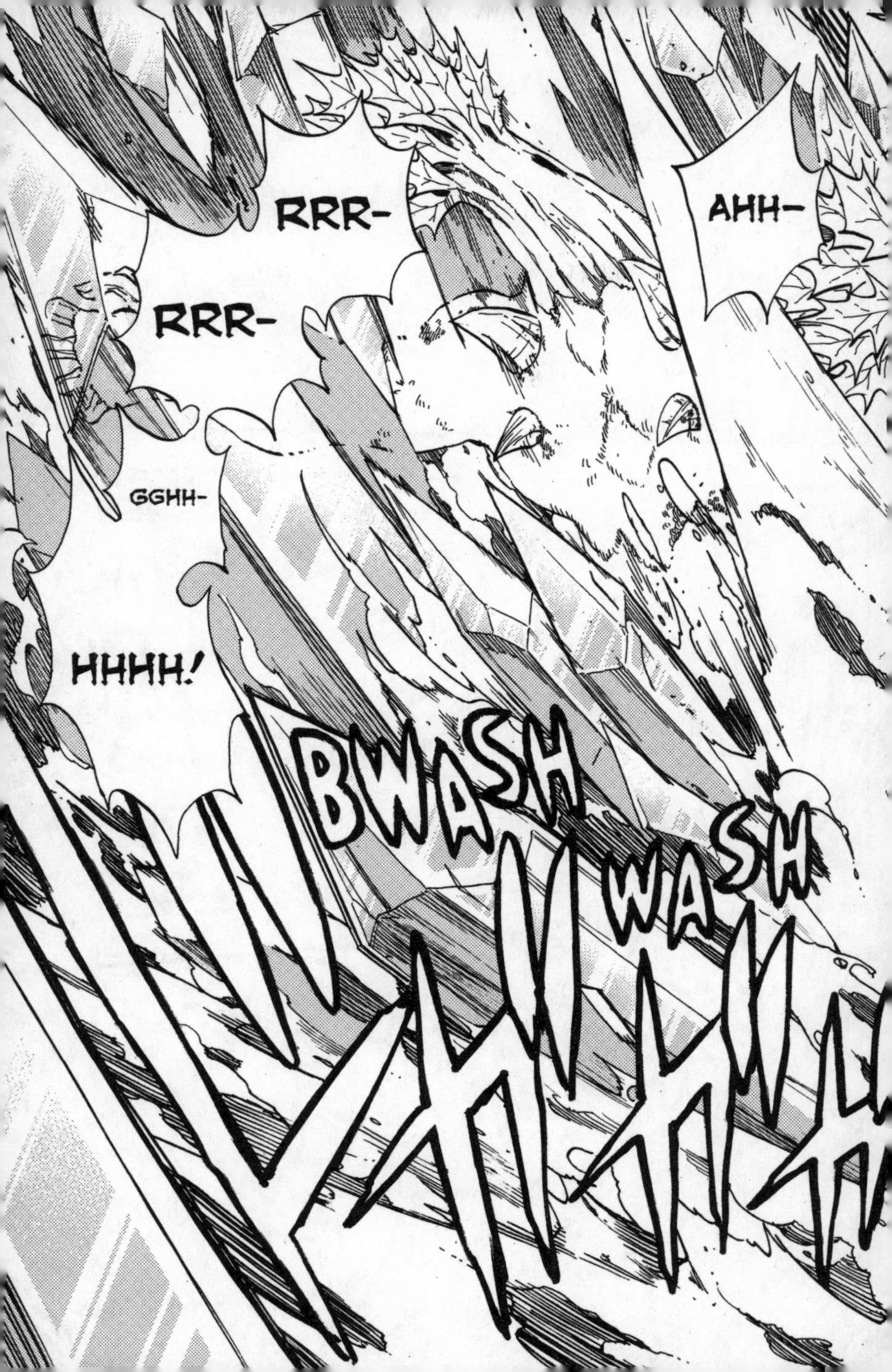
AHH-
RRR-
RRR-
GGHH-
HHHH!
BWASH
WASH

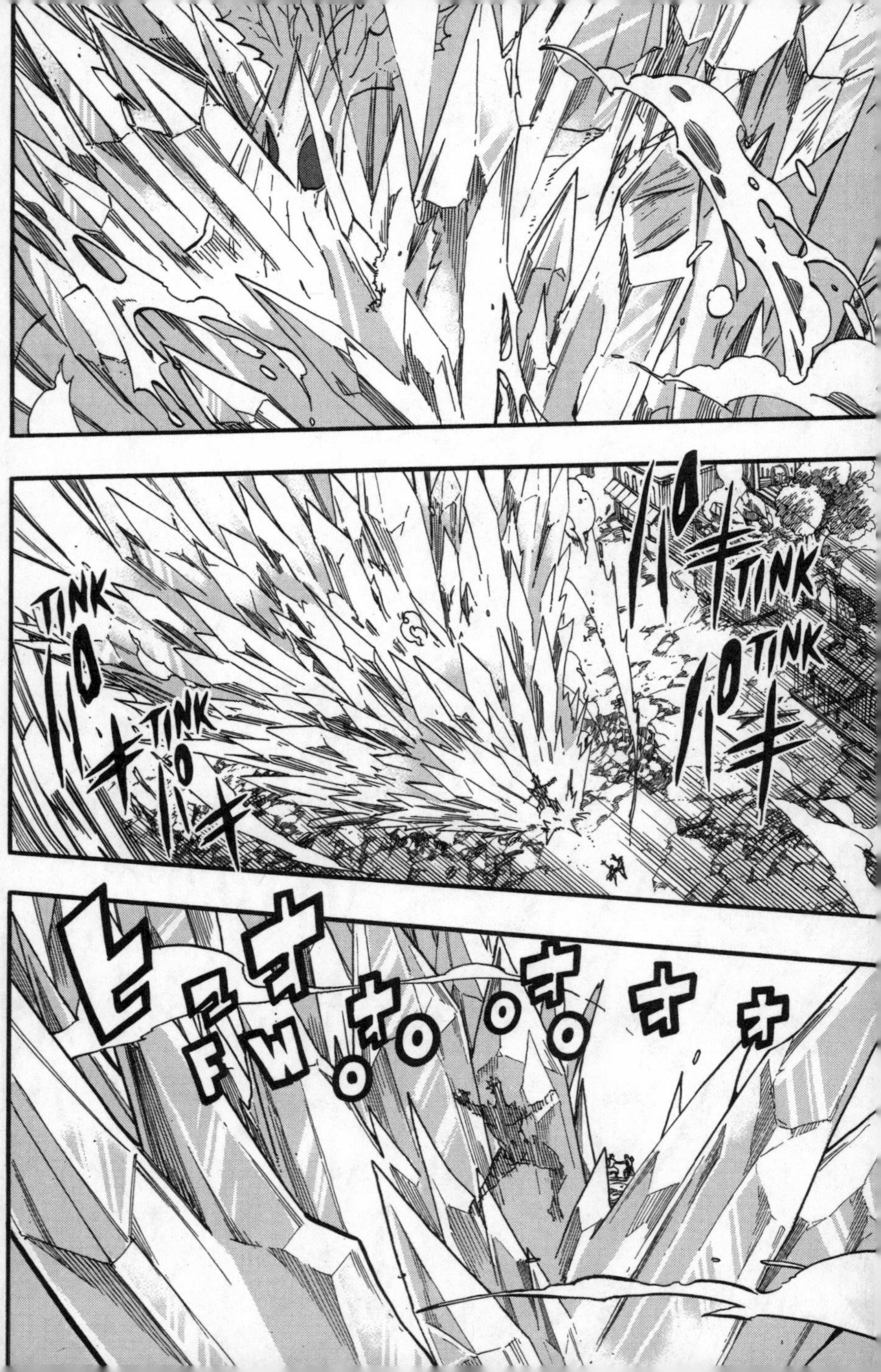

パキ TINK
パキ TINK
パキ TINK
パキ TINK
ヒュオオオオォ FWOOOO

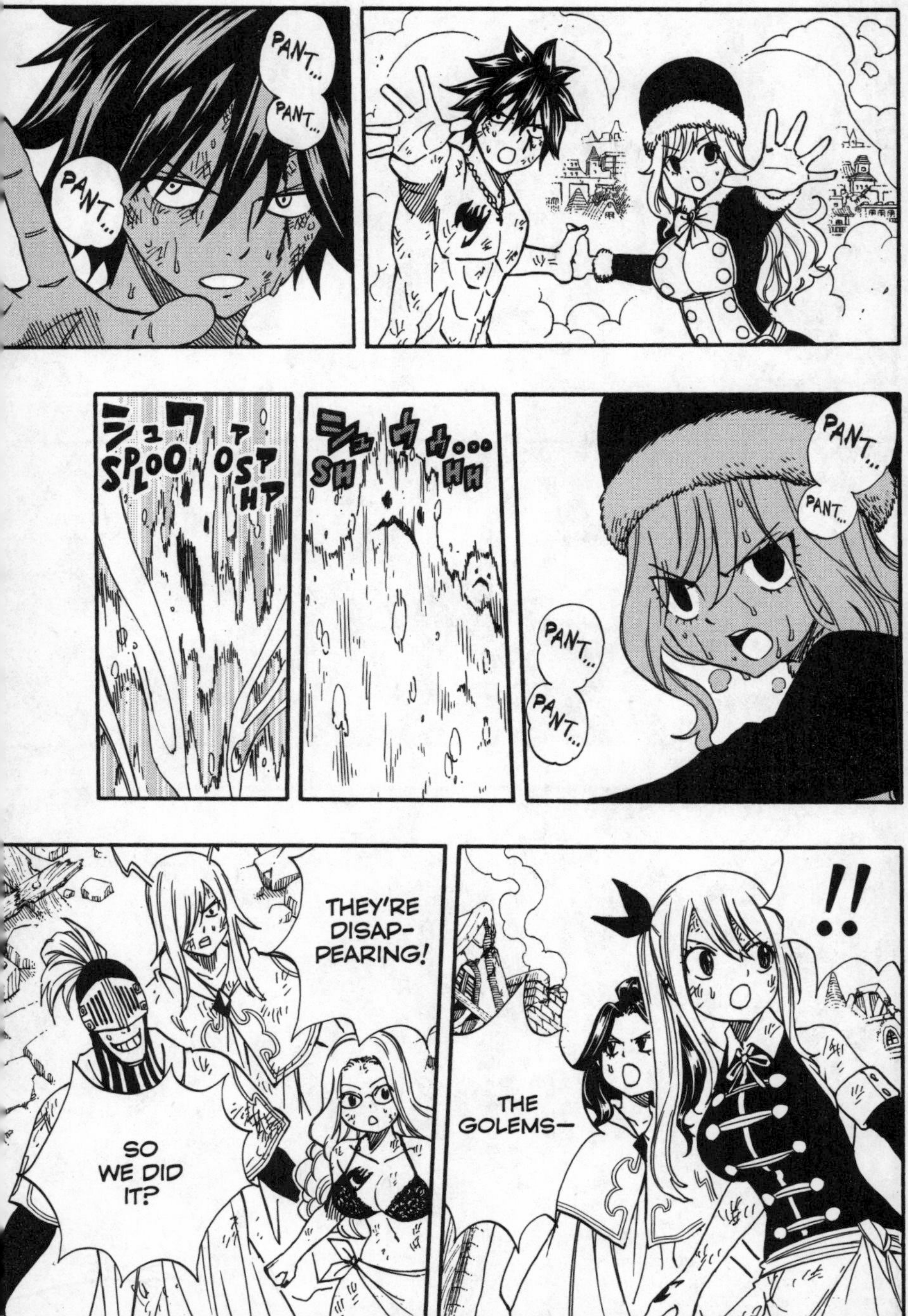
PANT...
PANT...
PANT...
PANT...
PANT...
PANT...
PANT...
シュゥゥ...
SHHH
シュワ
SPLOOOSHP
!!
THE GOLEMS—
THEY'RE DISAPPEARING!
SO WE DID IT?

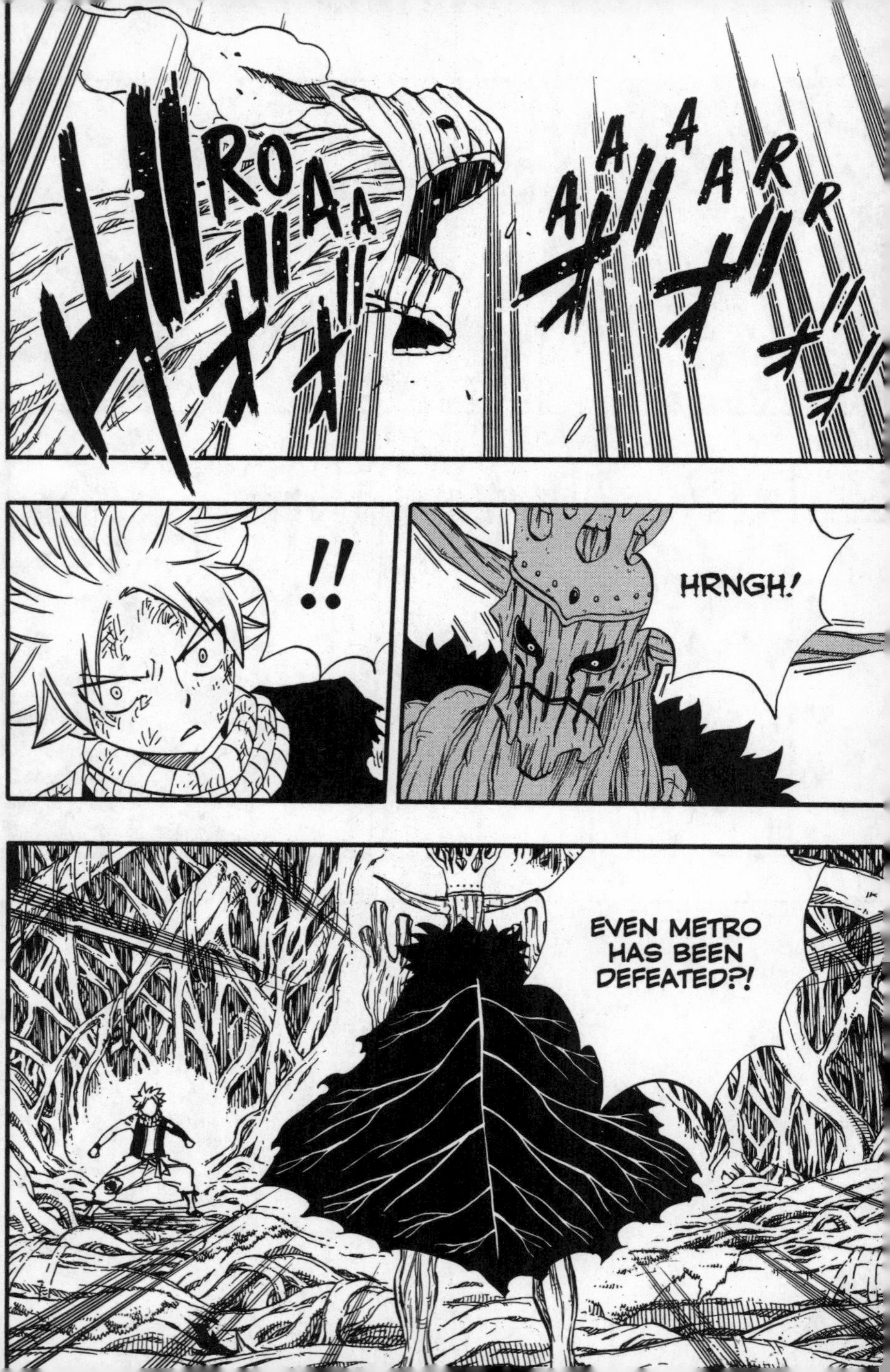
ROAAAAAARR
HRNGH!
!!
EVEN METRO HAS BEEN DEFEATED?!

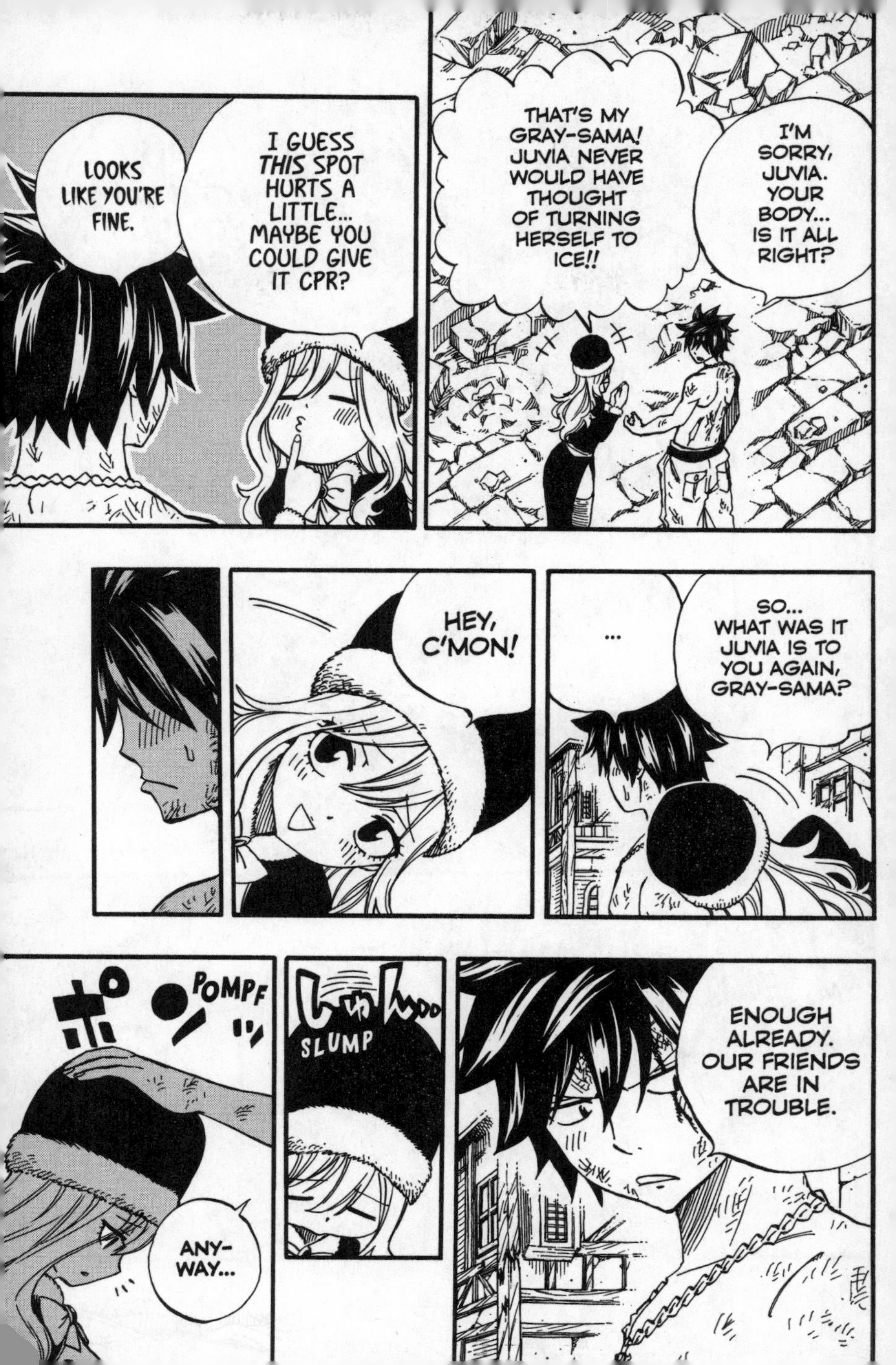
I'M SORRY, JUVIA. YOUR BODY... IS IT ALL RIGHT?
THAT'S MY GRAY-SAMA! JUVIA NEVER WOULD HAVE THOUGHT OF TURNING HERSELF TO ICE!!
I GUESS *THIS* SPOT HURTS A LITTLE... MAYBE YOU COULD GIVE IT CPR?
LOOKS LIKE YOU'RE FINE.
SO... WHAT WAS IT JUVIA IS TO YOU AGAIN, GRAY-SAMA?
...
HEY, C'MON!
ENOUGH ALREADY. OUR FRIENDS ARE IN TROUBLE.
SLUMP
POMPF
ANY-WAY...

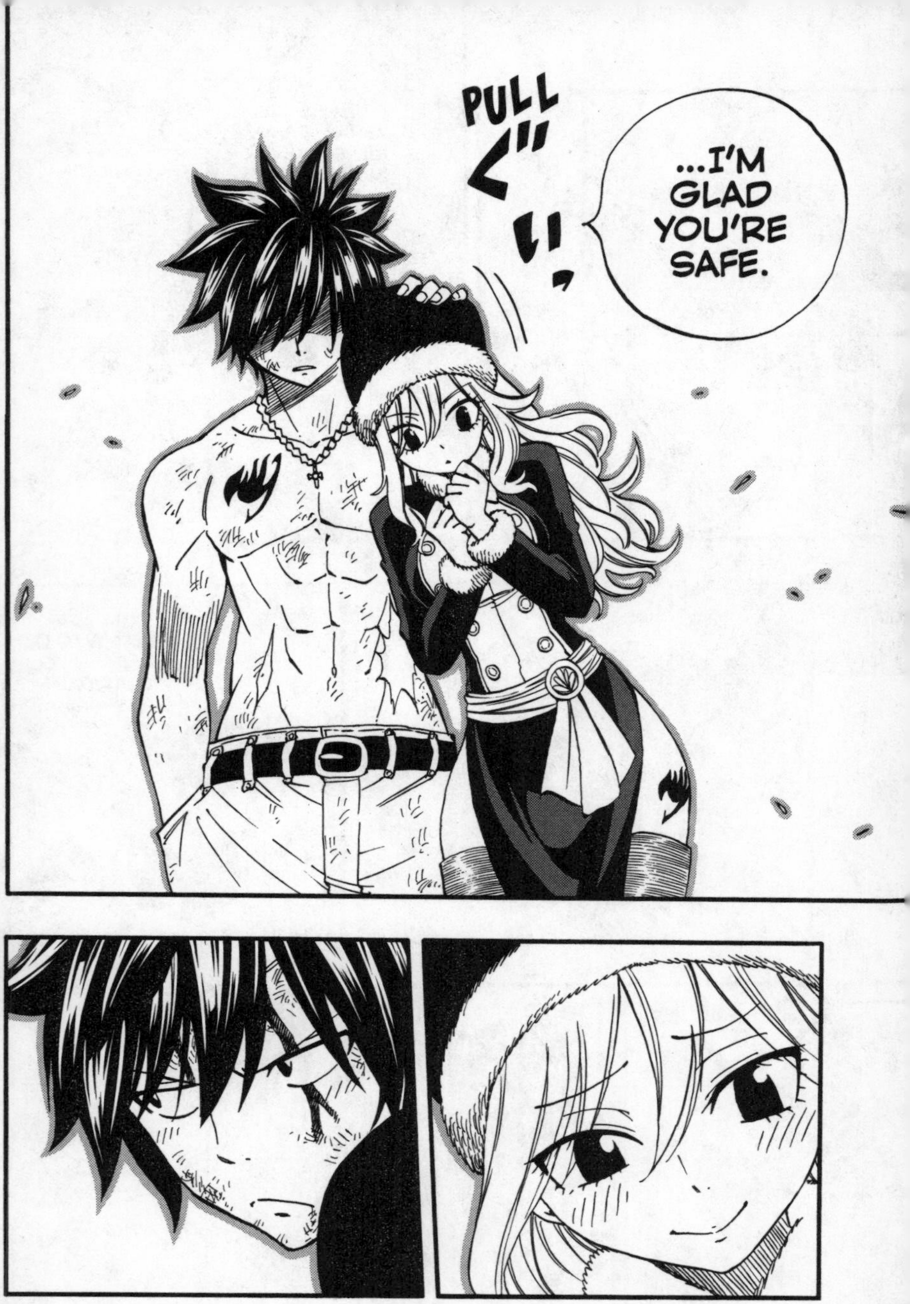
PULL
...I'M GLAD YOU'RE SAFE.

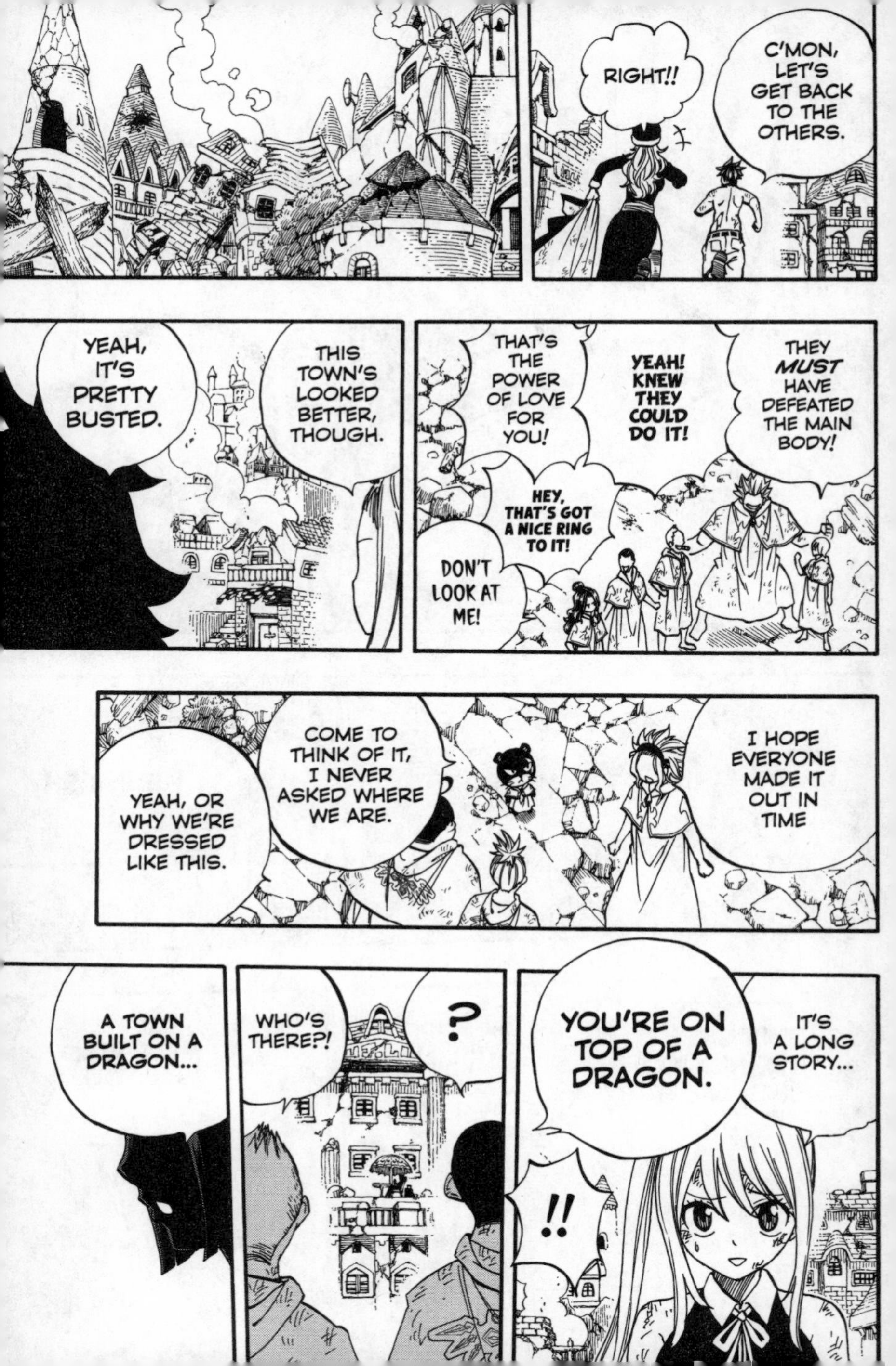
C'MON, LET'S GET BACK TO THE OTHERS.
RIGHT!!
THEY MUST HAVE DEFEATED THE MAIN BODY!
YEAH! KNEW THEY COULD DO IT!
THAT'S THE POWER OF LOVE FOR YOU!
HEY, THAT'S GOT A NICE RING TO IT!
DON'T LOOK AT ME!
THIS TOWN'S LOOKED BETTER, THOUGH.
YEAH, IT'S PRETTY BUSTED.
I HOPE EVERYONE MADE IT OUT IN TIME
COME TO THINK OF IT, I NEVER ASKED WHERE WE ARE.
YEAH, OR WHY WE'RE DRESSED LIKE THIS.
IT'S A LONG STORY...
YOU'RE ON TOP OF A DRAGON.
!!
?
WHO'S THERE?!
A TOWN BUILT ON A DRAGON...

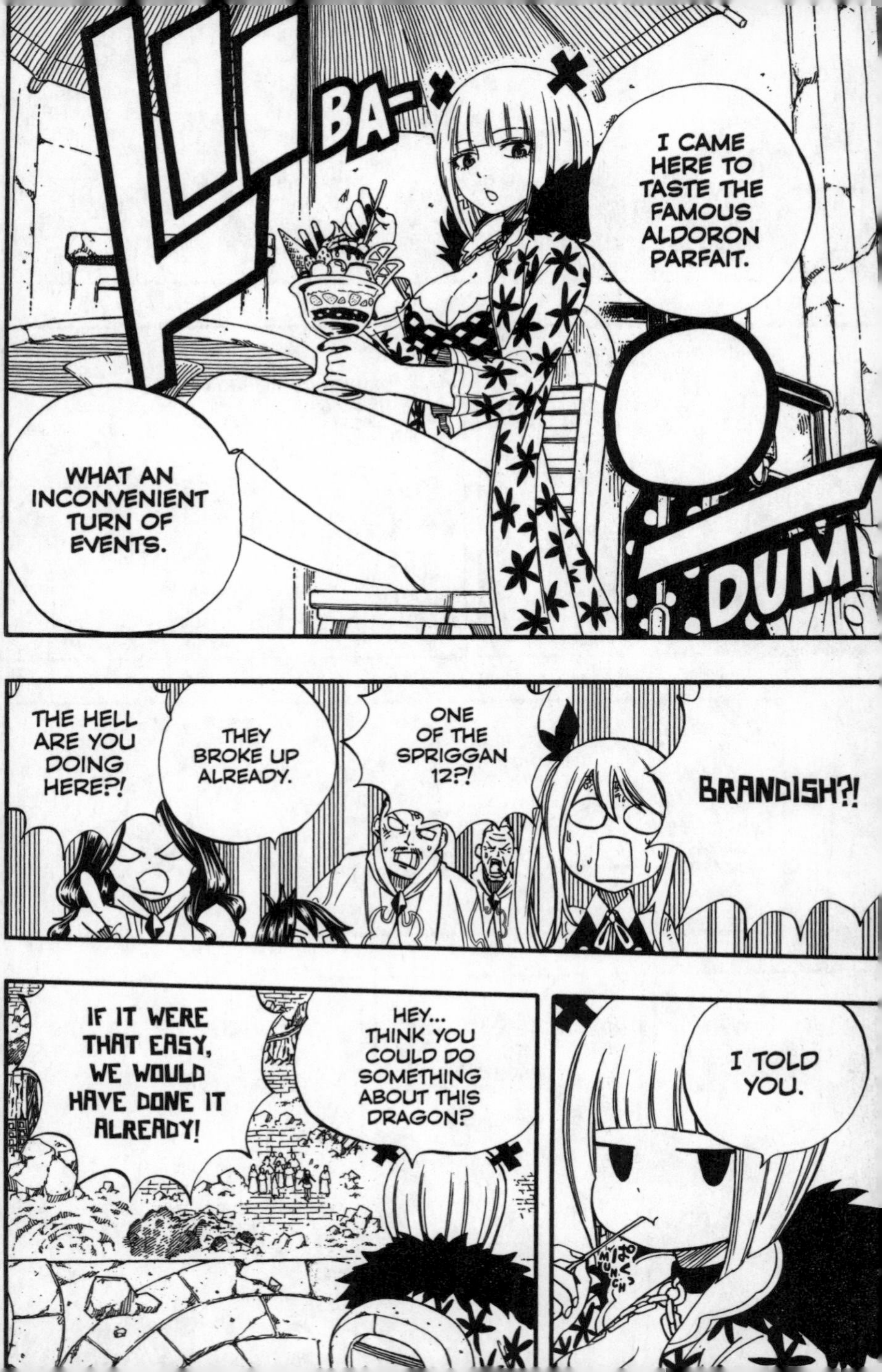
I CAME HERE TO TASTE THE FAMOUS ALDORON PARFAIT.
DUM
BA-
WHAT AN INCONVENIENT TURN OF EVENTS.
BRANDISH?!
ONE OF THE SPRIGGAN 12?!
THEY BROKE UP ALREADY.
THE HELL ARE YOU DOING HERE?!
I TOLD YOU.
HEY... THINK YOU COULD DO SOMETHING ABOUT THIS DRAGON?
IF IT WERE THAT EASY, WE WOULD HAVE DONE IT ALREADY!

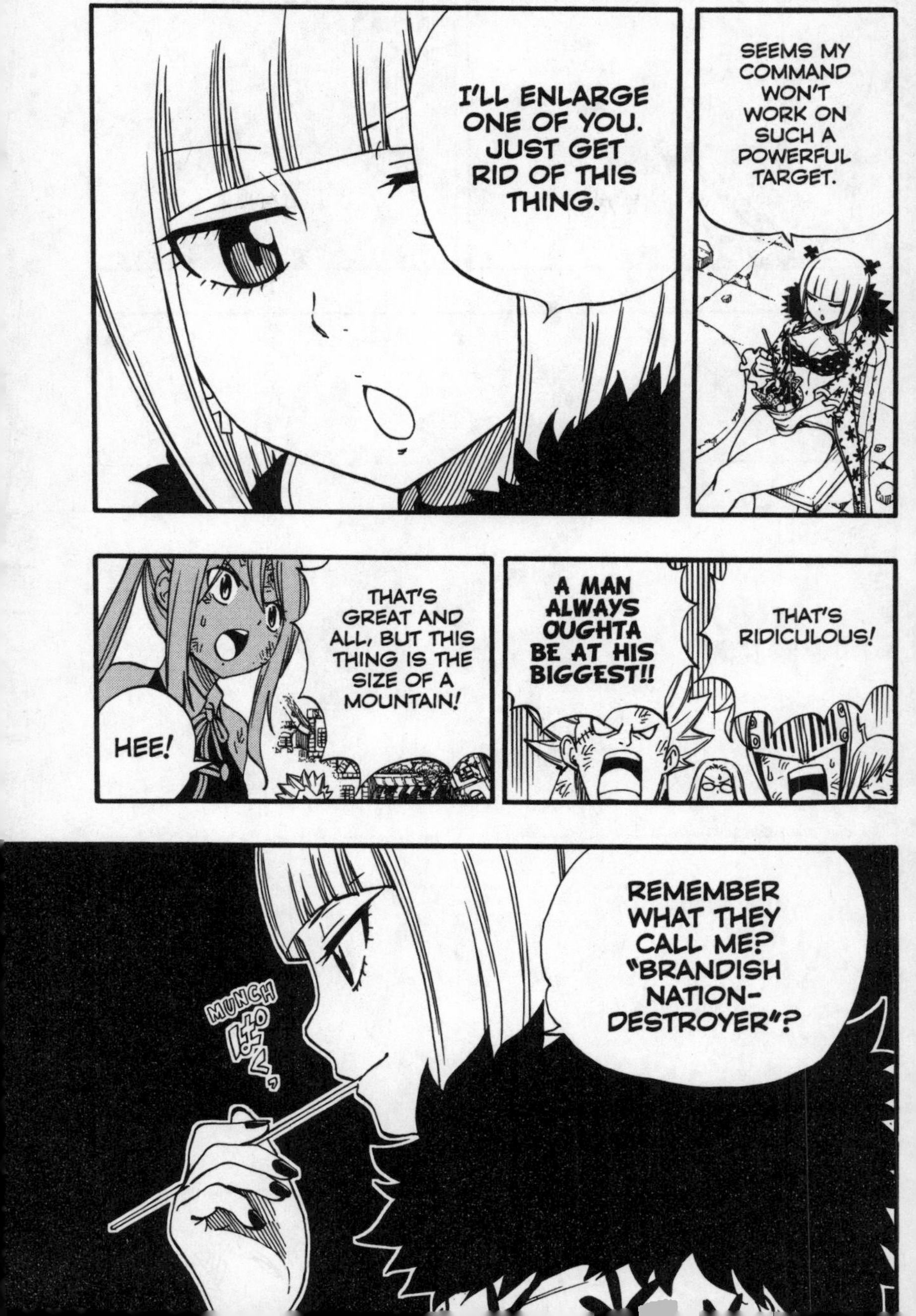
SEEMS MY COMMAND WON'T WORK ON SUCH A POWERFUL TARGET.
I'LL ENLARGE ONE OF YOU. JUST GET RID OF THIS THING.
THAT'S RIDICULOUS!
A MAN ALWAYS OUGHTA BE AT HIS BIGGEST!!
THAT'S GREAT AND ALL, BUT THIS THING IS THE SIZE OF A MOUNTAIN!
HEE!
REMEMBER WHAT THEY CALL ME? "BRANDISH NATION-DESTROYER"?
MUNCH

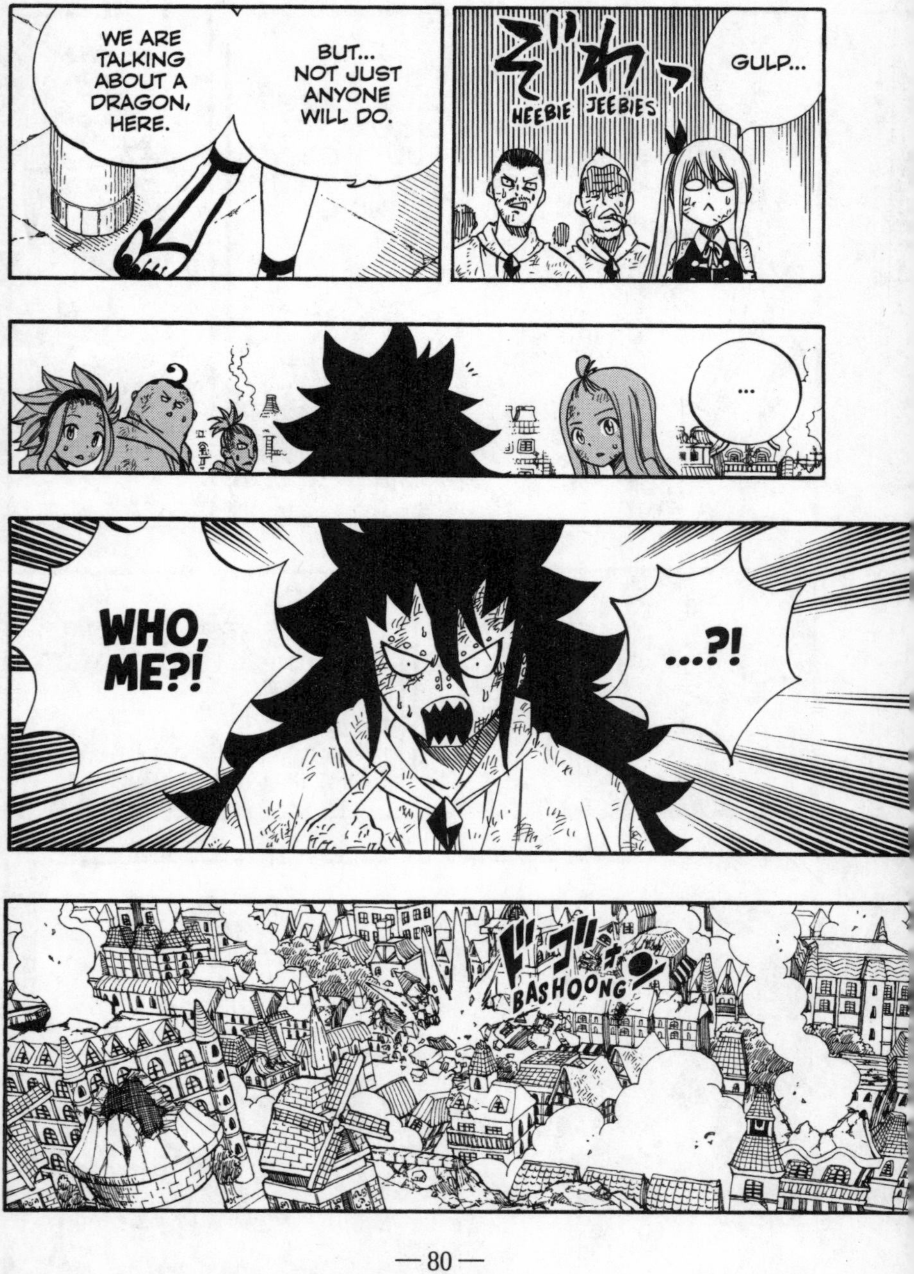
GULP...
ぞわっ
HEEBIE JEEBIES
BUT... NOT JUST ANYONE WILL DO.
WE ARE TALKING ABOUT A DRAGON, HERE.
...
...?!
WHO, ME?!
BASHOONG

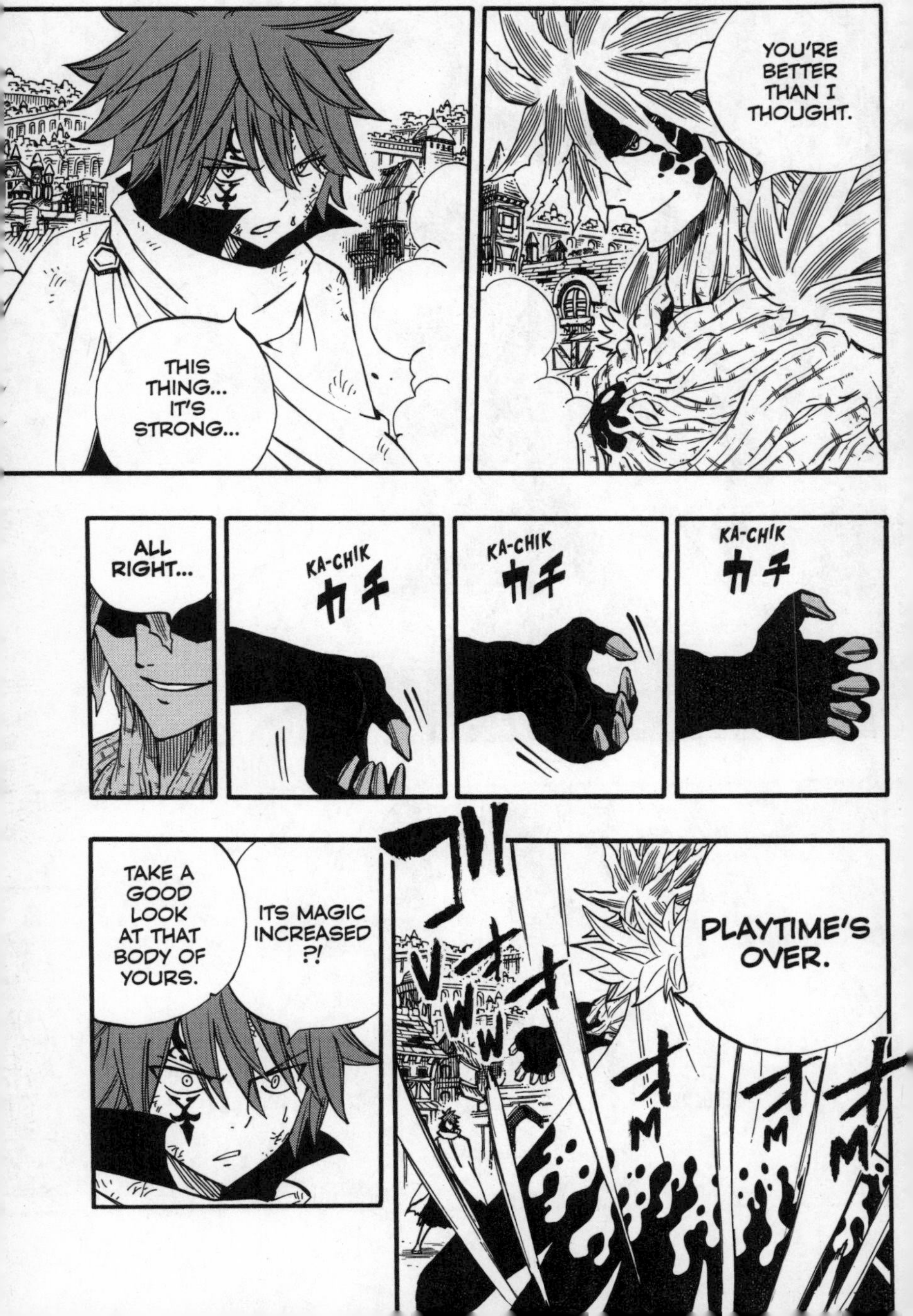
YOU'RE BETTER THAN I THOUGHT.
THIS THING... IT'S STRONG...
KA-CHIK
カチ
KA-CHIK
カチ
KA-CHIK
カチ
ALL RIGHT...
PLAYTIME'S OVER.
ゴオオ
VWWW
オオオ
MMM
ITS MAGIC INCREASED?!
TAKE A GOOD LOOK AT THAT BODY OF YOURS.

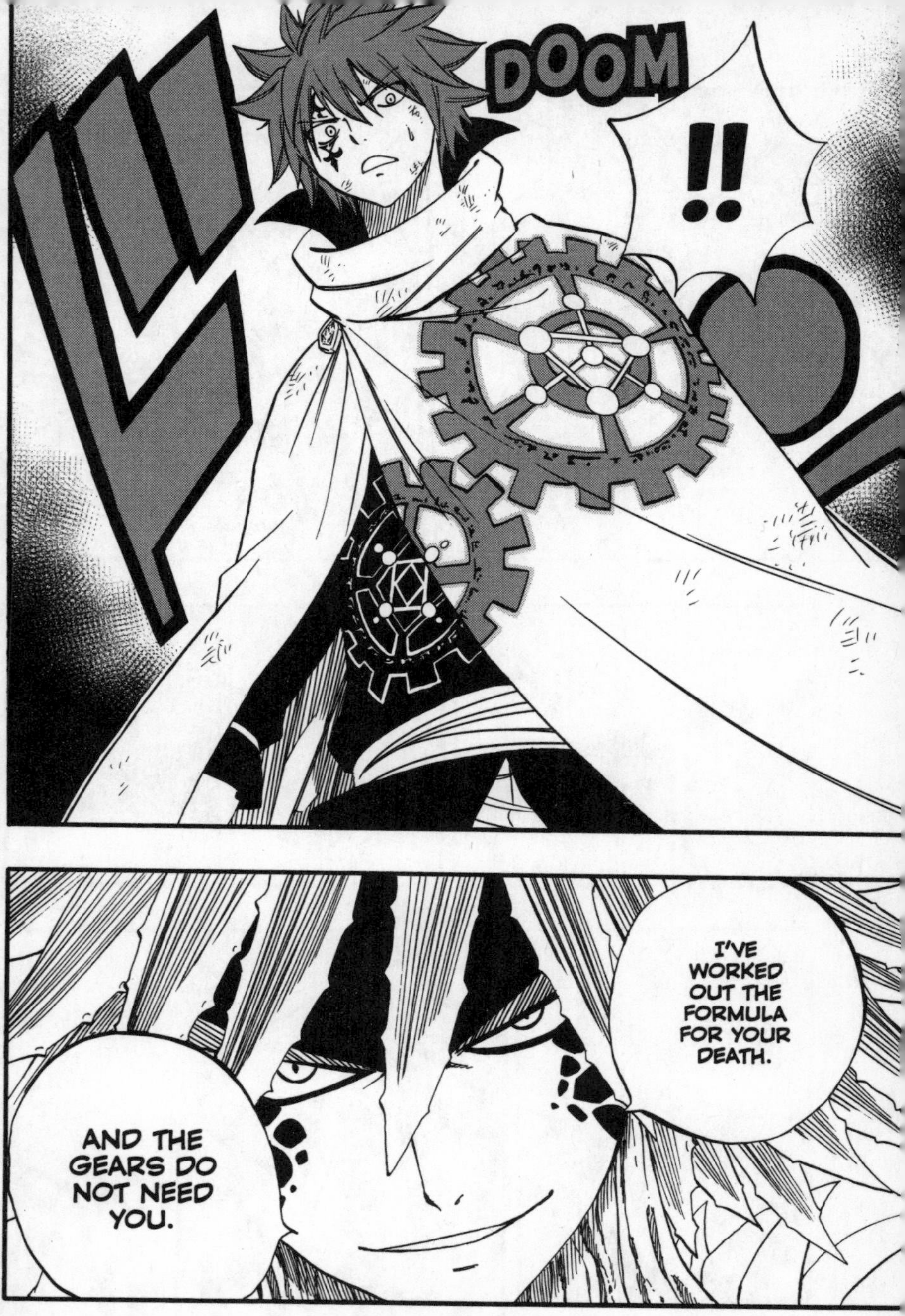
DOOM
!!
I'VE WORKED OUT THE FORMULA FOR YOUR DEATH.
AND THE GEARS DO NOT NEED YOU.

FAIRY TAIL
100 YEARS QUEST

Chapter 59: The Gears of Fate

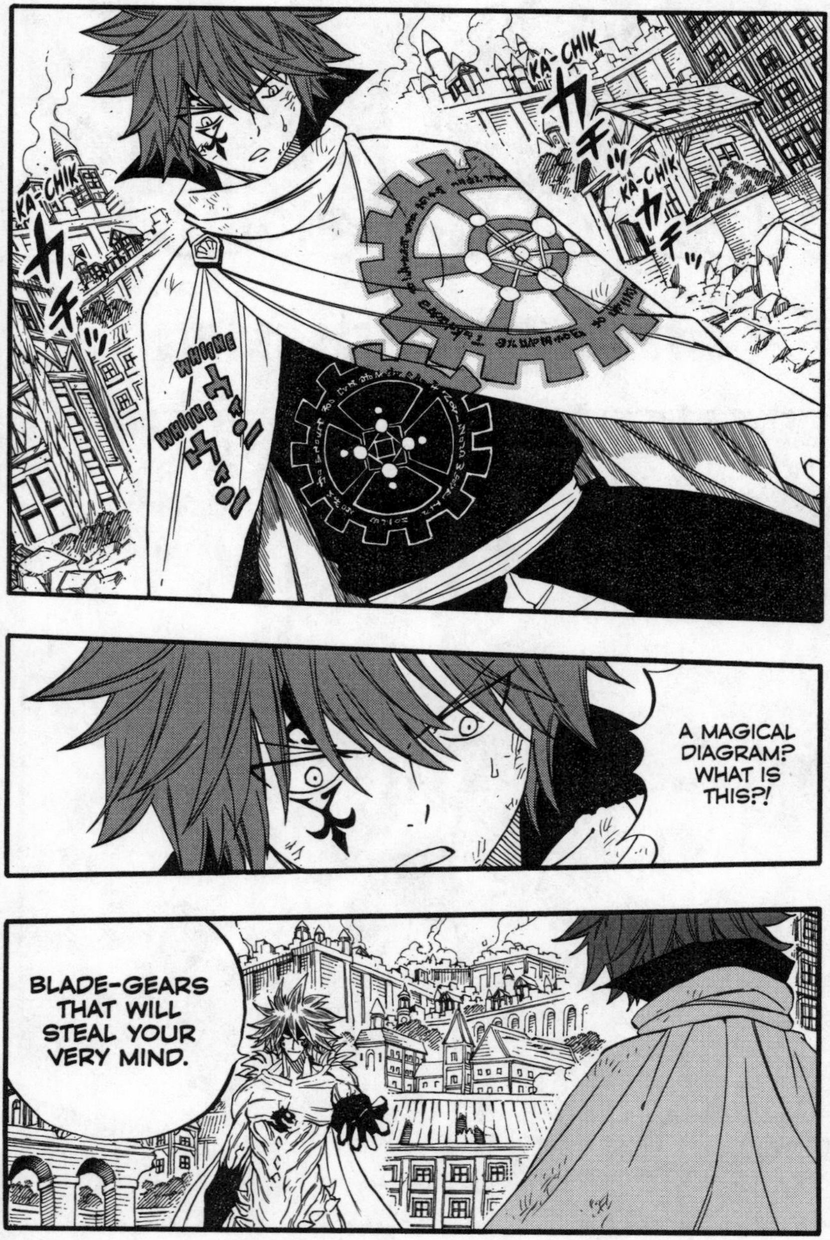
KA-CHIK
KA-CHIK
KA-CHIK
WHINE
WHINE
A MAGICAL DIAGRAM? WHAT IS THIS?!
BLADE-GEARS THAT WILL STEAL YOUR VERY MIND.

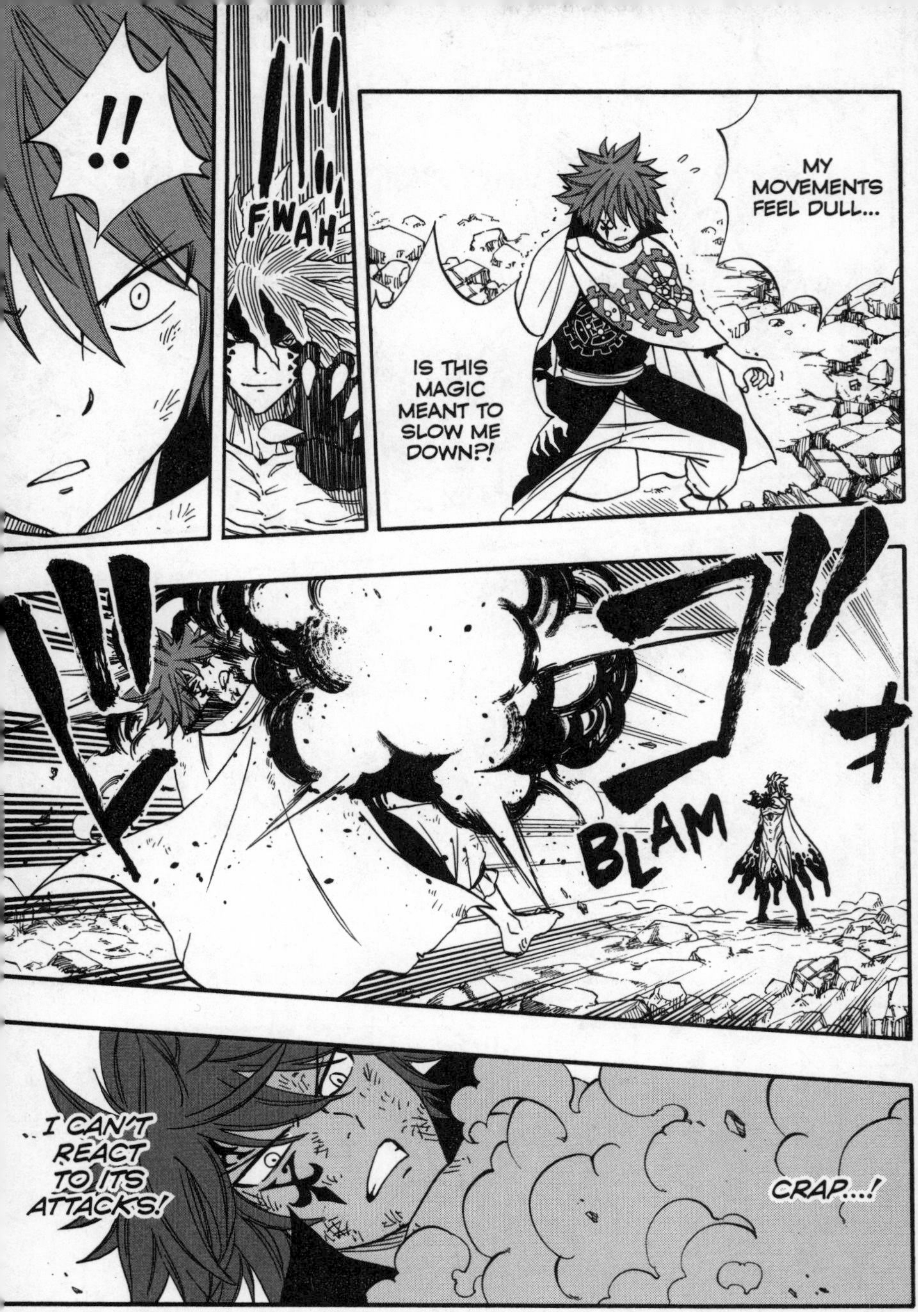
MY MOVEMENTS FEEL DULL...
IS THIS MAGIC MEANT TO SLOW ME DOWN?!
FWAH
!!
BLAM
CRAP...!
...I CAN'T REACT TO ITS ATTACKS!

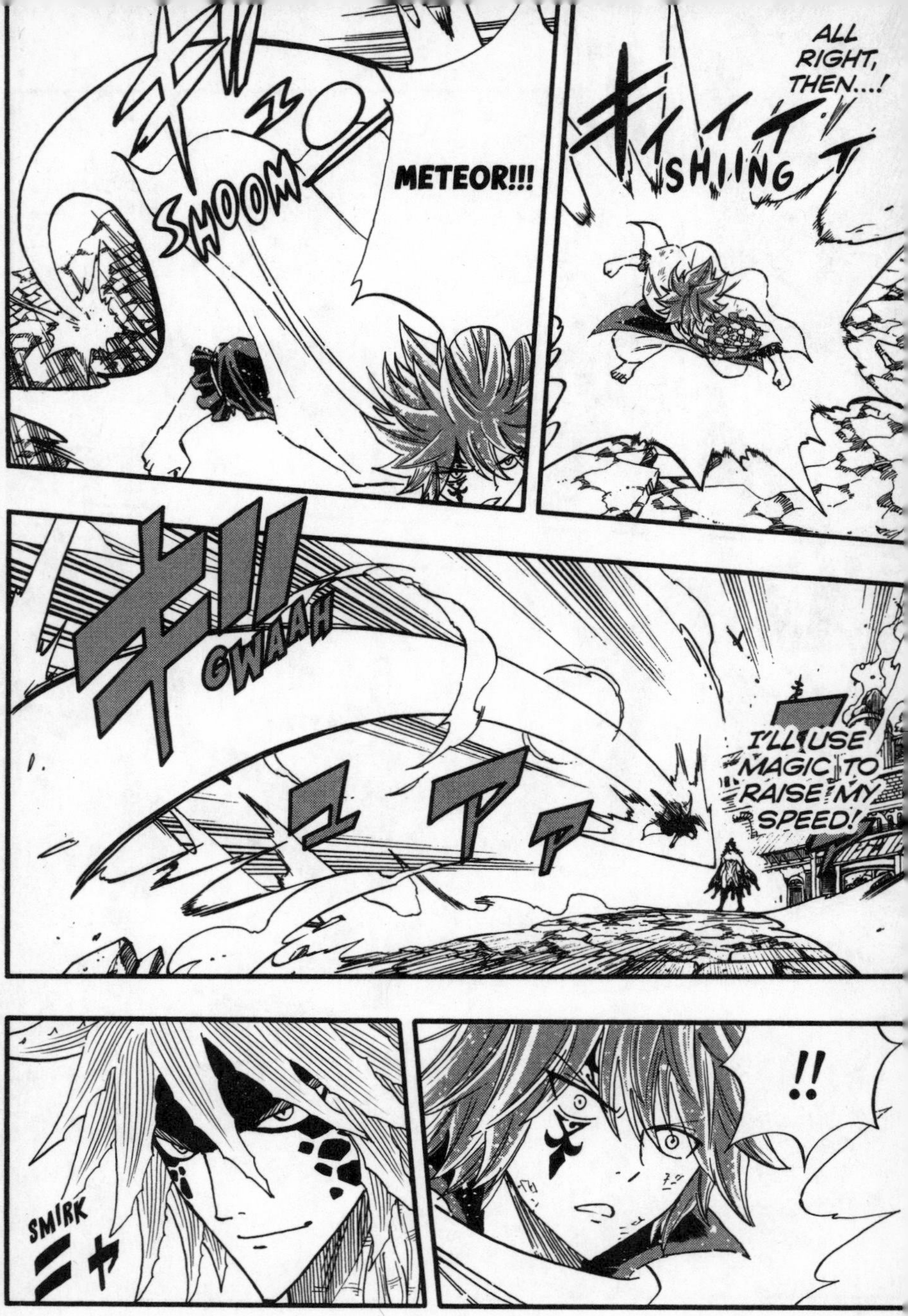
ALL RIGHT, THEN...!
SHIING
METEOR!!!
SHOOM
I'LL USE MAGIC TO RAISE MY SPEED!
GWAAH
!!
SMIRK

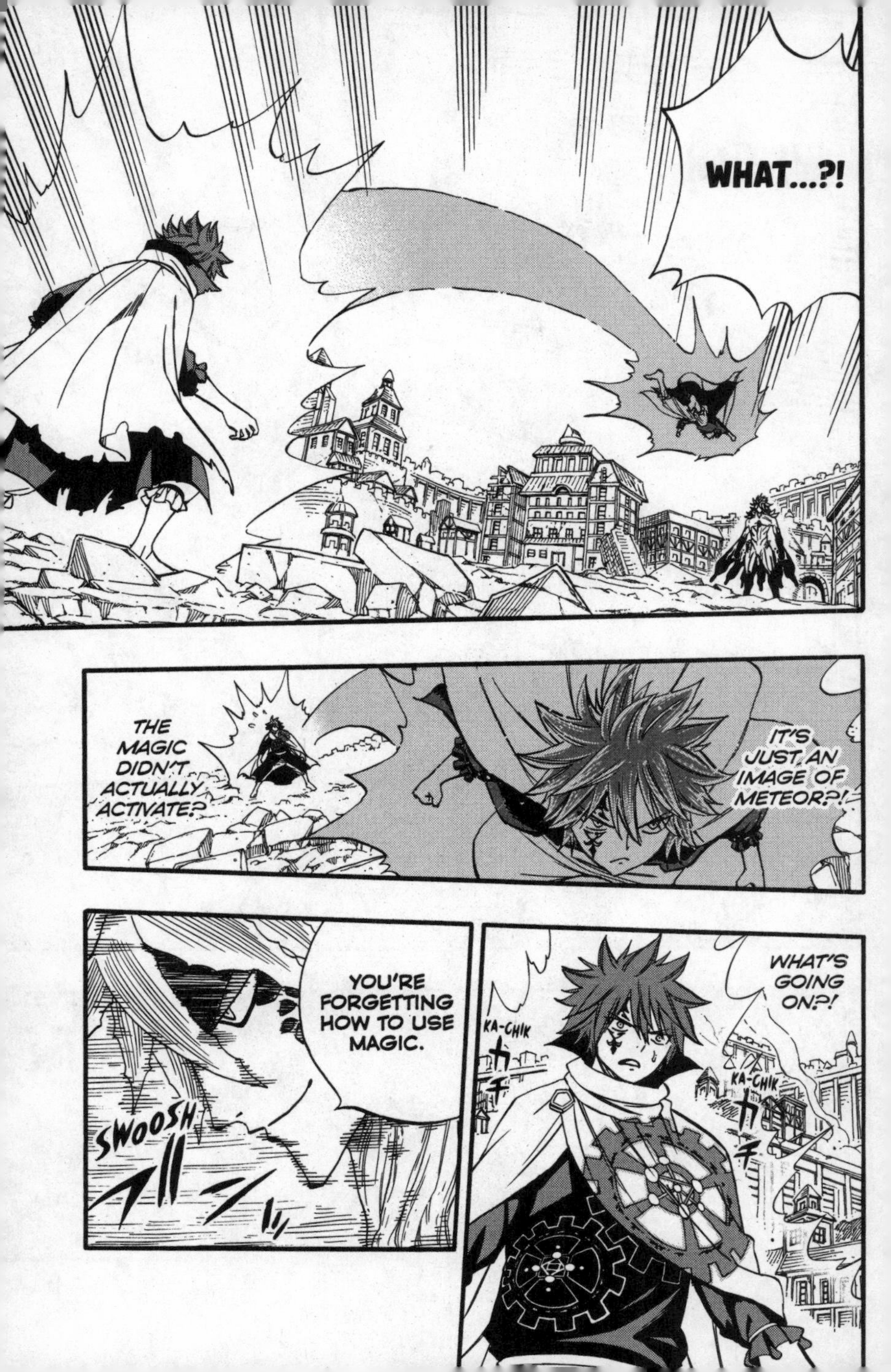
WHAT...?!
IT'S JUST AN IMAGE OF METEOR?!
THE MAGIC DIDN'T ACTUALLY ACTIVATE?
WHAT'S GOING ON?!
KA-CHIK
KA-CHIK
YOU'RE FORGETTING HOW TO USE MAGIC.
SWOOSH

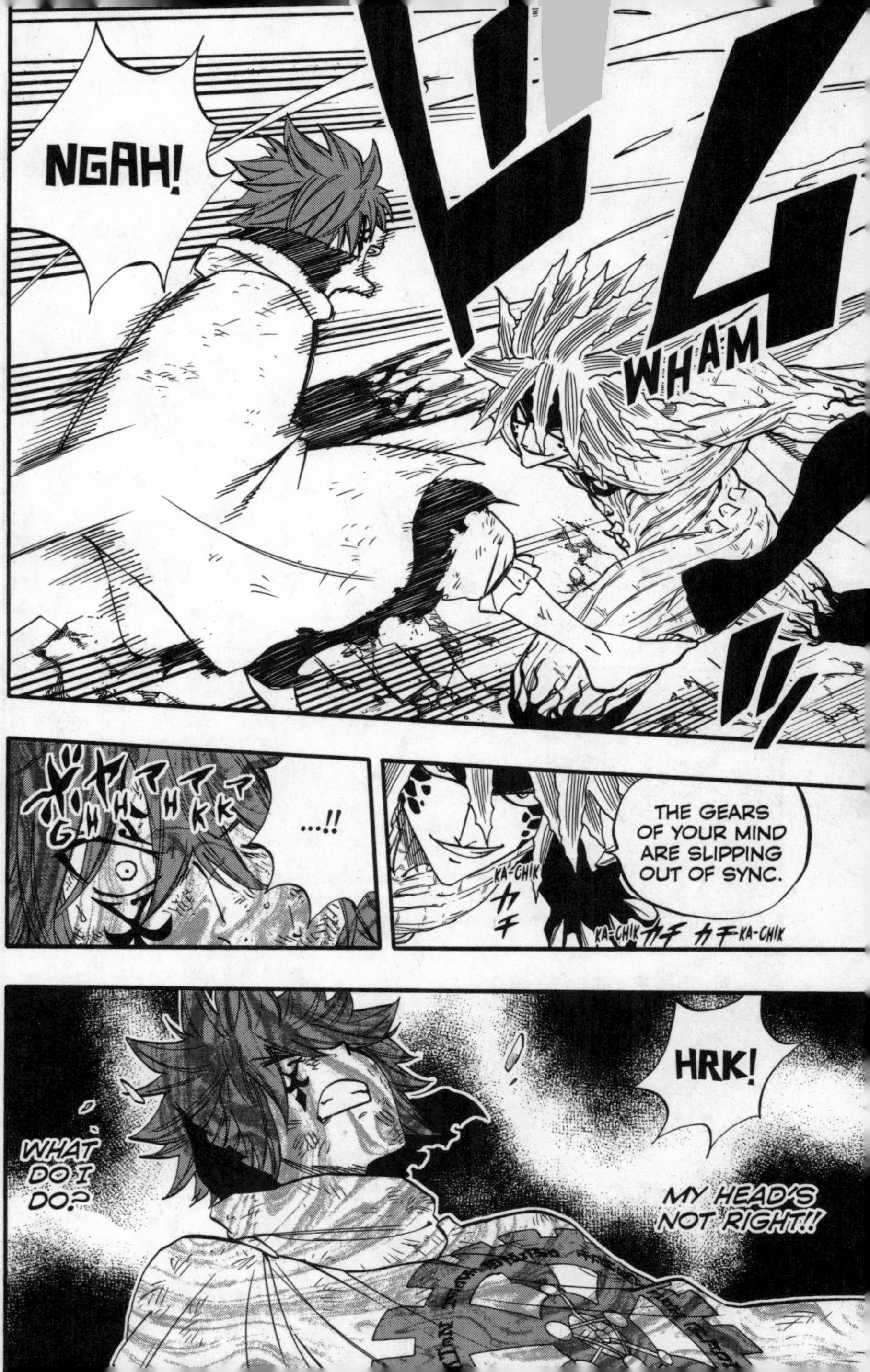
WHAM
NGAH!
THE GEARS OF YOUR MIND ARE SLIPPING OUT OF SYNC.
KA-CHIK
KA-CHIK
KA-CHIK
GHHKK
...!!
HRK!
MY HEAD'S NOT RIGHT!!
WHAT DO I DO?

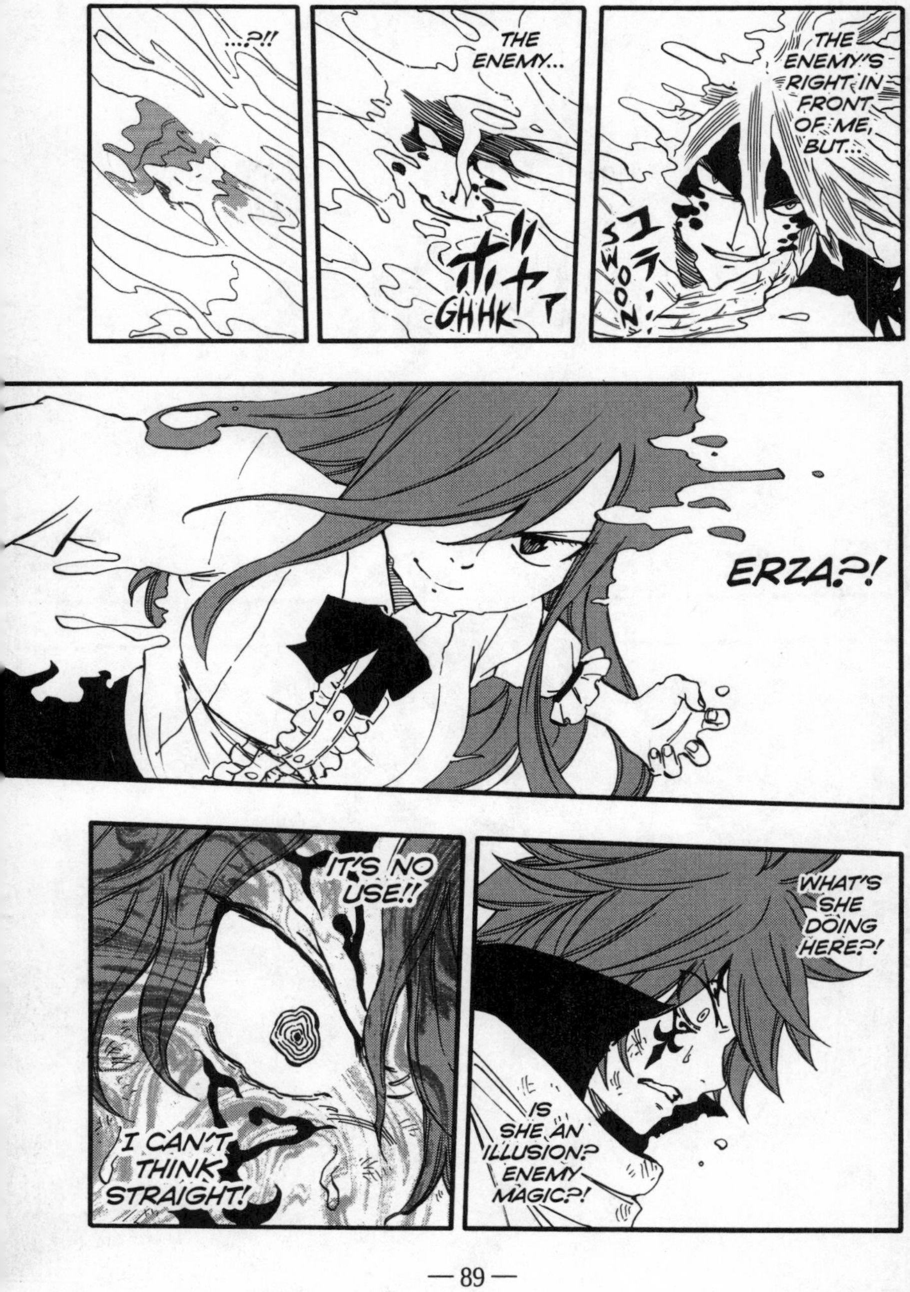
THE ENEMY'S RIGHT IN FRONT OF ME, BUT...
SWOON
THE ENEMY...
GHHK
...?!!
ERZA?!
WHAT'S SHE DOING HERE?!
IS SHE AN ILLUSION? ENEMY MAGIC?!
IT'S NO USE!!
I CAN'T THINK STRAIGHT!

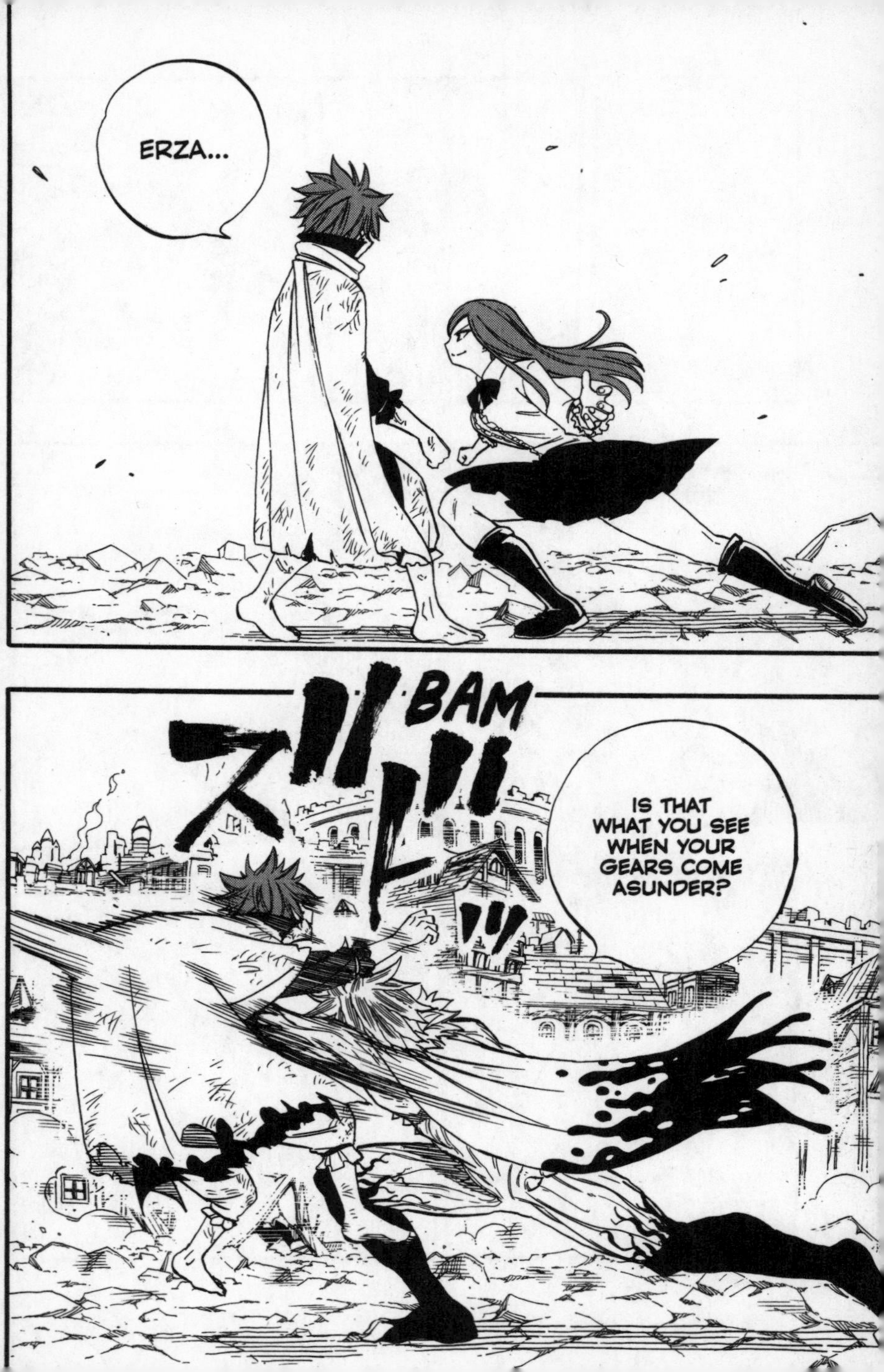
ERZA...
BAM
IS THAT WHAT YOU SEE WHEN YOUR GEARS COME ASUNDER?

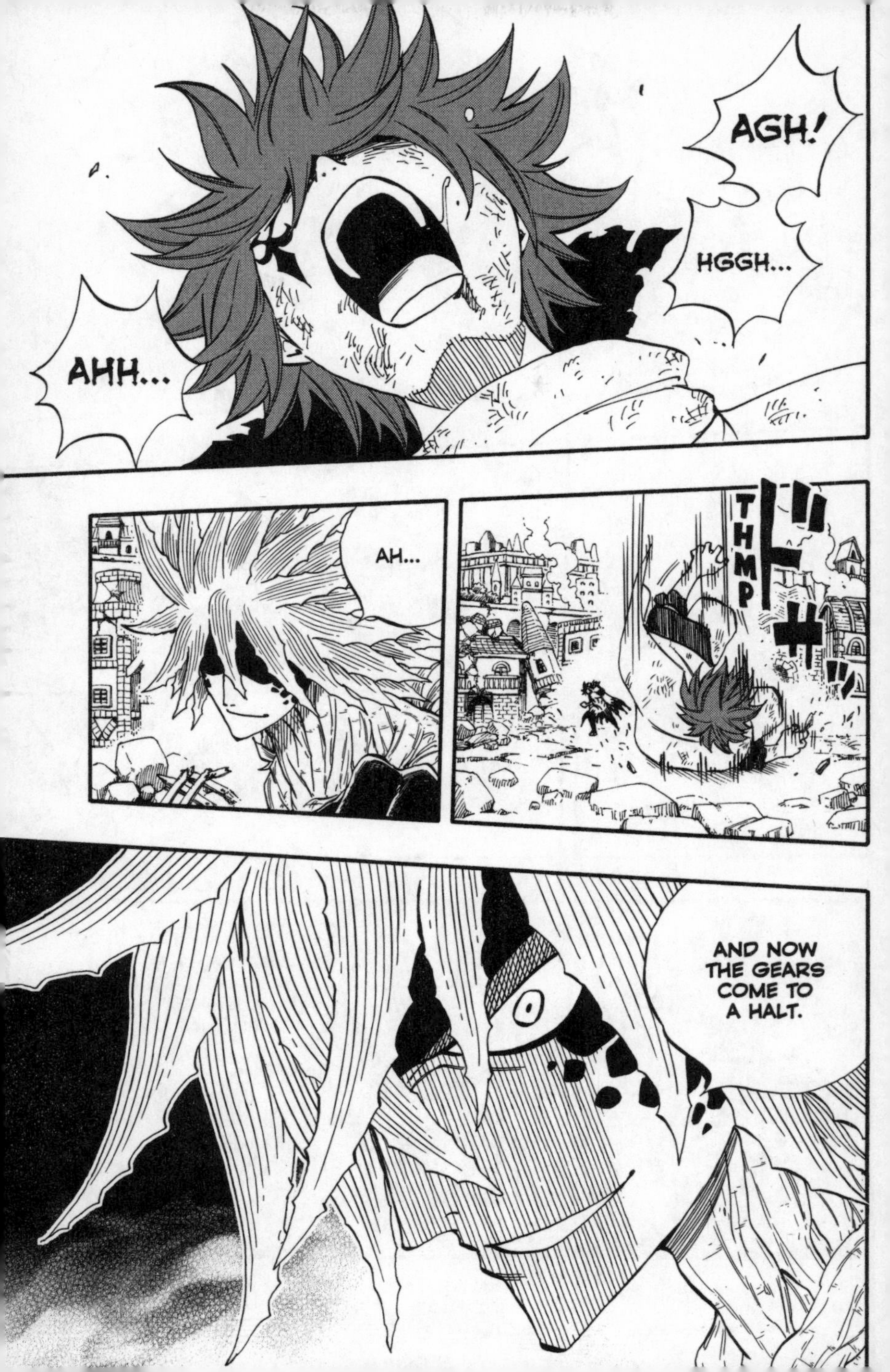
AGH!
HGGH...
AHH...
THMP
AH...
AND NOW THE GEARS COME TO A HALT.

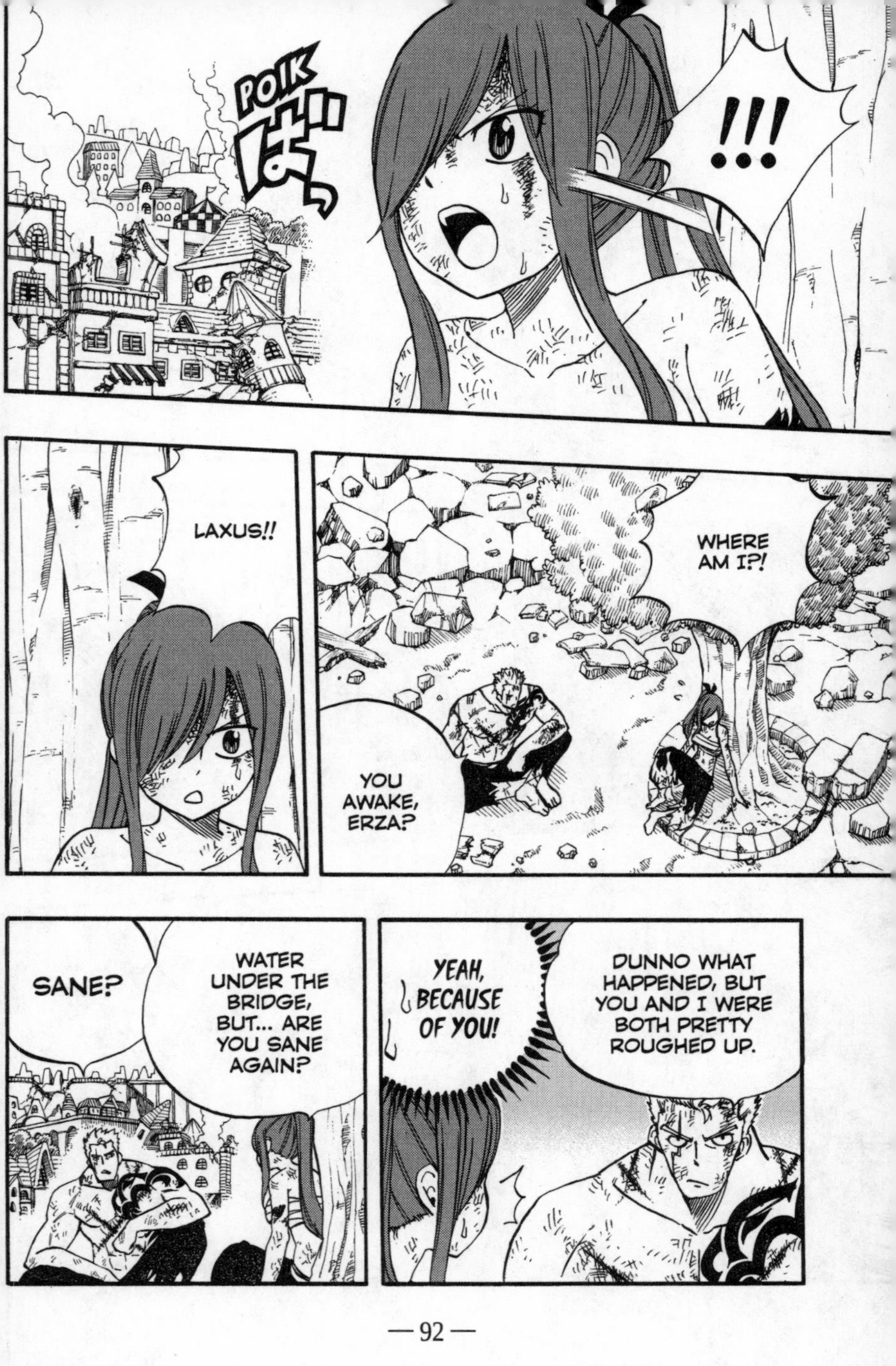
!!!
POIK
ぱっ
WHERE AM I?!
YOU AWAKE, ERZA?
LAXUS!!
DUNNO WHAT HAPPENED, BUT YOU AND I WERE BOTH PRETTY ROUGHED UP.
YEAH, BECAUSE OF YOU!
WATER UNDER THE BRIDGE, BUT... ARE YOU SANE AGAIN?
SANE?

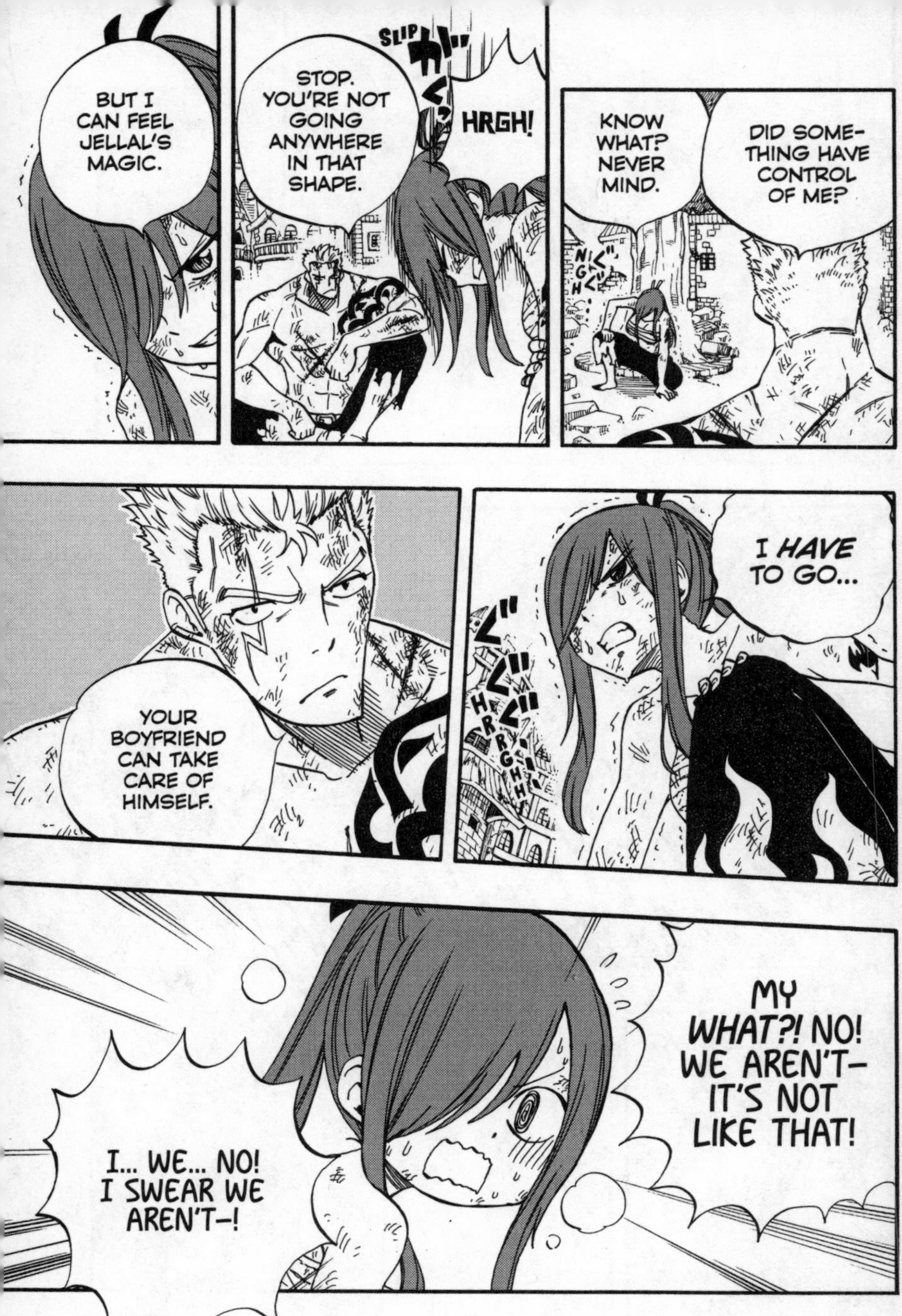
DID SOME-THING HAVE CONTROL OF ME?
KNOW WHAT? NEVER MIND.
NGH
SLIP
HRGH!
STOP. YOU'RE NOT GOING ANYWHERE IN THAT SHAPE.
BUT I CAN FEEL JELLAL'S MAGIC.
I *HAVE* TO GO...
HRRGHH
YOUR BOYFRIEND CAN TAKE CARE OF HIMSELF.
MY *WHAT?!* NO! WE AREN'T– IT'S NOT LIKE THAT!
I... WE... NO! I SWEAR WE AREN'T–!

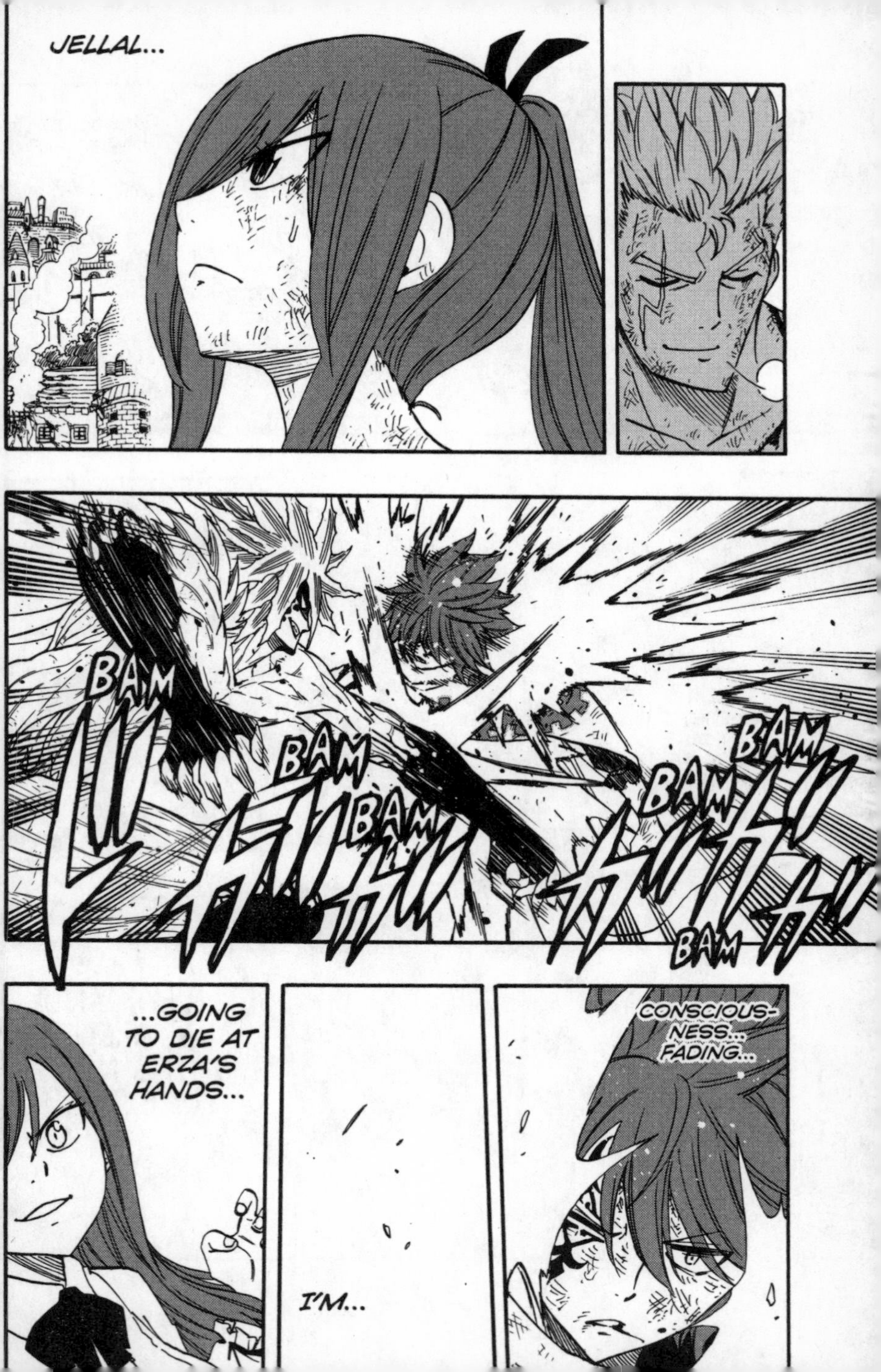
JELLAL...
BAM
BAM
BAM
BAM
BAM
BAM
CONSCIOUS-NESS... FADING...
I'M...
...GOING TO DIE AT ERZA'S HANDS...

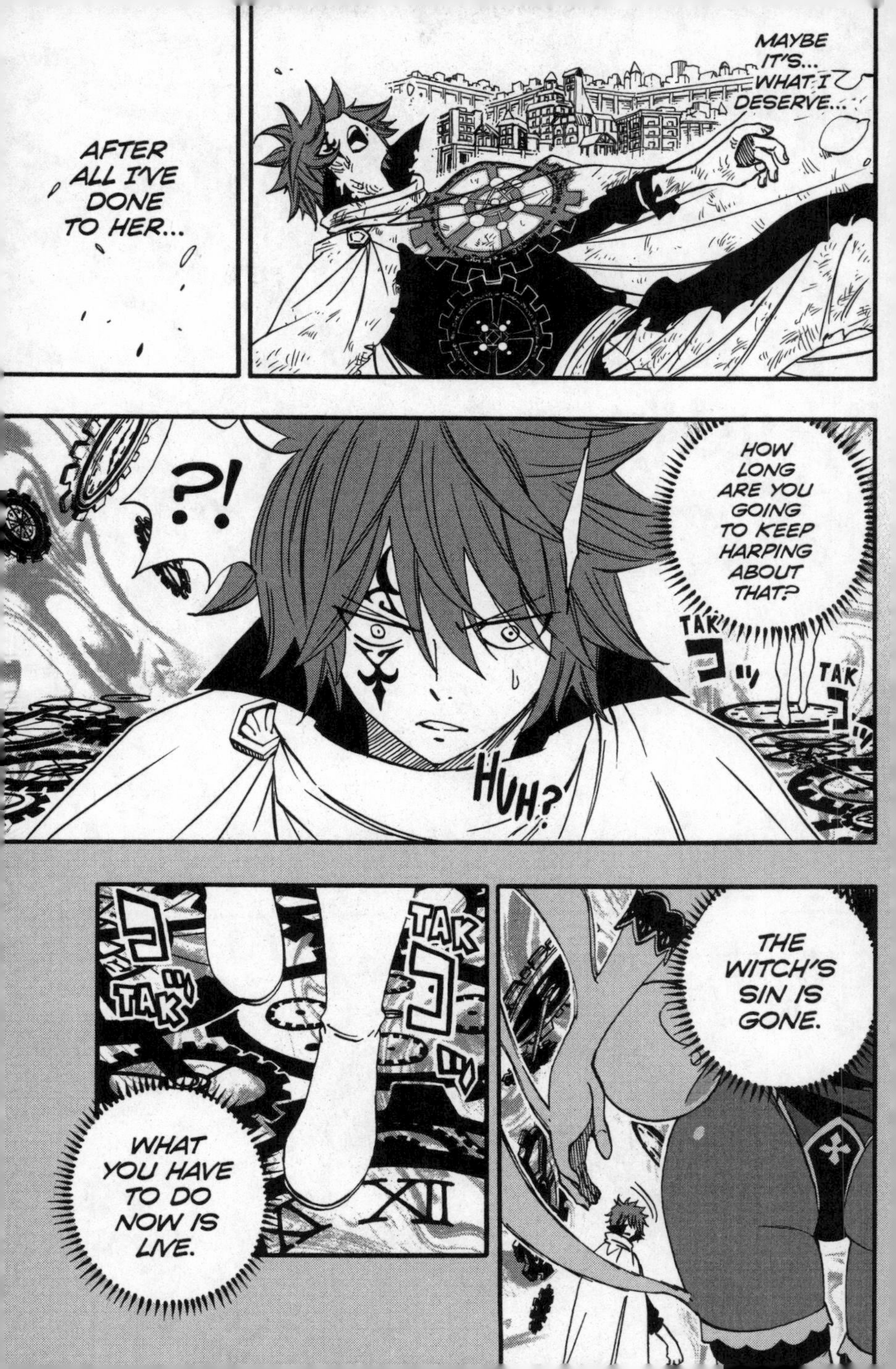
MAYBE IT'S... WHAT I DESERVE...
AFTER ALL I'VE DONE TO HER...
HOW LONG ARE YOU GOING TO KEEP HARPING ABOUT THAT?
TAK
TAK
?!
HUH?
THE WITCH'S SIN IS GONE.
TAK
TAK
WHAT YOU HAVE TO DO NOW IS LIVE.

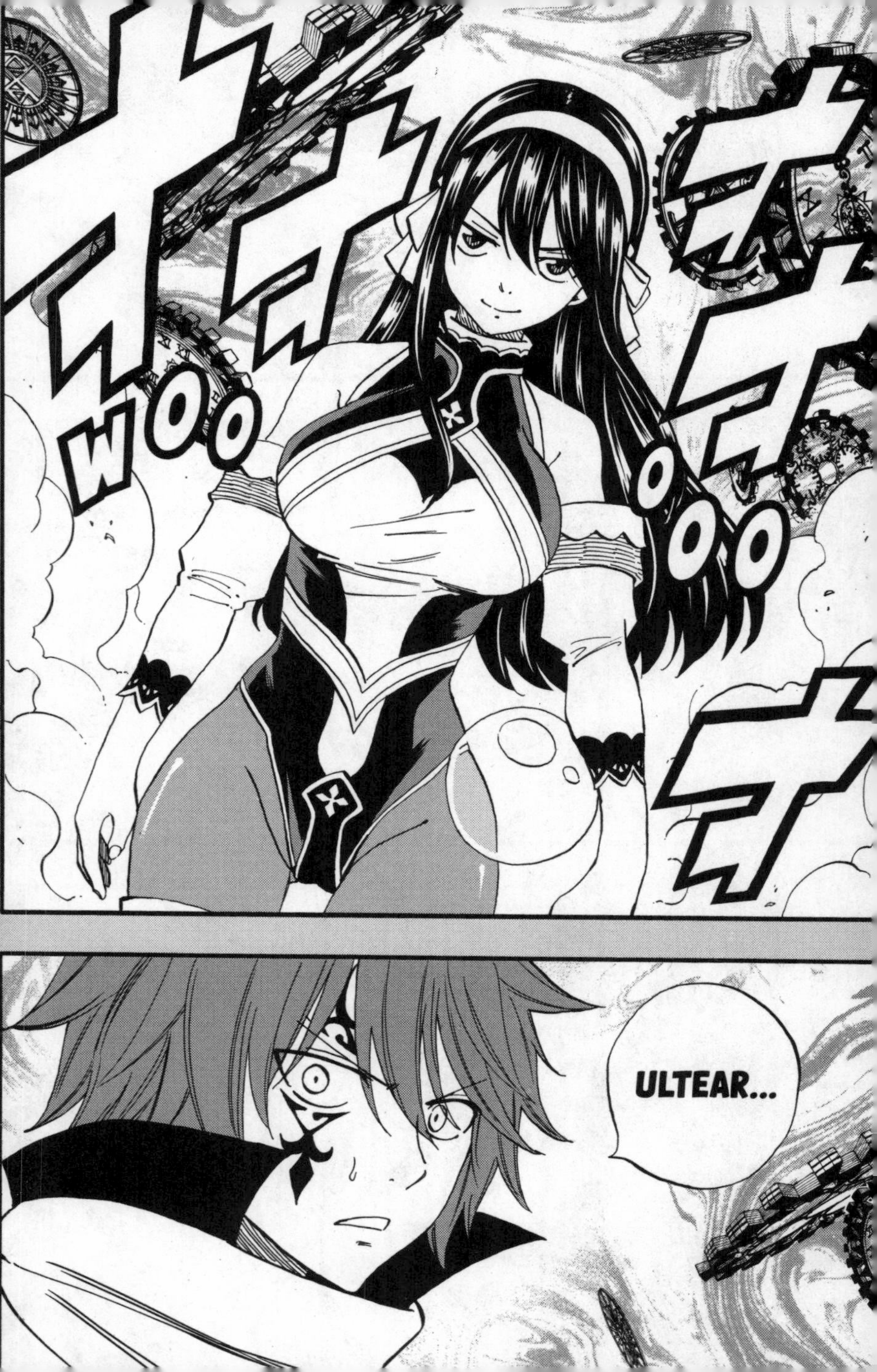
WOO
OOO
ULTEAR...

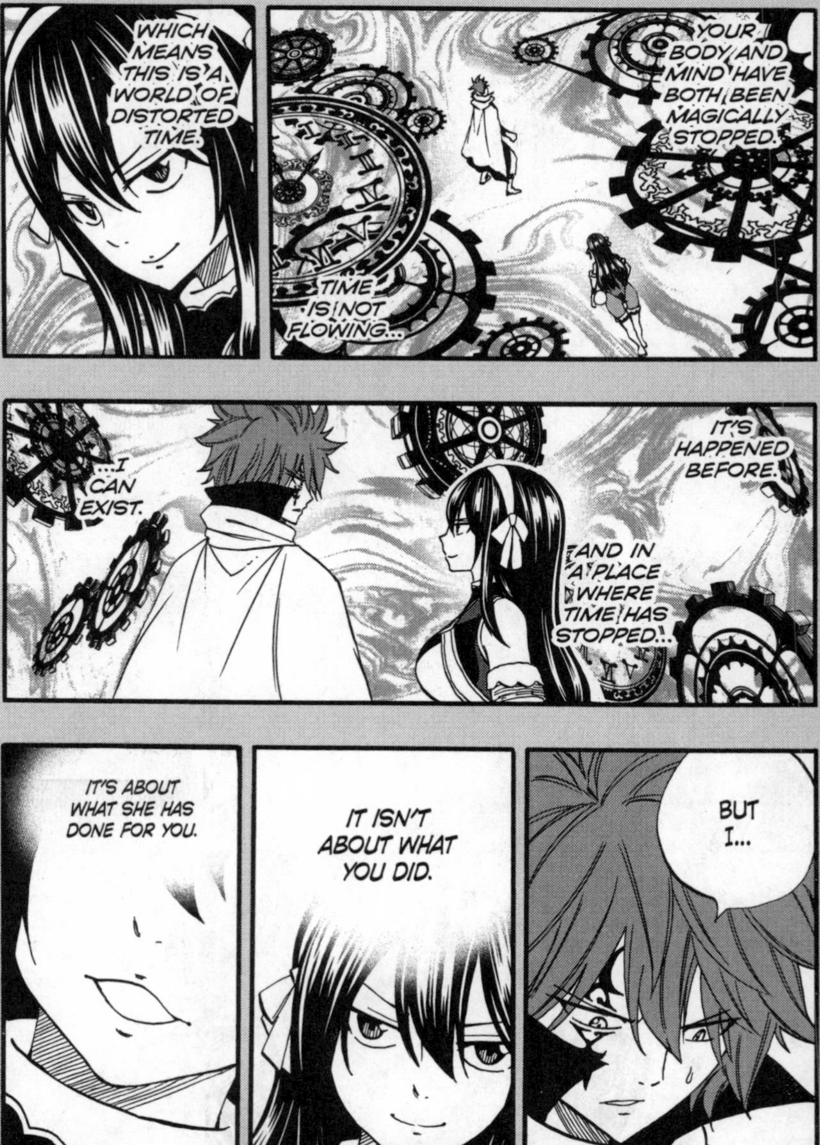
YOUR BODY AND MIND HAVE BOTH BEEN MAGICALLY STOPPED.
TIME IS NOT FLOWING...
WHICH MEANS THIS IS A WORLD OF DISTORTED TIME.
IT'S HAPPENED BEFORE.
AND IN A PLACE WHERE TIME HAS STOPPED...
...I CAN EXIST.
BUT I...
IT ISN'T ABOUT WHAT YOU DID.
IT'S ABOUT WHAT SHE HAS DONE FOR YOU.

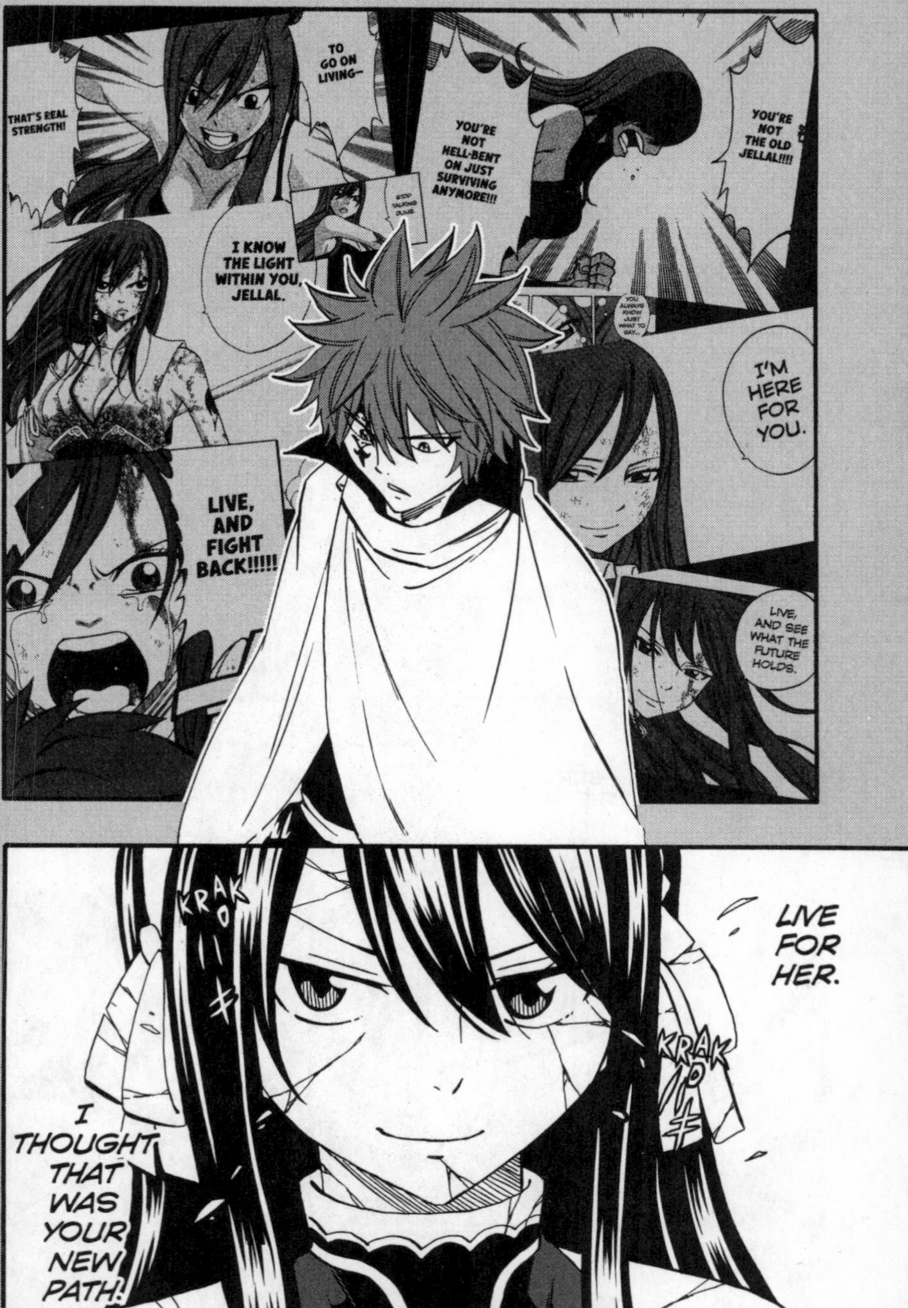
YOU'RE NOT THE OLD JELLAL!!!!
YOU'RE NOT HELL-BENT ON JUST SURVIVING ANYMORE!!!
TO GO ON LIVING—
THAT'S REAL STRENGTH!
YOU ALWAYS KNOW JUST WHAT TO SAY...
I'M HERE FOR YOU.
I KNOW THE LIGHT WITHIN YOU, JELLAL.
LIVE, AND SEE WHAT THE FUTURE HOLDS.
LIVE, AND FIGHT BACK!!!!!
LIVE FOR HER.
KRAK
KRAK
I THOUGHT THAT WAS YOUR NEW PATH!

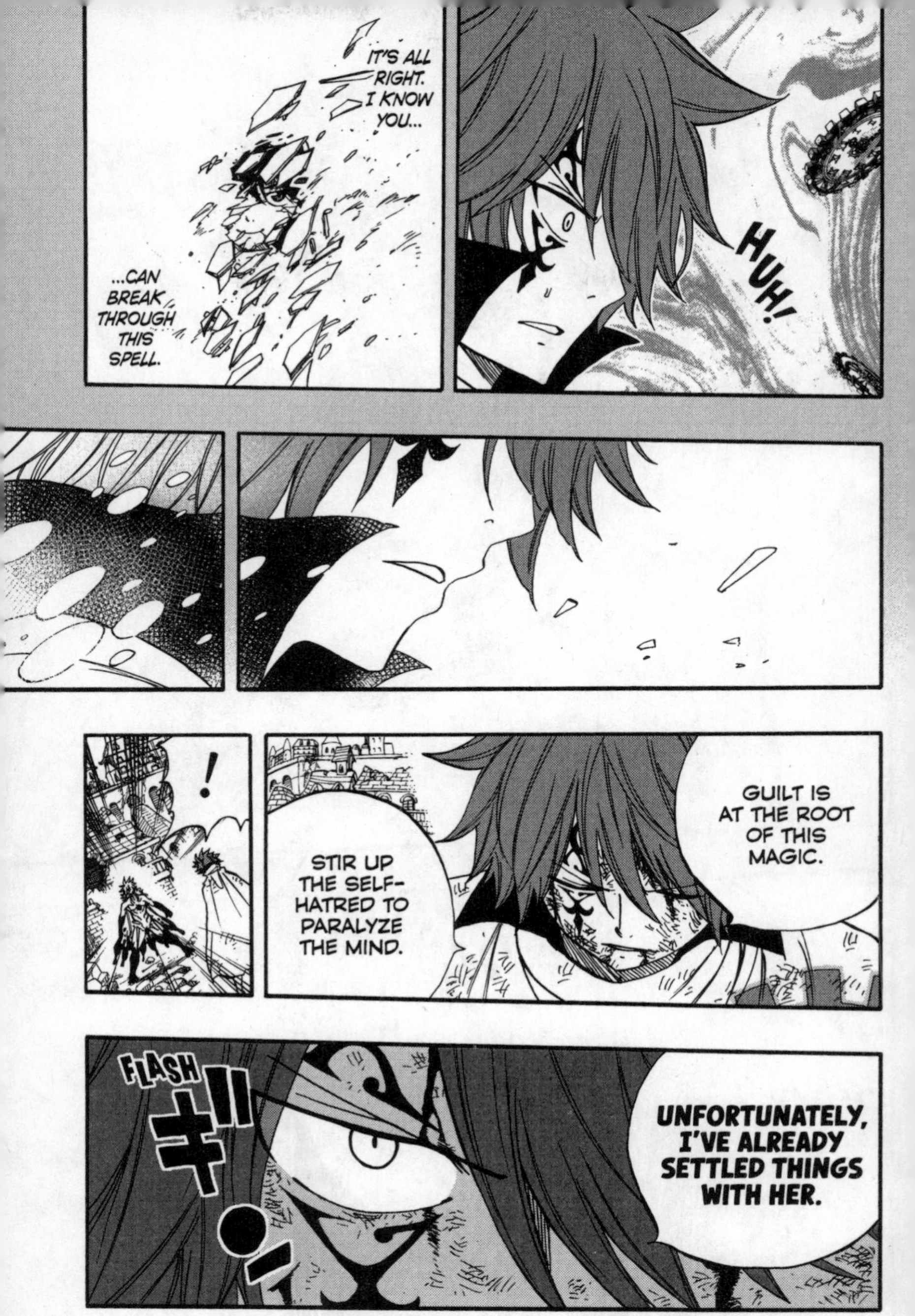
HUH!
IT'S ALL RIGHT. I KNOW YOU...
...CAN BREAK THROUGH THIS SPELL.
GUILT IS AT THE ROOT OF THIS MAGIC.
STIR UP THE SELF-HATRED TO PARALYZE THE MIND.
!
UNFORTUNATELY, I'VE ALREADY SETTLED THINGS WITH HER.
FLASH

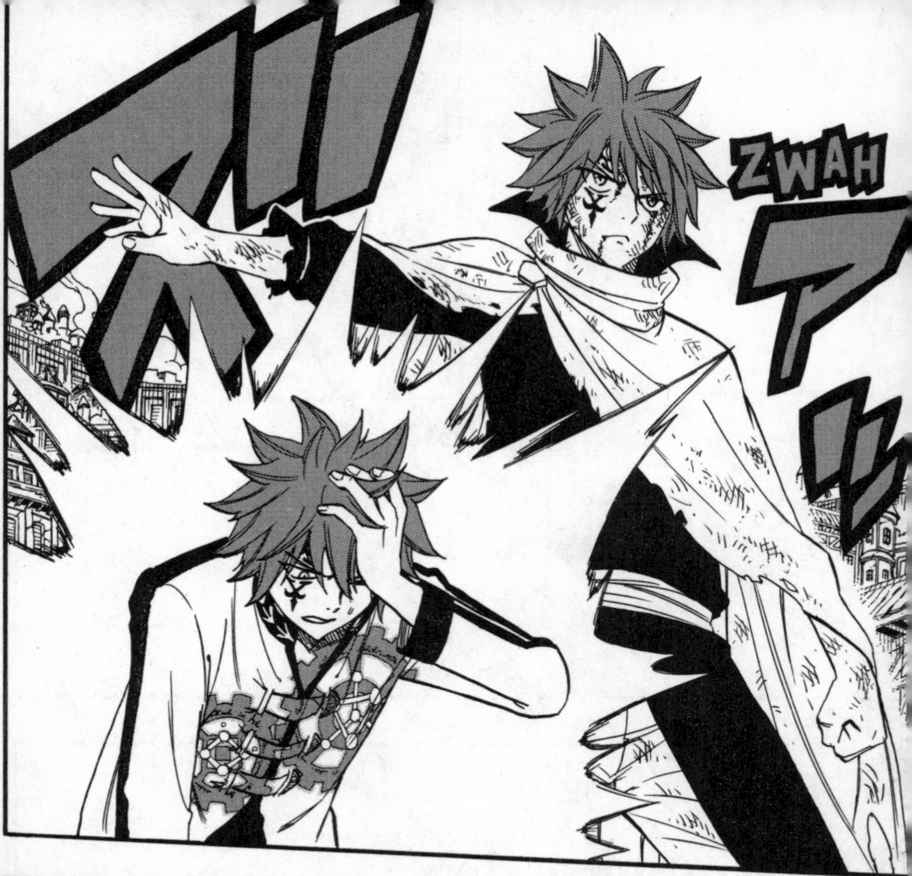
ZWAH

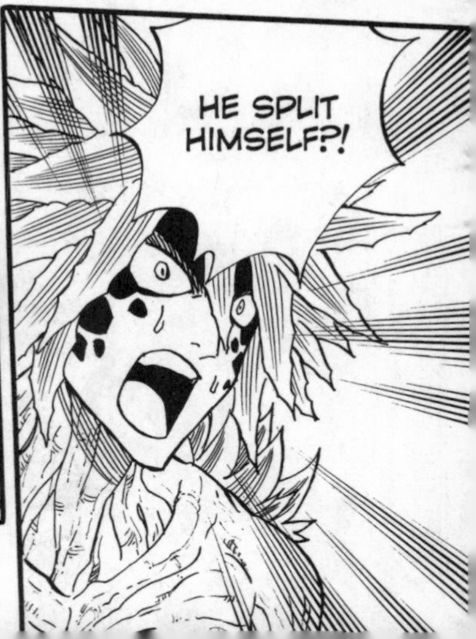
HE SPLIT HIMSELF?!

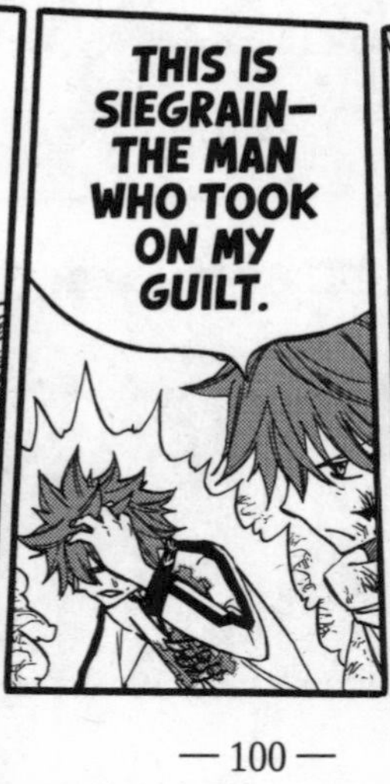
THIS IS SIEGRAIN—THE MAN WHO TOOK ON MY GUILT.

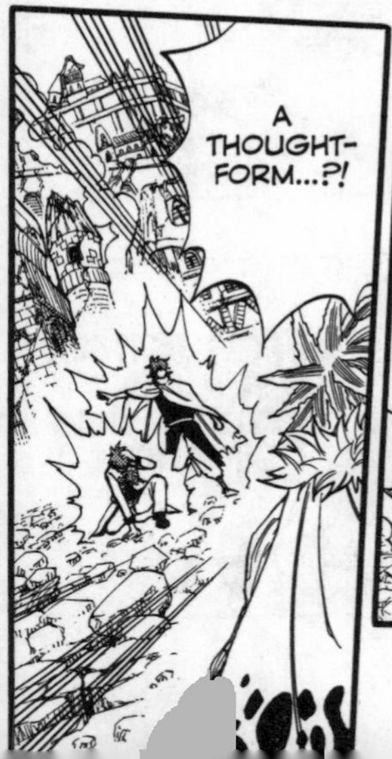
A THOUGHT-FORM...?!

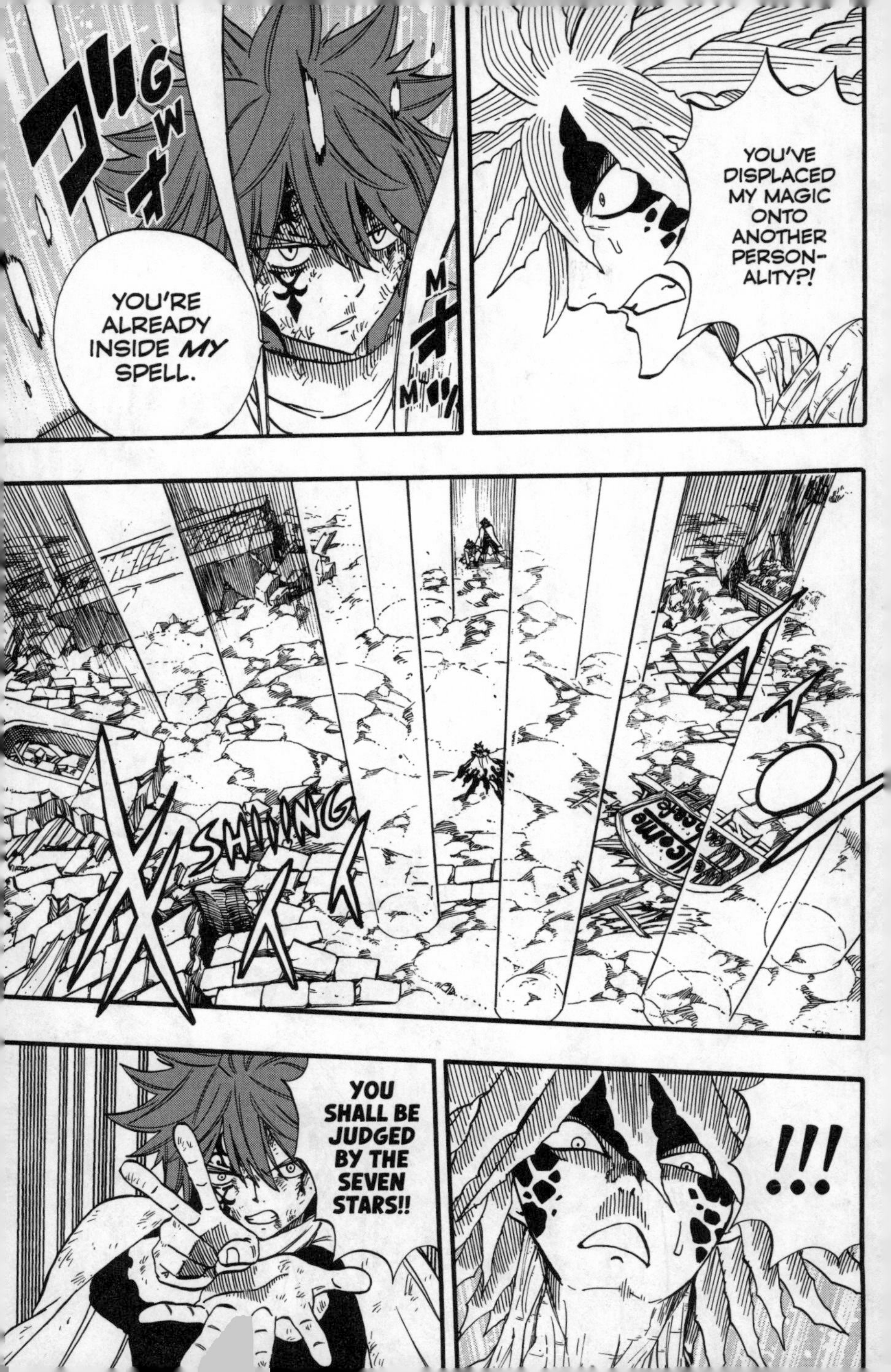
YOU'VE DISPLACED MY MAGIC ONTO ANOTHER PERSONALITY?!
YOU'RE ALREADY INSIDE *MY* SPELL.
SHIIING
!!!
YOU SHALL BE JUDGED BY THE SEVEN STARS!!

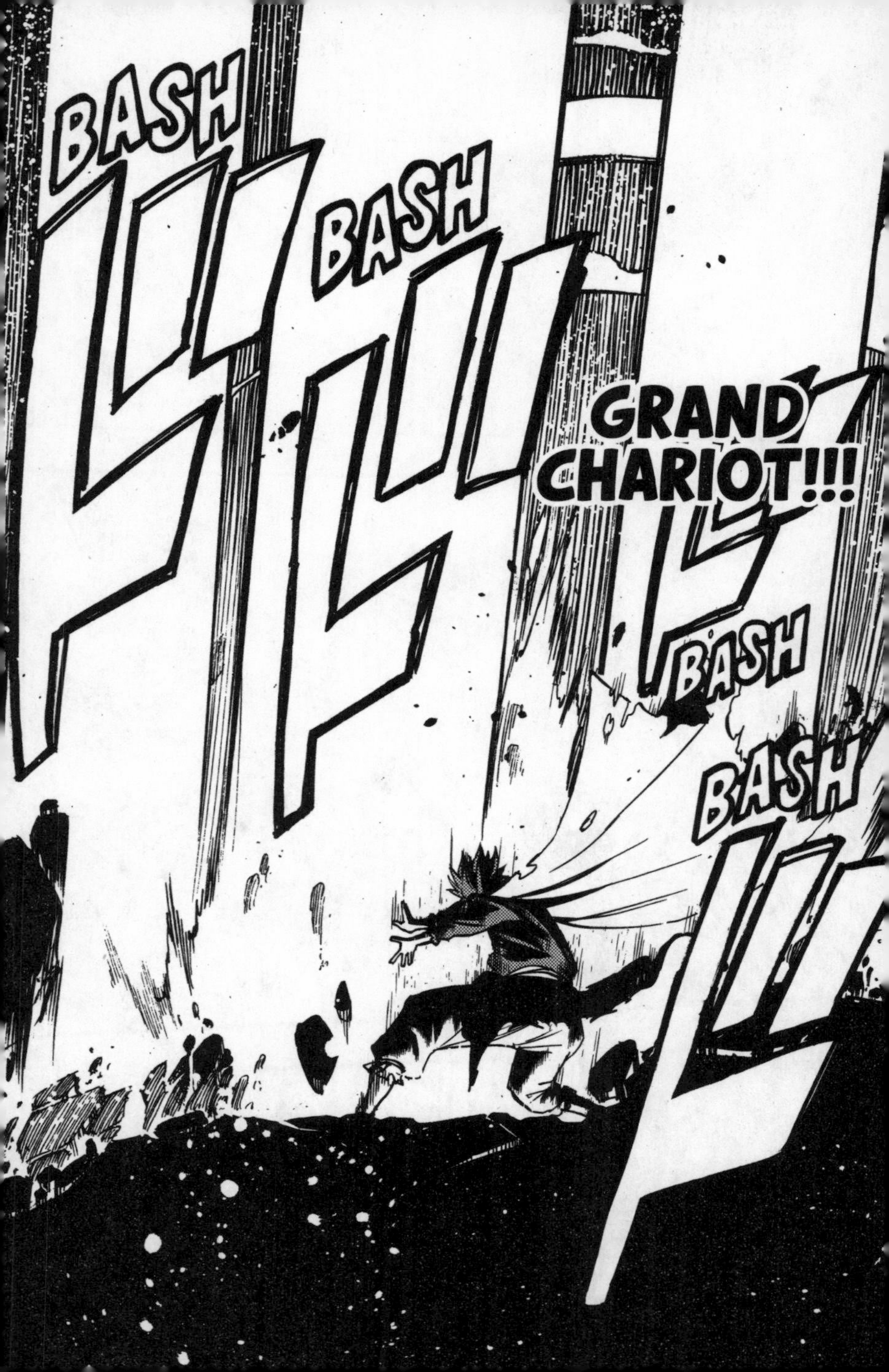
BASH
BASH
GRAND CHARIOT!!!
BASH
BASH

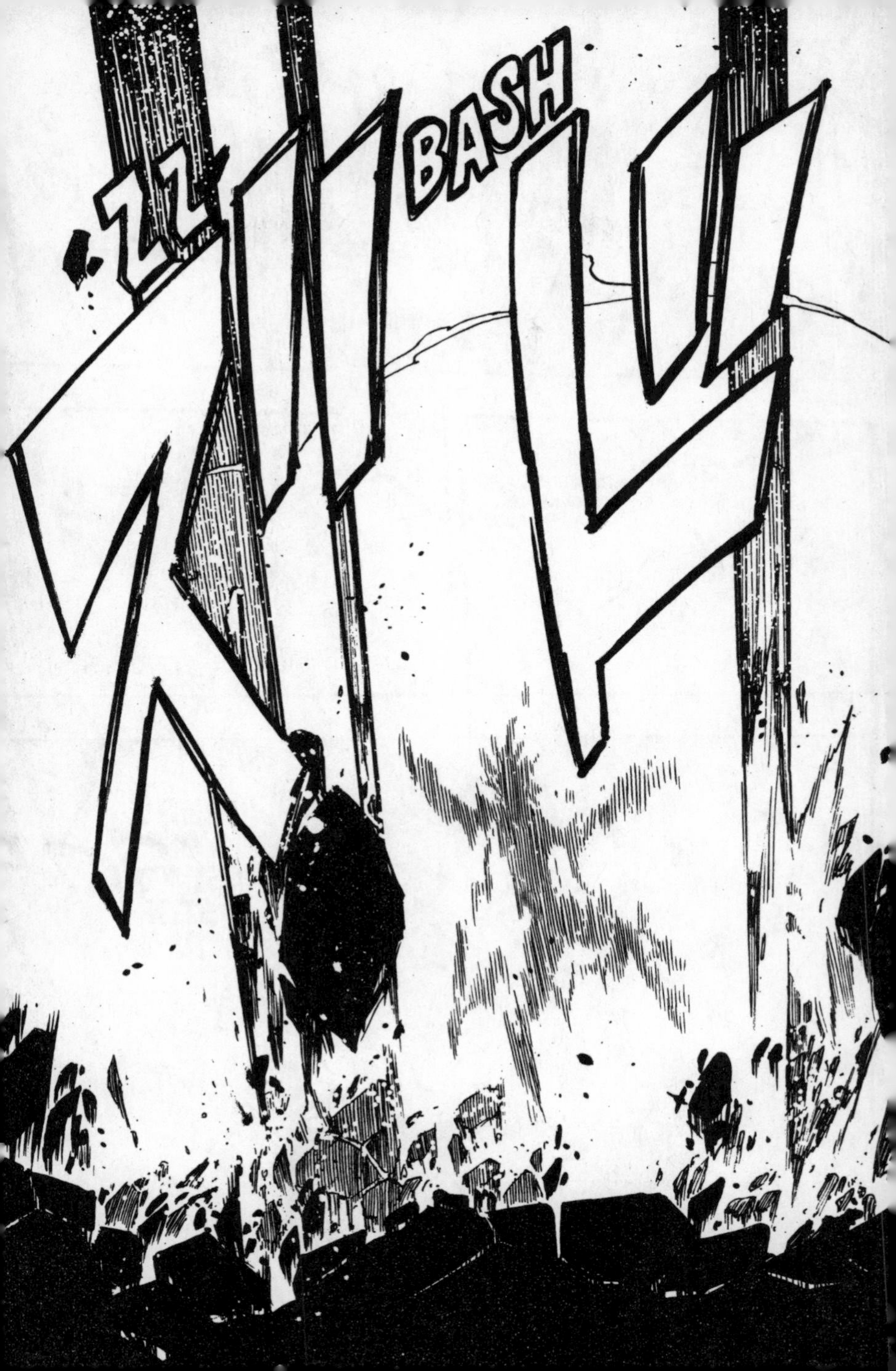
BASH

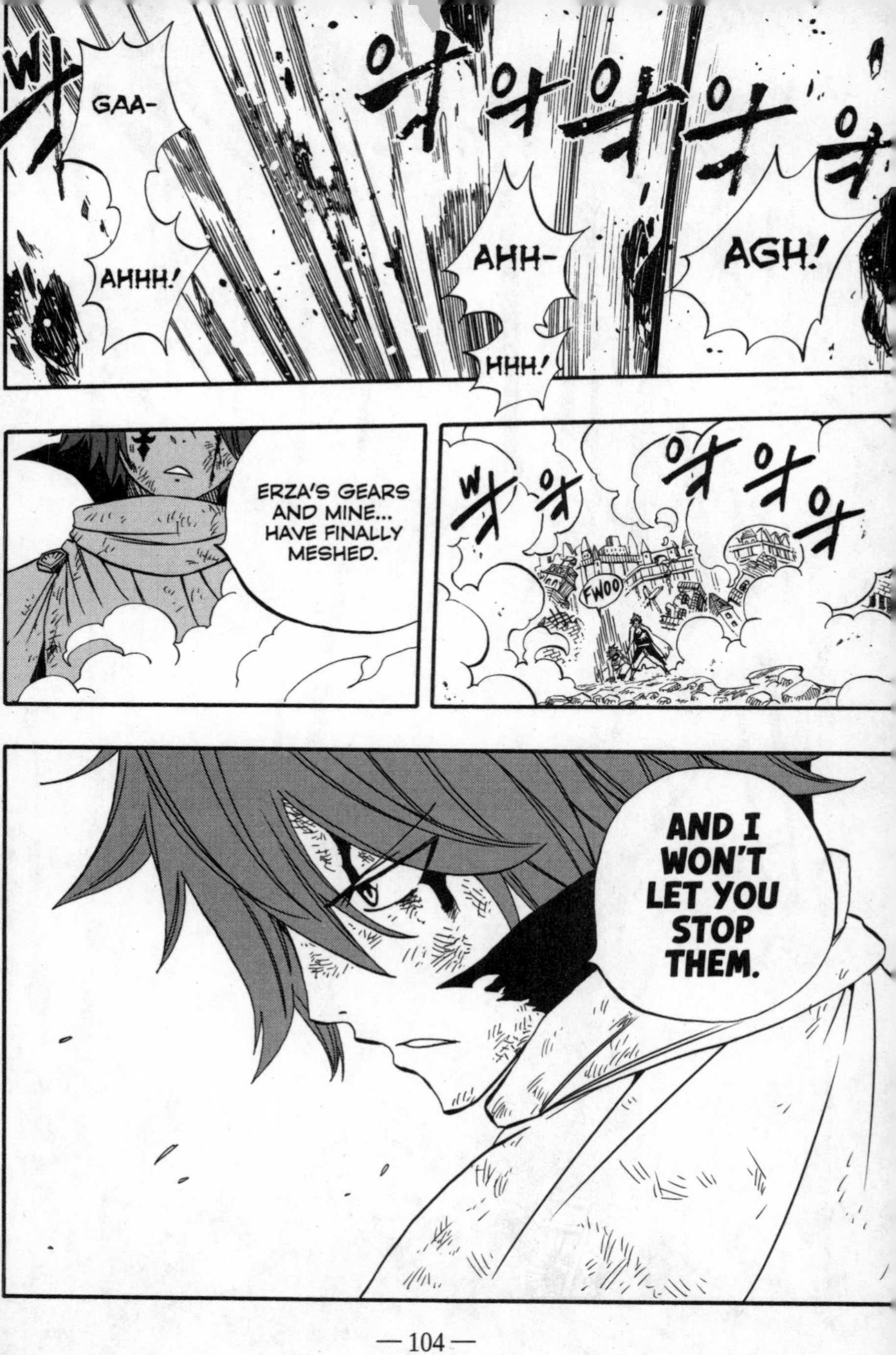
AGH!
AHH- HHH!
GAA- AHHH!
FWOO
ERZA'S GEARS AND MINE... HAVE FINALLY MESHED.
AND I WON'T LET YOU STOP THEM.

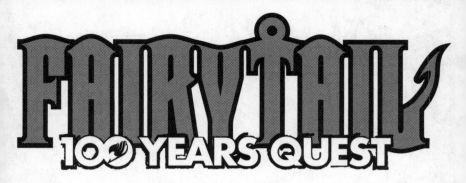

FAIRY TAIL

100 YEARS QUEST

CHAPTER 60: GIGANTIFY

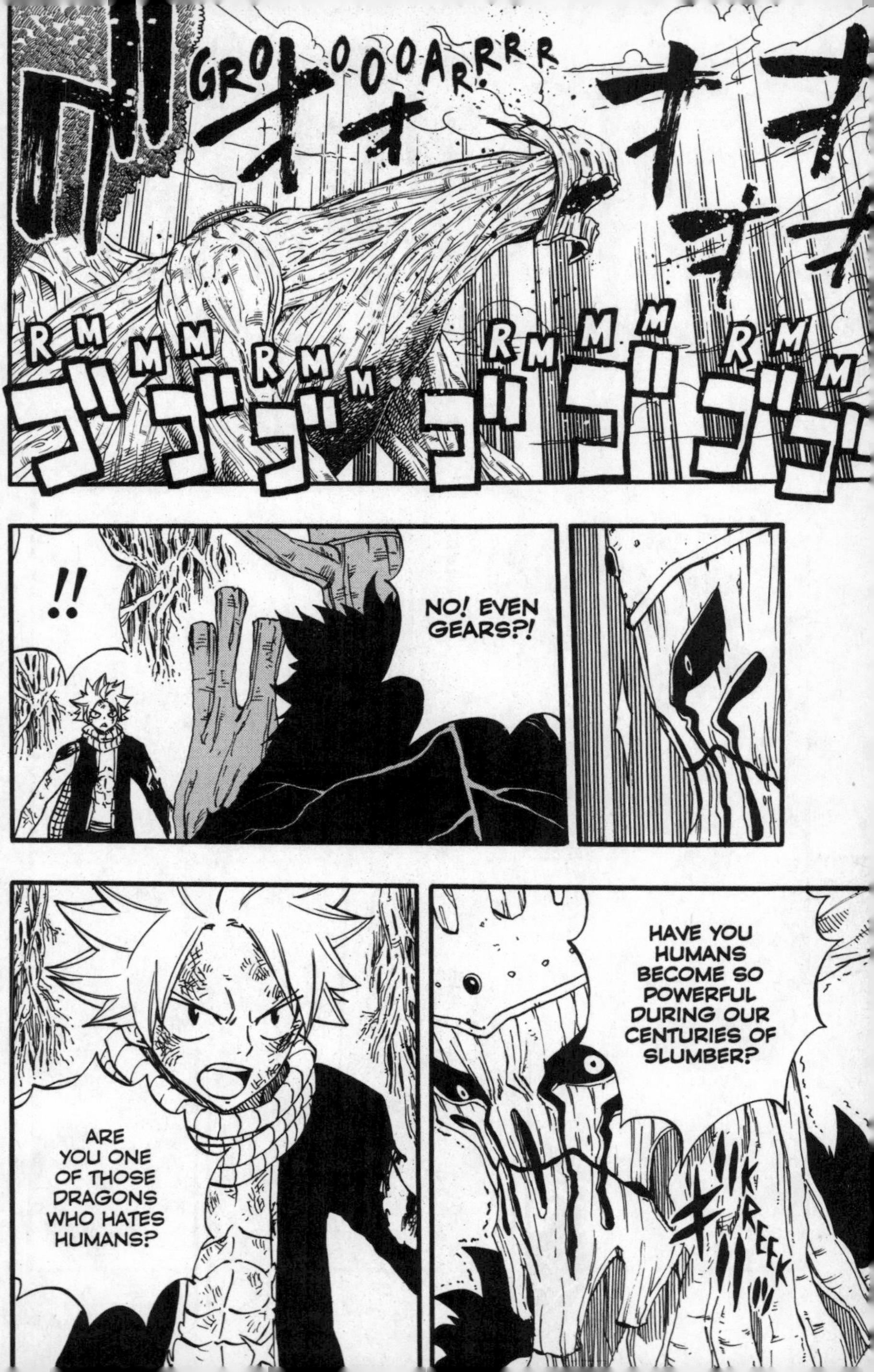
GROOOOARRRR
RMMM RMMM.. RMMM RMMM
!!
NO! EVEN GEARS?!
HAVE YOU HUMANS BECOME SO POWERFUL DURING OUR CENTURIES OF SLUMBER?
KREEK
ARE YOU ONE OF THOSE DRAGONS WHO HATES HUMANS?

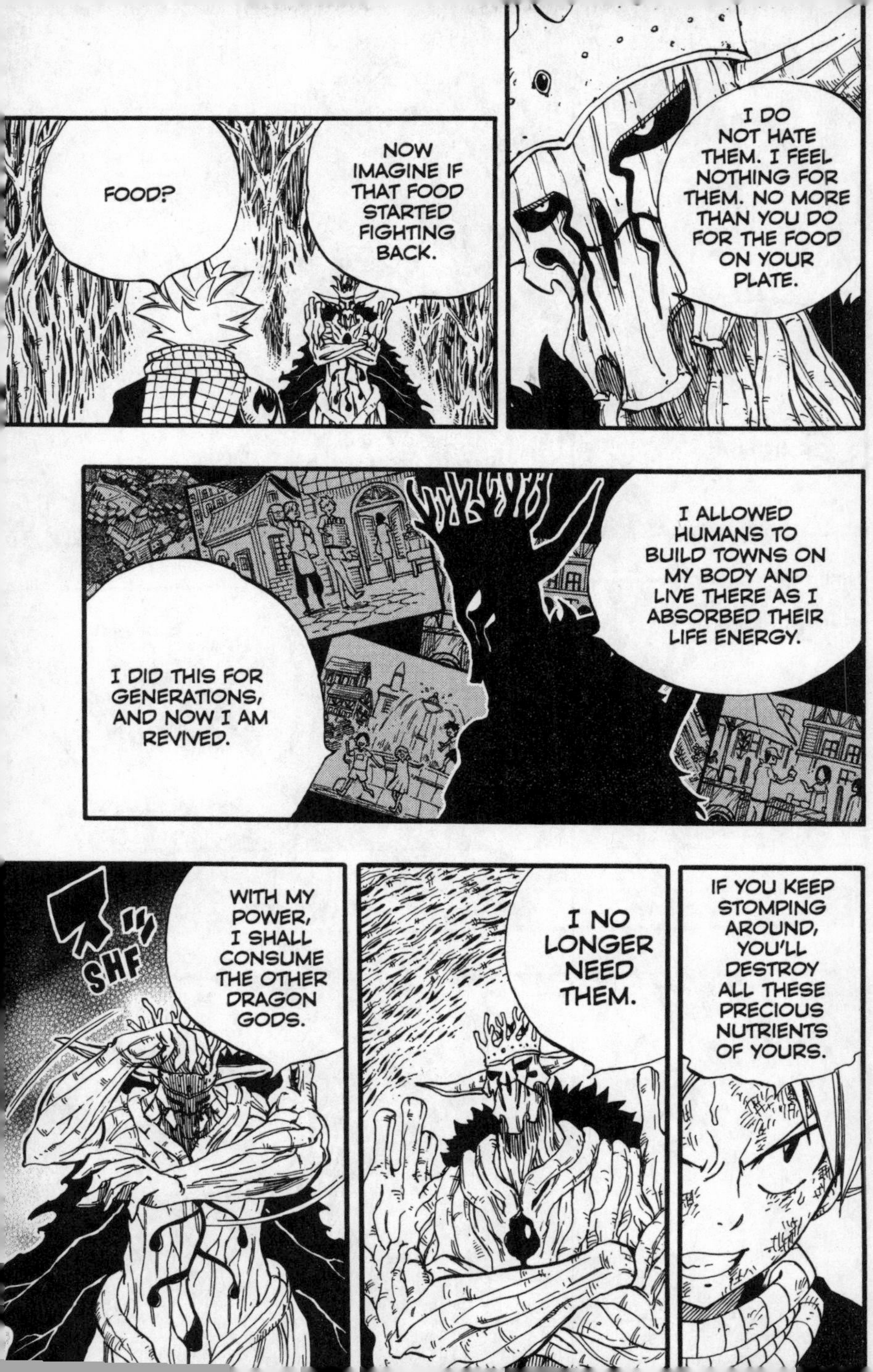
I DO NOT HATE THEM. I FEEL NOTHING FOR THEM. NO MORE THAN YOU DO FOR THE FOOD ON YOUR PLATE.
FOOD?
NOW IMAGINE IF THAT FOOD STARTED FIGHTING BACK.
I ALLOWED HUMANS TO BUILD TOWNS ON MY BODY AND LIVE THERE AS I ABSORBED THEIR LIFE ENERGY.
I DID THIS FOR GENERATIONS, AND NOW I AM REVIVED.
IF YOU KEEP STOMPING AROUND, YOU'LL DESTROY ALL THESE PRECIOUS NUTRIENTS OF YOURS.
I NO LONGER NEED THEM.
WITH MY POWER, I SHALL CONSUME THE OTHER DRAGON GODS.
SHF

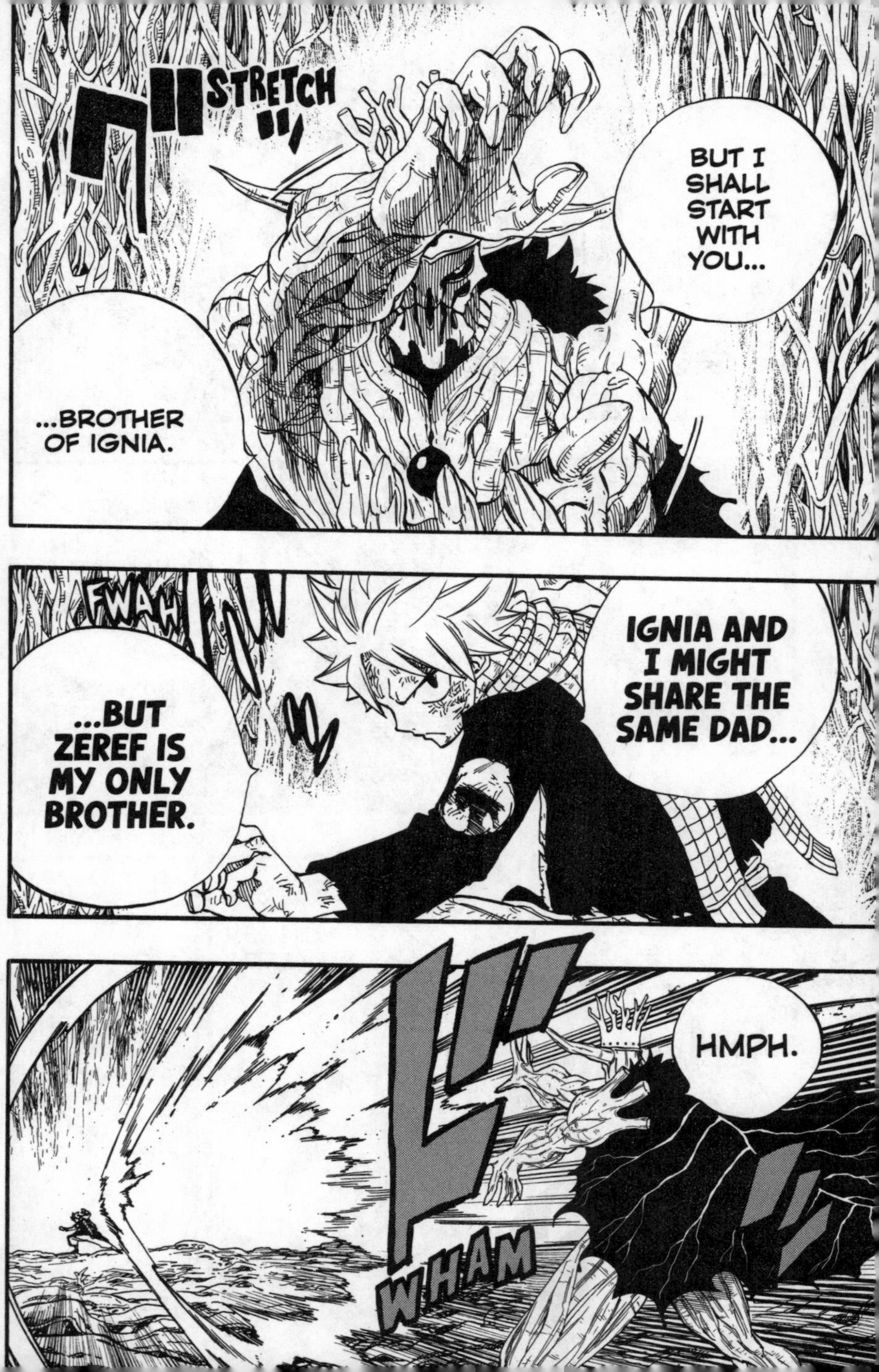
STRETCH
BUT I SHALL START WITH YOU...
...BROTHER OF IGNIA.
FWAH
IGNIA AND I MIGHT SHARE THE SAME DAD...
...BUT ZEREF IS MY ONLY BROTHER.
HMPH.
WHAM

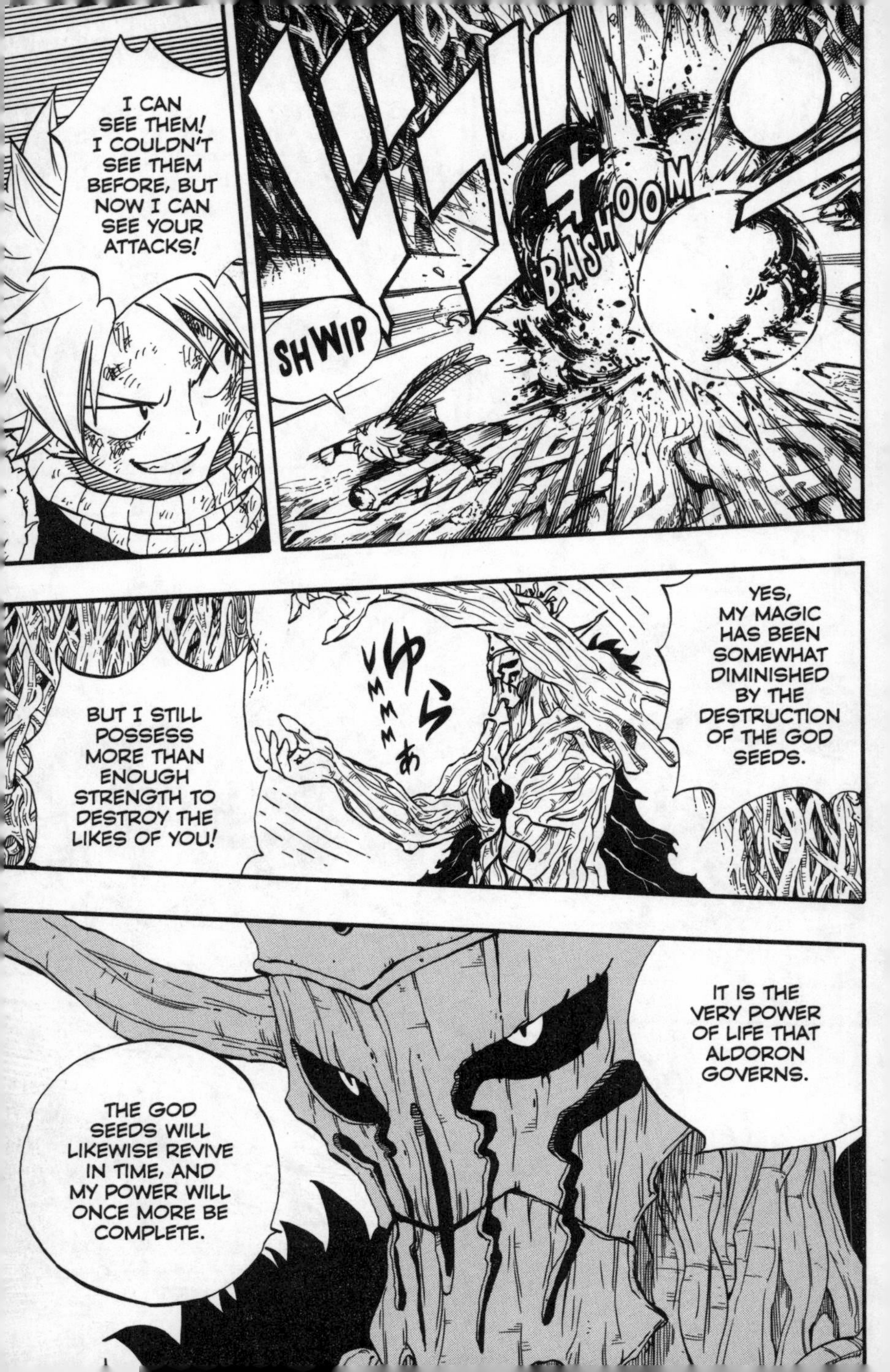
BASHOOM
SHWIP
I CAN SEE THEM! I COULDN'T SEE THEM BEFORE, BUT NOW I CAN SEE YOUR ATTACKS!
YES, MY MAGIC HAS BEEN SOMEWHAT DIMINISHED BY THE DESTRUCTION OF THE GOD SEEDS.
ゆらあ
VMMMM
BUT I STILL POSSESS MORE THAN ENOUGH STRENGTH TO DESTROY THE LIKES OF YOU!
IT IS THE VERY POWER OF LIFE THAT ALDORON GOVERNS.
THE GOD SEEDS WILL LIKEWISE REVIVE IN TIME, AND MY POWER WILL ONCE MORE BE COMPLETE.

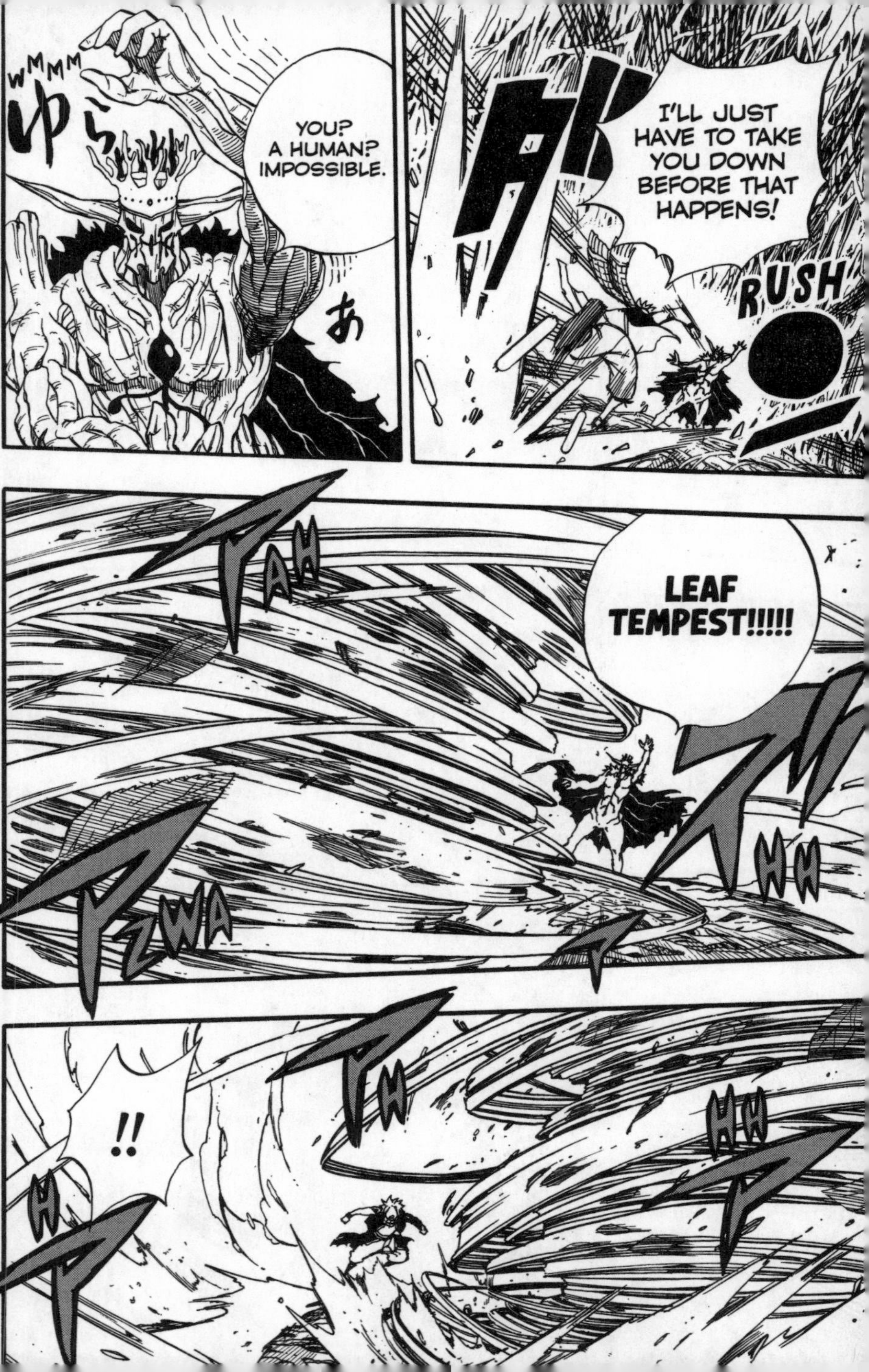
I'LL JUST HAVE TO TAKE YOU DOWN BEFORE THAT HAPPENS!
RUSH
YOU? A HUMAN? IMPOSSIBLE.
WMMM
ゆら
あ
LEAF TEMPEST!!!!!
WHH
TAH
ZWA
HH
TH
!!
H

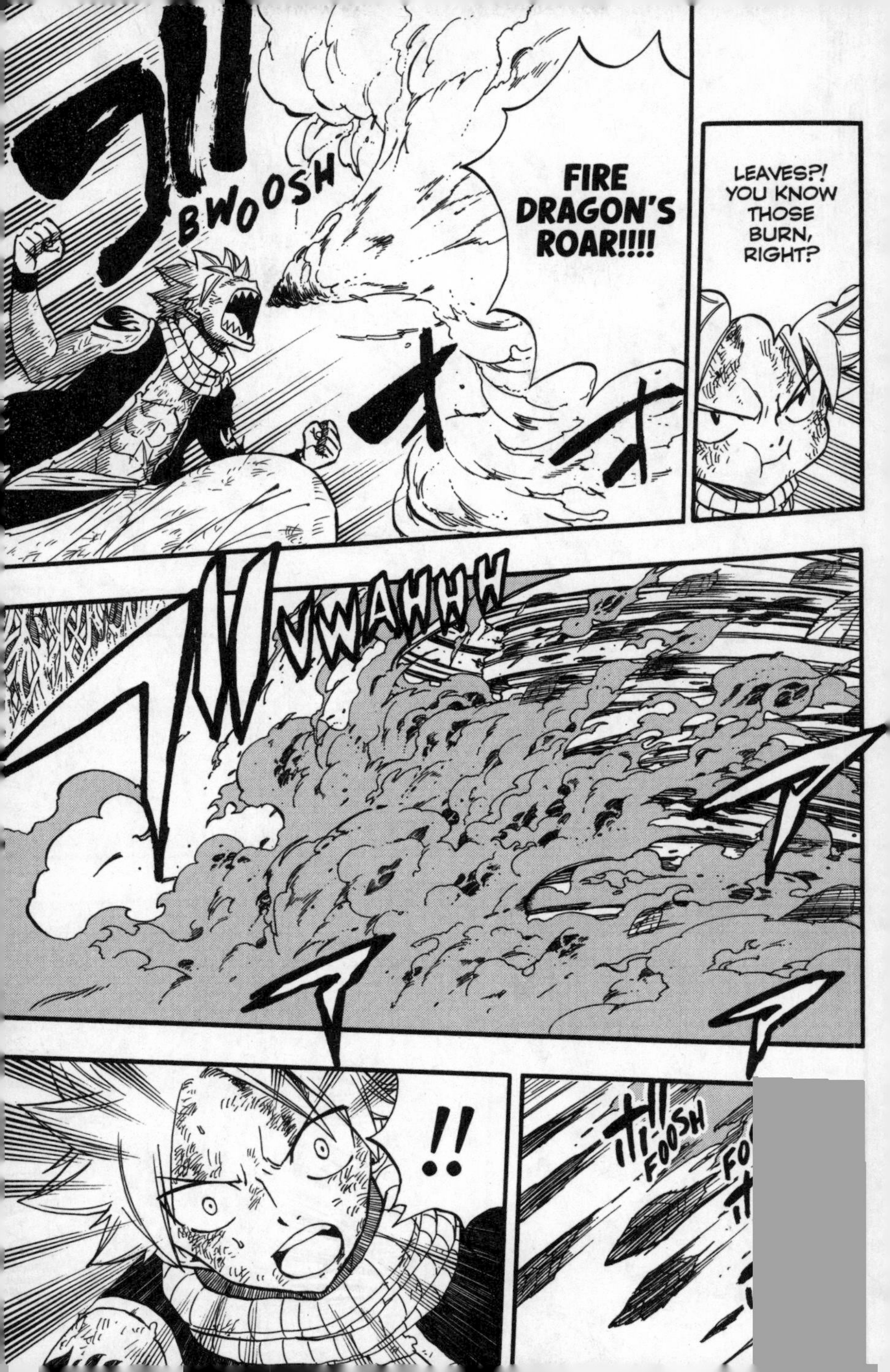
LEAVES?! YOU KNOW THOSE BURN, RIGHT?
FIRE DRAGON'S ROAR!!!!
BWOOSH
VWAHHH
FOOSH
!!

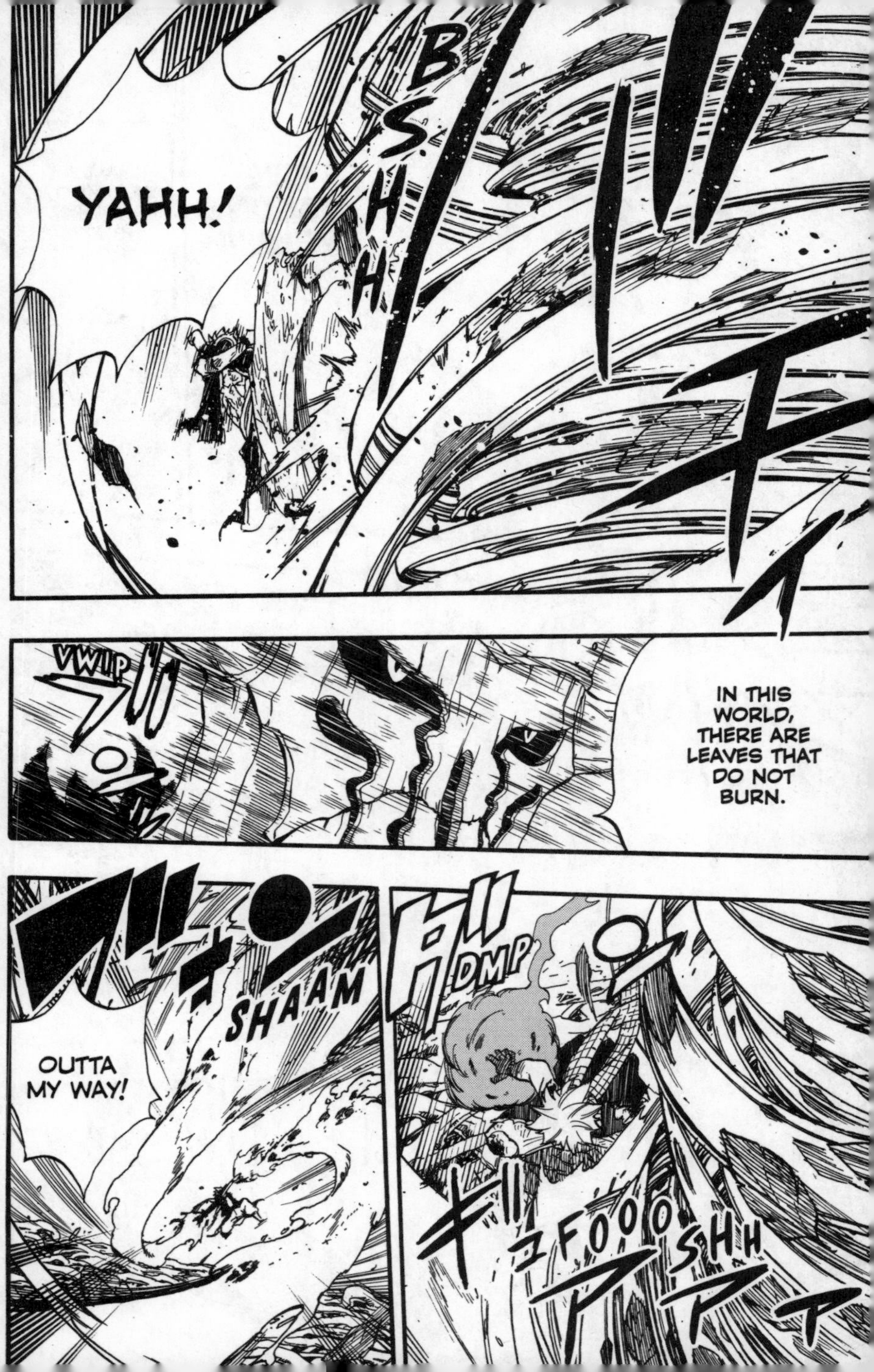
BSHHH
YAHH!
IN THIS WORLD, THERE ARE LEAVES THAT DO NOT BURN.
VWIP
DMP
FOOOSHH
SHAAM
OUTTA MY WAY!

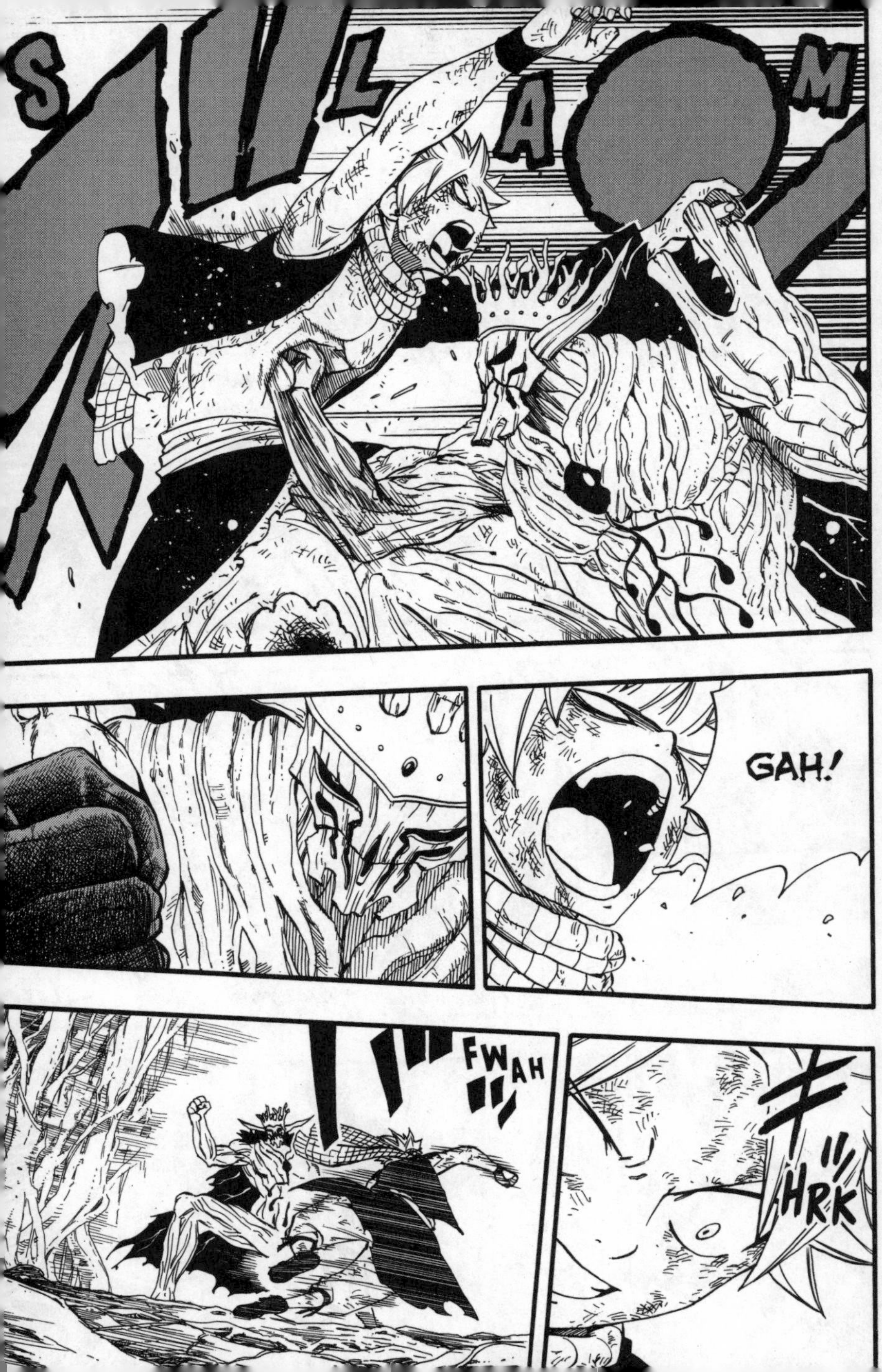
SLAM
GAH!
HRK
FWAH

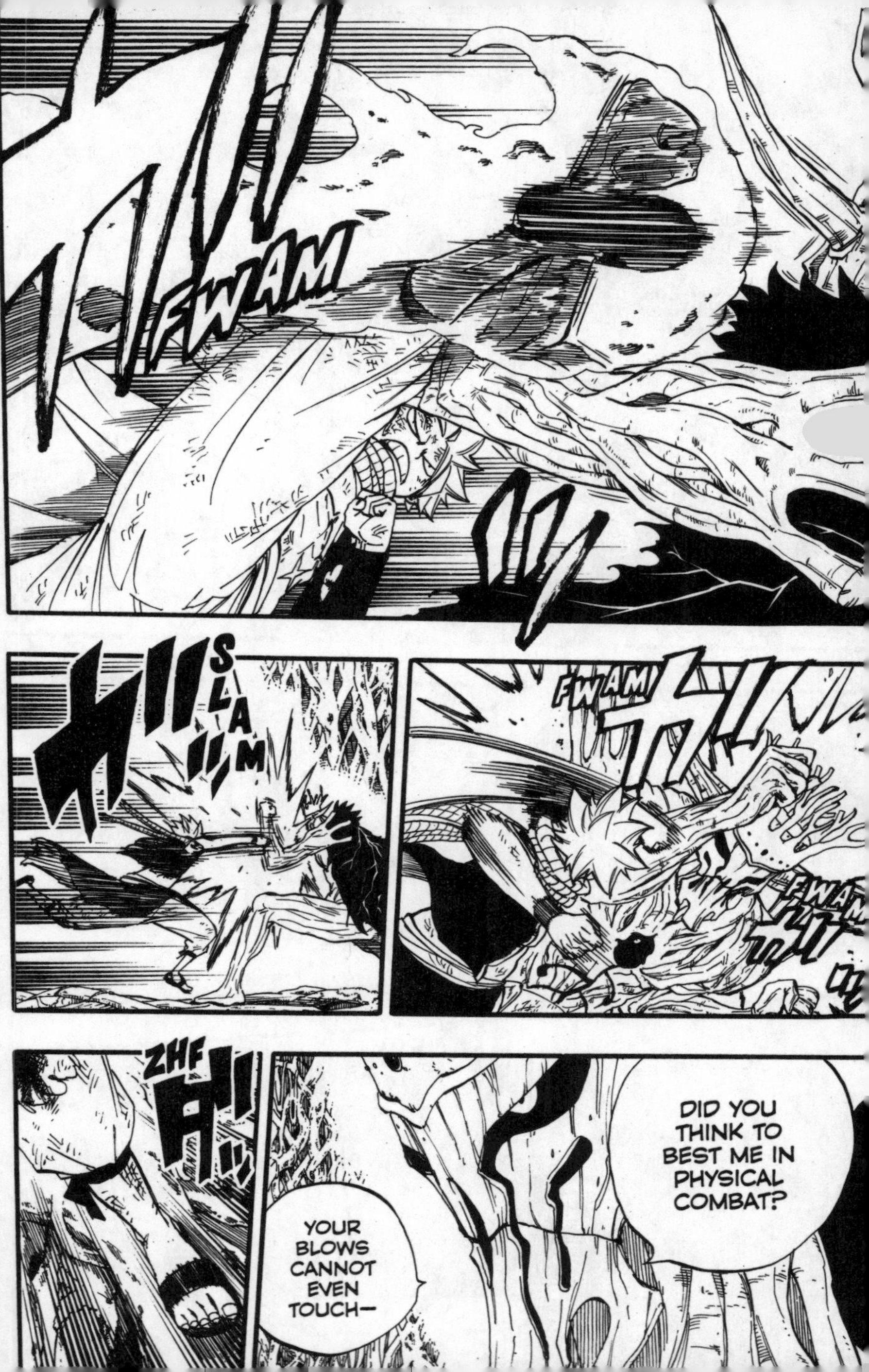
FWAM
FWAM
FWAM
SLAM
DID YOU THINK TO BEST ME IN PHYSICAL COMBAT?
YOUR BLOWS CANNOT EVEN TOUCH—
ZHF

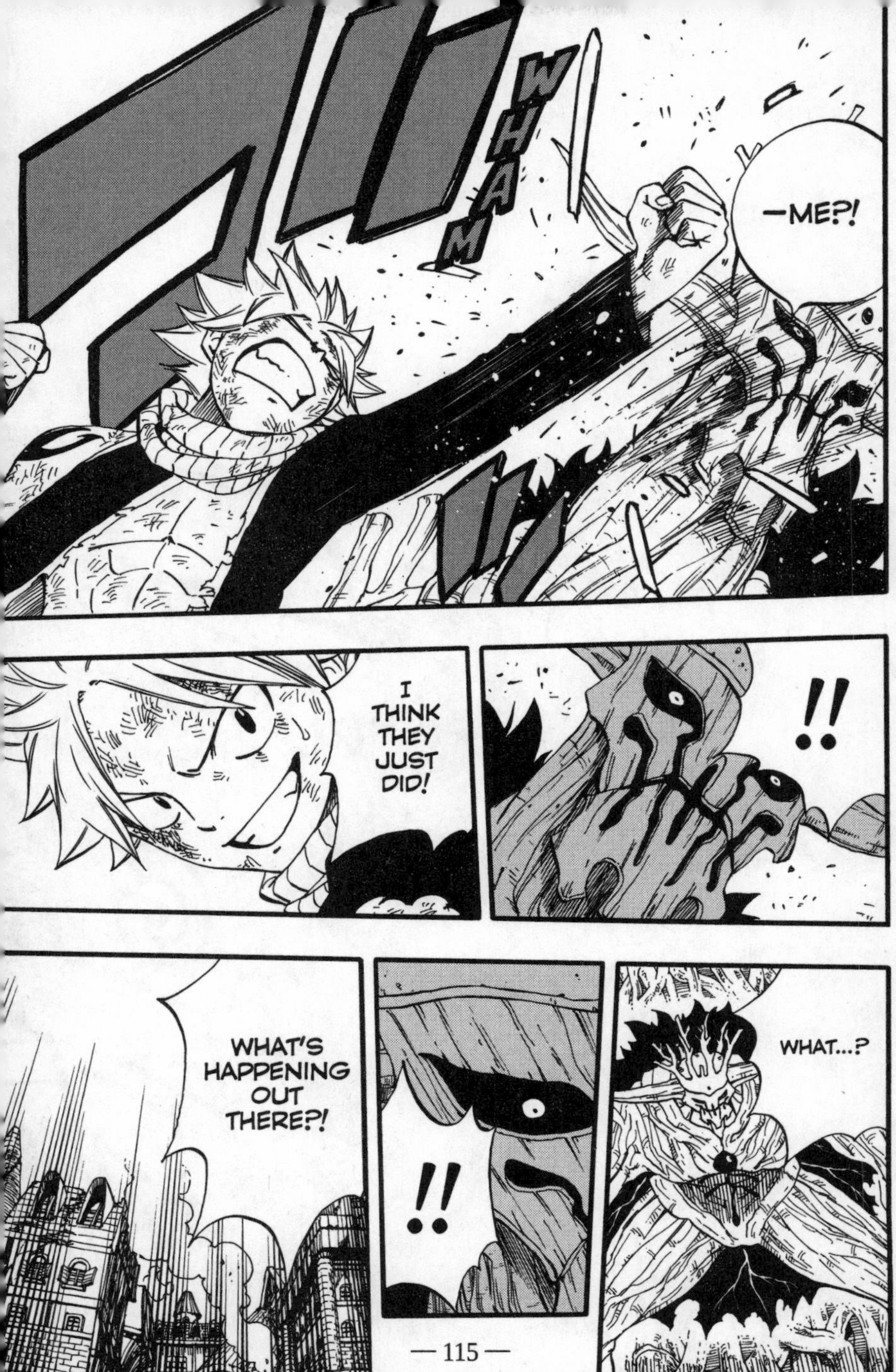
—ME?!
WHAM
!!
I THINK THEY JUST DID!
WHAT...?
!!
WHAT'S HAPPENING OUT THERE?!

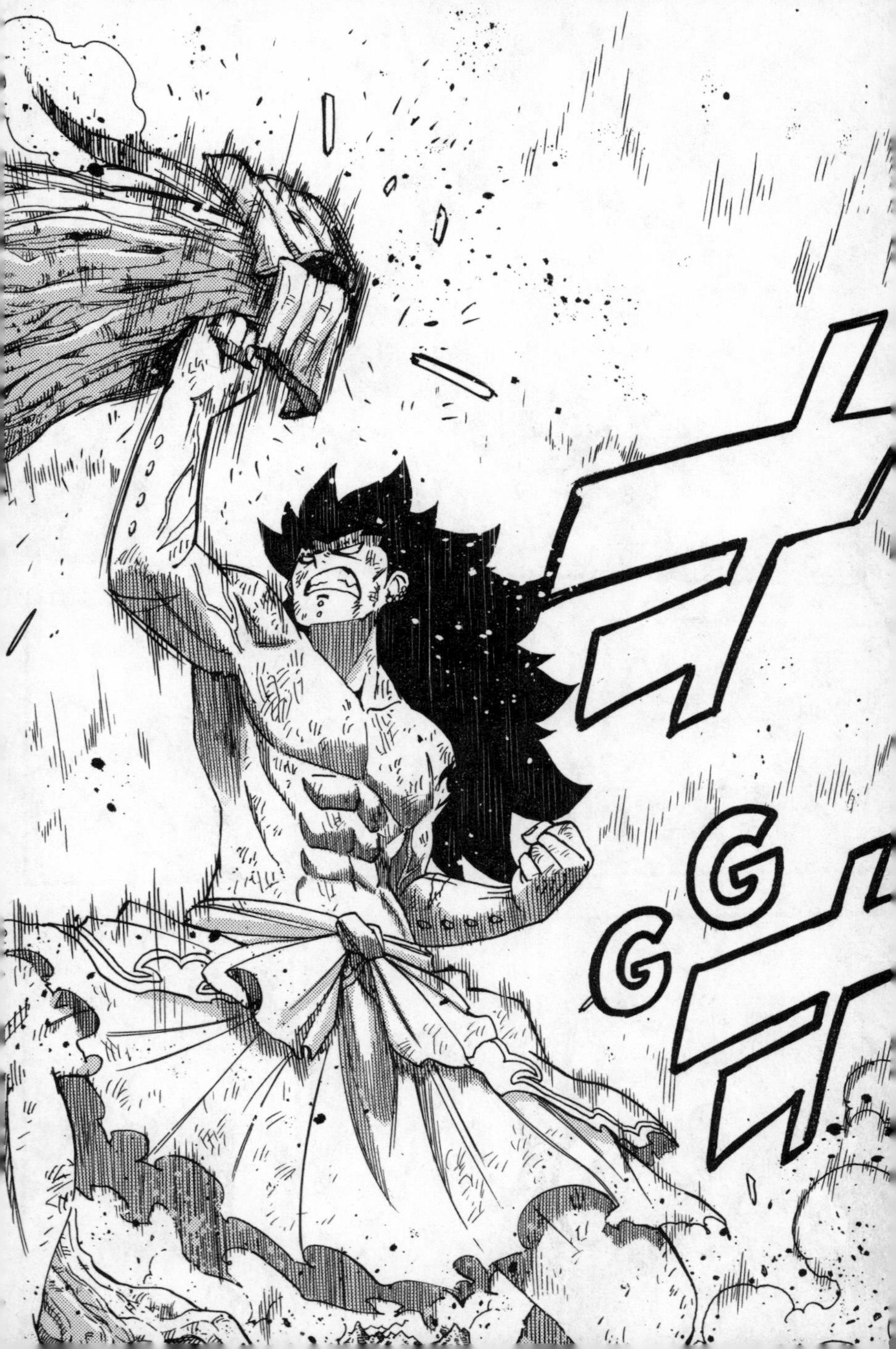
GG

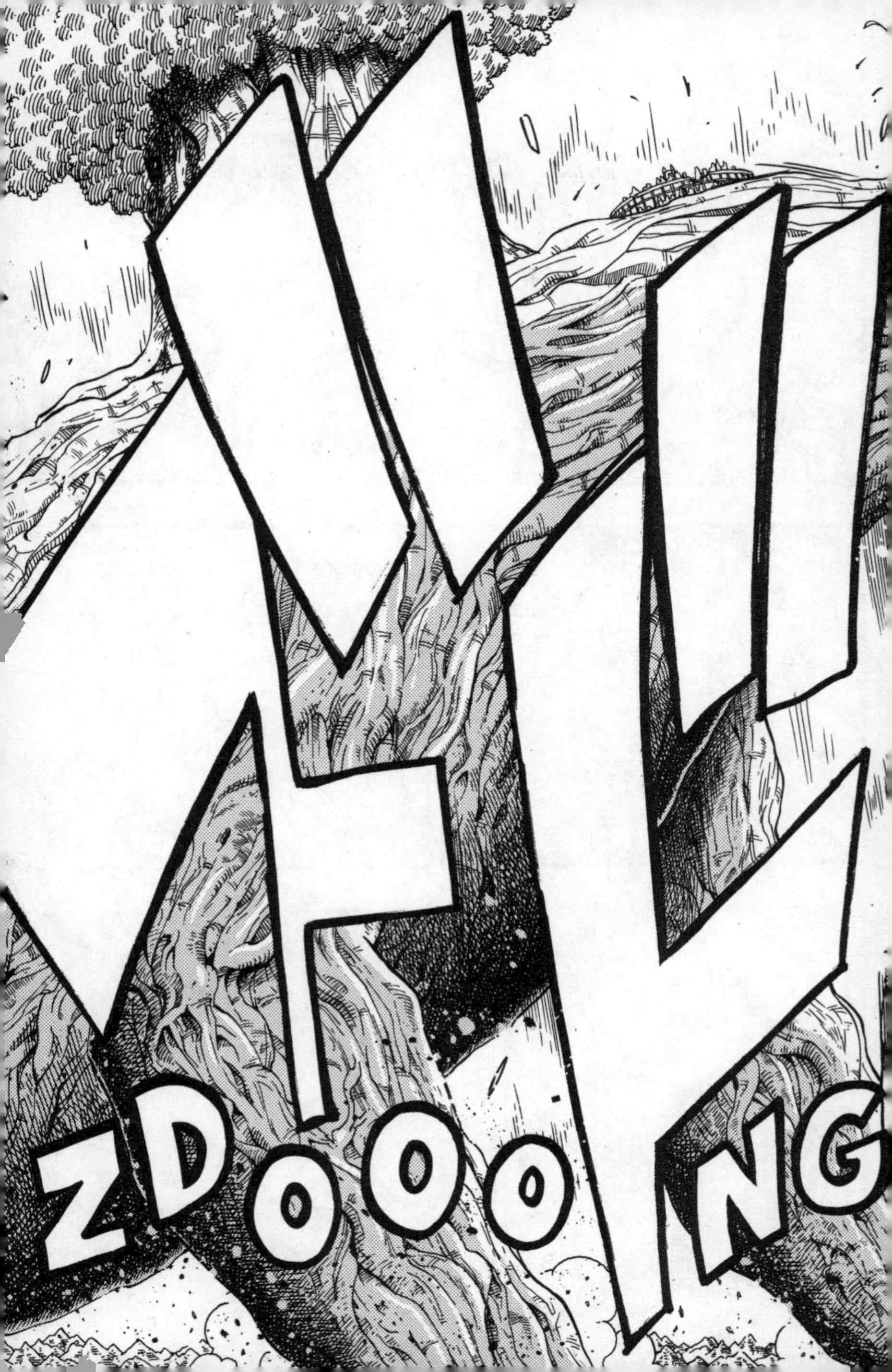
ZDOOOONG

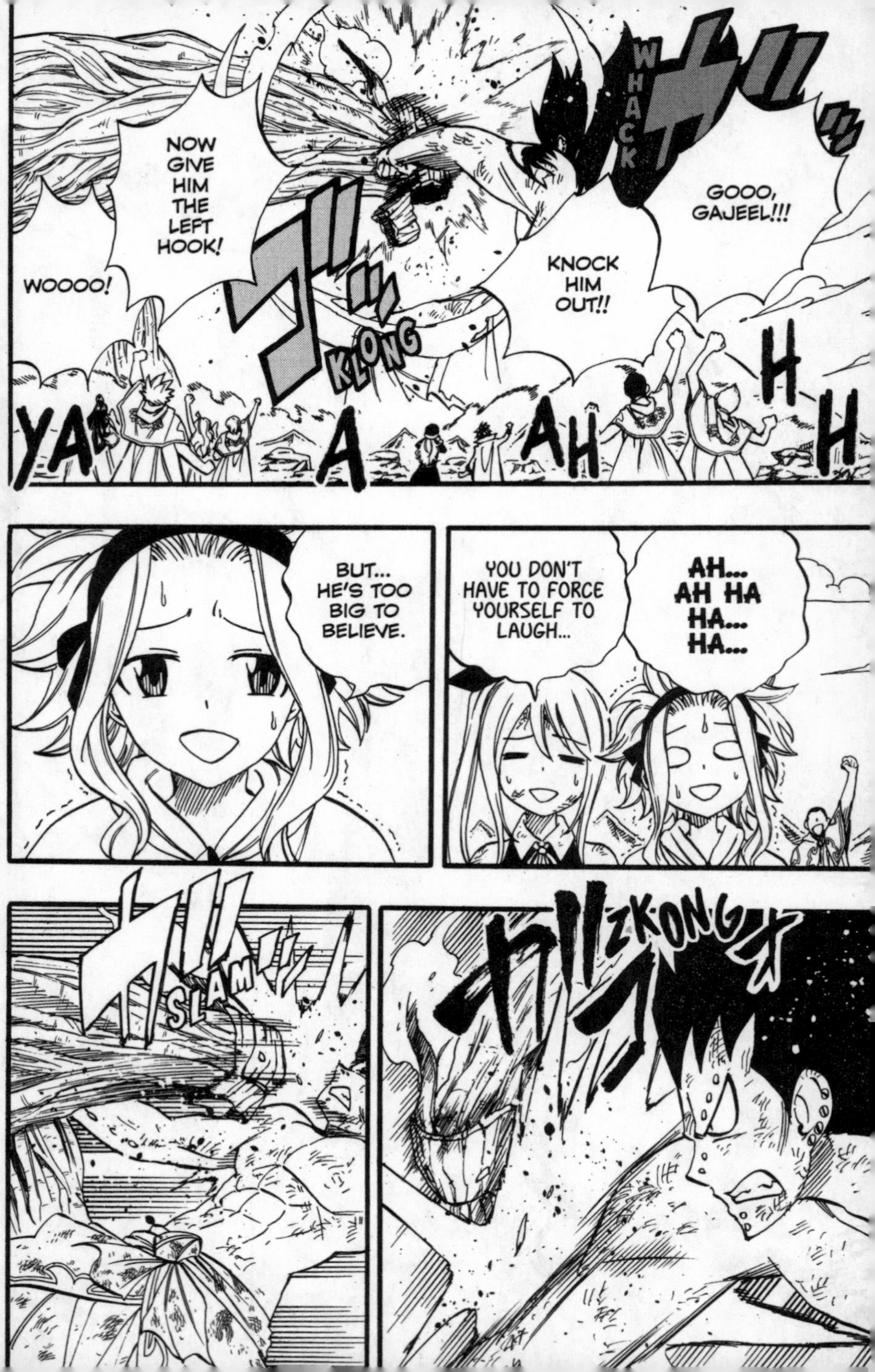
WHACK
GOOO, GAJEEL!!!
KNOCK HIM OUT!!
NOW GIVE HIM THE LEFT HOOK!
WOOOO!
KLONG
YAAAHHHH
AH... AH HA HA... HA...
YOU DON'T HAVE TO FORCE YOURSELF TO LAUGH...
BUT... HE'S TOO BIG TO BELIEVE.
KONG
SLAM

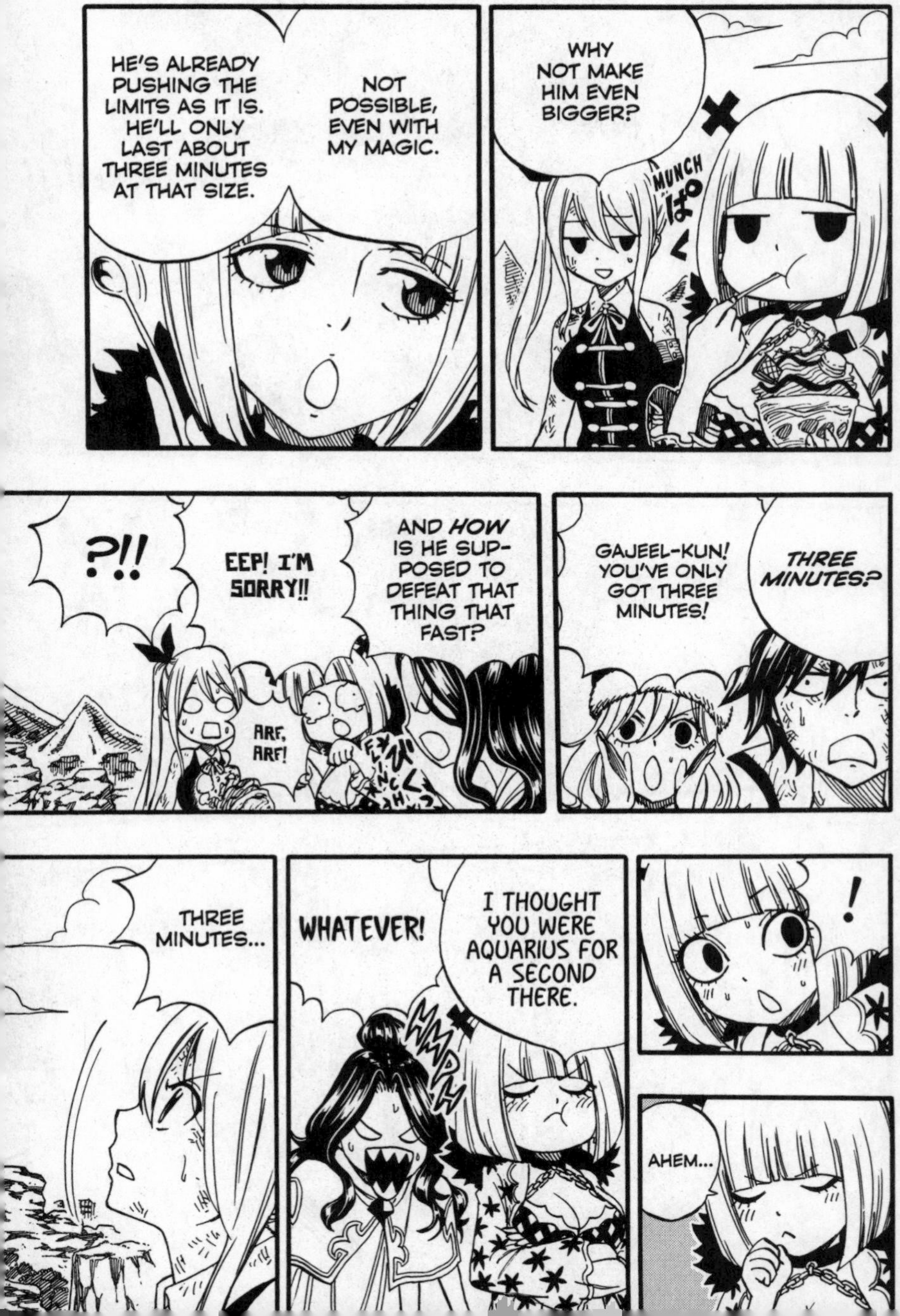
WHY NOT MAKE HIM EVEN BIGGER?
MUNCH
NOT POSSIBLE, EVEN WITH MY MAGIC.
HE'S ALREADY PUSHING THE LIMITS AS IT IS. HE'LL ONLY LAST ABOUT THREE MINUTES AT THAT SIZE.
THREE MINUTES?
GAJEEL-KUN! YOU'VE ONLY GOT THREE MINUTES!
AND *HOW* IS HE SUPPOSED TO DEFEAT THAT THING THAT FAST?
EEP! I'M SORRY!!
?!!
ARF, ARF!
FLINCH
!
AHEM...
I THOUGHT YOU WERE AQUARIUS FOR A SECOND THERE.
HMPH
WHATEVER!
THREE MINUTES...

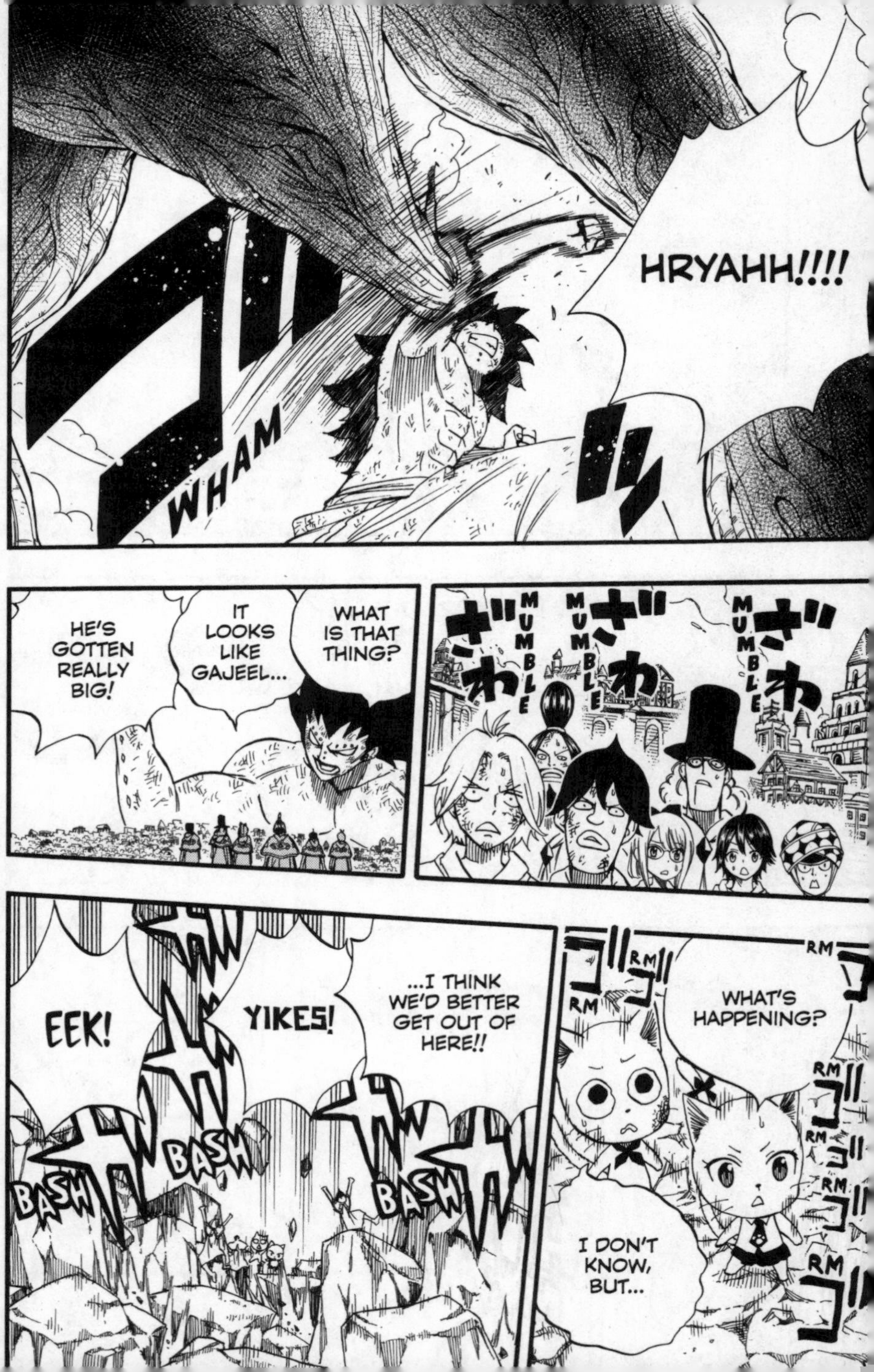
HRYAHH!!!!
WHAM
ざわ MUMBLE
ざわ MUMBLE
ざわ MUMBLE
WHAT IS THAT THING?
IT LOOKS LIKE GAJEEL...
HE'S GOTTEN REALLY BIG!
RM RM RM RM RM RM RM
WHAT'S HAPPENING?
I DON'T KNOW, BUT...
...I THINK WE'D BETTER GET OUT OF HERE!!
YIKES!
EEK!
BASH
BASH
BASH

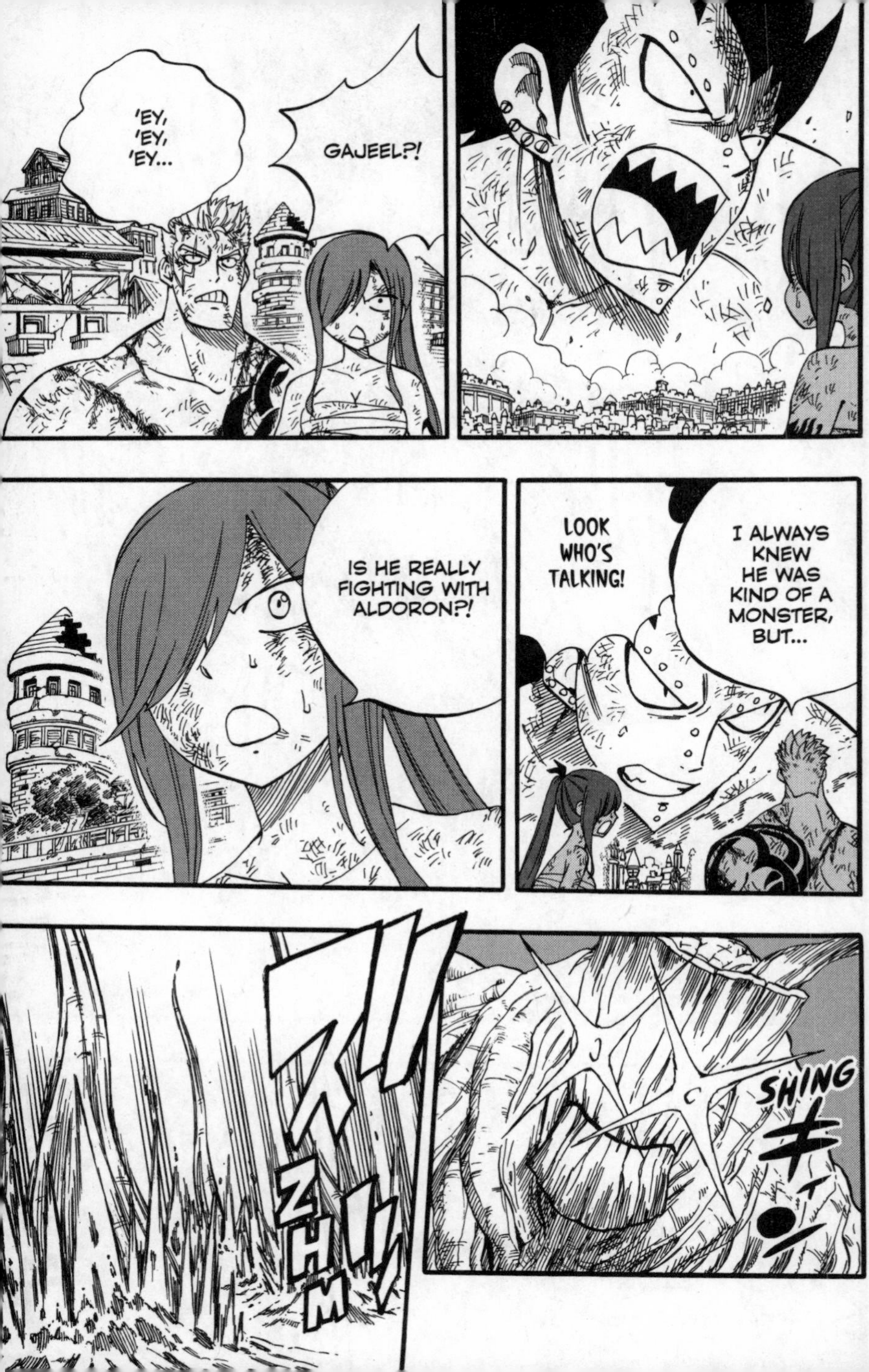
GAJEEL?!
'EY, 'EY, 'EY...
I ALWAYS KNEW HE WAS KIND OF A MONSTER, BUT...
LOOK WHO'S TALKING!
IS HE REALLY FIGHTING WITH ALDORON?!
SHING
ZHM

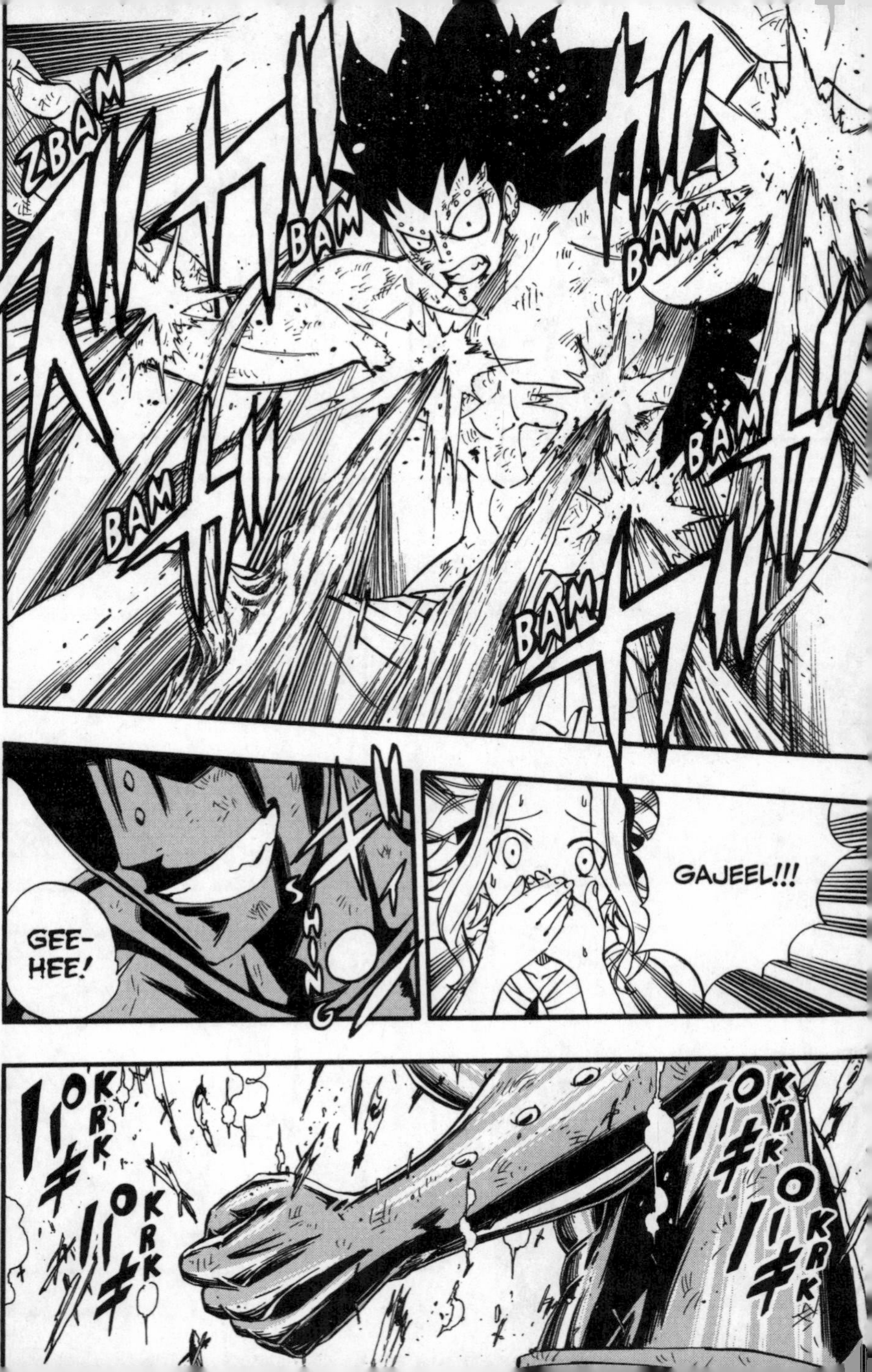
BAM
BAM
ZBAM
BAM
BAM
BAM
GAJEEL!!!
SHING
GEE-HEE!
OKRK
OKRK
OKRK
OKRK

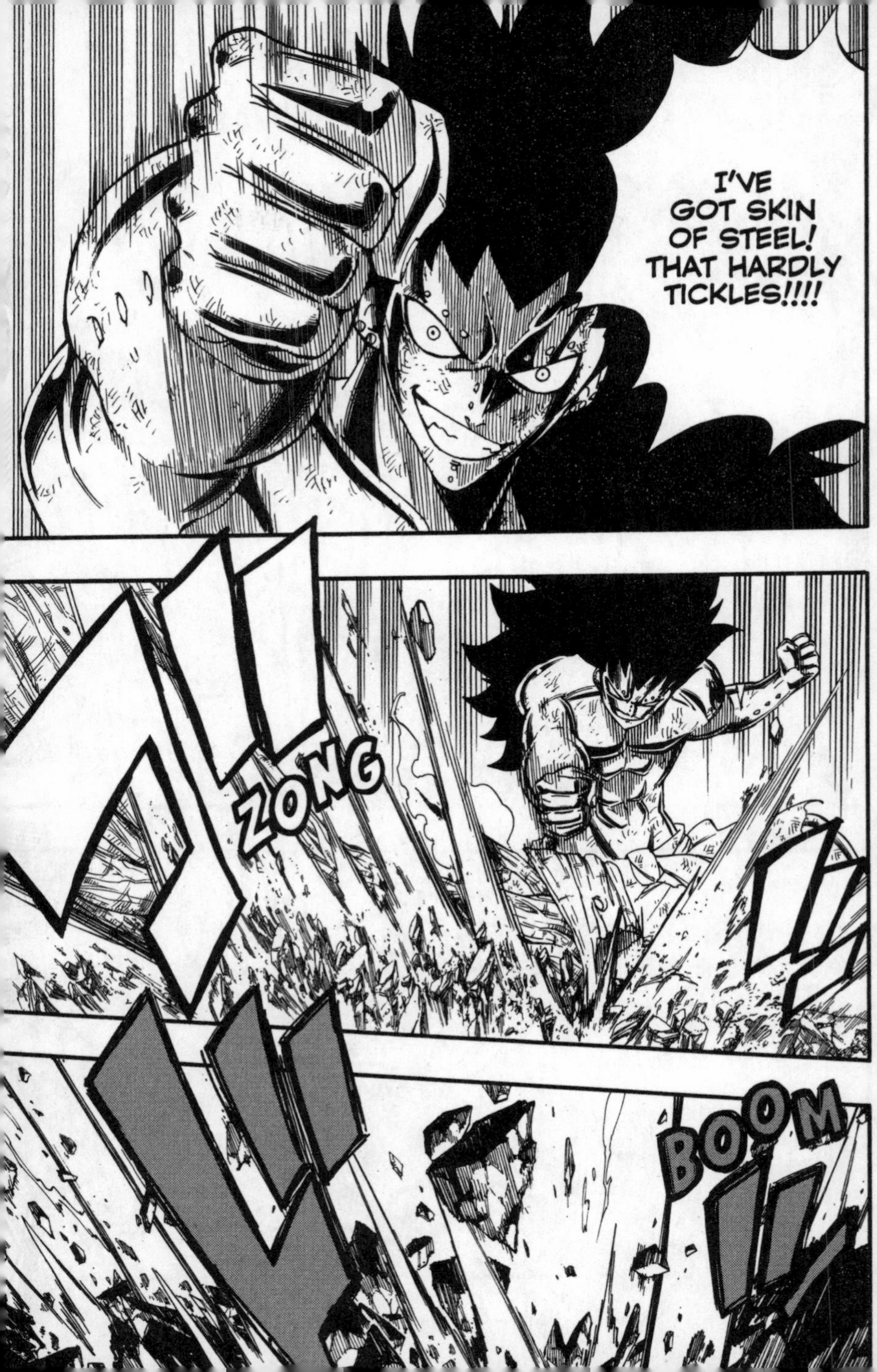

I'VE GOT SKIN OF STEEL! THAT HARDLY TICKLES!!!!
ZONG
BOOM

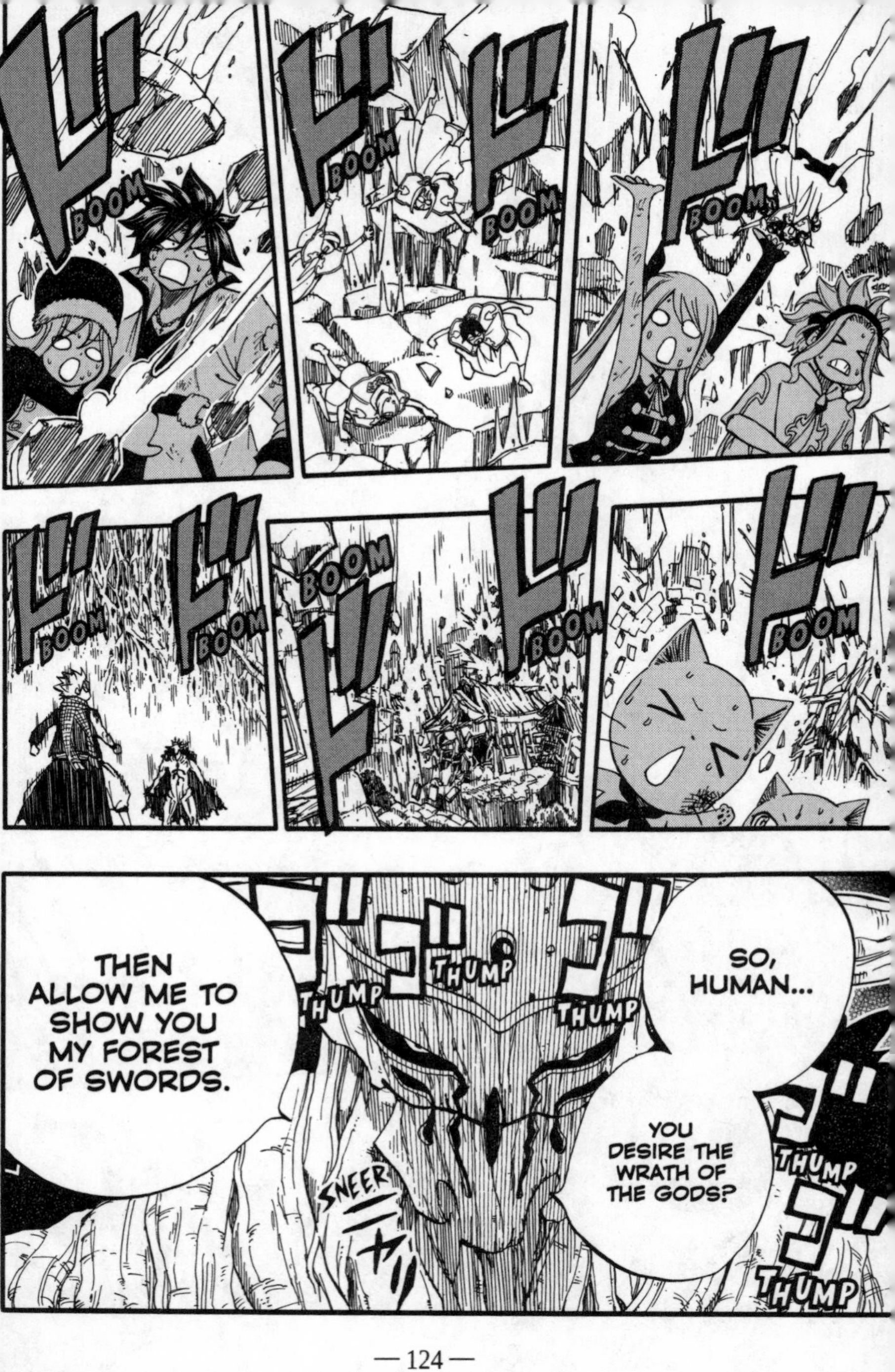
BOOM
BOOM
BOOM
BOOM
BOOM
BOOM
BOOM
BOOM
BOOM
THUMP
THUMP
THUMP
SO, HUMAN...
YOU DESIRE THE WRATH OF THE GODS?
THUMP
THUMP
SNEER
THEN ALLOW ME TO SHOW YOU MY FOREST OF SWORDS.

FAIRY TAIL 100 YEARS QUEST

Chapter 61: Forest of Swords

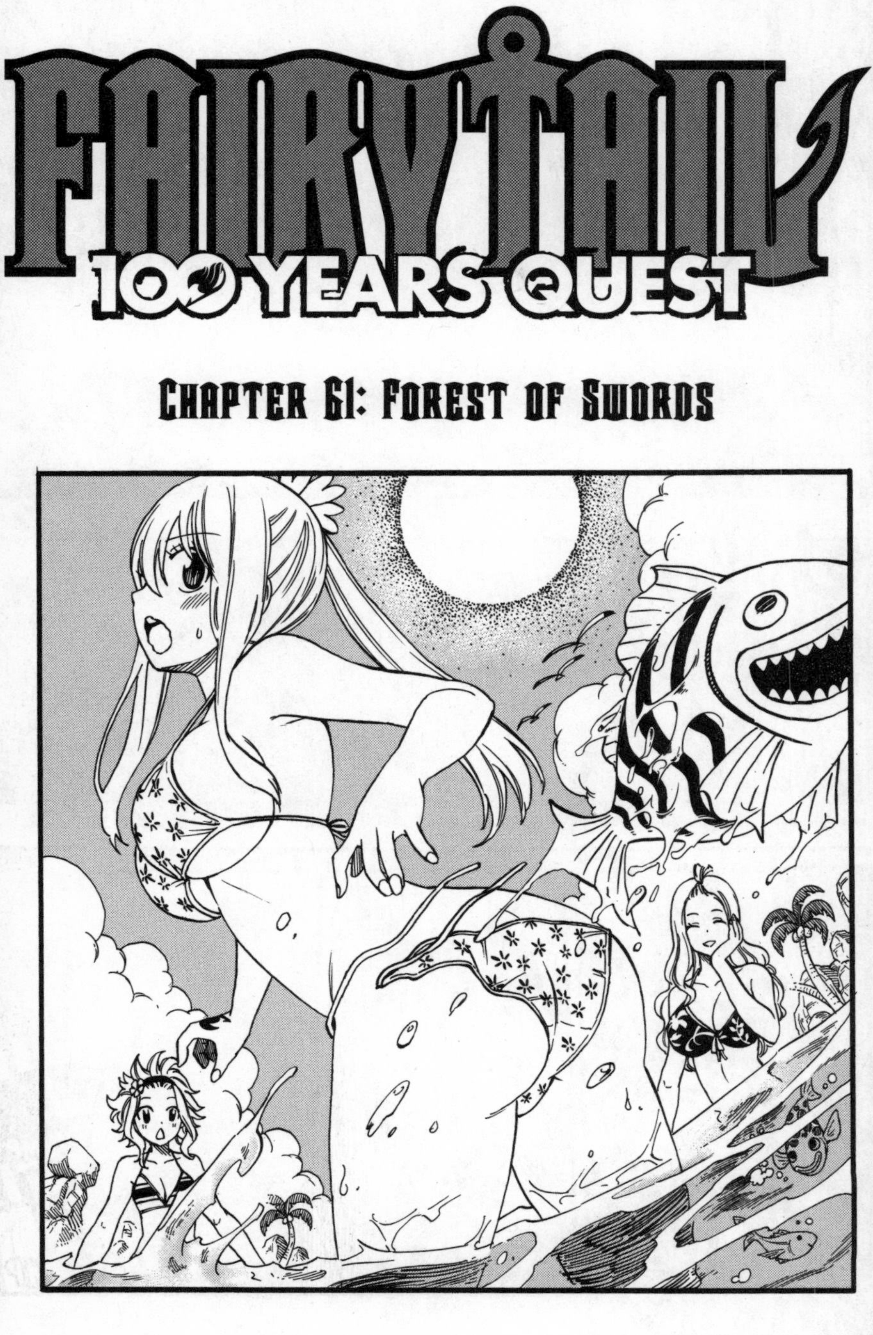

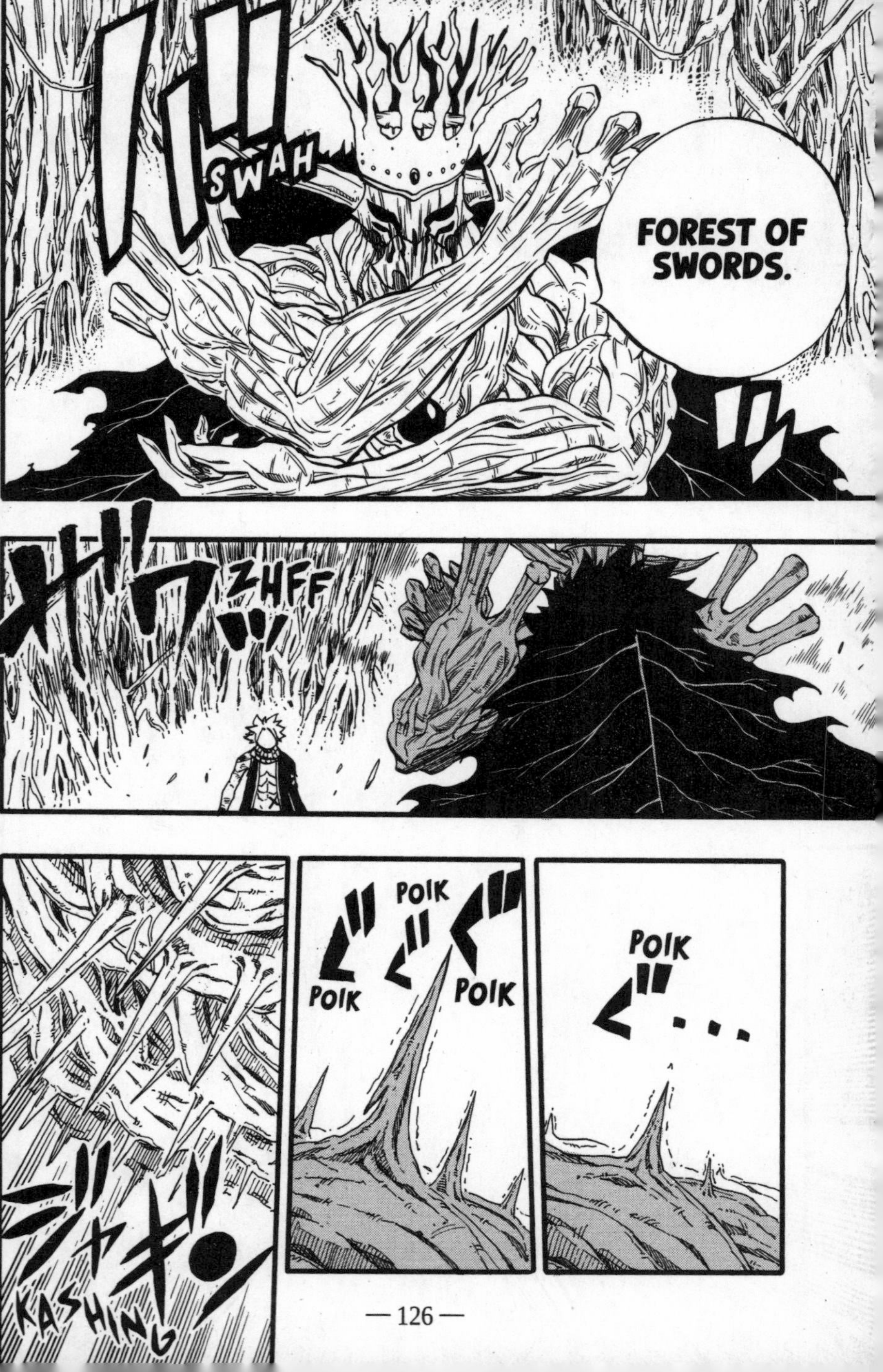
SWAH
FOREST OF SWORDS.
ZHFF
POIK
POIK
POIK
POIK
KASHING

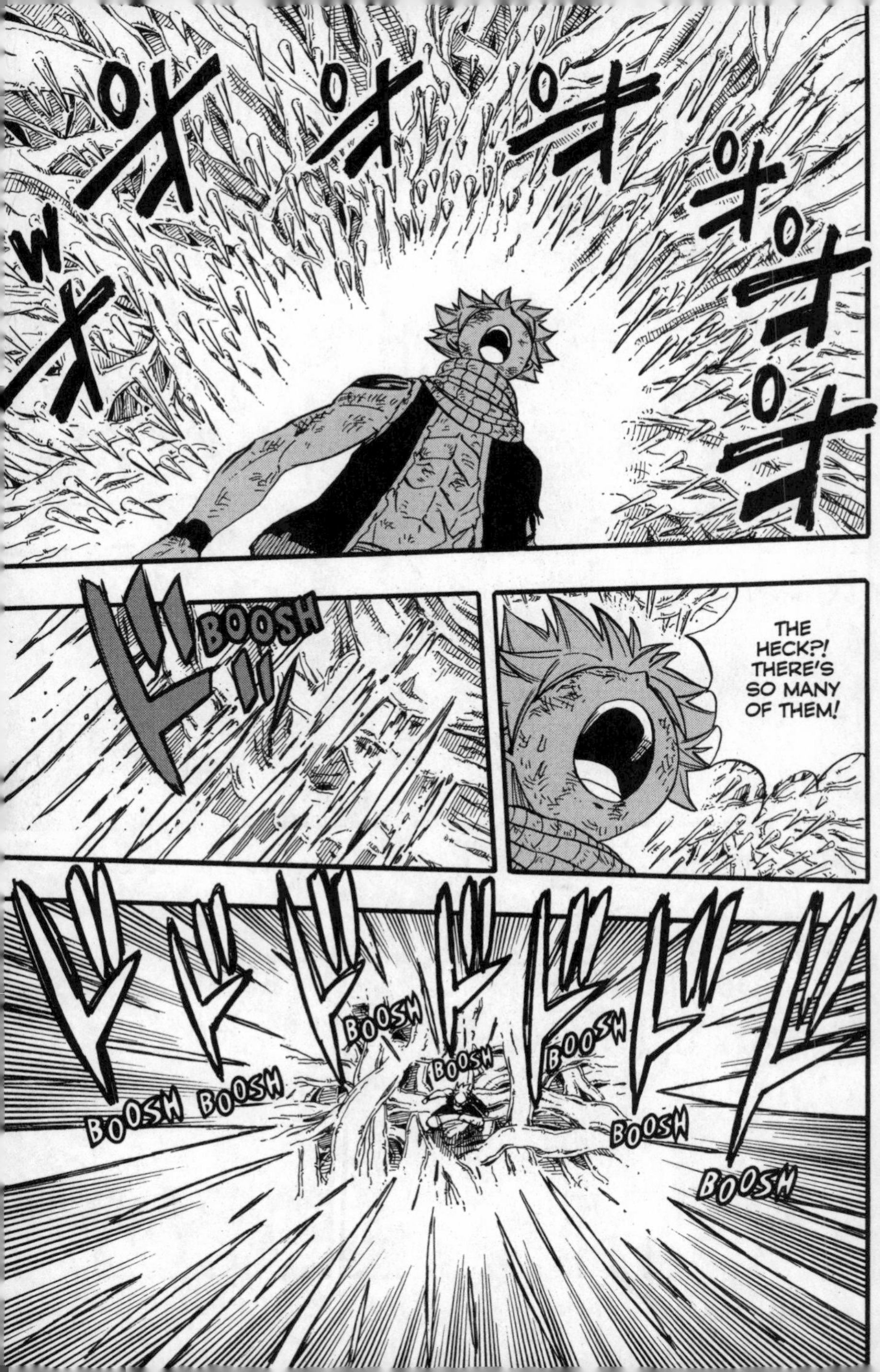
WOOOOOO
THE HECK?! THERE'S SO MANY OF THEM!
BOOSH
BOOSH
BOOSH
BOOSH
BOOSH
BOOSH
BOOSH
BOOSH
BOOSH

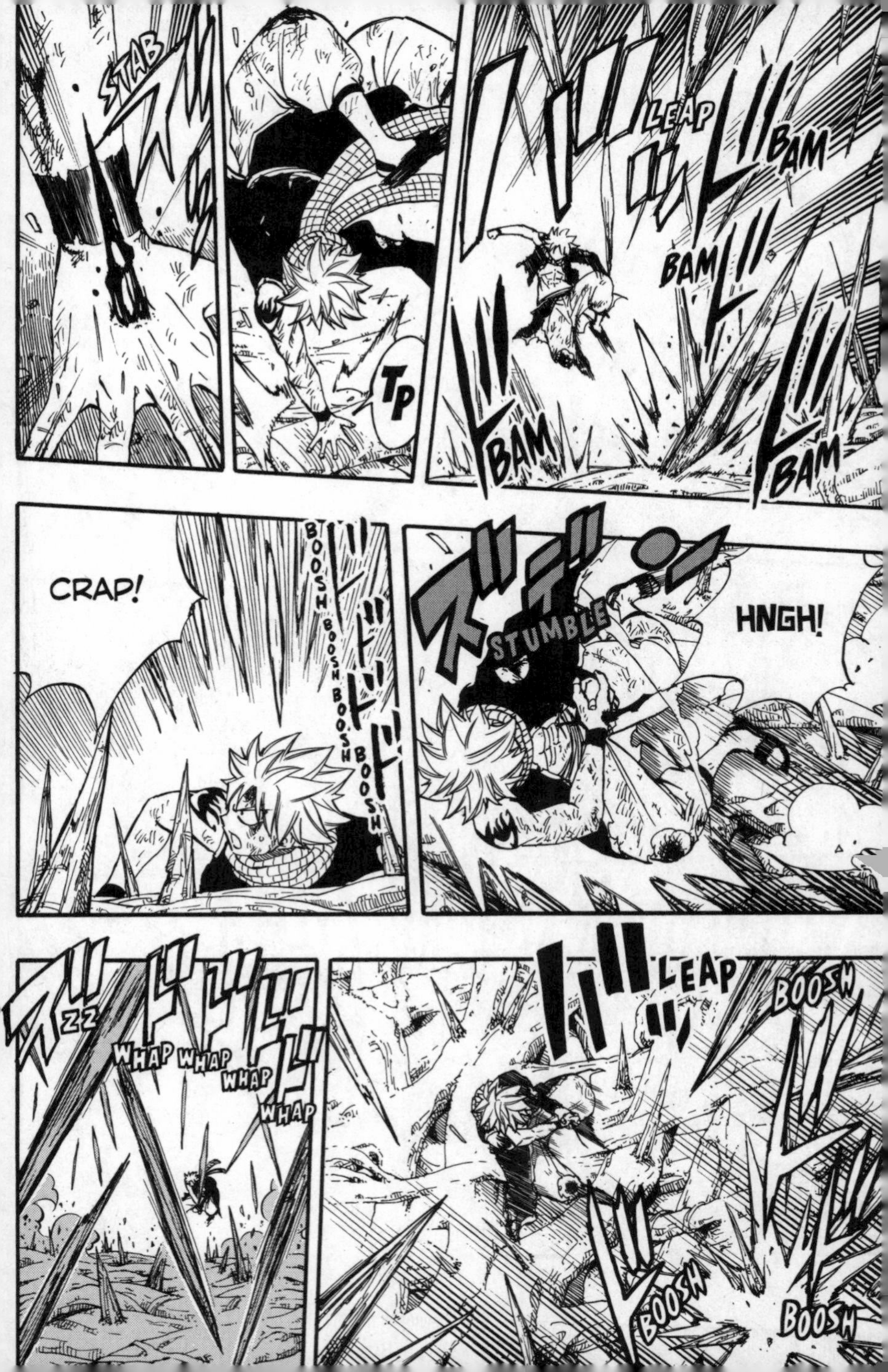
LEAP
BAM
BAM
BAM
BAM
TP
STAB
STUMBLE
HNGH!
CRAP!
BOOSH BOOSH BOOSH BOOSH
LEAP
BOOSH
BOOSH
BOOSH
WHAP WHAP WHAP WHAP

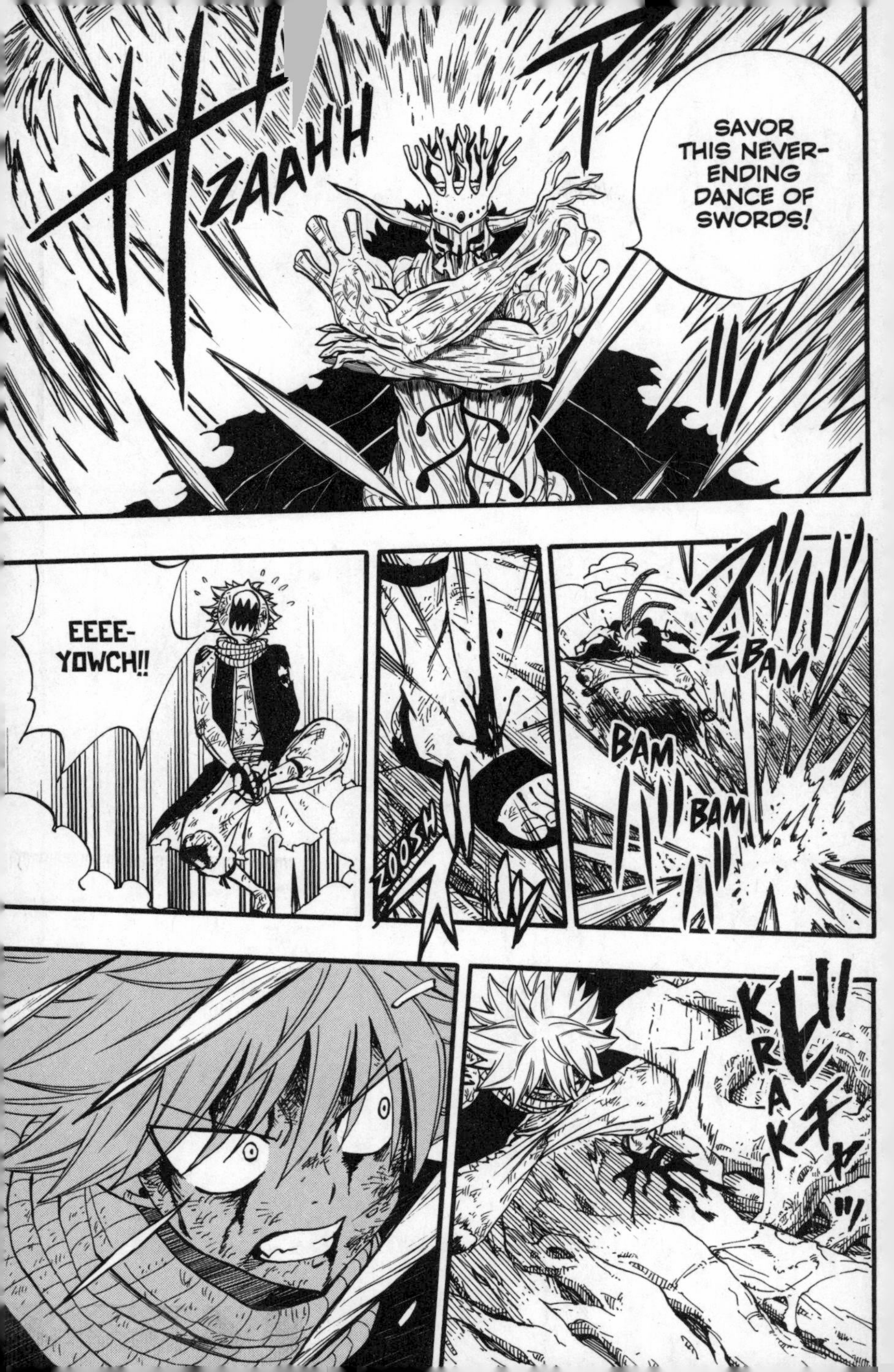
ZAAHH
SAVOR THIS NEVER-ENDING DANCE OF SWORDS!
ZBAM
BAM
BAM
ZOOSH
EEEE-YOWCH!!
KRAK

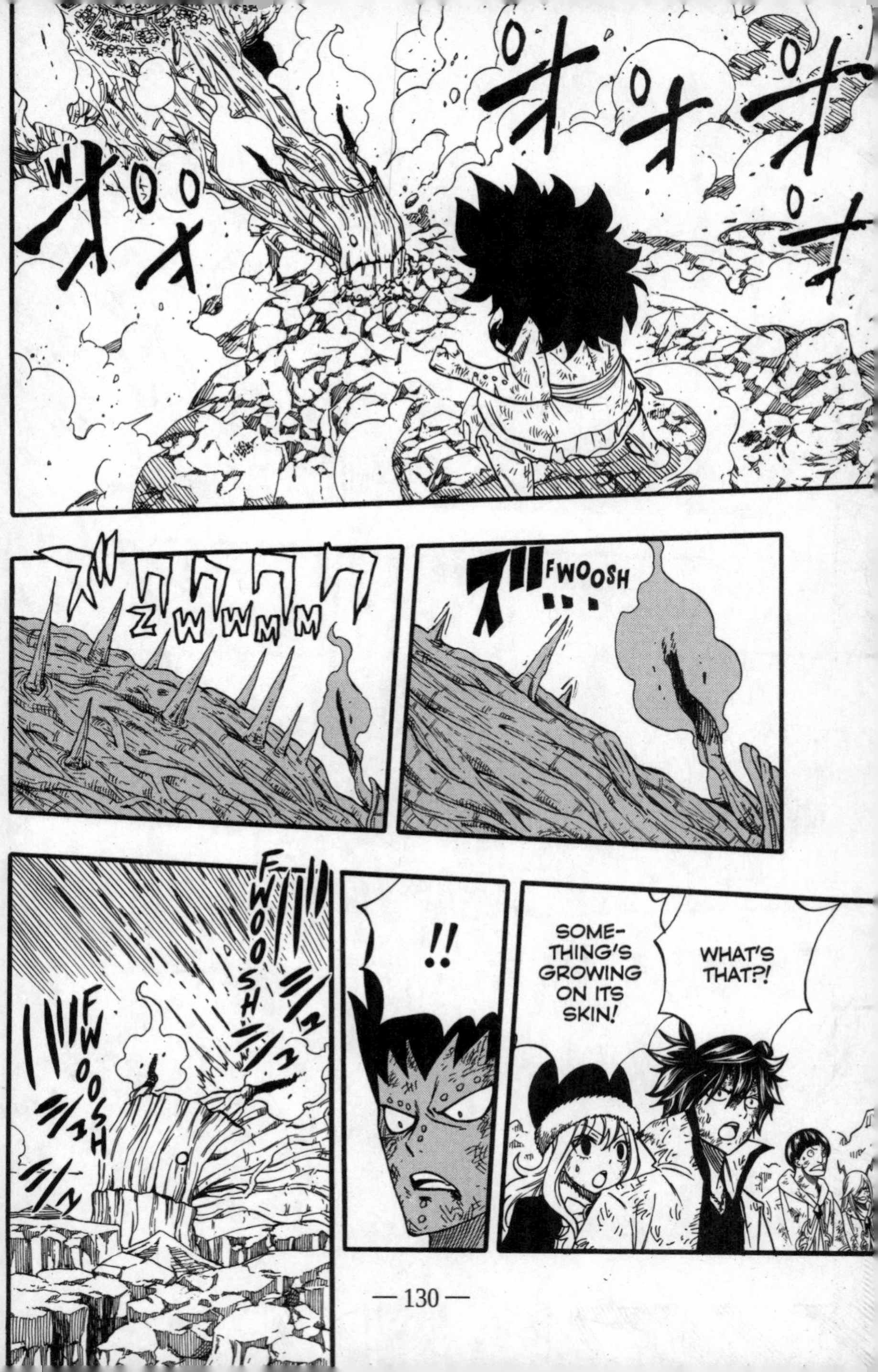
WOOO
FWOOSH...
ZWWMMM
WHAT'S THAT?!
SOME-THING'S GROWING ON ITS SKIN!
!!
FWOOSH
FWOOSH

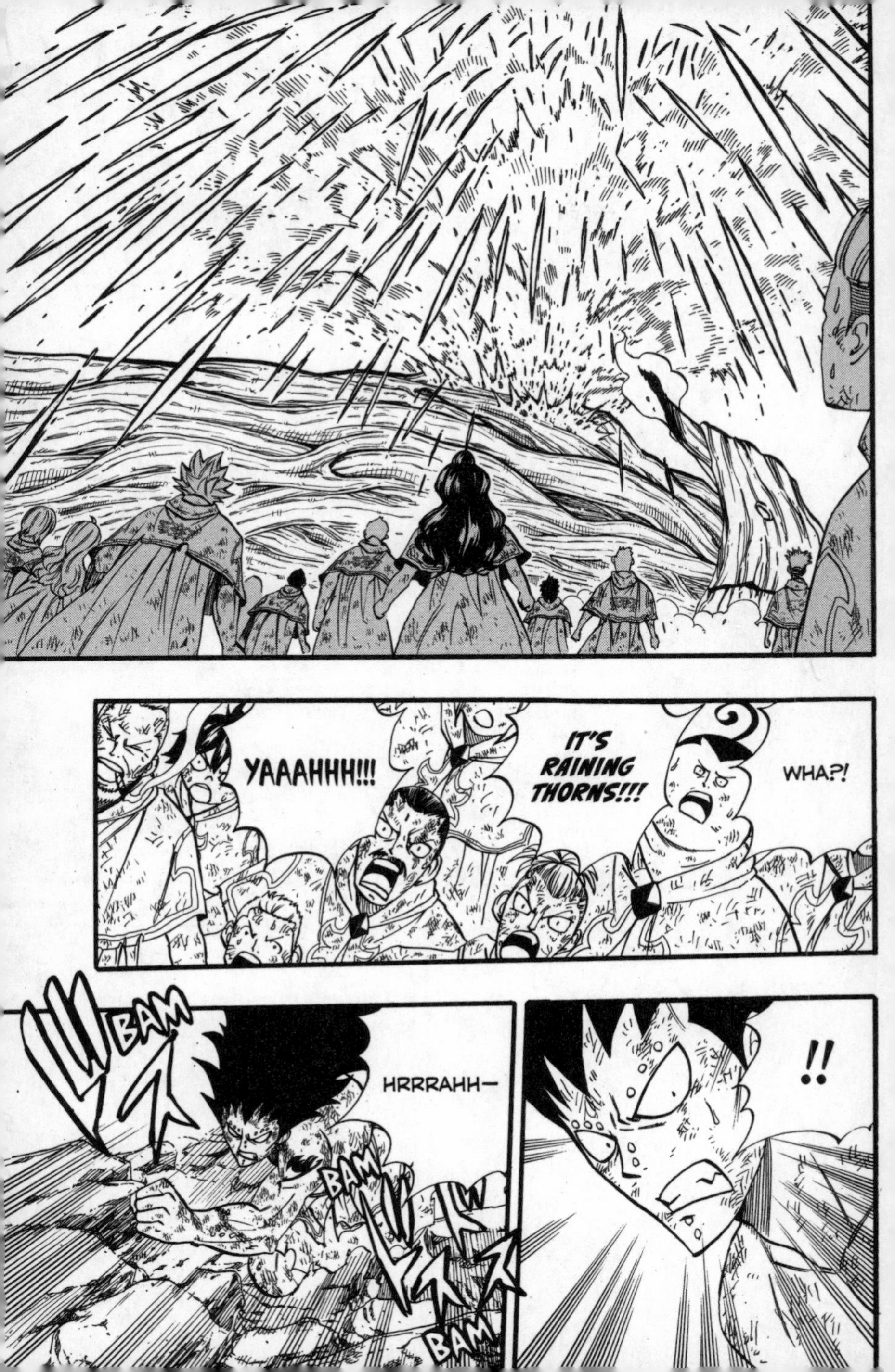
WHA?!
IT'S RAINING THORNS!!!
YAAAHHH!!!
!!
HRRRAHH—
BAM
BAM
BAM

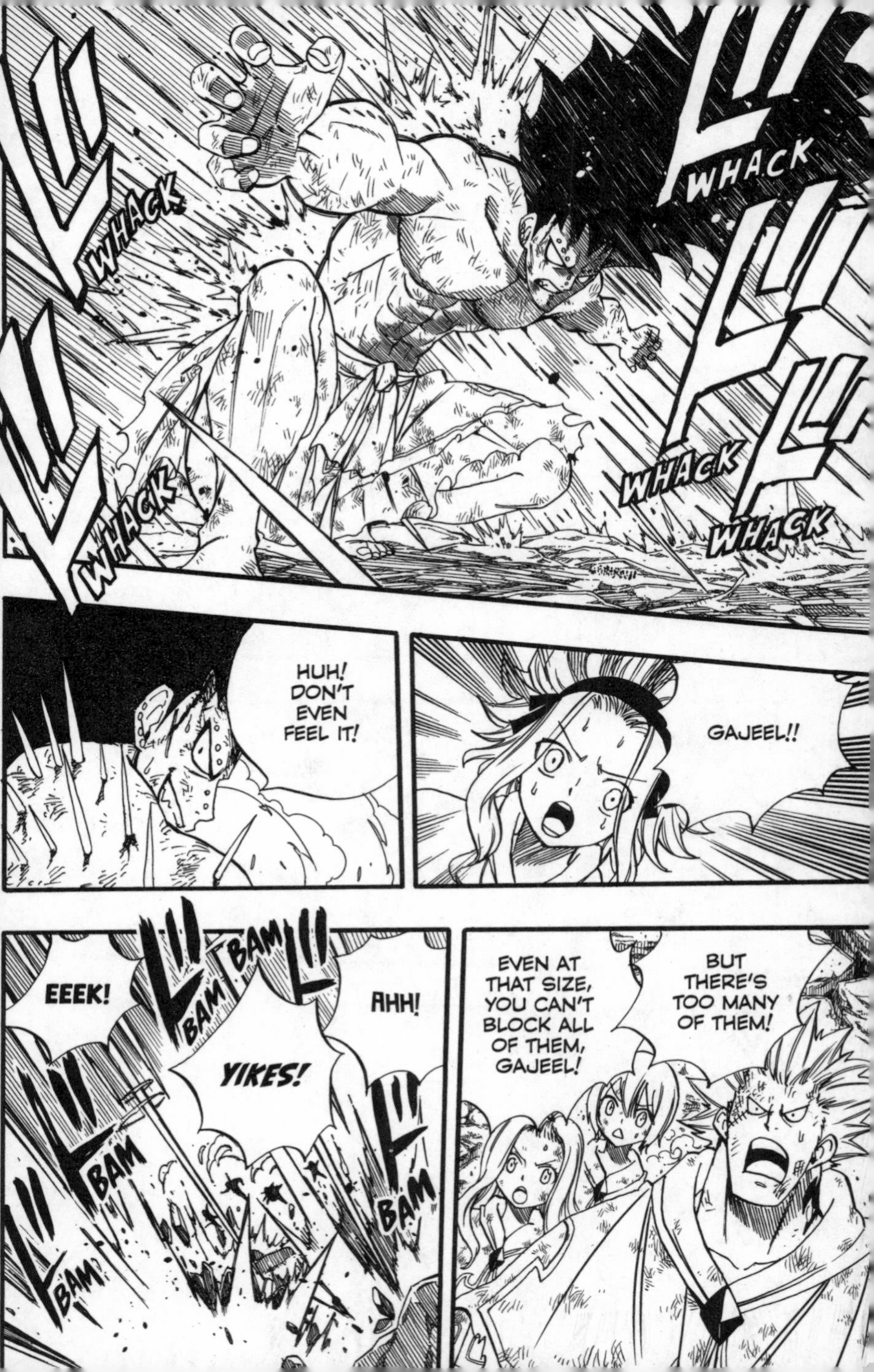
WHACK
WHACK
WHACK
WHACK
WHACK
GAJEEL!!
HUH! DON'T EVEN FEEL IT!
BUT THERE'S TOO MANY OF THEM!
EVEN AT THAT SIZE, YOU CAN'T BLOCK ALL OF THEM, GAJEEL!
AHH!
BAM
BAM
BAM
EEEK!
YIKES!
BAM
BAM
BAM

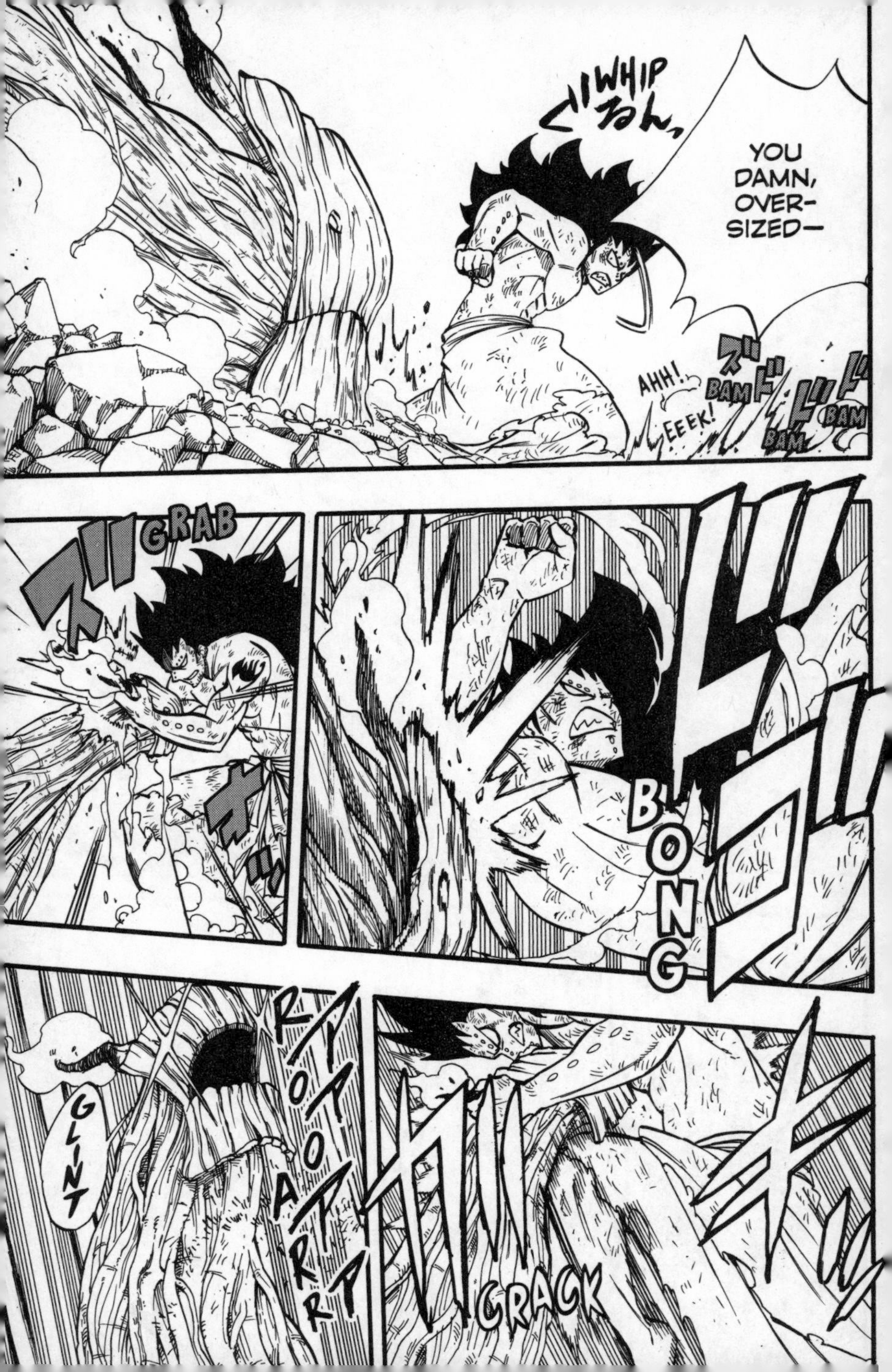
YOU DAMN, OVER-SIZED—
WHIP
AHH!
EEEK!
BAM
BAM
BAM
BAM
BONG
GRAB
CRACK
ROOARR
GLINT

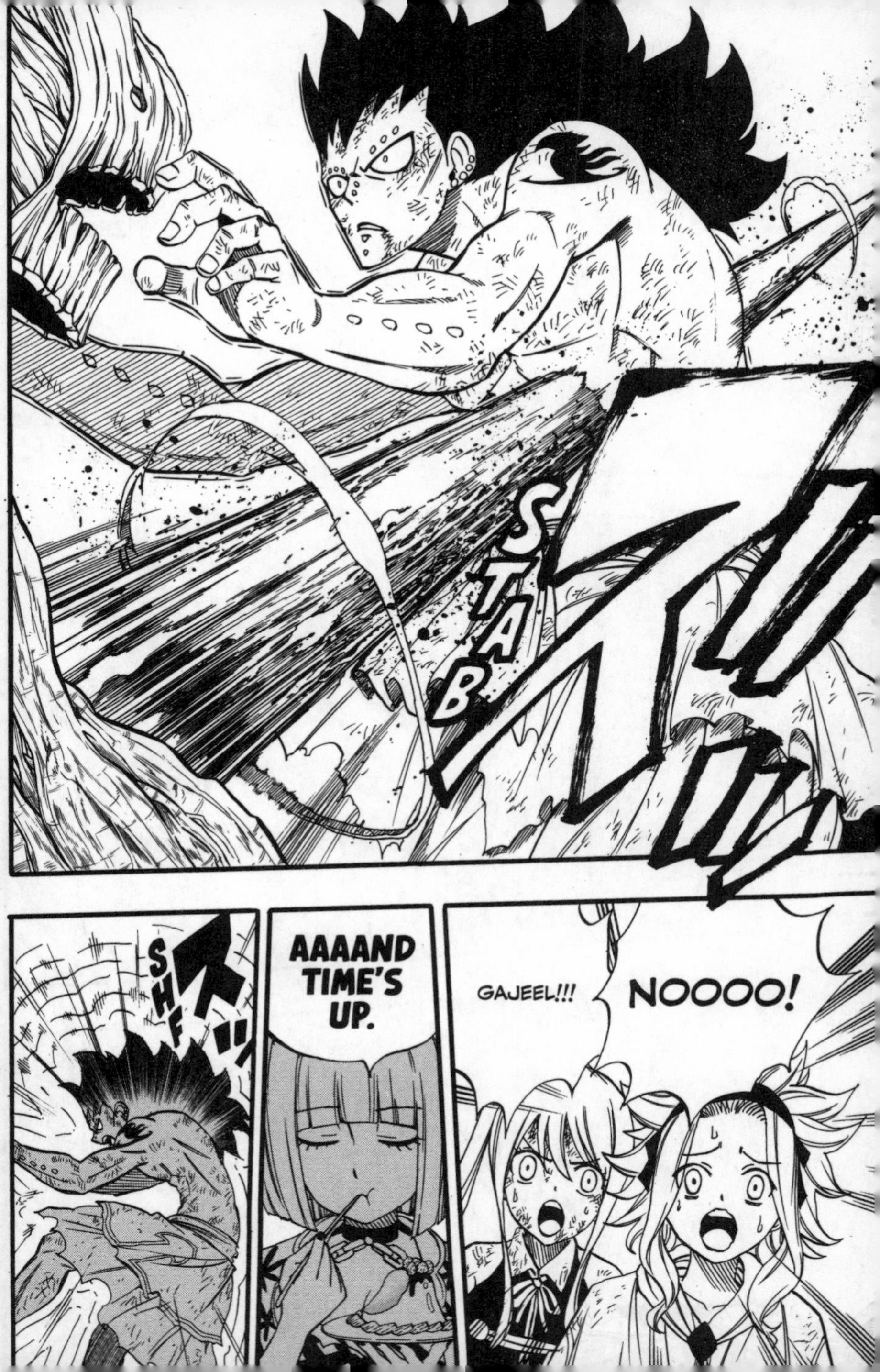
STAB
NOOOO!
GAJEEL!!!
AAAAND TIME'S UP.
SHF!!

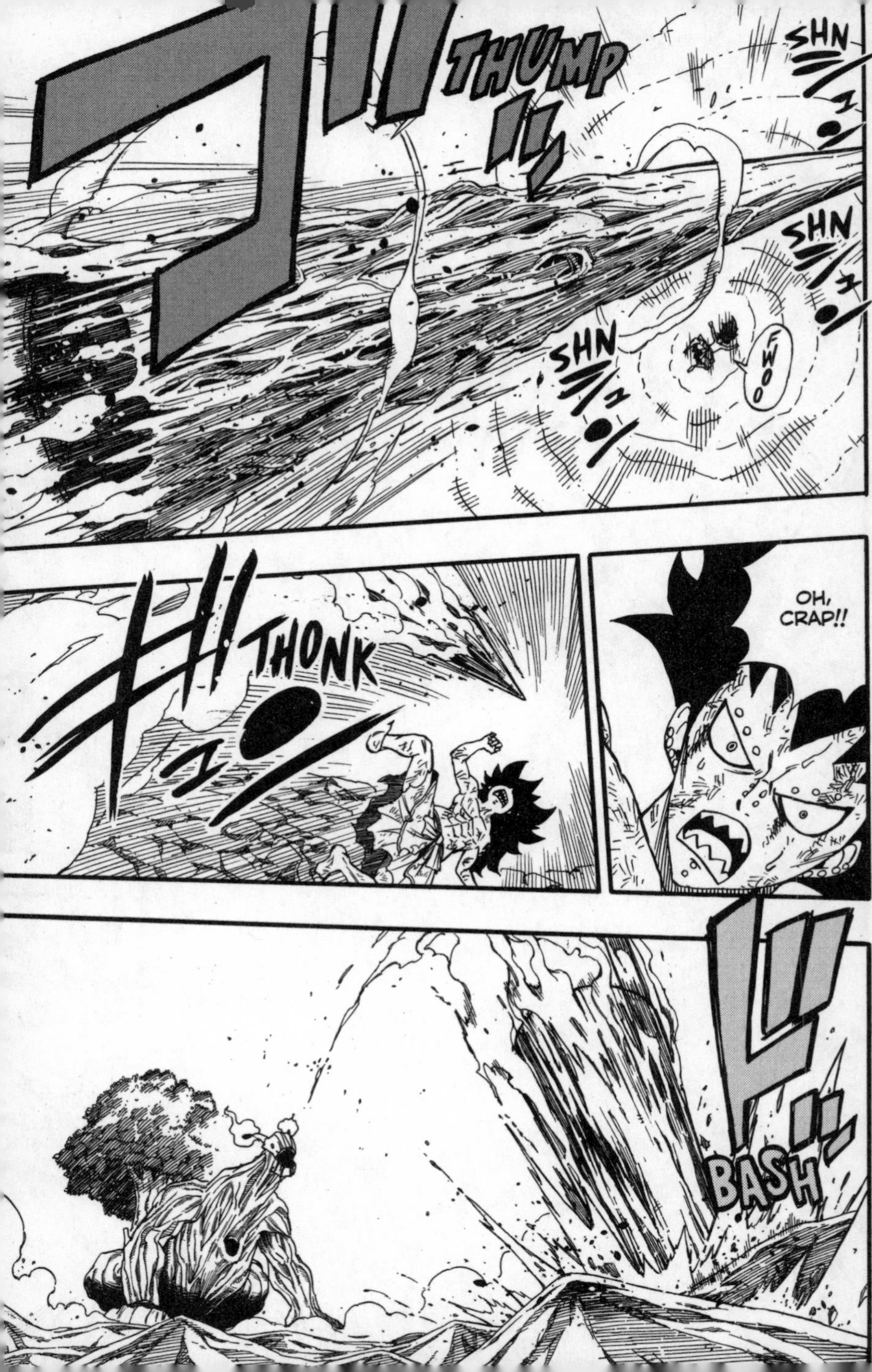
SHN
THUMP
SHN
FWOO
SHN
OH, CRAP!!
THONK
BASH

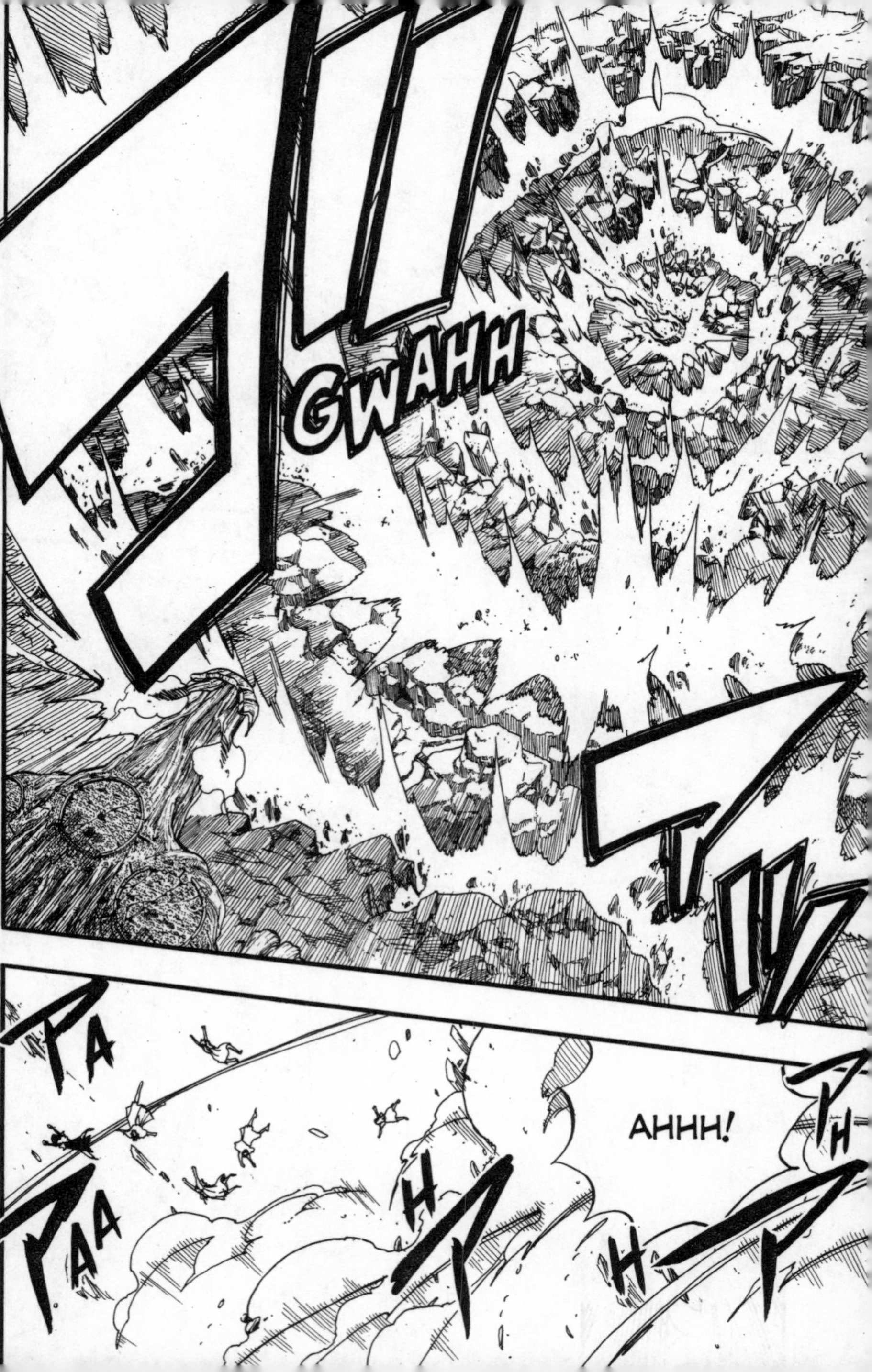
GWAHH
AHHH!
PA
PAA

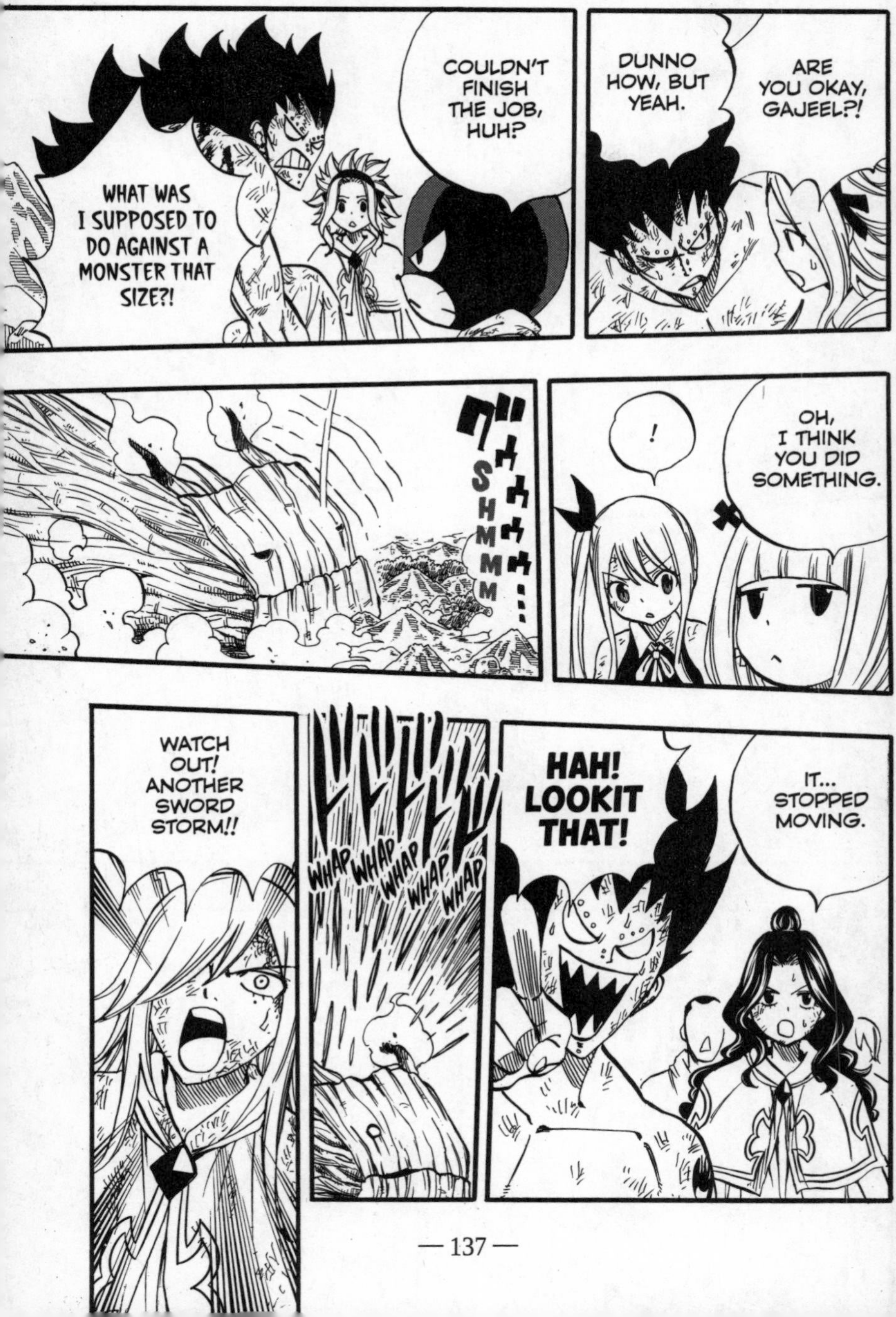
ARE YOU OKAY, GAJEEL?!
DUNNO HOW, BUT YEAH.
COULDN'T FINISH THE JOB, HUH?
WHAT WAS I SUPPOSED TO DO AGAINST A MONSTER THAT SIZE?!
OH, I THINK YOU DID SOMETHING.
!
SHMMM
IT... STOPPED MOVING.
HAH! LOOKIT THAT!
WHAP WHAP WHAP WHAP WHAP
WATCH OUT! ANOTHER SWORD STORM!!

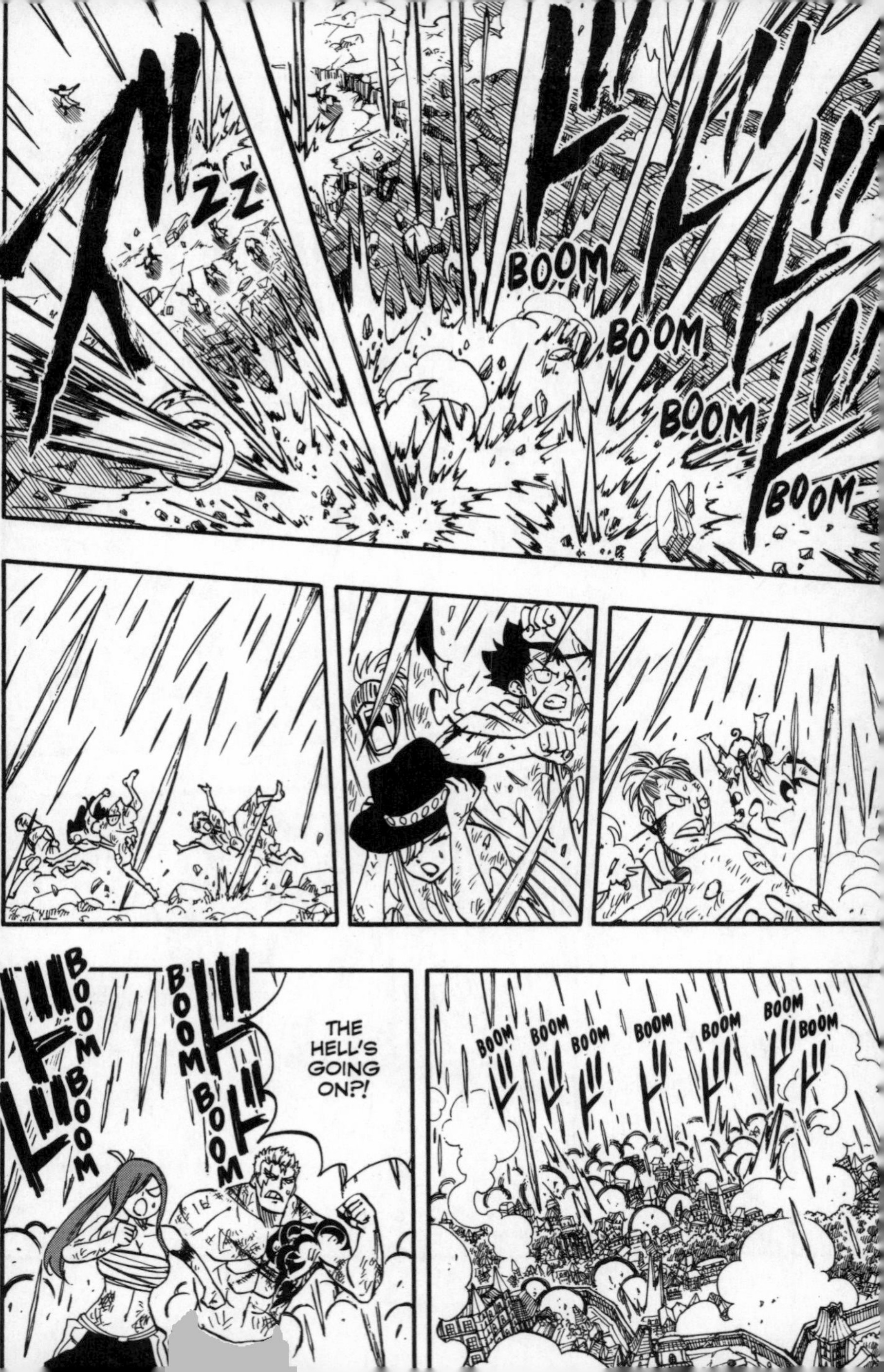
BOOM
BOOM
BOOM
BOOM
BOOM
BOOM
BOOM
BOOM
BOOM
BOOM
BOOM
BOOM BOOM
BOOM BOOM
THE HELL'S GOING ON?!
BOOM BOOM

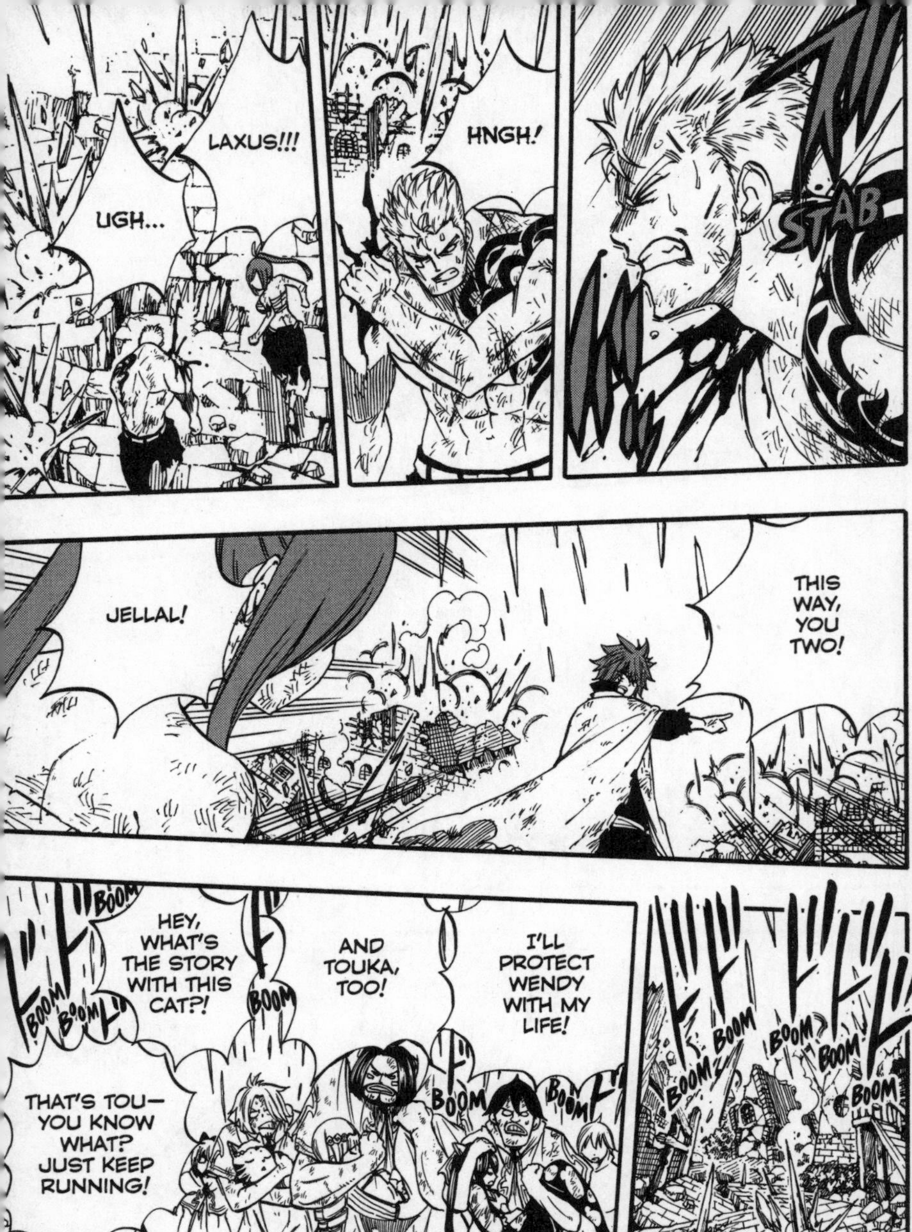
STAB
HNGH!
LAXUS!!!
UGH...
THIS WAY, YOU TWO!
JELLAL!
BOOM BOOM BOOM BOOM BOOM BOOM
I'LL PROTECT WENDY WITH MY LIFE!
AND TOUKA, TOO!
BOOM BOOM
HEY, WHAT'S THE STORY WITH THIS CAT?!
BOOM
BOOM BOOM BOOM
THAT'S TOU— YOU KNOW WHAT? JUST KEEP RUNNING!

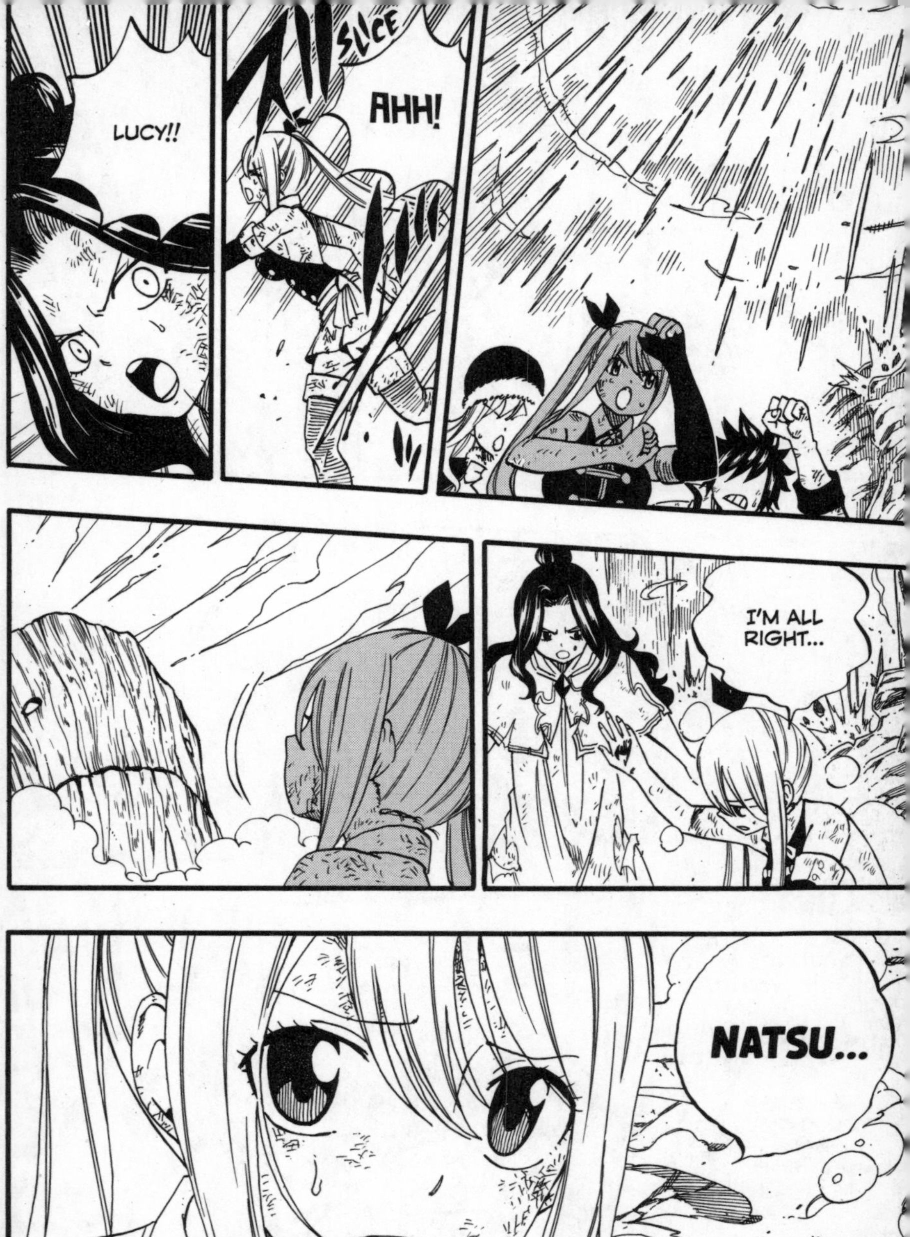
SLICE
AHH!
LUCY!!
I'M ALL RIGHT...
NATSU...

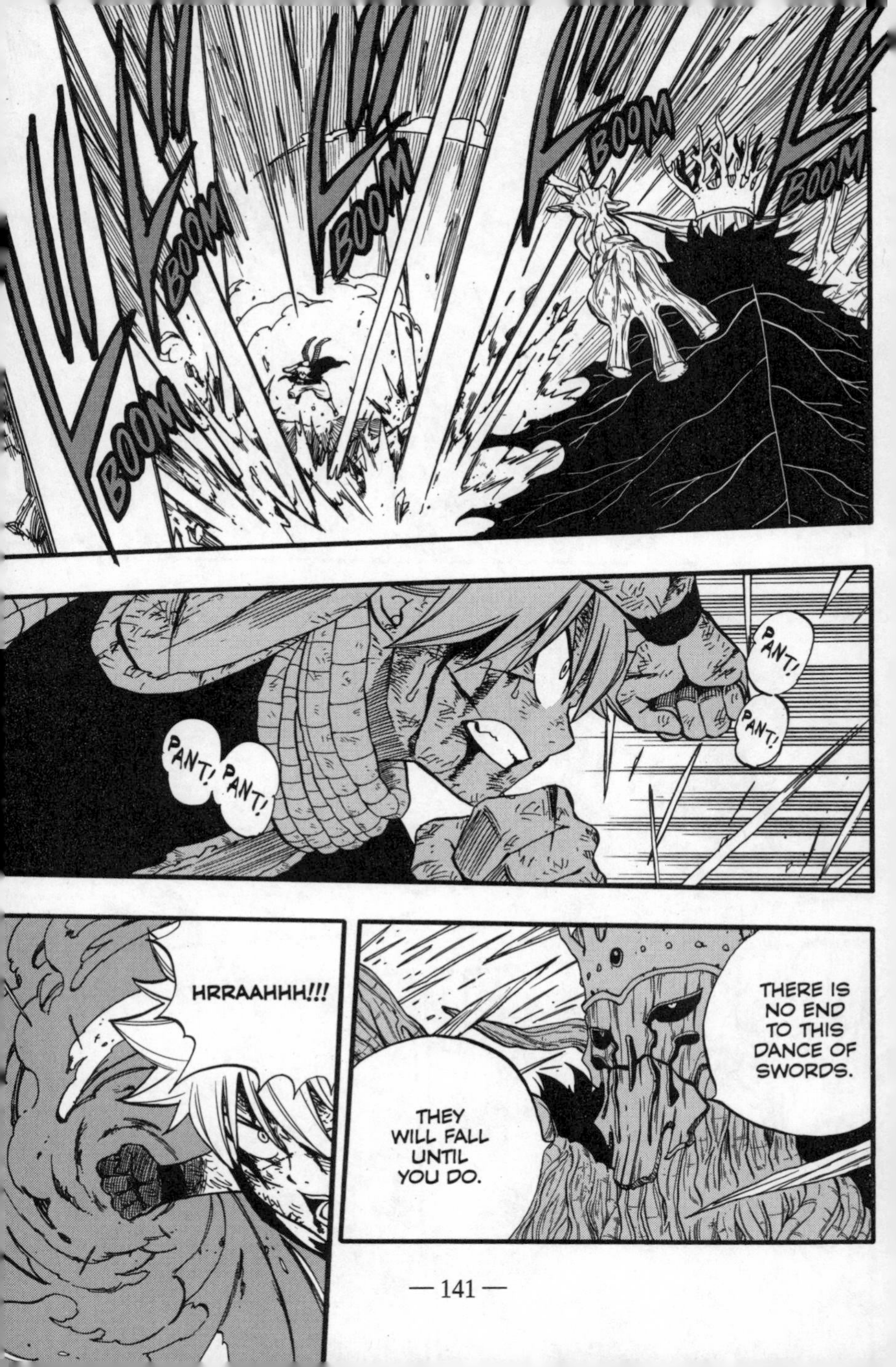
BOOM
BOOM
BOOM
BOOM
BOOM
PANT!
PANT!
PANT!
PANT!
THERE IS NO END TO THIS DANCE OF SWORDS.
THEY WILL FALL UNTIL YOU DO.
HRRAAHHH!!!

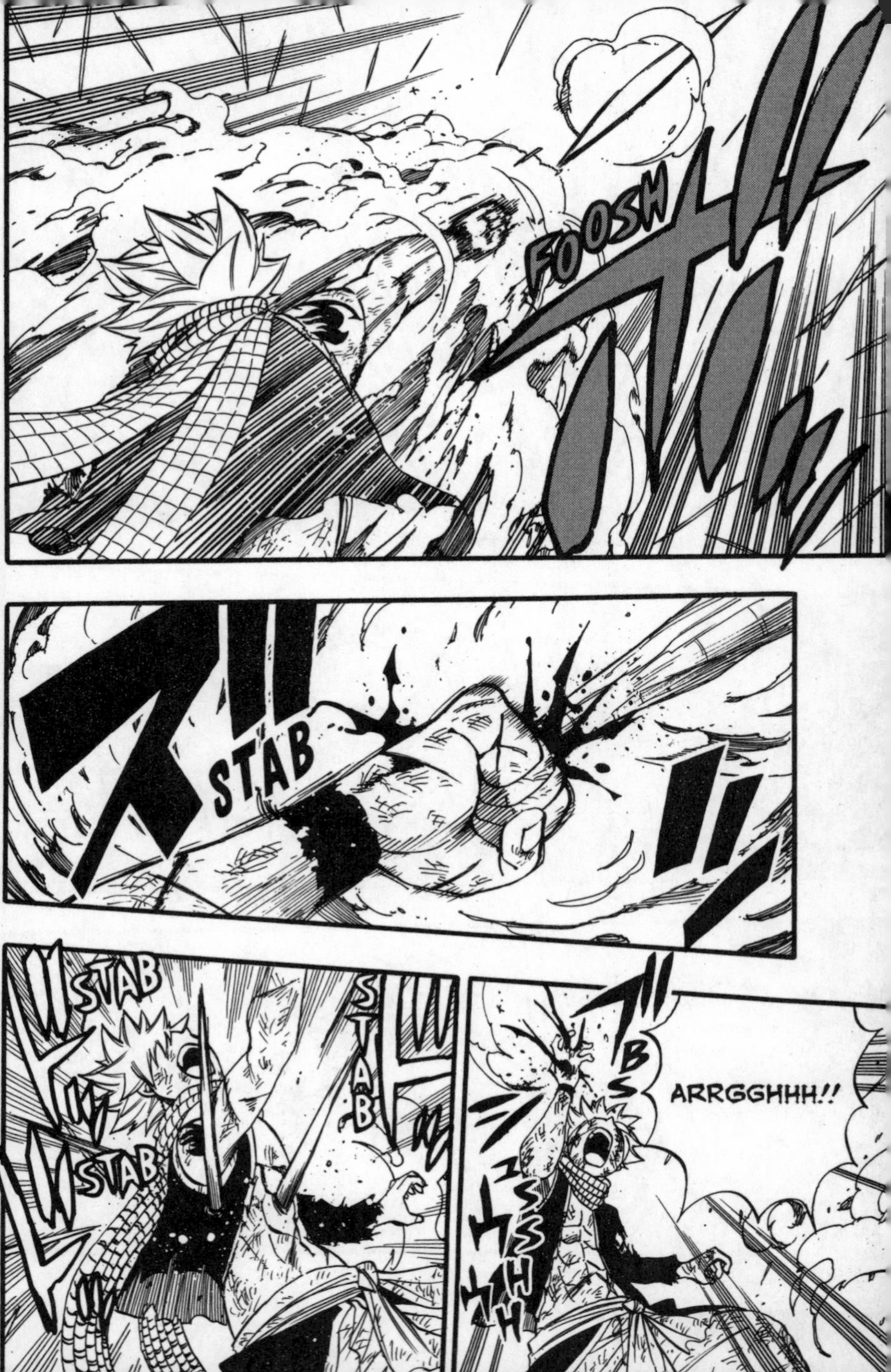
FOOSH
STAB
BS
ARRGGHHH!!
SSSHHH
STAB
STAB
STAB

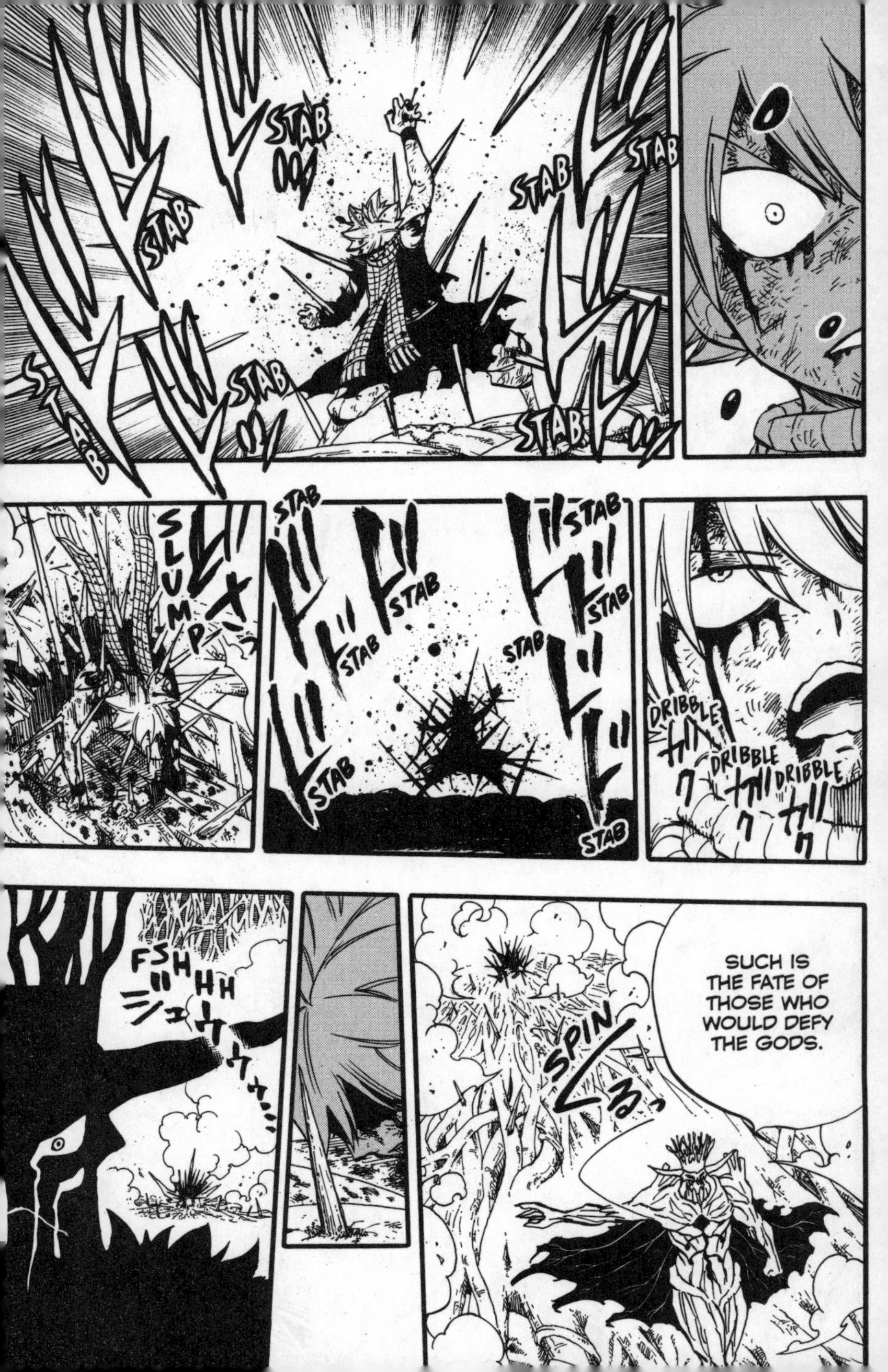
STAB
STAB
STAB
STAB
STAB
STAB
STAB
DRIBBLE
DRIBBLE
DRIBBLE
STAB
STAB
STAB
STAB
STAB
STAB
STAB
STAB
SLUMP
SUCH IS THE FATE OF THOSE WHO WOULD DEFY THE GODS.
SPIN
FSHHHH

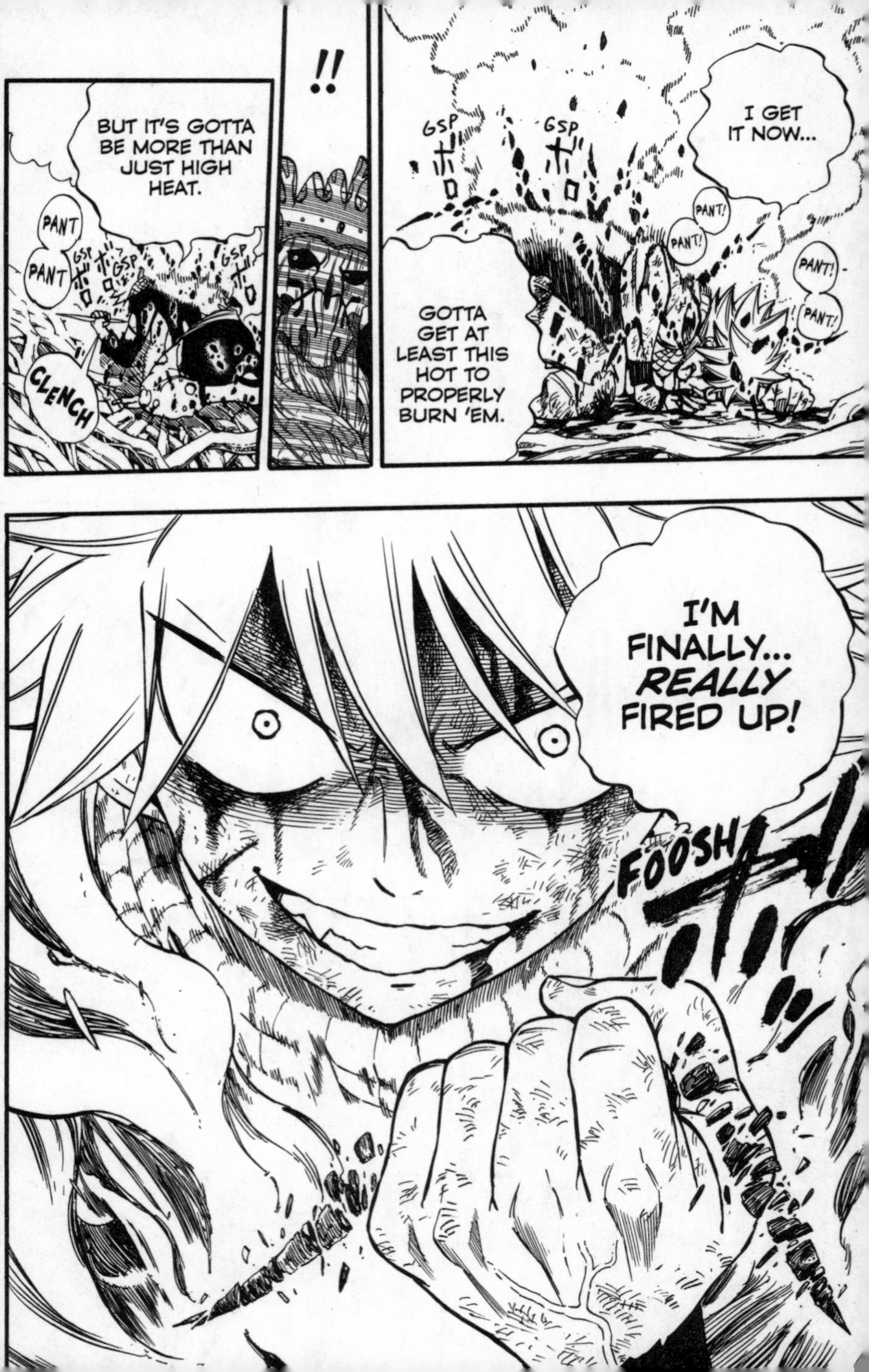
I GET IT NOW...
PANT!
PANT!
PANT!
PANT!
GSP
GSP
GOTTA GET AT LEAST THIS HOT TO PROPERLY BURN 'EM.
!!
BUT IT'S GOTTA BE MORE THAN JUST HIGH HEAT.
PANT
PANT
GSP
GSP
GSP
CLENCH
I'M FINALLY... *REALLY* FIRED UP!
FOOSH

FAIRY TAIL 100 YEARS QUEST

Chapter 62: Burning Will

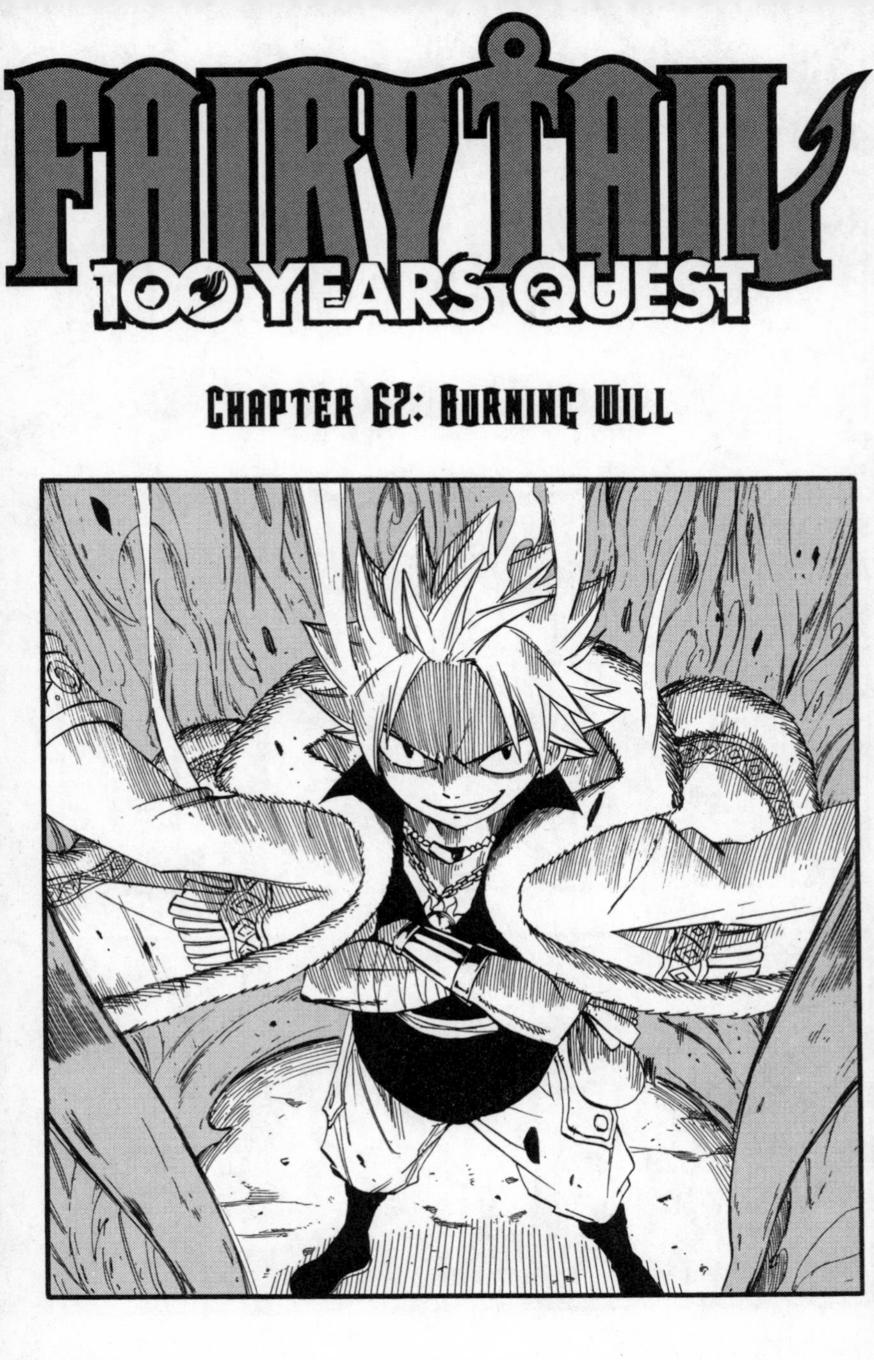

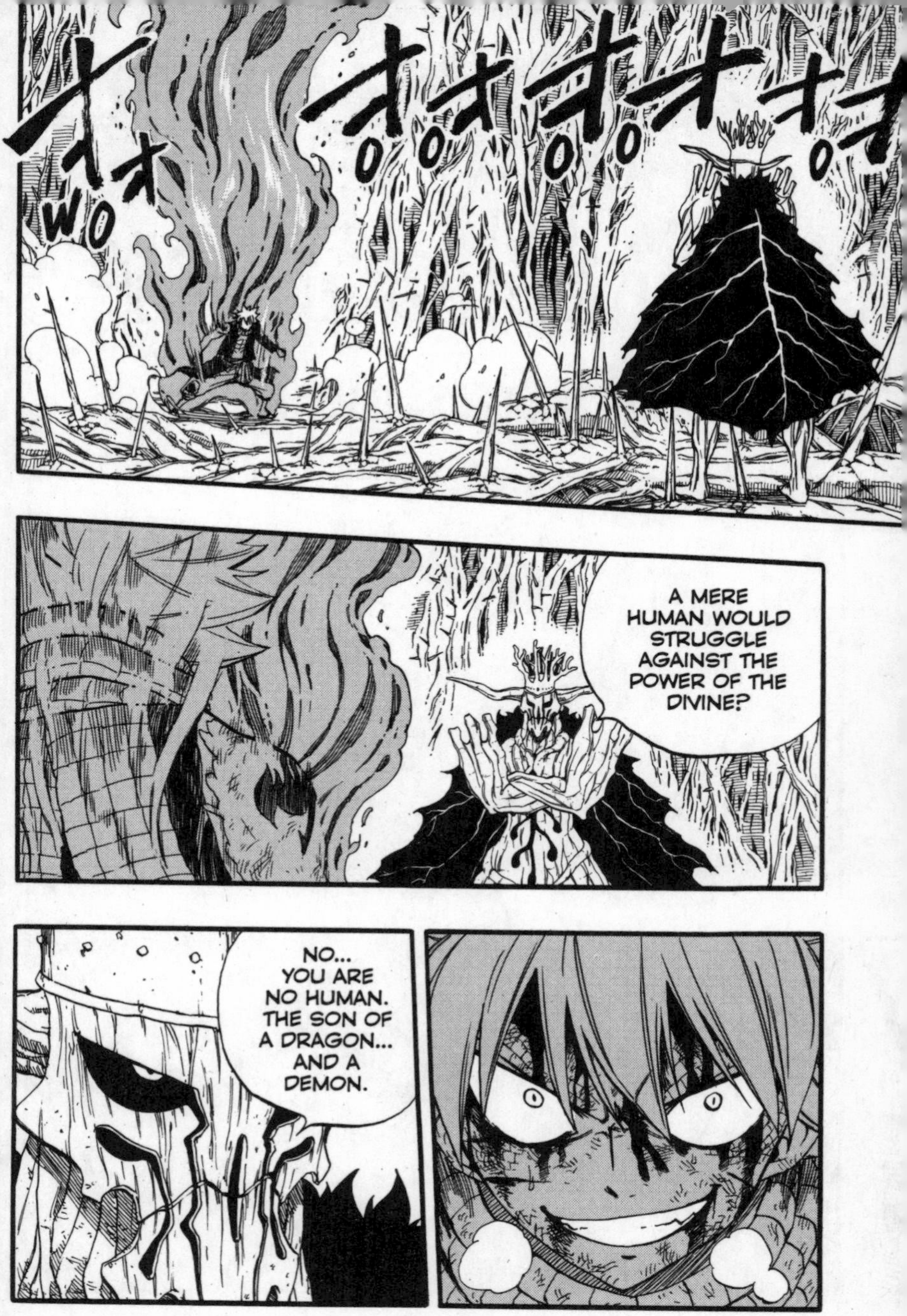
WO O O O O O
A MERE HUMAN WOULD STRUGGLE AGAINST THE POWER OF THE DIVINE?
NO... YOU ARE NO HUMAN. THE SON OF A DRAGON... AND A DEMON.

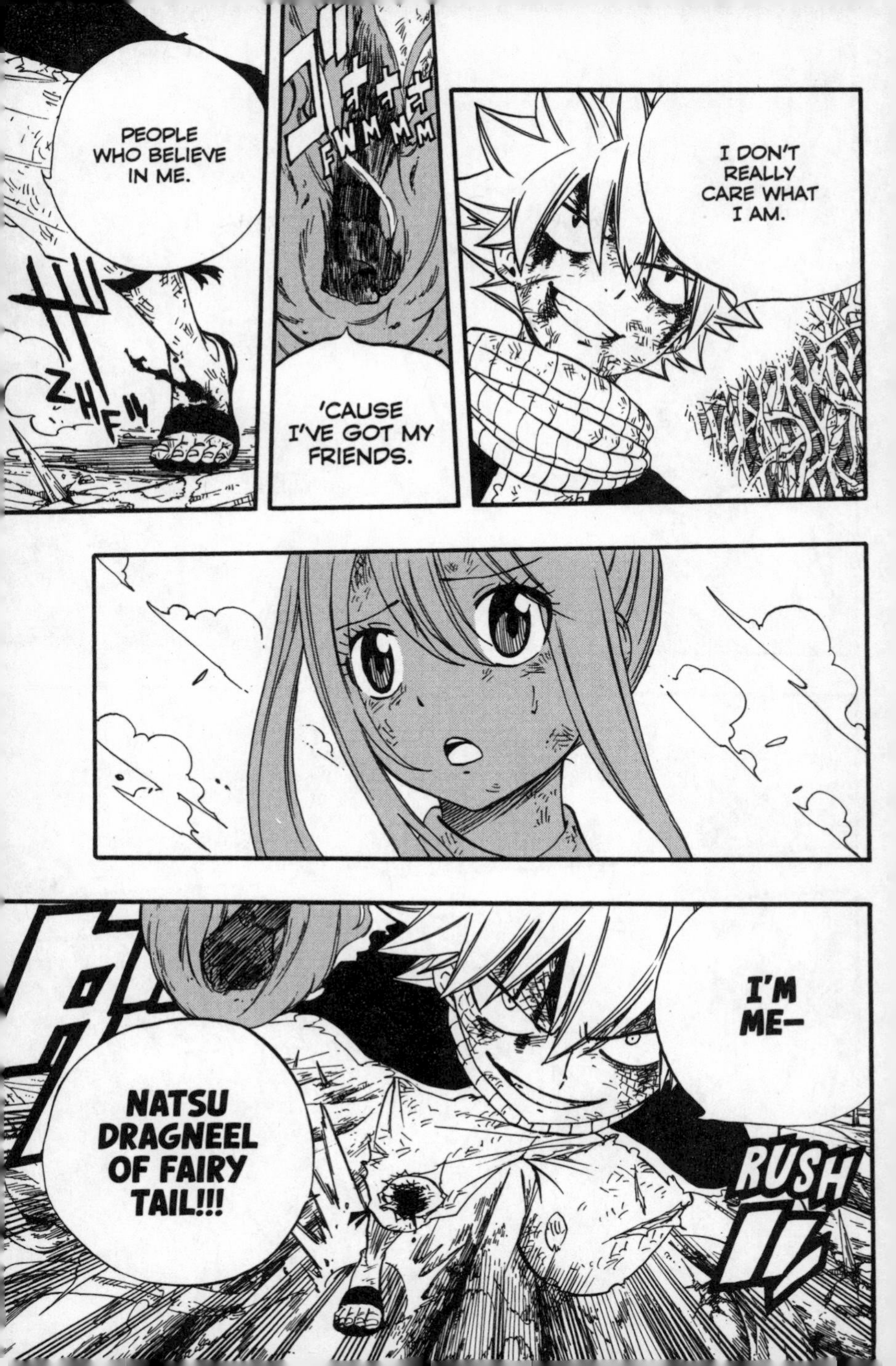
I DON'T REALLY CARE WHAT I AM.
FWMMMM
'CAUSE I'VE GOT MY FRIENDS.
PEOPLE WHO BELIEVE IN ME.
ZHF
I'M ME–
NATSU DRAGNEEL OF FAIRY TAIL!!!
RUSH!!

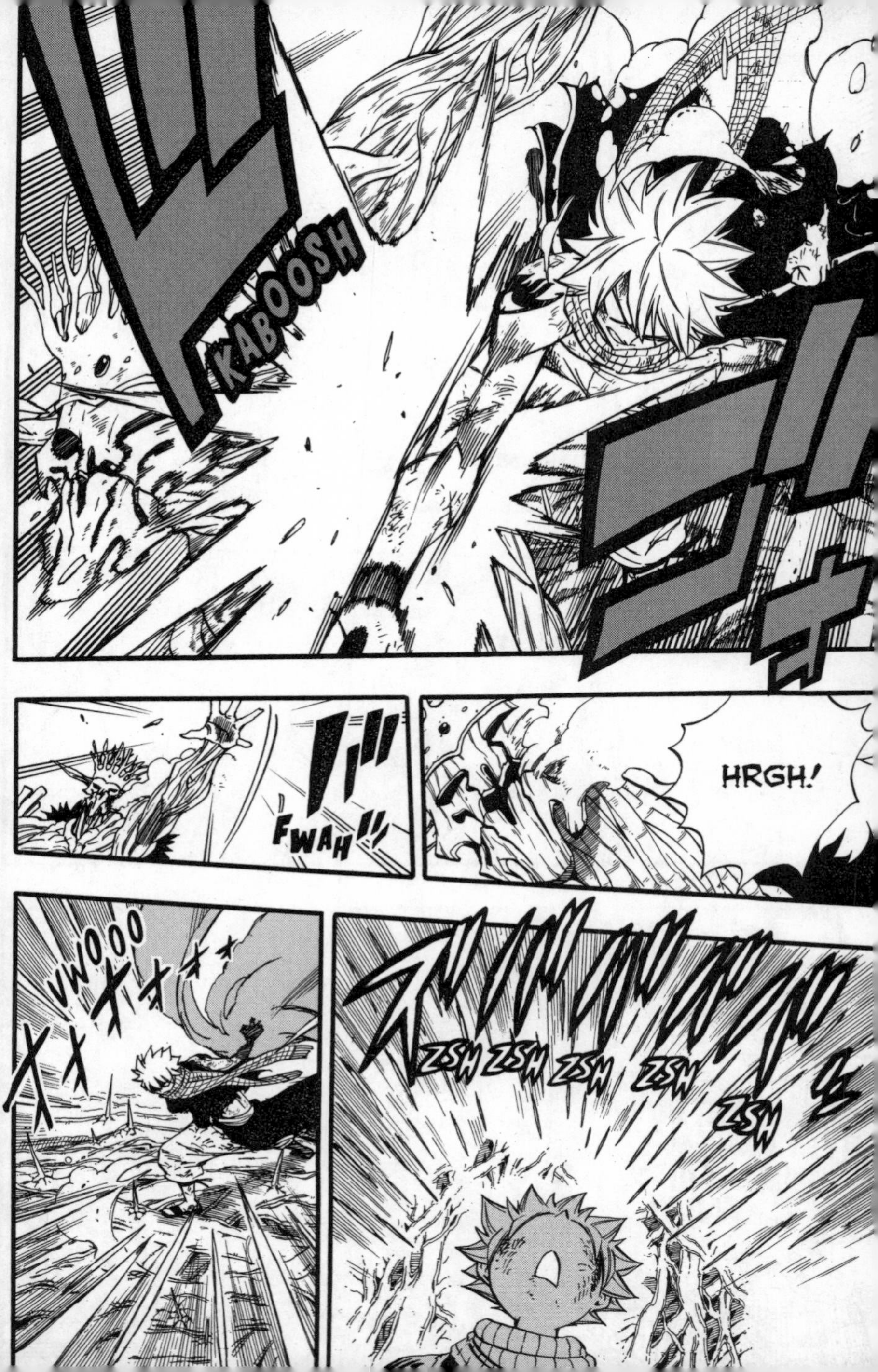
KABOOSH
HRGH!
FWAH!!!
VWOOO
ZSH ZSH ZSH ZSH
ZSH

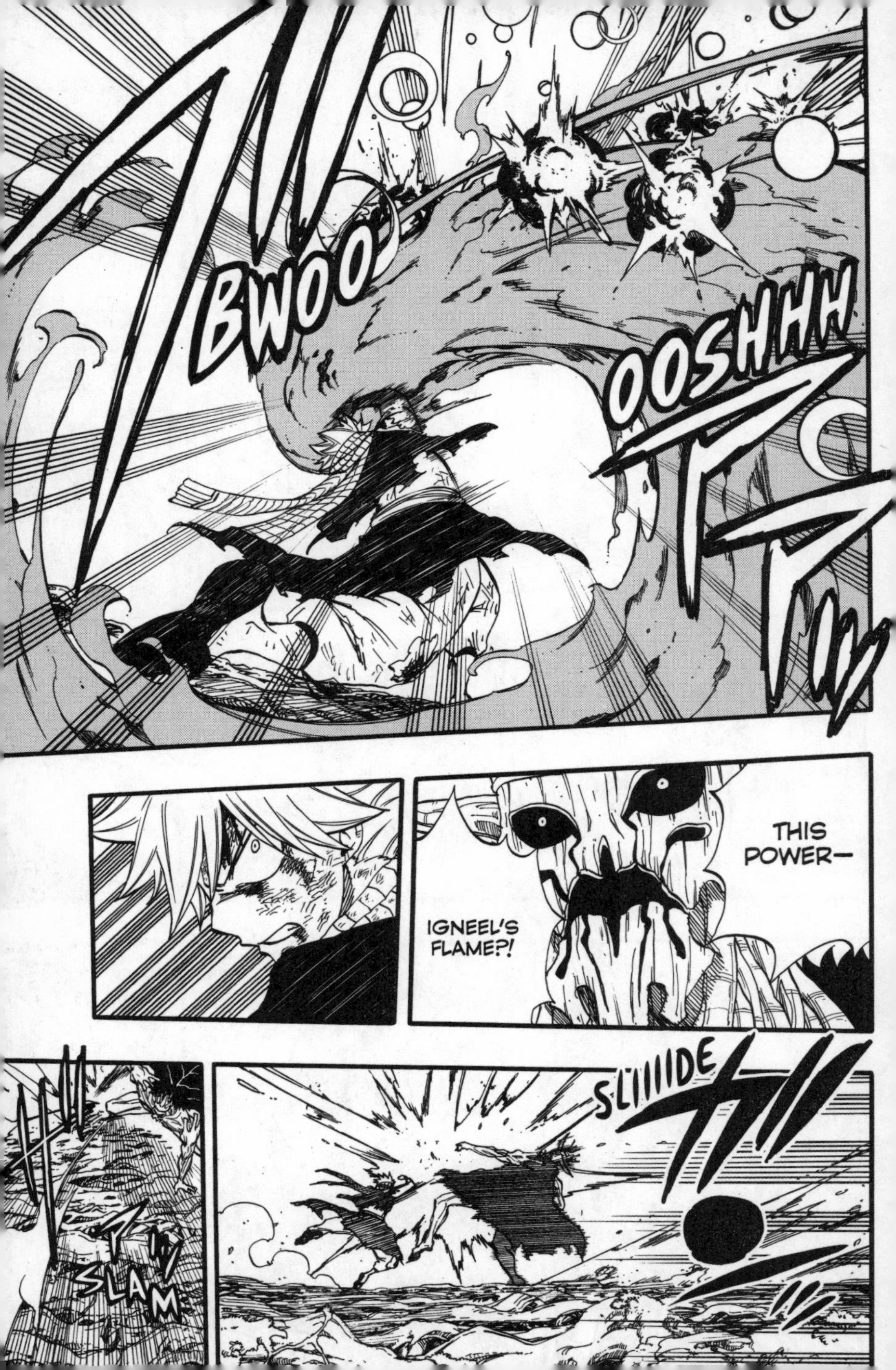
BWOO
OOSHHH
THIS POWER—
IGNEEL'S FLAME?!
SLIIIIDE
SLAM

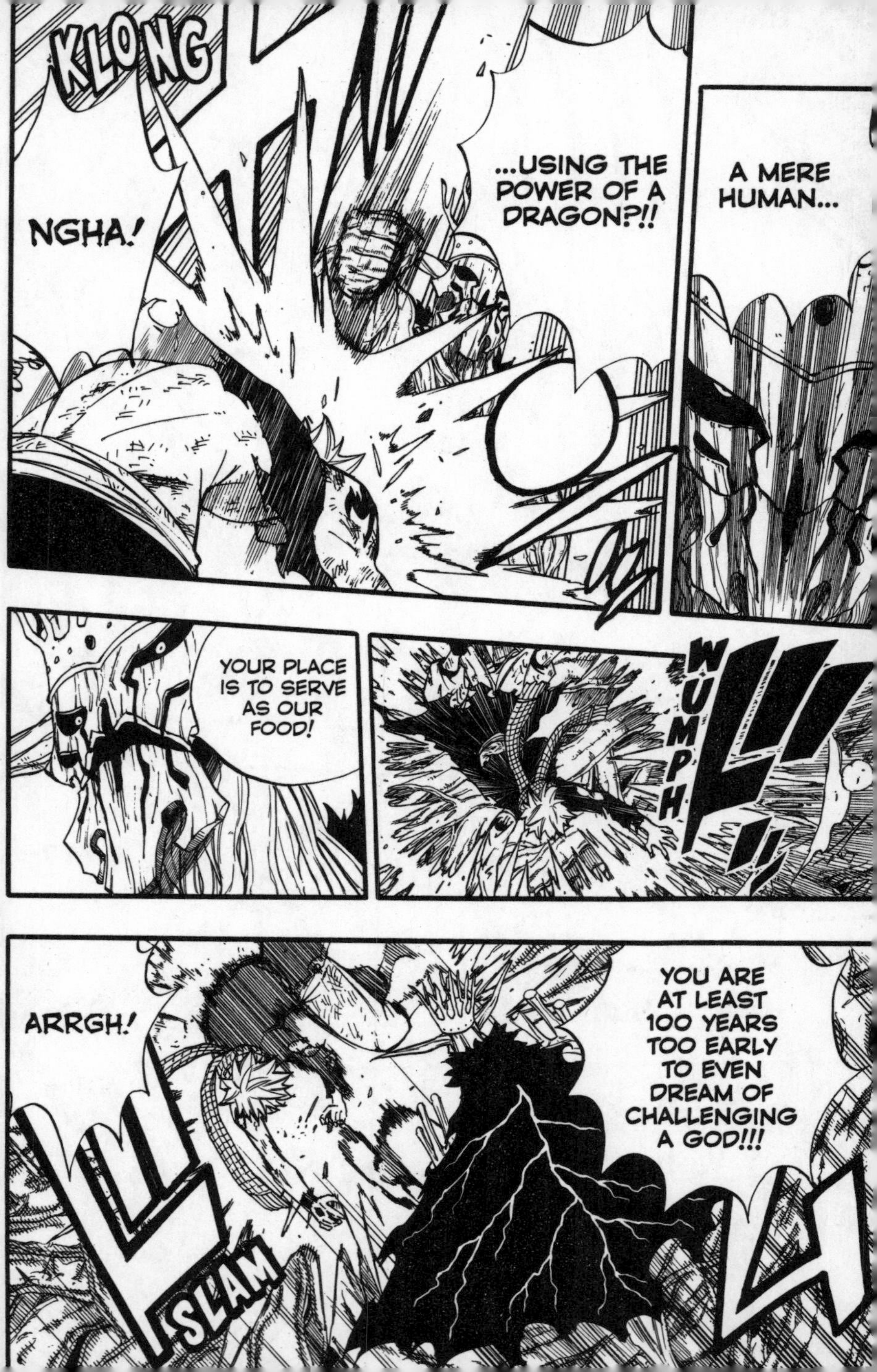
A MERE HUMAN...
...USING THE POWER OF A DRAGON?!!
KLONG
NGHA!
WUMPH
YOUR PLACE IS TO SERVE AS OUR FOOD!
YOU ARE AT LEAST 100 YEARS TOO EARLY TO EVEN DREAM OF CHALLENGING A GOD!!!
ARRGH!
SLAM

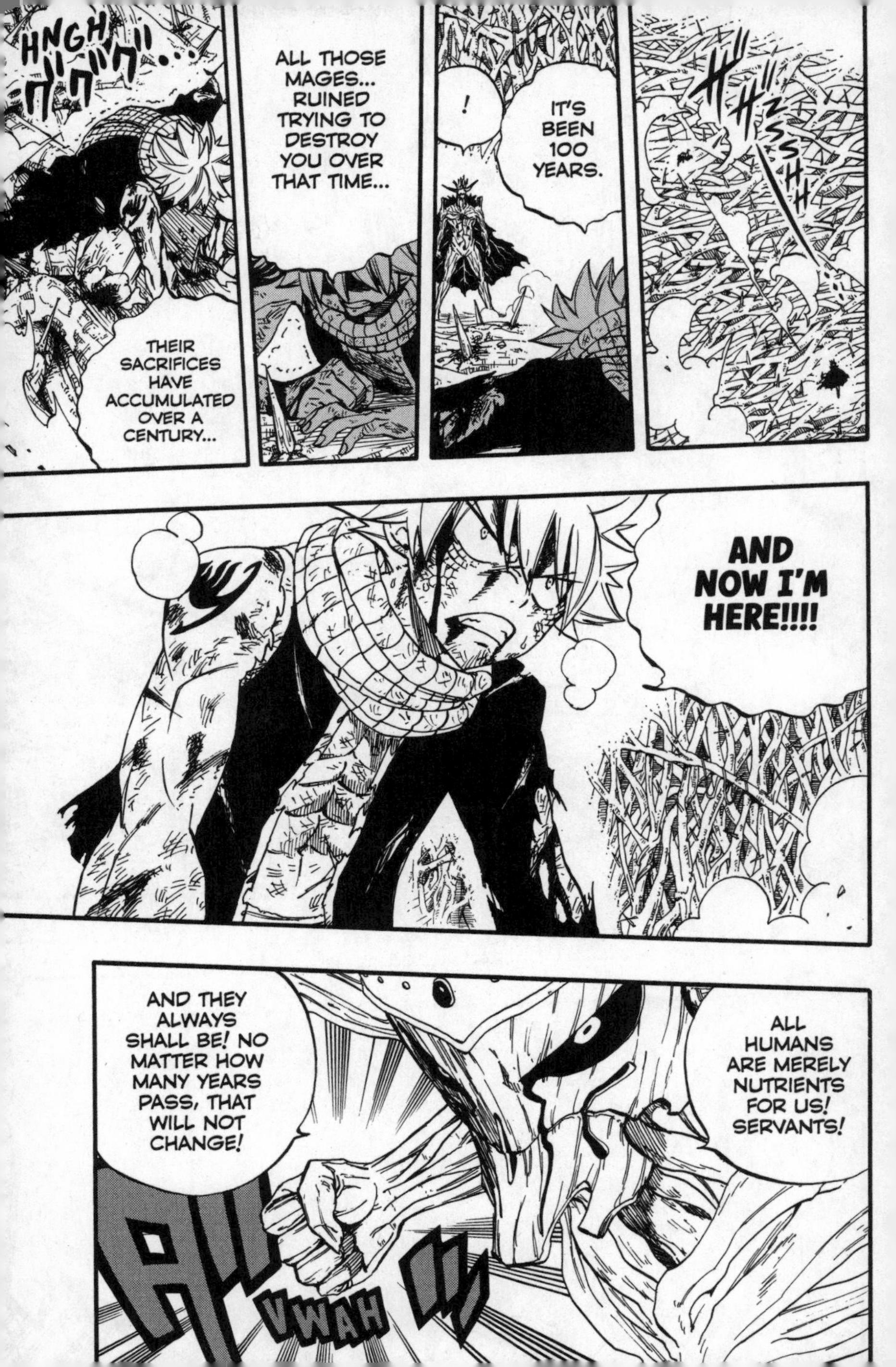
!
IT'S BEEN 100 YEARS.
ALL THOSE MAGES... RUINED TRYING TO DESTROY YOU OVER THAT TIME...
HNGH...
THEIR SACRIFICES HAVE ACCUMULATED OVER A CENTURY...
AND NOW I'M HERE!!!!
ALL HUMANS ARE MERELY NUTRIENTS FOR US! SERVANTS!
AND THEY ALWAYS SHALL BE! NO MATTER HOW MANY YEARS PASS, THAT WILL NOT CHANGE!
VWAH

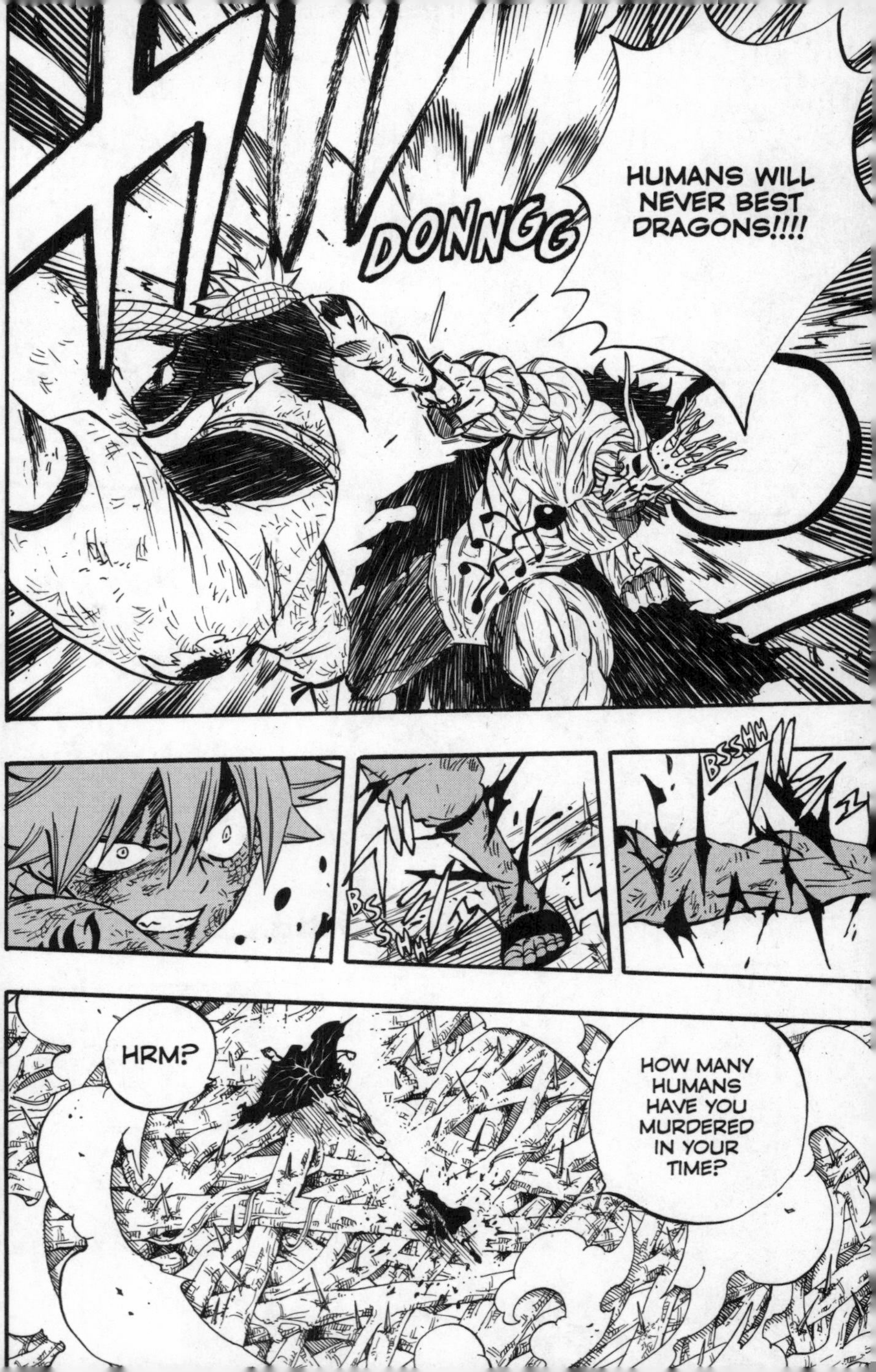
HUMANS WILL NEVER BEST DRAGONS!!!!
DONNGG
BSSHH
BSSHH
HOW MANY HUMANS HAVE YOU MURDERED IN YOUR TIME?
HRM?

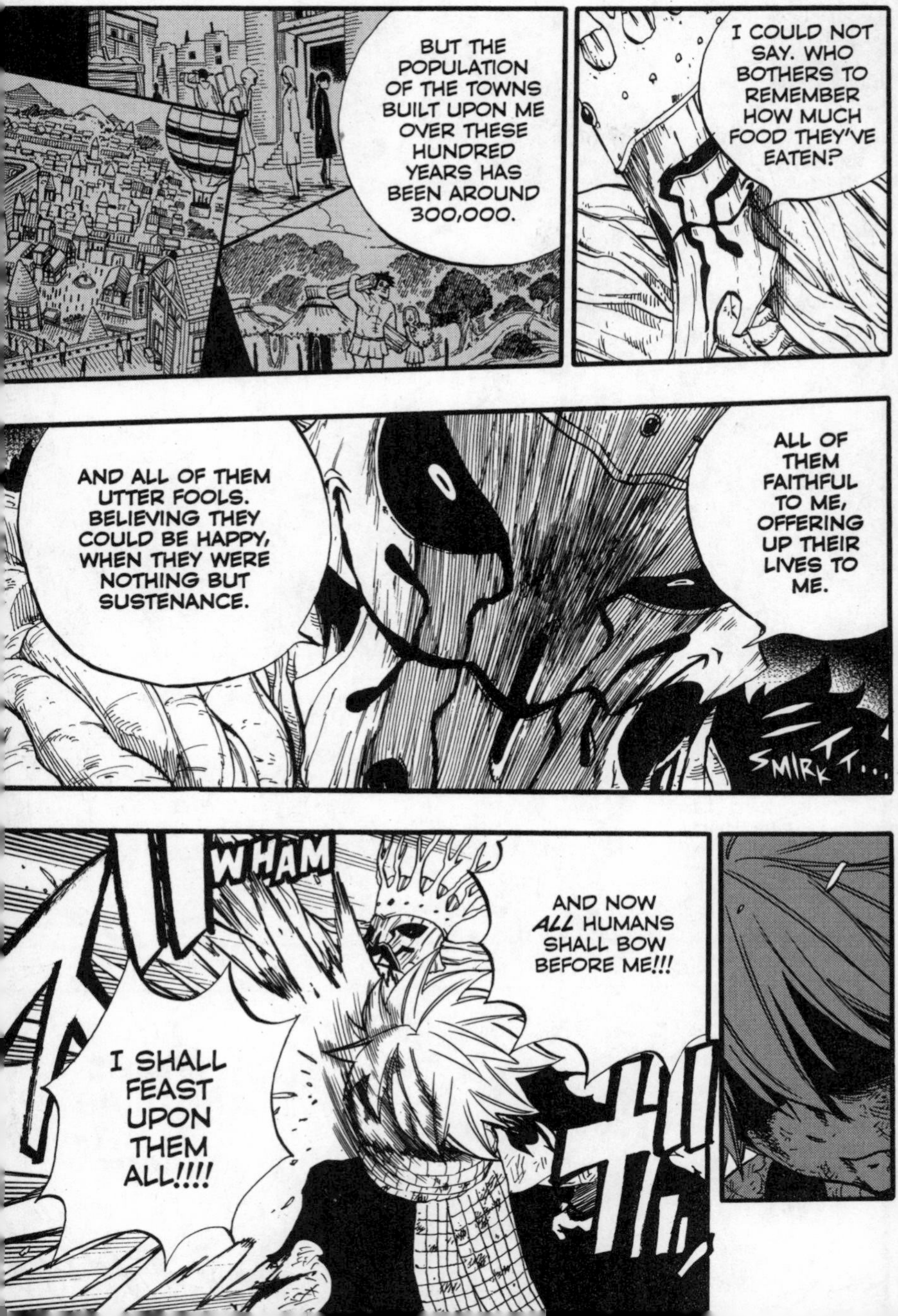
I COULD NOT SAY. WHO BOTHERS TO REMEMBER HOW MUCH FOOD THEY'VE EATEN?
BUT THE POPULATION OF THE TOWNS BUILT UPON ME OVER THESE HUNDRED YEARS HAS BEEN AROUND 300,000.
ALL OF THEM FAITHFUL TO ME, OFFERING UP THEIR LIVES TO ME.
AND ALL OF THEM UTTER FOOLS. BELIEVING THEY COULD BE HAPPY, WHEN THEY WERE NOTHING BUT SUSTENANCE.
SMIRKTT...
WHAM
AND NOW *ALL* HUMANS SHALL BOW BEFORE ME!!!
I SHALL FEAST UPON THEM ALL!!!!

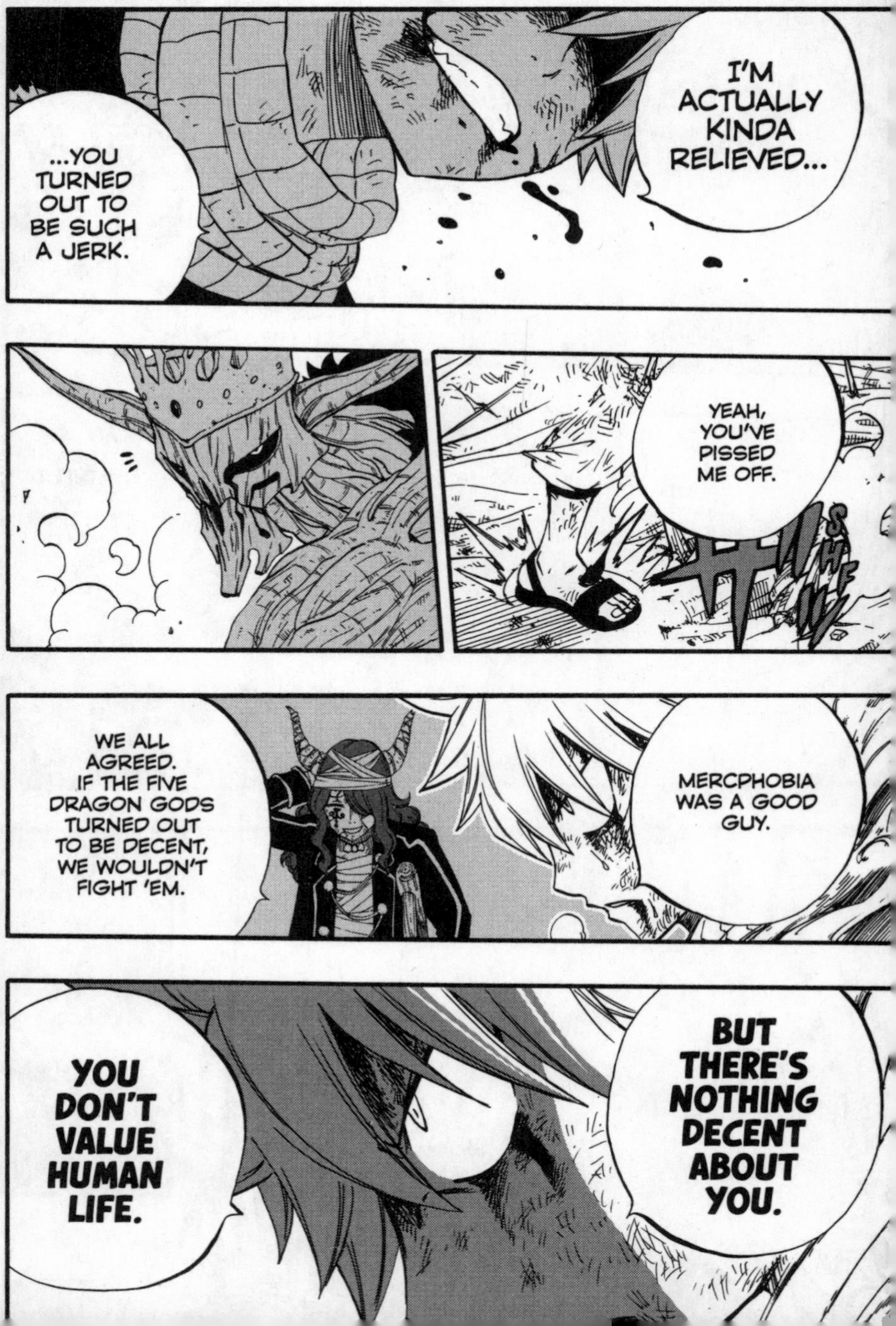
I'M ACTUALLY KINDA RELIEVED...
...YOU TURNED OUT TO BE SUCH A JERK.
YEAH, YOU'VE PISSED ME OFF.
MERCPHOBIA WAS A GOOD GUY.
WE ALL AGREED. IF THE FIVE DRAGON GODS TURNED OUT TO BE DECENT, WE WOULDN'T FIGHT 'EM.
BUT THERE'S NOTHING DECENT ABOUT YOU.
YOU DON'T VALUE HUMAN LIFE.

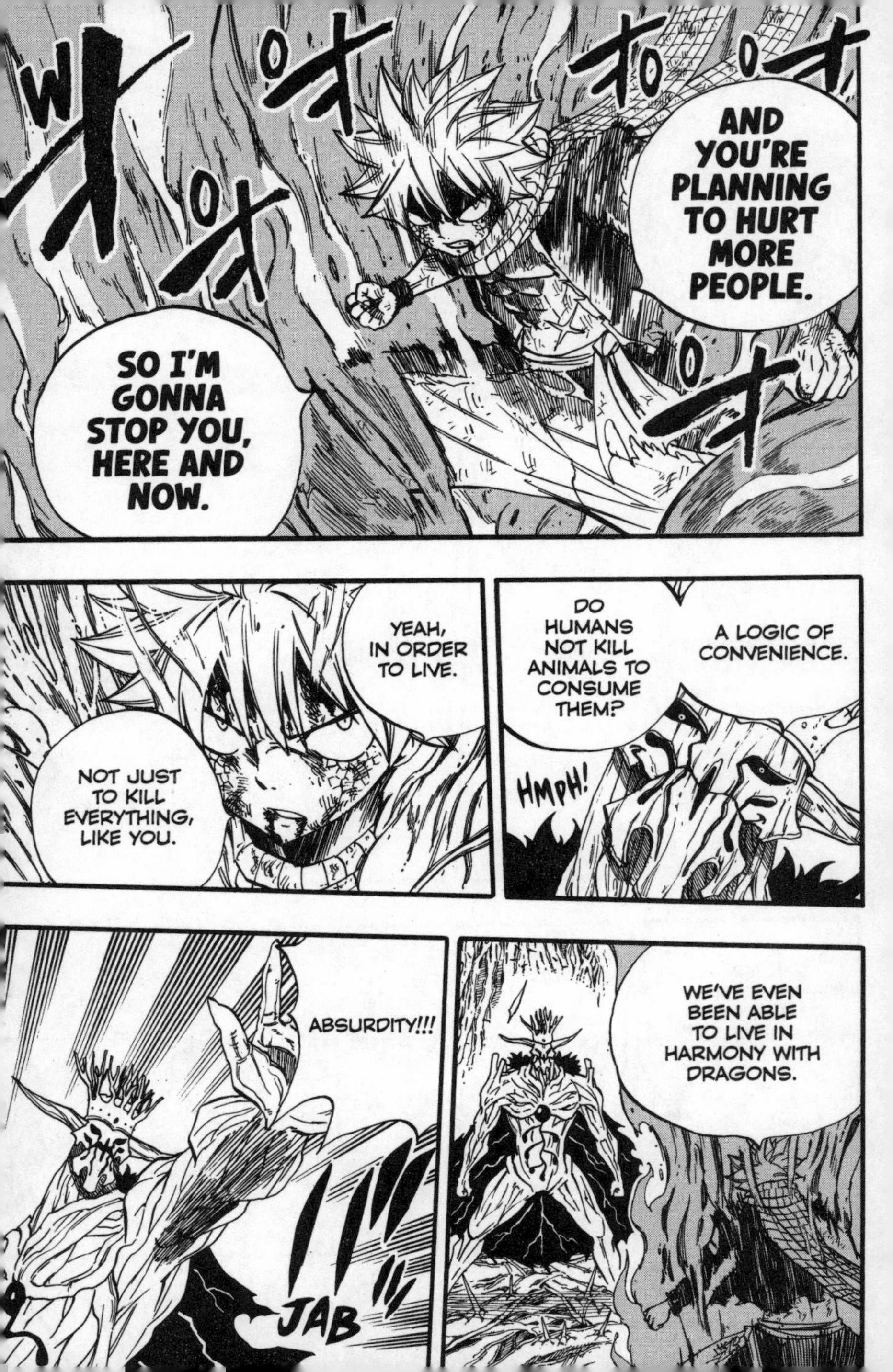
AND YOU'RE PLANNING TO HURT MORE PEOPLE.
SO I'M GONNA STOP YOU, HERE AND NOW.
A LOGIC OF CONVENIENCE.
DO HUMANS NOT KILL ANIMALS TO CONSUME THEM?
HMPH!
YEAH, IN ORDER TO LIVE.
NOT JUST TO KILL EVERYTHING, LIKE YOU.
WE'VE EVEN BEEN ABLE TO LIVE IN HARMONY WITH DRAGONS.
ABSURDITY!!!
JAB

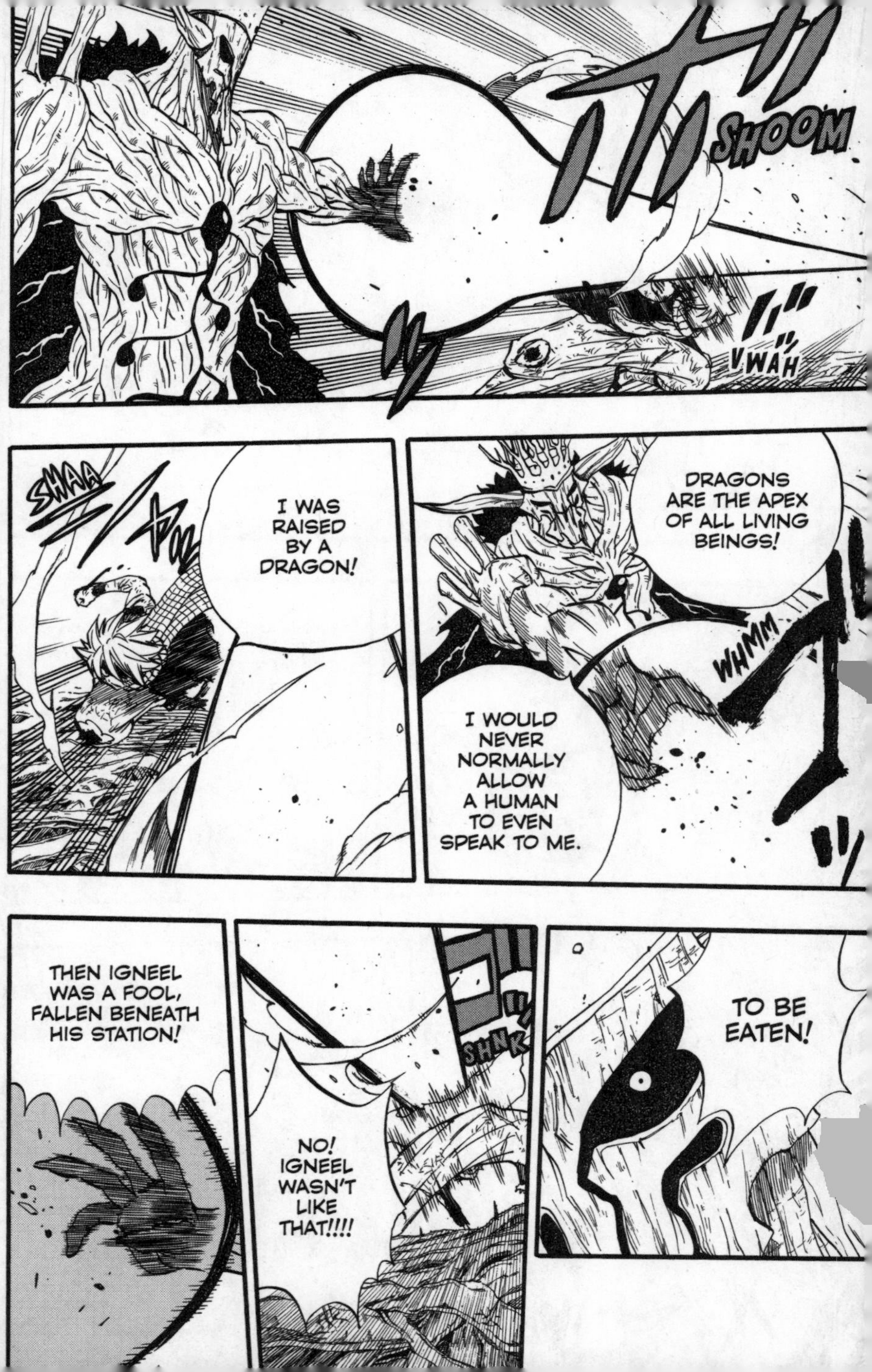
SHOOM
VWAH
DRAGONS ARE THE APEX OF ALL LIVING BEINGS!
WHMM
I WOULD NEVER NORMALLY ALLOW A HUMAN TO EVEN SPEAK TO ME.
SHAA
I WAS RAISED BY A DRAGON!
TO BE EATEN!
SHNK
NO! IGNEEL WASN'T LIKE THAT!!!!
THEN IGNEEL WAS A FOOL, FALLEN BENEATH HIS STATION!

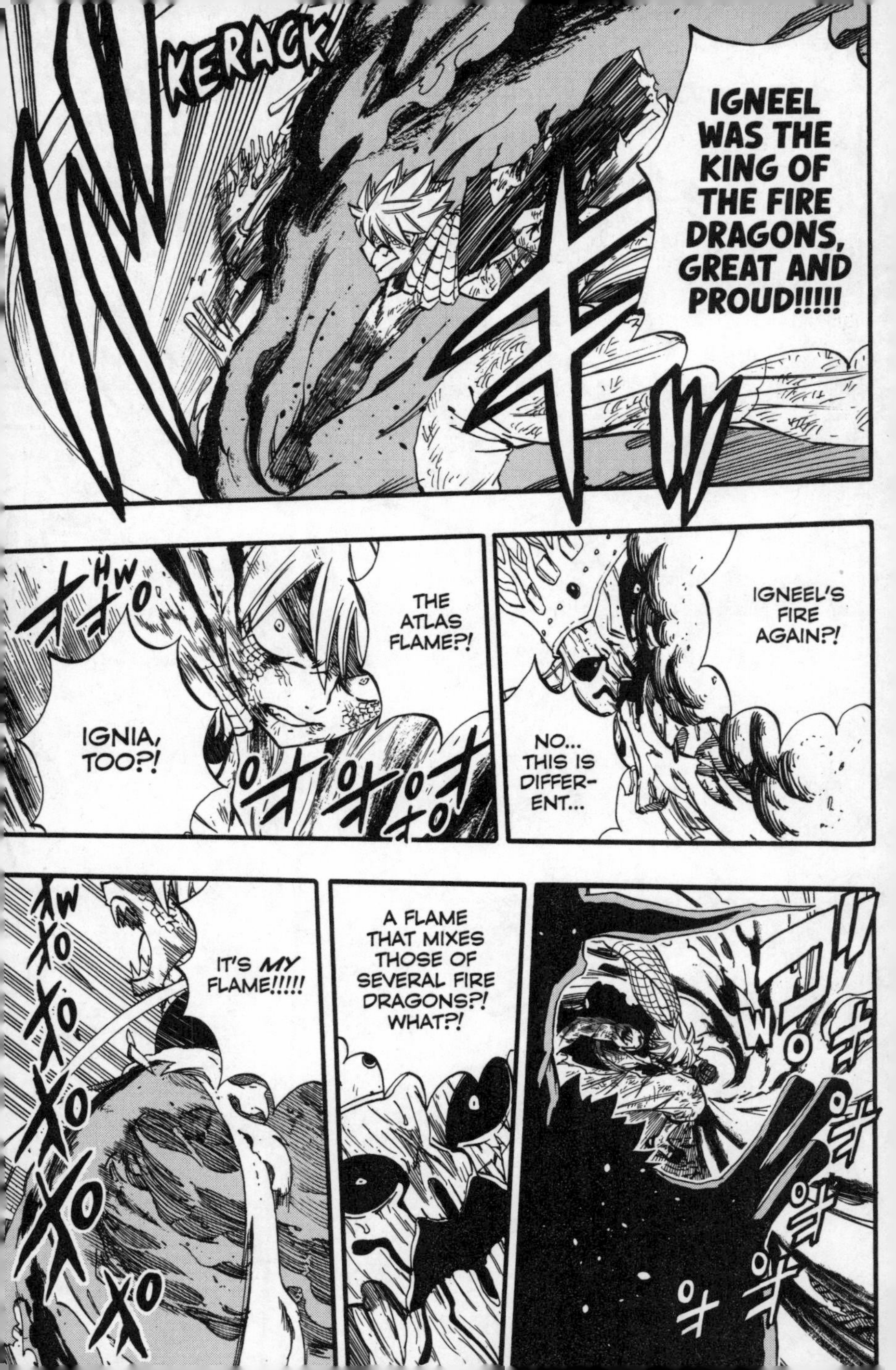
IGNEEL WAS THE KING OF THE FIRE DRAGONS, GREAT AND PROUD!!!!!
KERACK
IGNEEL'S FIRE AGAIN?!
NO... THIS IS DIFFER-ENT...
HWO
THE ATLAS FLAME?!
IGNIA, TOO?!
WO
A FLAME THAT MIXES THOSE OF SEVERAL FIRE DRAGONS?! WHAT?!
HWO
IT'S MY FLAME!!!!!

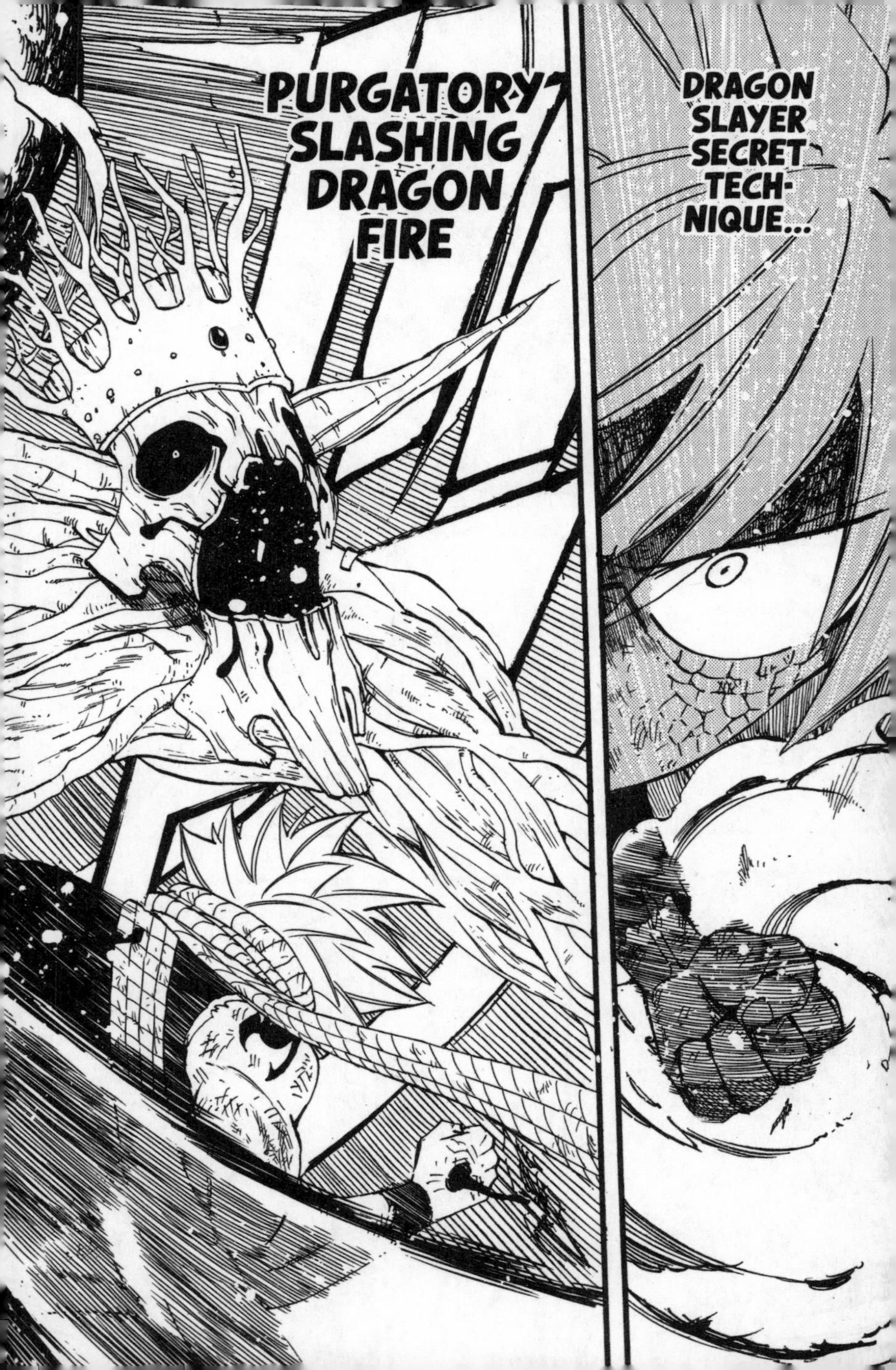
DRAGON SLAYER SECRET TECHNIQUE...
PURGATORY-SLASHING DRAGON FIRE

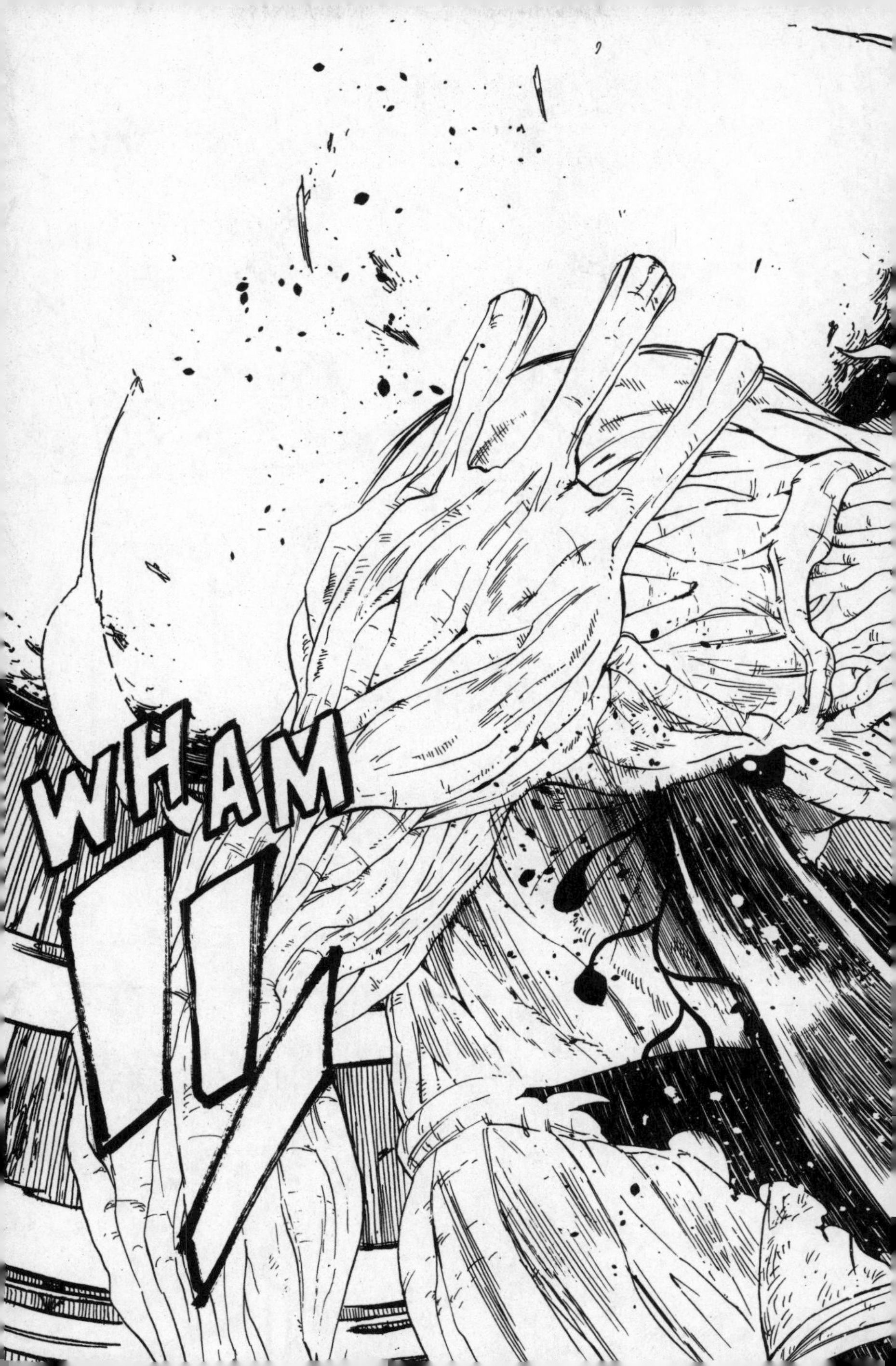
WHAM

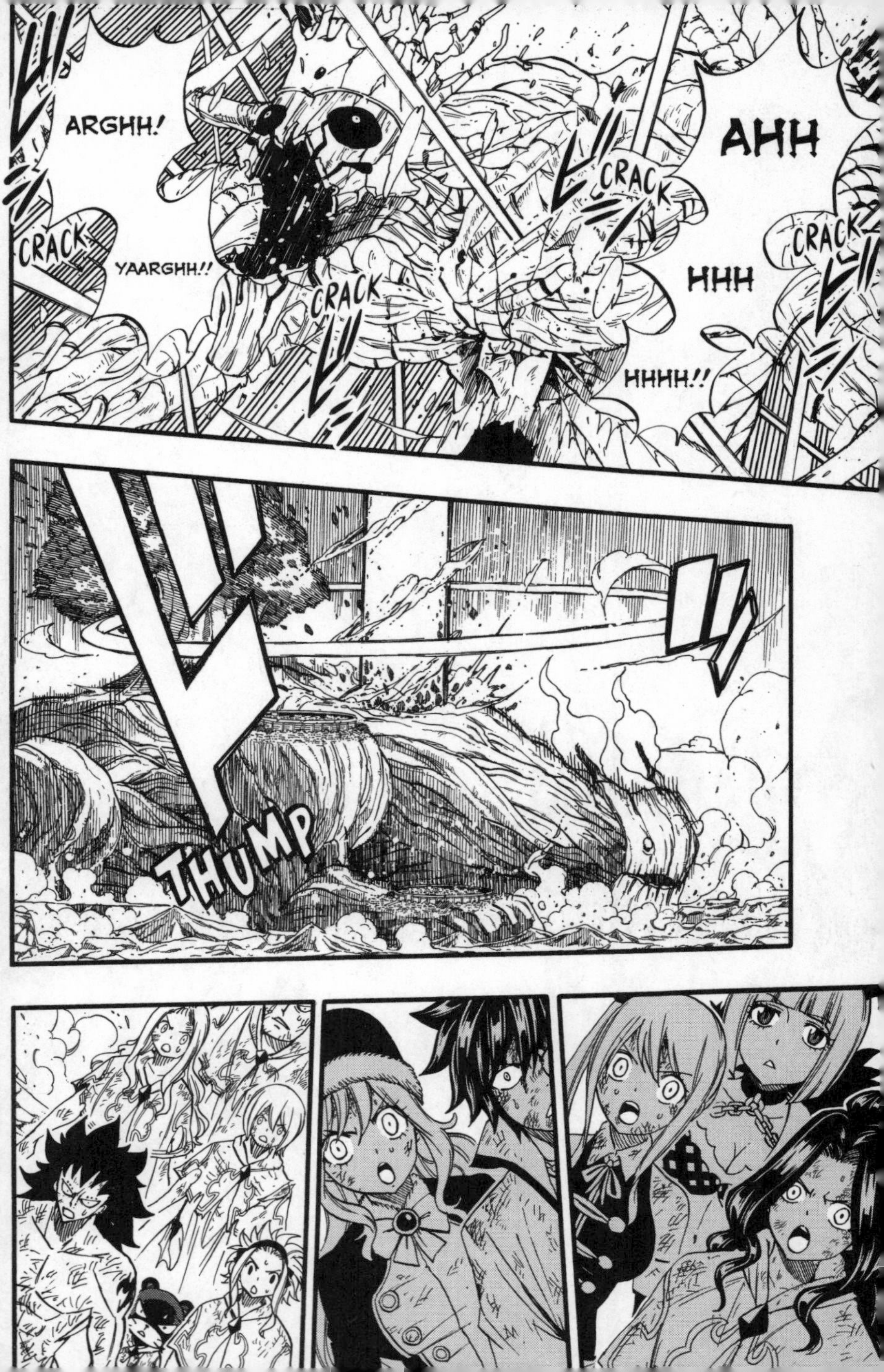
AHH
HHH
CRACK
CRACK
HHHH!!
ARGHH!
CRACK
YAARGHH!!
CRACK
THUMP

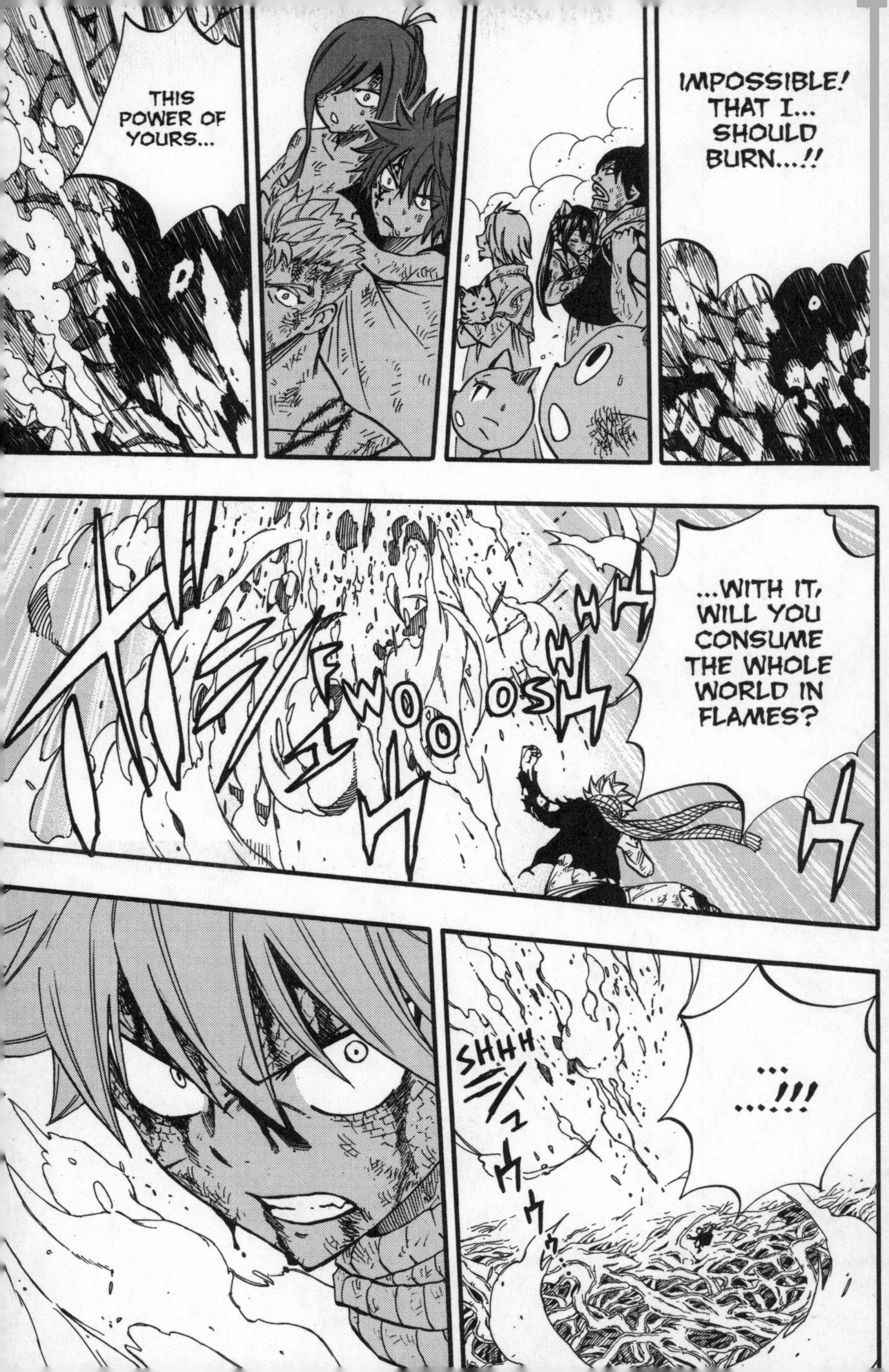
IMPOSSIBLE! THAT I... SHOULD BURN...!!
THIS POWER OF YOURS...
...WITH IT, WILL YOU CONSUME THE WHOLE WORLD IN FLAMES?
FWOOOOSH
...
...!!!
SHHH

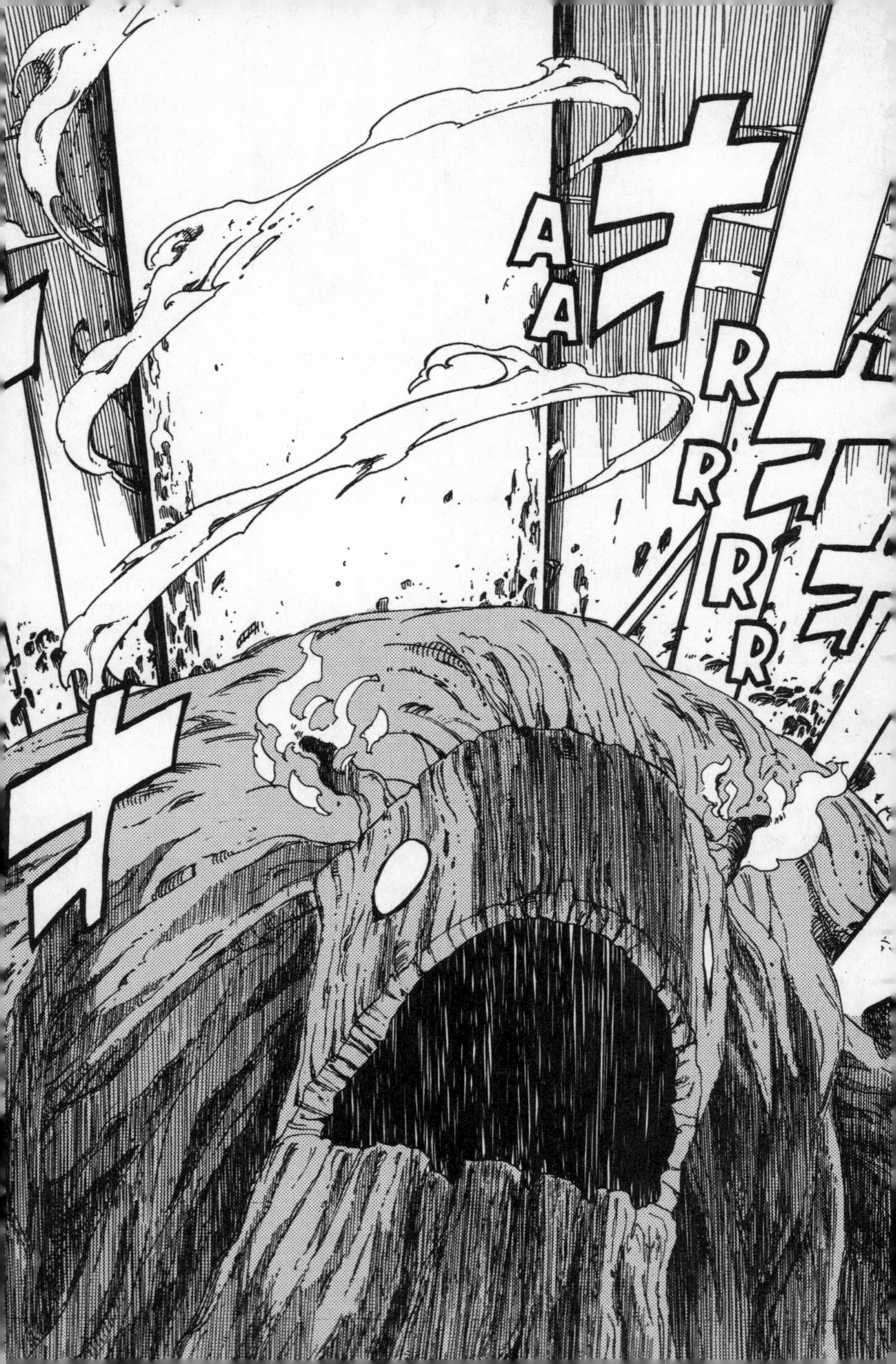
AARRRR

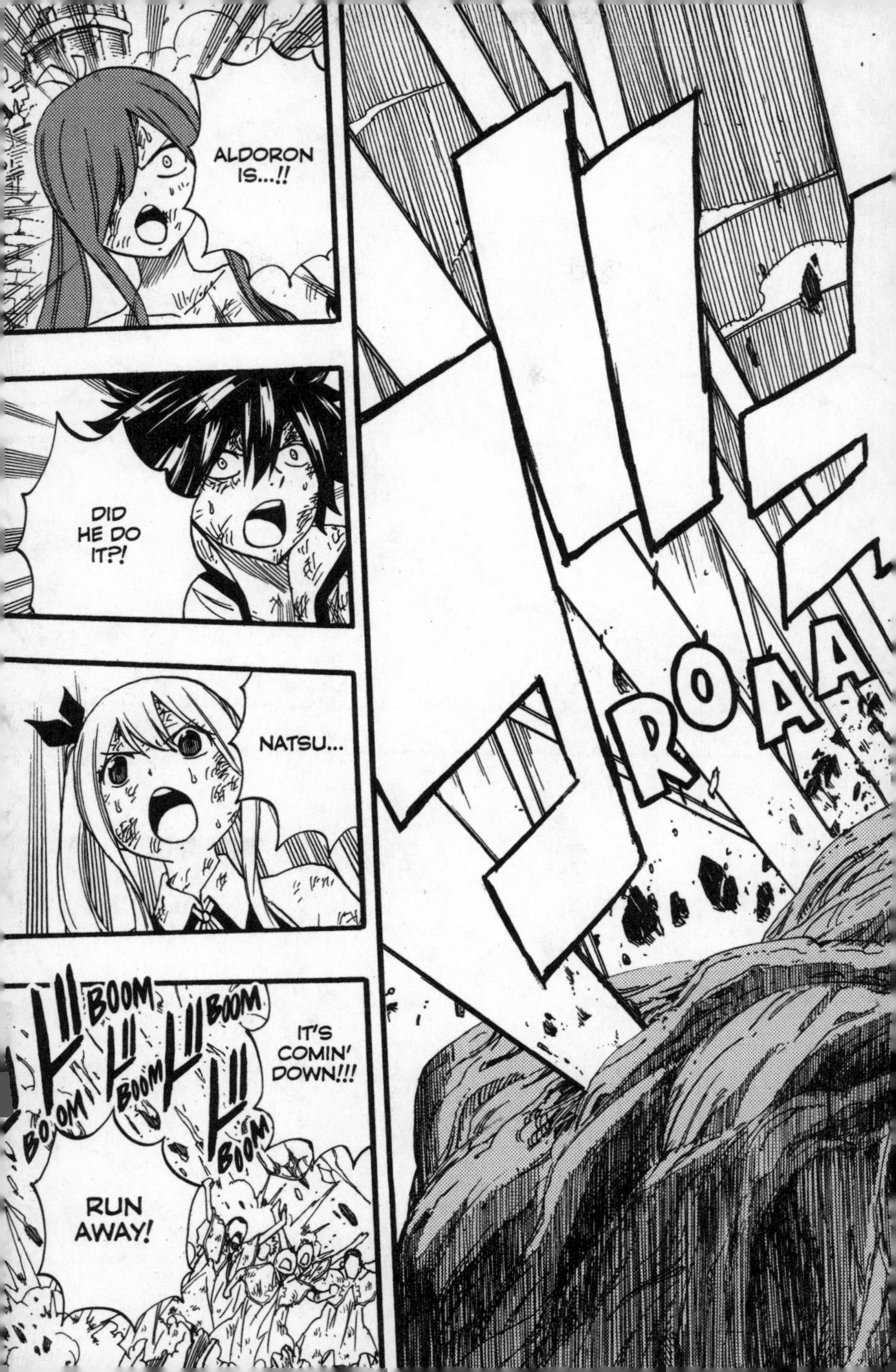
ROAA
ALDORON IS...!!
DID HE DO IT?!
NATSU...
IT'S COMIN' DOWN!!!
BOOM
BOOM
BOOM
BOOM
BOOM
RUN AWAY!

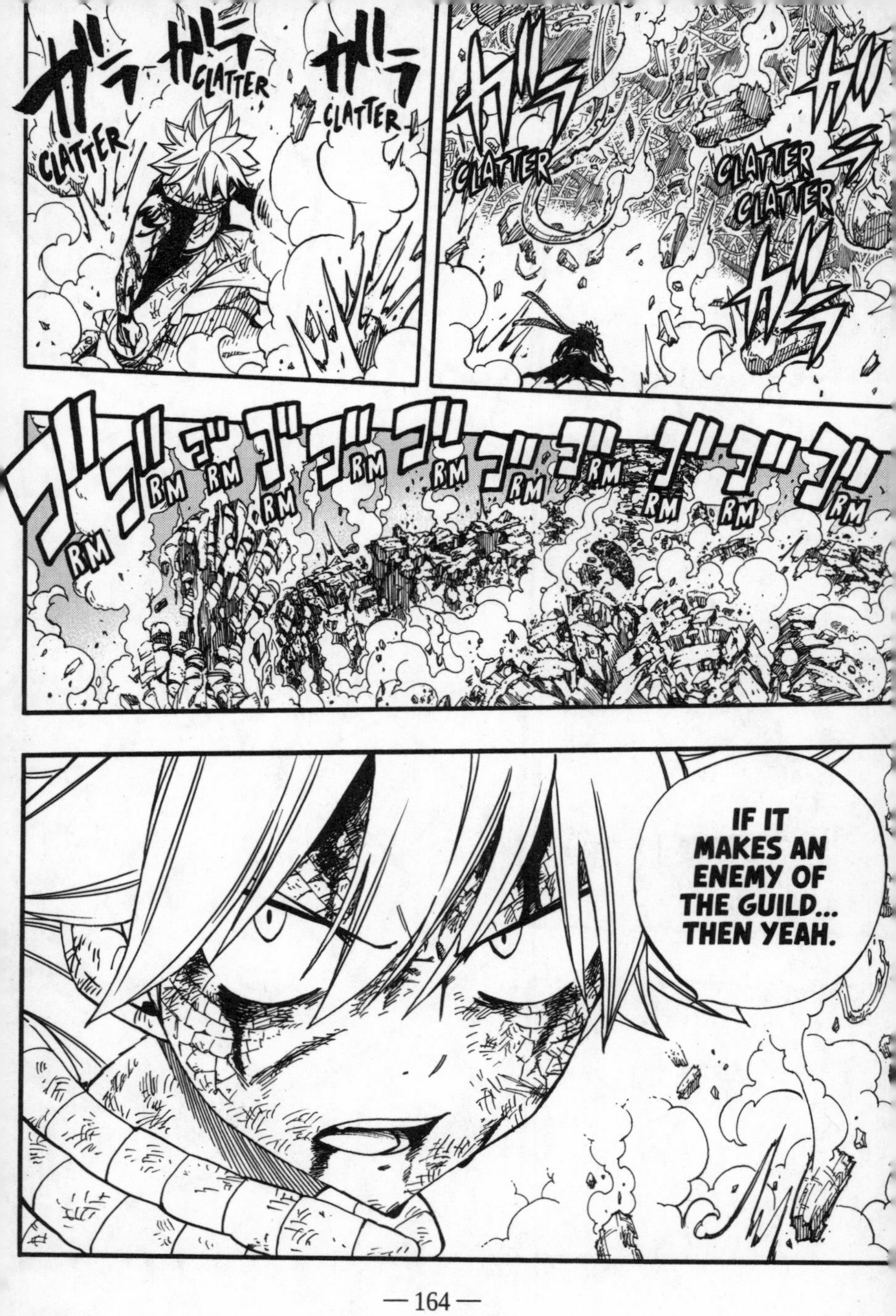

CLATTER
CLATTER
CLATTER
CLATTER
CLATTER
CLATTER
RM RM RM RM RM RM RM RM RM RM RM
IF IT MAKES AN ENEMY OF THE GUILD... THEN YEAH.

FAIRY TAIL 100 YEARS QUEST

Chapter 63: Celebration in Dramil

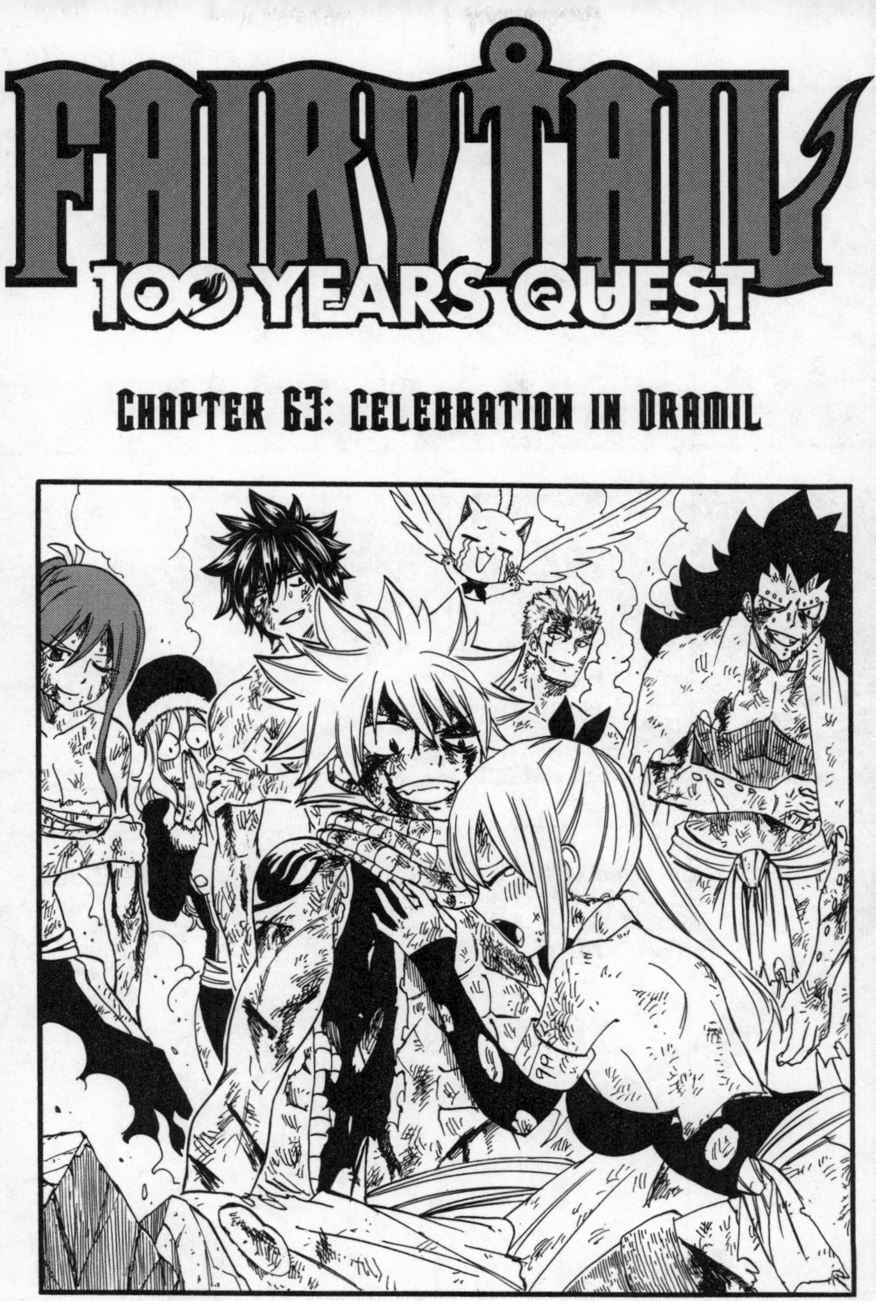

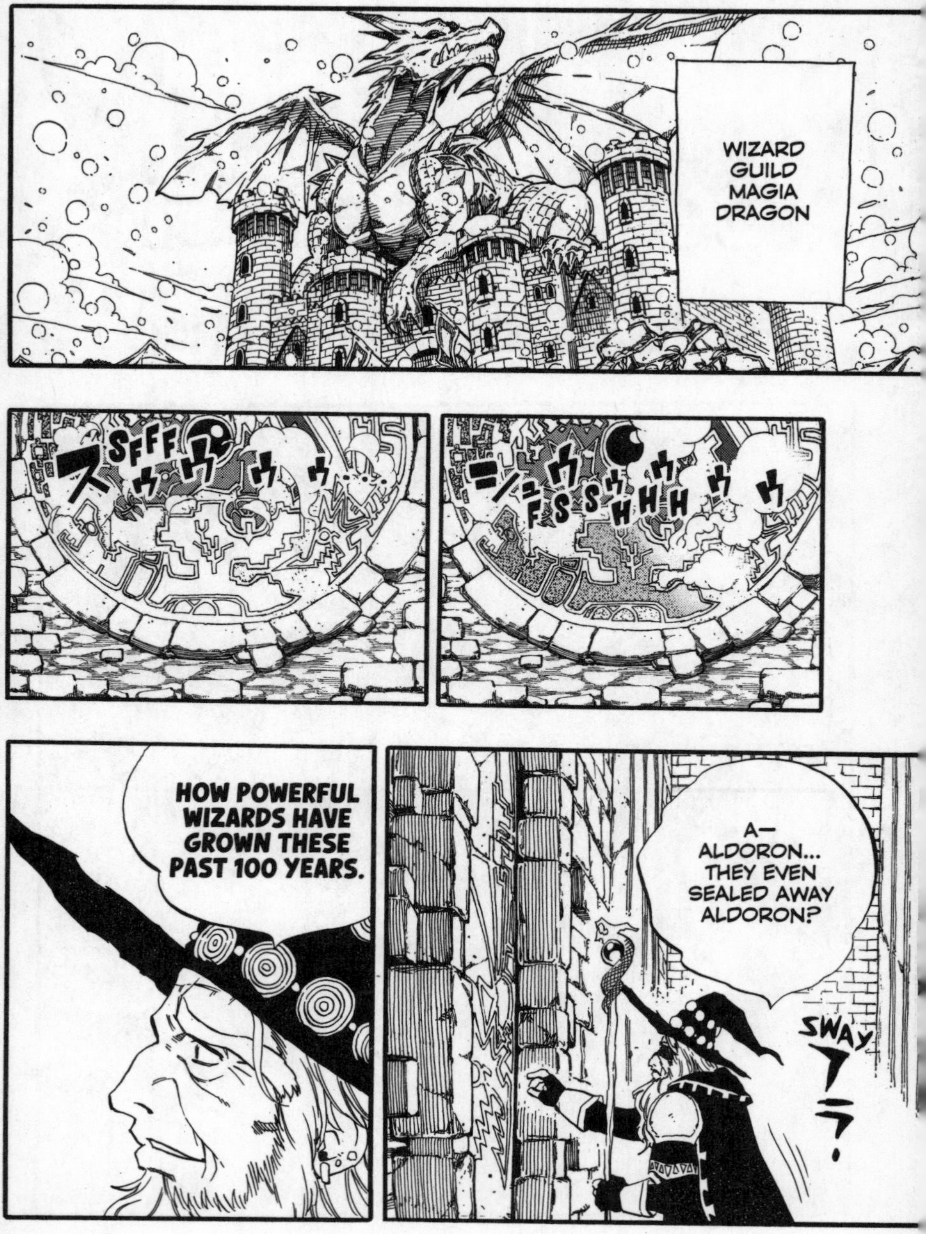
WIZARD GUILD MAGIA DRAGON
FSSHHH
SFFF
A— ALDORON... THEY EVEN SEALED AWAY ALDORON?
SWAY
HOW POWERFUL WIZARDS HAVE GROWN THESE PAST 100 YEARS.

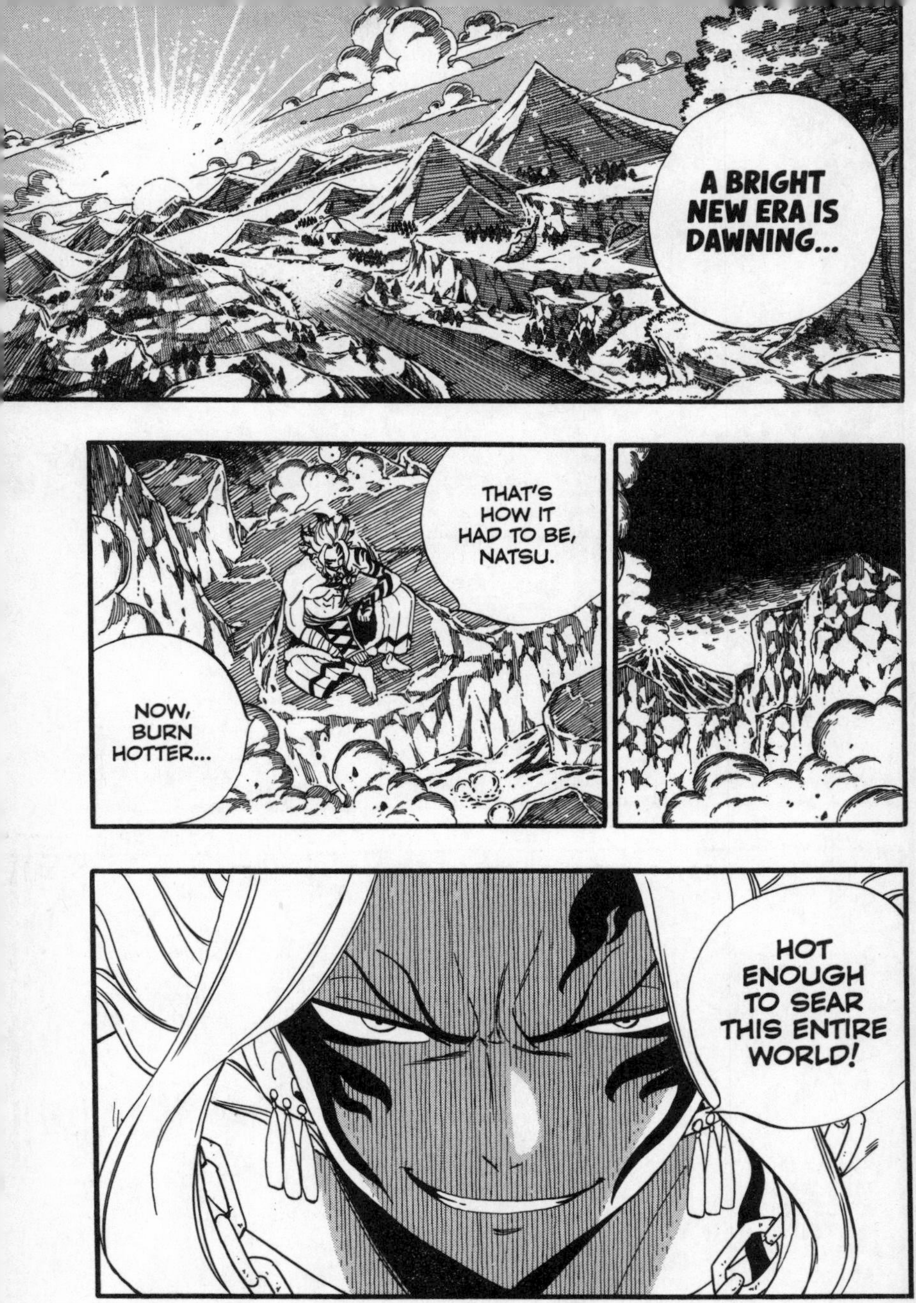
A BRIGHT NEW ERA IS DAWNING...
THAT'S HOW IT HAD TO BE, NATSU.
NOW, BURN HOTTER...
HOT ENOUGH TO SEAR THIS ENTIRE WORLD!

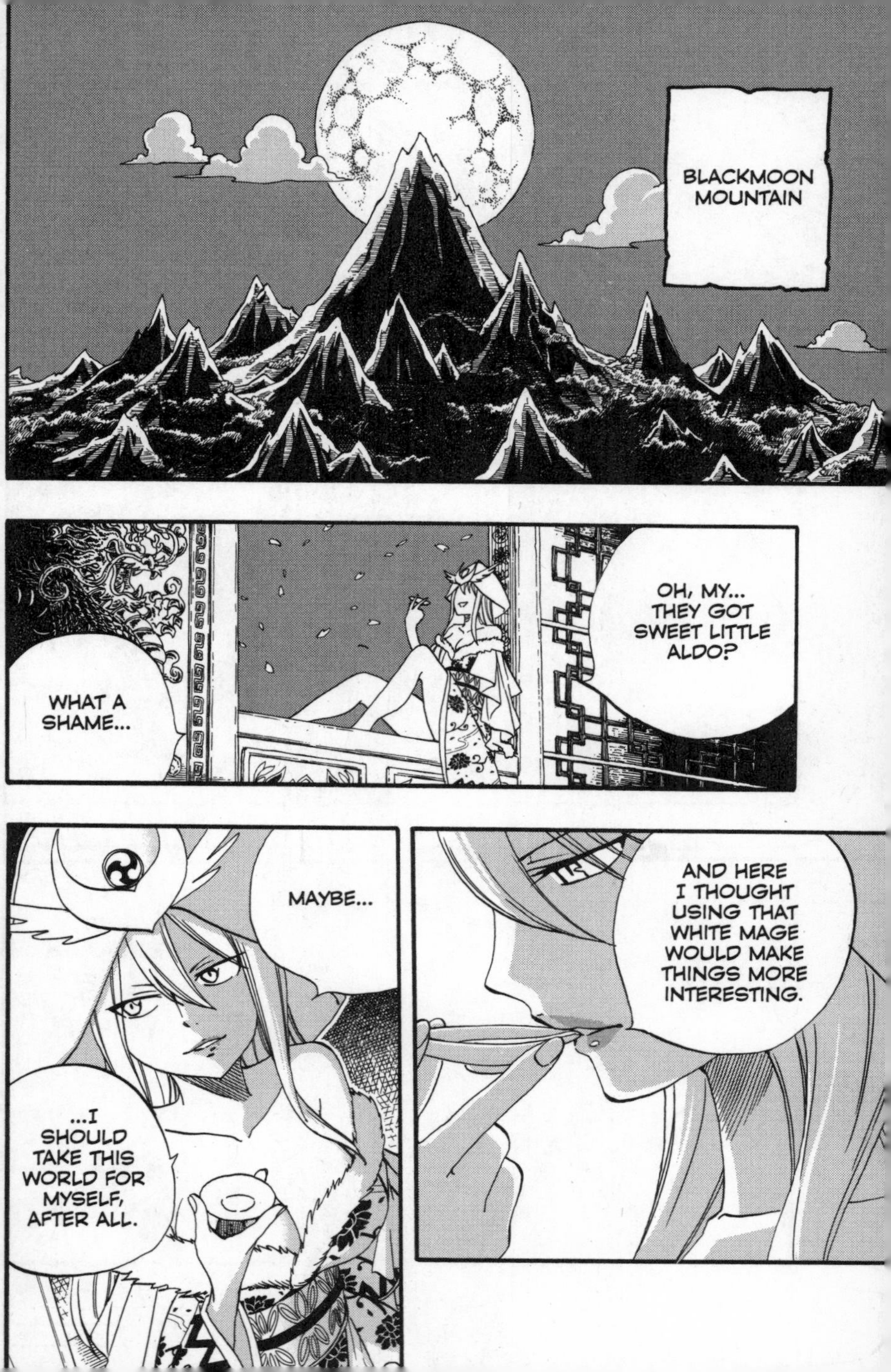
BLACKMOON MOUNTAIN
OH, MY... THEY GOT SWEET LITTLE ALDO?
WHAT A SHAME...
AND HERE I THOUGHT USING THAT WHITE MAGE WOULD MAKE THINGS MORE INTERESTING.
MAYBE...
...I SHOULD TAKE THIS WORLD FOR MYSELF, AFTER ALL.

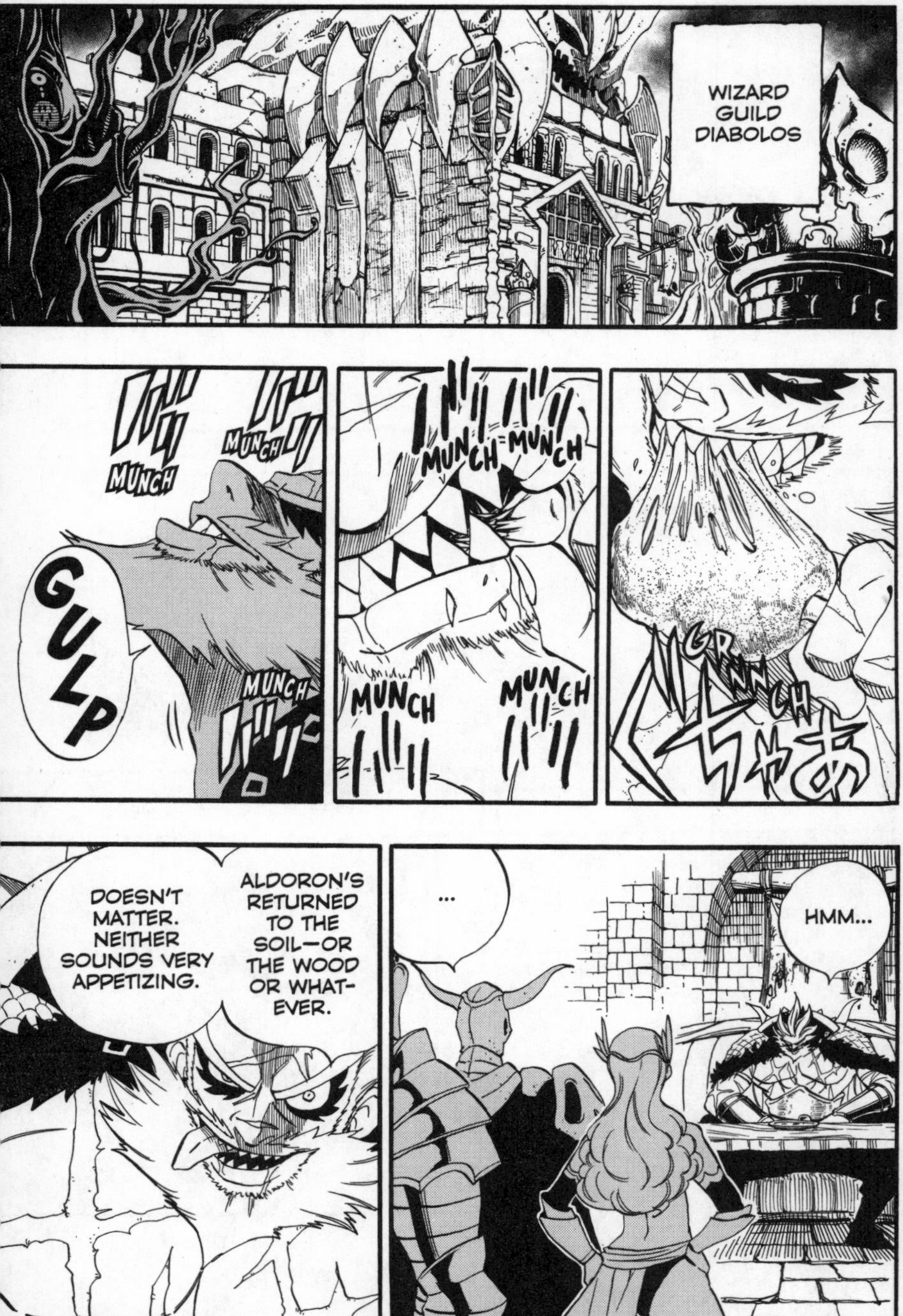
WIZARD GUILD DIABOLOS
GRNNCH
ちゃあ
MUNCH
MUNCH
MUNCH
MUNCH
MUNCH
MUNCH
GULP
MUNCH
HMM...
...
ALDORON'S RETURNED TO THE SOIL—OR THE WOOD OR WHATEVER.
DOESN'T MATTER. NEITHER SOUNDS VERY APPETIZING.

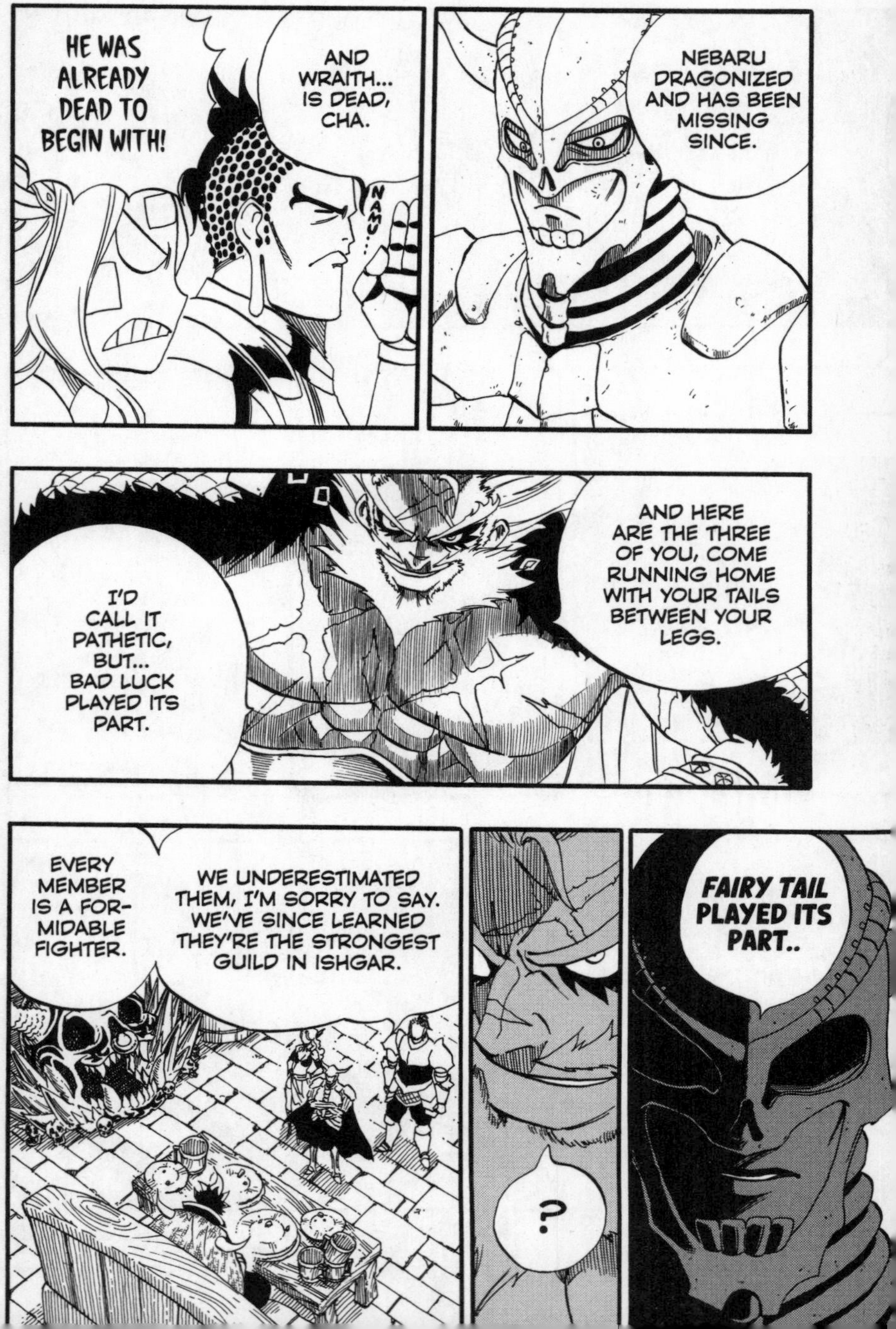
NEBARU DRAGONIZED AND HAS BEEN MISSING SINCE.
AND WRAITH... IS DEAD, CHA.
NAMU...
HE WAS ALREADY DEAD TO BEGIN WITH!
AND HERE ARE THE THREE OF YOU, COME RUNNING HOME WITH YOUR TAILS BETWEEN YOUR LEGS.
I'D CALL IT PATHETIC, BUT... BAD LUCK PLAYED ITS PART.
FAIRY TAIL PLAYED ITS PART..
?
WE UNDERESTIMATED THEM, I'M SORRY TO SAY. WE'VE SINCE LEARNED THEY'RE THE STRONGEST GUILD IN ISHGAR.
EVERY MEMBER IS A FOR-MIDABLE FIGHTER.

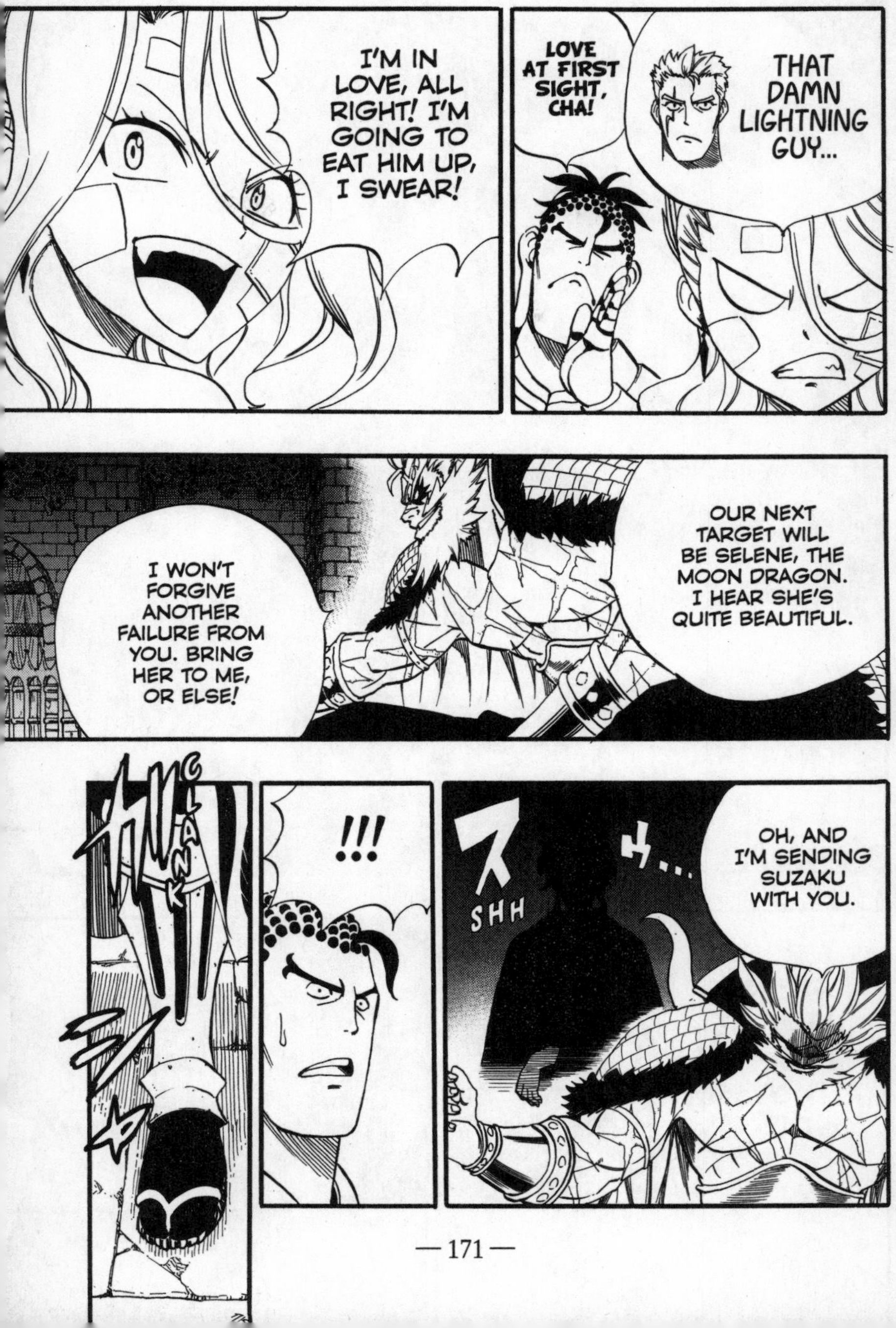
THAT DAMN LIGHTNING GUY...
LOVE AT FIRST SIGHT, CHA!
I'M IN LOVE, ALL RIGHT! I'M GOING TO EAT HIM UP, I SWEAR!
OUR NEXT TARGET WILL BE SELENE, THE MOON DRAGON. I HEAR SHE'S QUITE BEAUTIFUL.
I WON'T FORGIVE ANOTHER FAILURE FROM YOU. BRING HER TO ME, OR ELSE!
OH, AND I'M SENDING SUZAKU WITH YOU.
SHH
!!!
CLANK

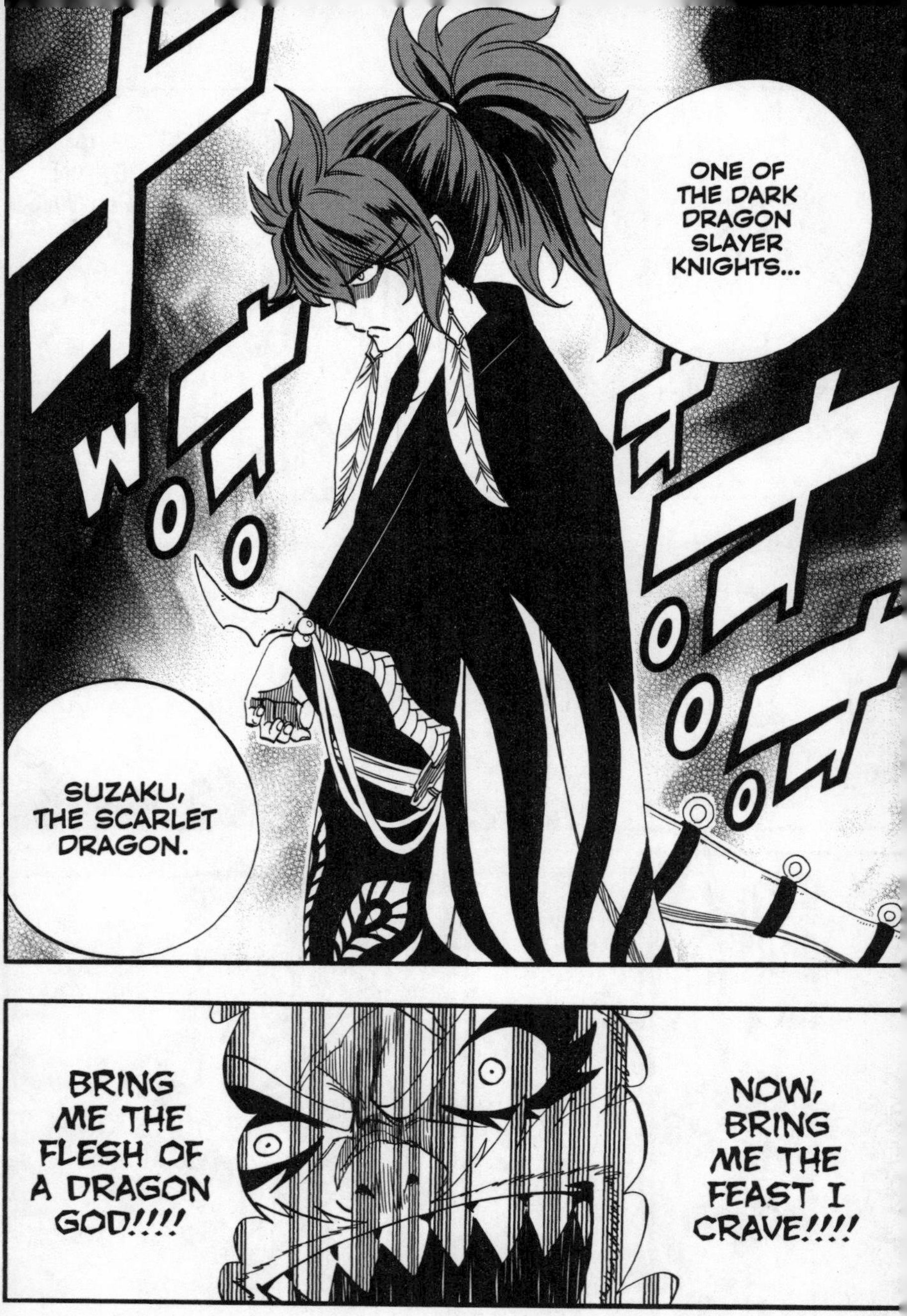
ONE OF THE DARK DRAGON SLAYER KNIGHTS...
OOO
WOO
SUZAKU, THE SCARLET DRAGON.
NOW, BRING ME THE FEAST I CRAVE!!!!
BRING ME THE FLESH OF A DRAGON GOD!!!!

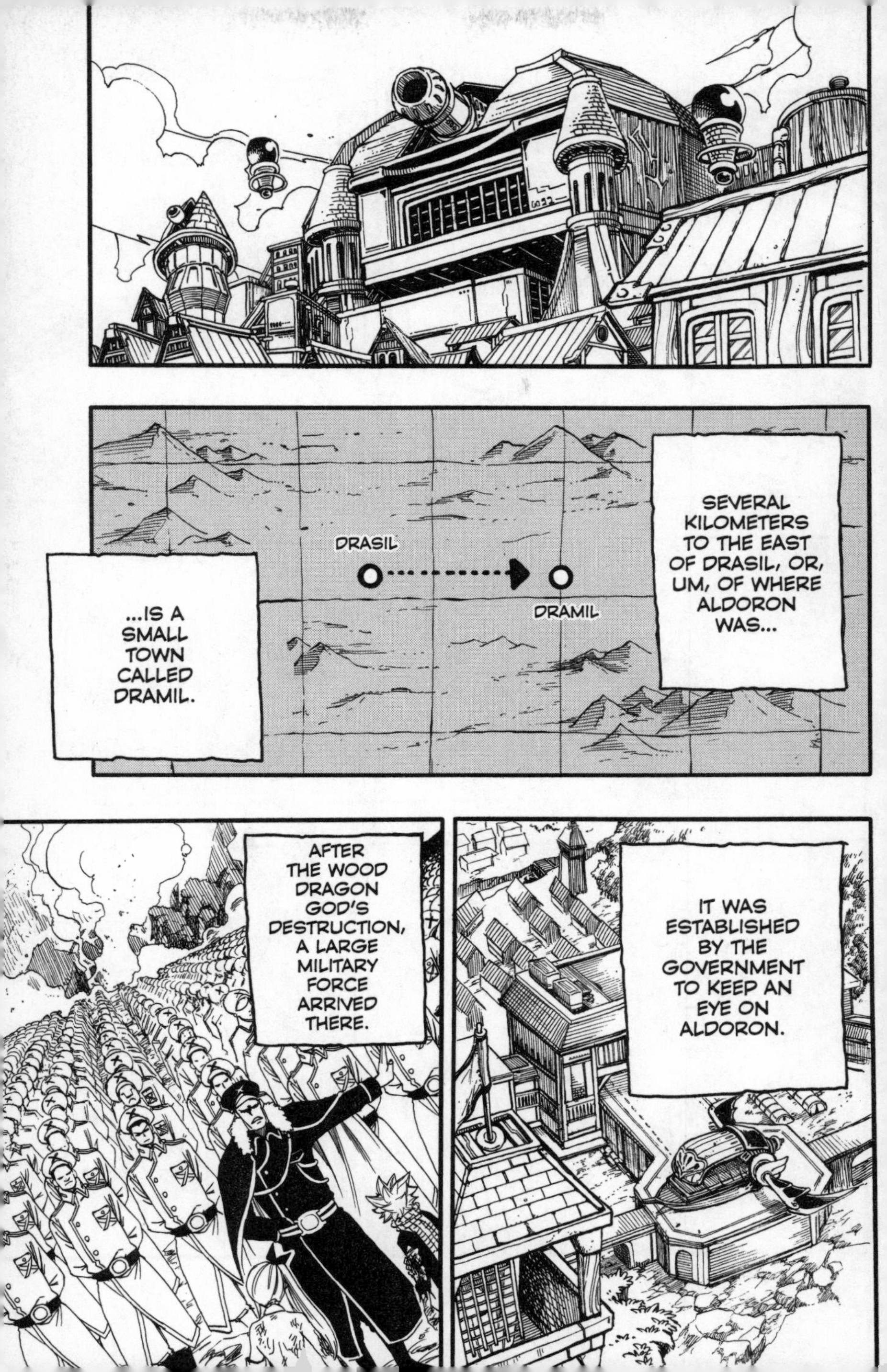
SEVERAL KILOMETERS TO THE EAST OF DRASIL, OR, UM, OF WHERE ALDORON WAS...
DRASIL
DRAMIL
...IS A SMALL TOWN CALLED DRAMIL.
IT WAS ESTABLISHED BY THE GOVERNMENT TO KEEP AN EYE ON ALDORON.
AFTER THE WOOD DRAGON GOD'S DESTRUCTION, A LARGE MILITARY FORCE ARRIVED THERE.

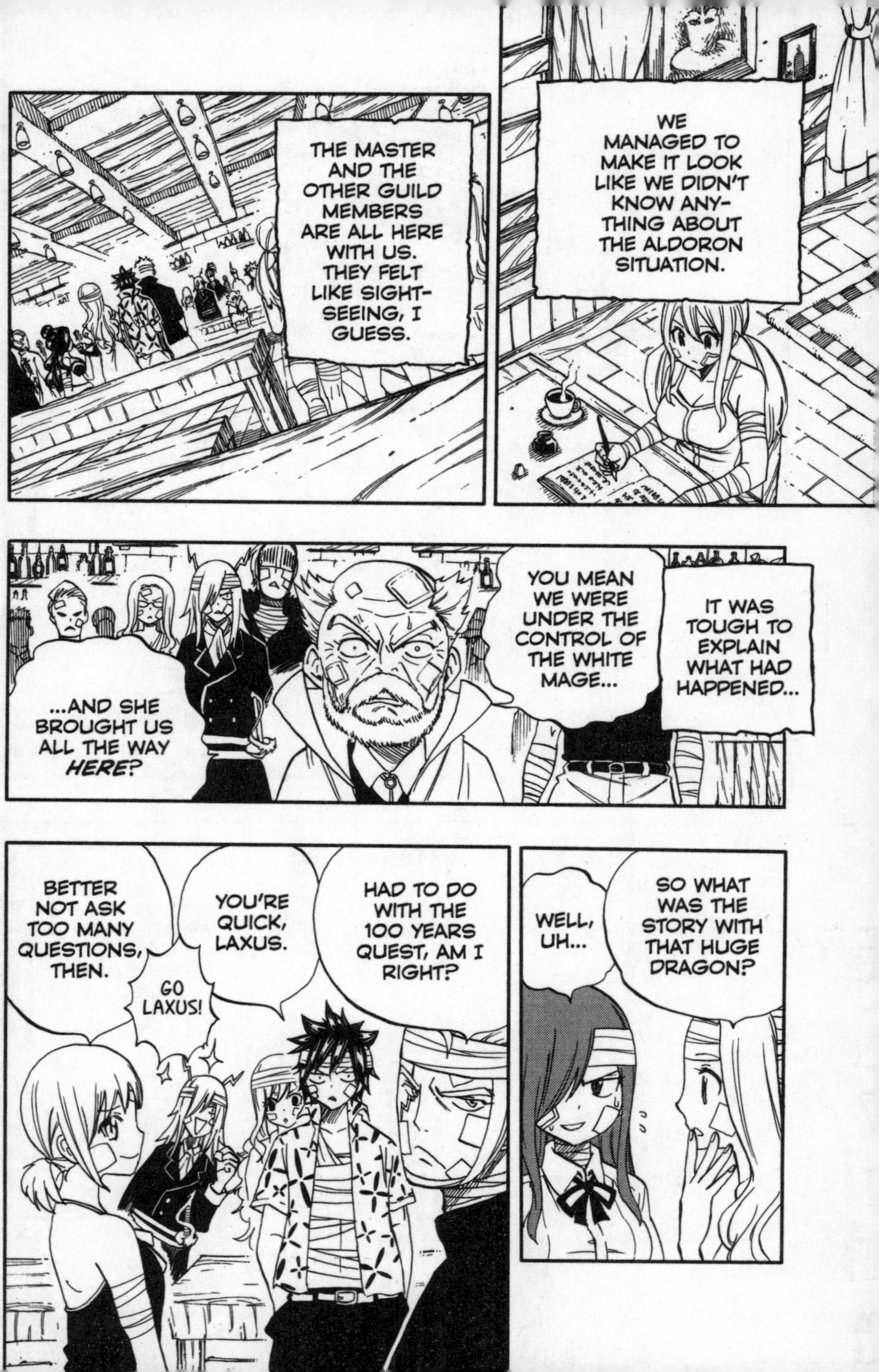
WE MANAGED TO MAKE IT LOOK LIKE WE DIDN'T KNOW ANY-THING ABOUT THE ALDORON SITUATION.
THE MASTER AND THE OTHER GUILD MEMBERS ARE ALL HERE WITH US. THEY FELT LIKE SIGHT-SEEING, I GUESS.
IT WAS TOUGH TO EXPLAIN WHAT HAD HAPPENED...
YOU MEAN WE WERE UNDER THE CONTROL OF THE WHITE MAGE...
...AND SHE BROUGHT US ALL THE WAY *HERE*?
SO WHAT WAS THE STORY WITH THAT HUGE DRAGON?
WELL, UH...
HAD TO DO WITH THE 100 YEARS QUEST, AM I RIGHT?
YOU'RE QUICK, LAXUS.
GO LAXUS!
BETTER NOT ASK TOO MANY QUESTIONS, THEN.

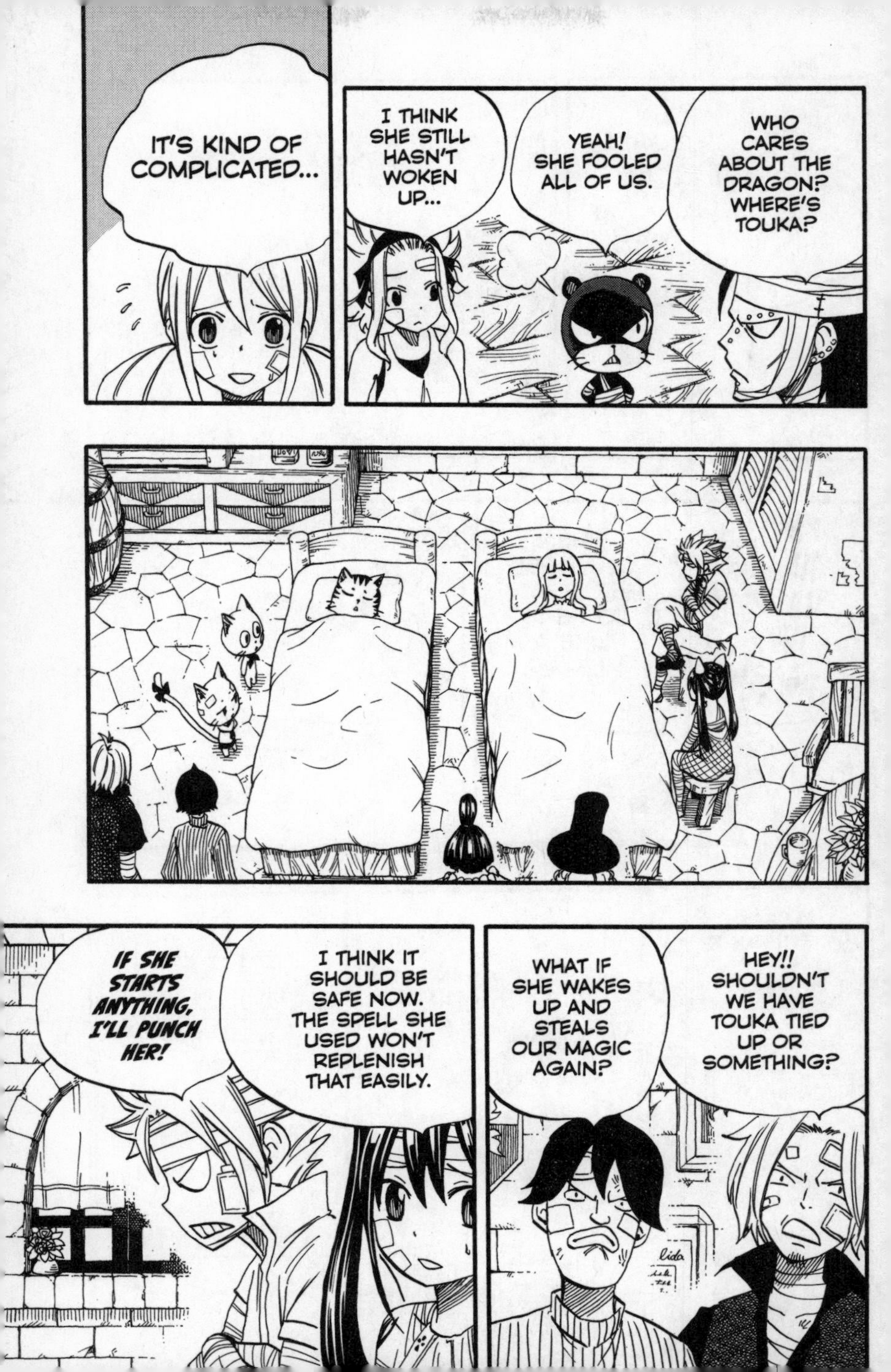
WHO CARES ABOUT THE DRAGON? WHERE'S TOUKA?
YEAH! SHE FOOLED ALL OF US.
I THINK SHE STILL HASN'T WOKEN UP...
IT'S KIND OF COMPLICATED...
HEY!! SHOULDN'T WE HAVE TOUKA TIED UP OR SOMETHING?
WHAT IF SHE WAKES UP AND STEALS OUR MAGIC AGAIN?
I THINK IT SHOULD BE SAFE NOW. THE SPELL SHE USED WON'T REPLENISH THAT EASILY.
IF SHE STARTS ANYTHING, I'LL PUNCH HER!

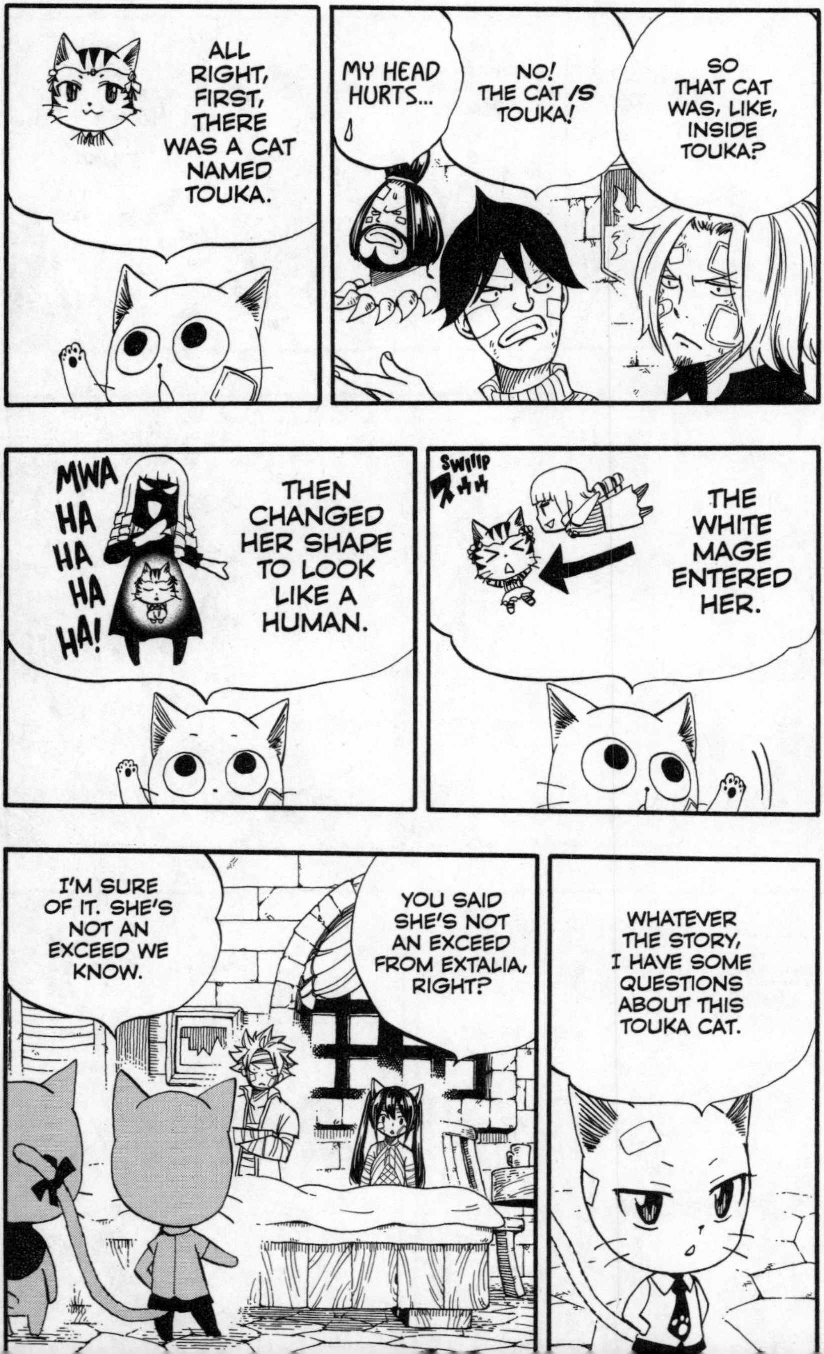
SO THAT CAT WAS, LIKE, INSIDE TOUKA?
NO! THE CAT IS TOUKA!
MY HEAD HURTS...
ALL RIGHT, FIRST, THERE WAS A CAT NAMED TOUKA.
Swllp
THE WHITE MAGE ENTERED HER.
MWA HA HA HA HA!
THEN CHANGED HER SHAPE TO LOOK LIKE A HUMAN.
WHATEVER THE STORY, I HAVE SOME QUESTIONS ABOUT THIS TOUKA CAT.
YOU SAID SHE'S NOT AN EXCEED FROM EXTALIA, RIGHT?
I'M SURE OF IT. SHE'S NOT AN EXCEED WE KNOW.

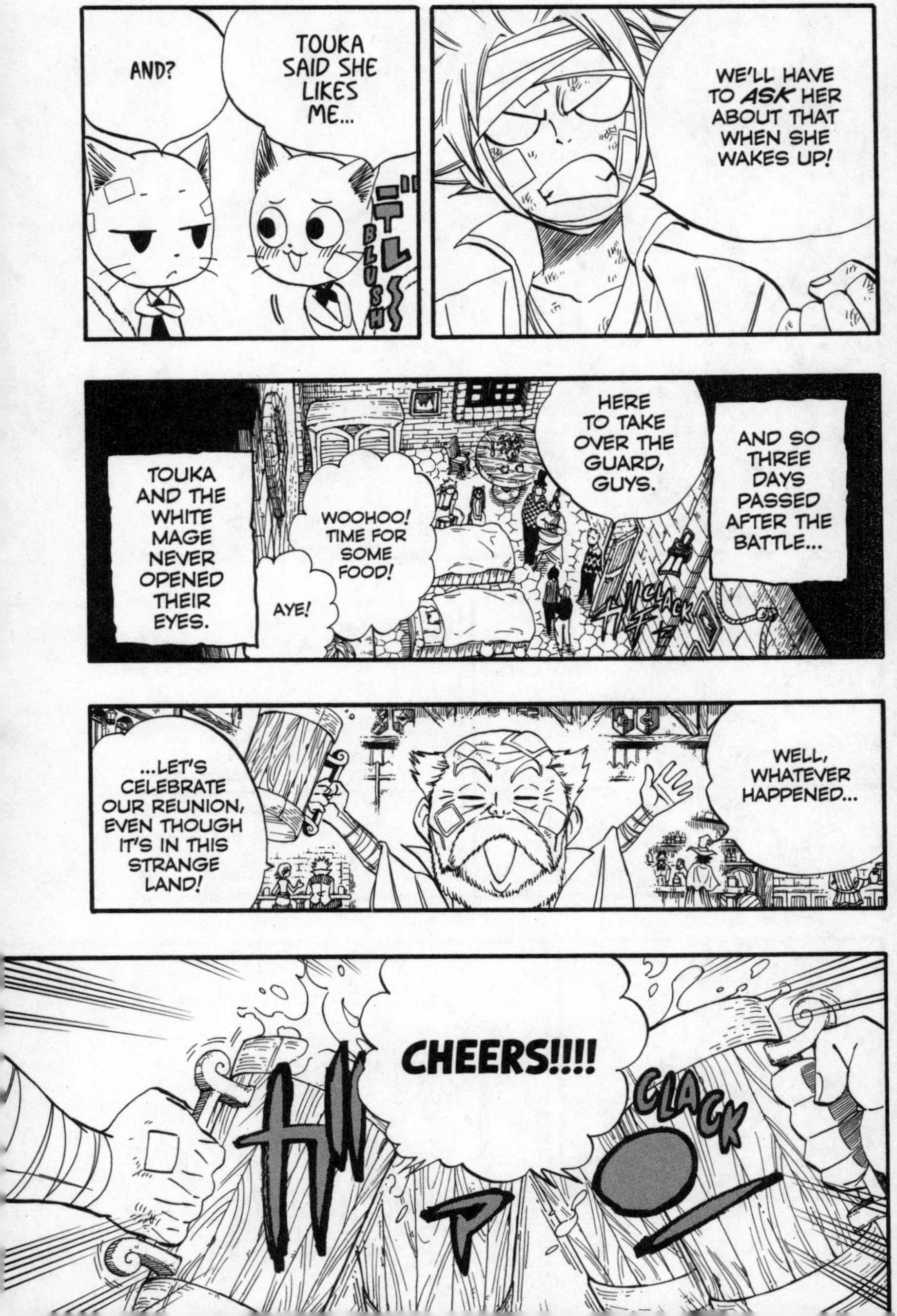
WE'LL HAVE TO ASK HER ABOUT THAT WHEN SHE WAKES UP!
TOUKA SAID SHE LIKES ME...
AND?
BLUSH
AND SO THREE DAYS PASSED AFTER THE BATTLE...
HERE TO TAKE OVER THE GUARD, GUYS.
CLACK
WOOHOO! TIME FOR SOME FOOD!
AYE!
TOUKA AND THE WHITE MAGE NEVER OPENED THEIR EYES.
WELL, WHATEVER HAPPENED...
...LET'S CELEBRATE OUR REUNION, EVEN THOUGH IT'S IN THIS STRANGE LAND!
CLACK
CHEERS!!!!

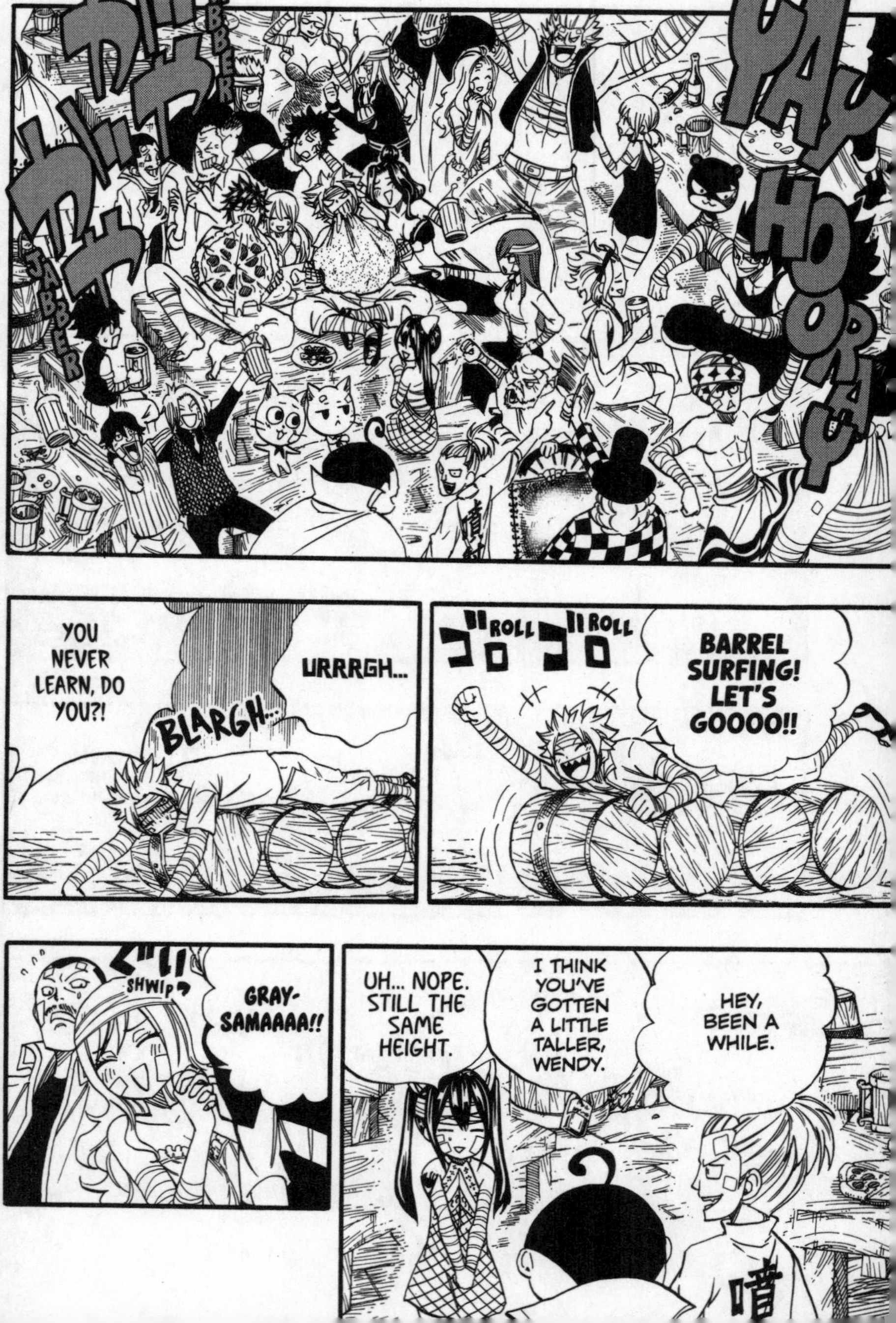
YAY, HOORAY
JABBER
JABBER
ROLL ROLL
BARREL SURFING! LET'S GOOOO!!
YOU NEVER LEARN, DO YOU?!
URRRGH...
BLARGH...
HEY, BEEN A WHILE.
I THINK YOU'VE GOTTEN A LITTLE TALLER, WENDY.
UH... NOPE. STILL THE SAME HEIGHT.
SHWIP
GRAY-SAMAAAA!!

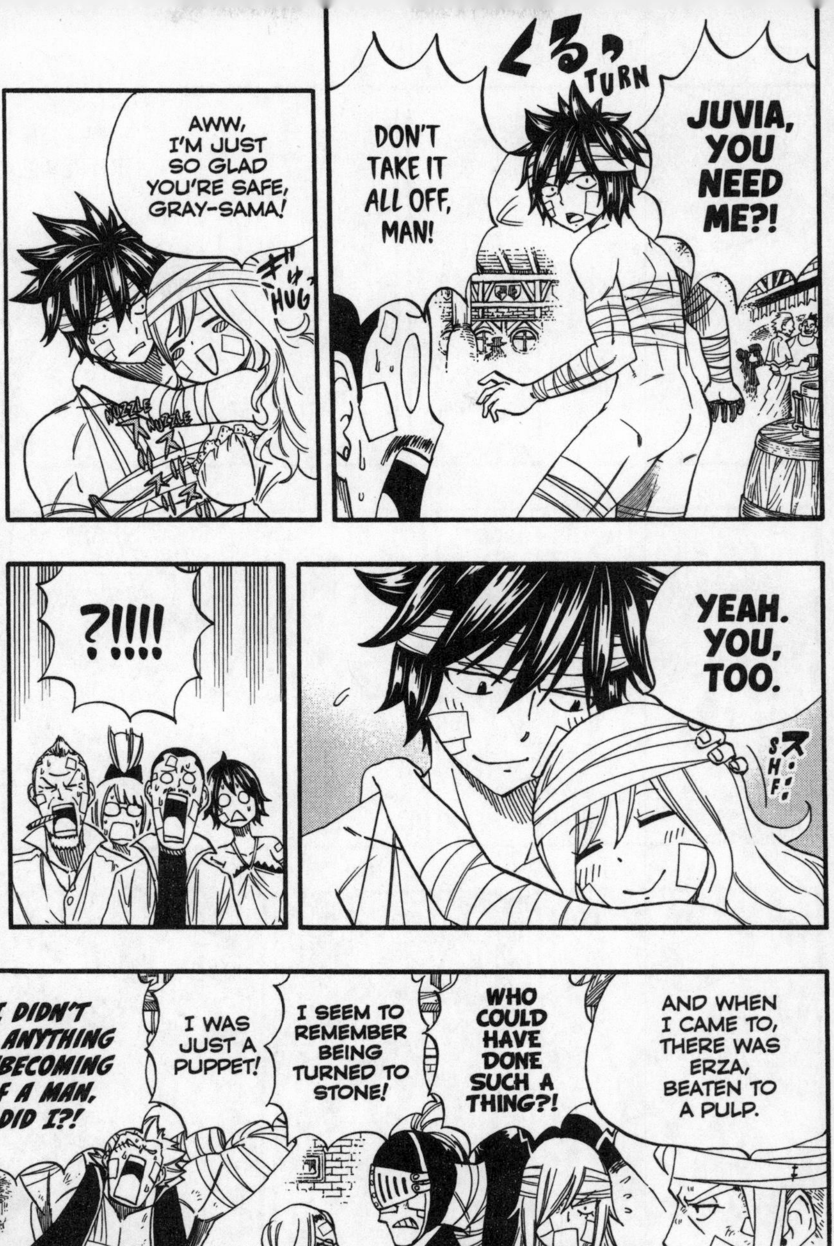

くるっ
TURN
JUVIA, YOU NEED ME?!
DON'T TAKE IT ALL OFF, MAN!
AWW, I'M JUST SO GLAD YOU'RE SAFE, GRAY-SAMA!
HUG
NUZZLE NUZZLE
YEAH. YOU, TOO.
SHF
?!!!!
AND WHEN I CAME TO, THERE WAS ERZA, BEATEN TO A PULP.
WHO COULD HAVE DONE SUCH A THING?!
I SEEM TO REMEMBER BEING TURNED TO STONE!
I WAS JUST A PUPPET!
I DIDN'T DO ANYTHING UNBECOMING OF A MAN, DID I?!

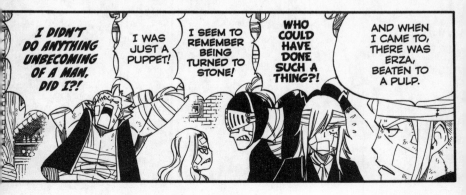

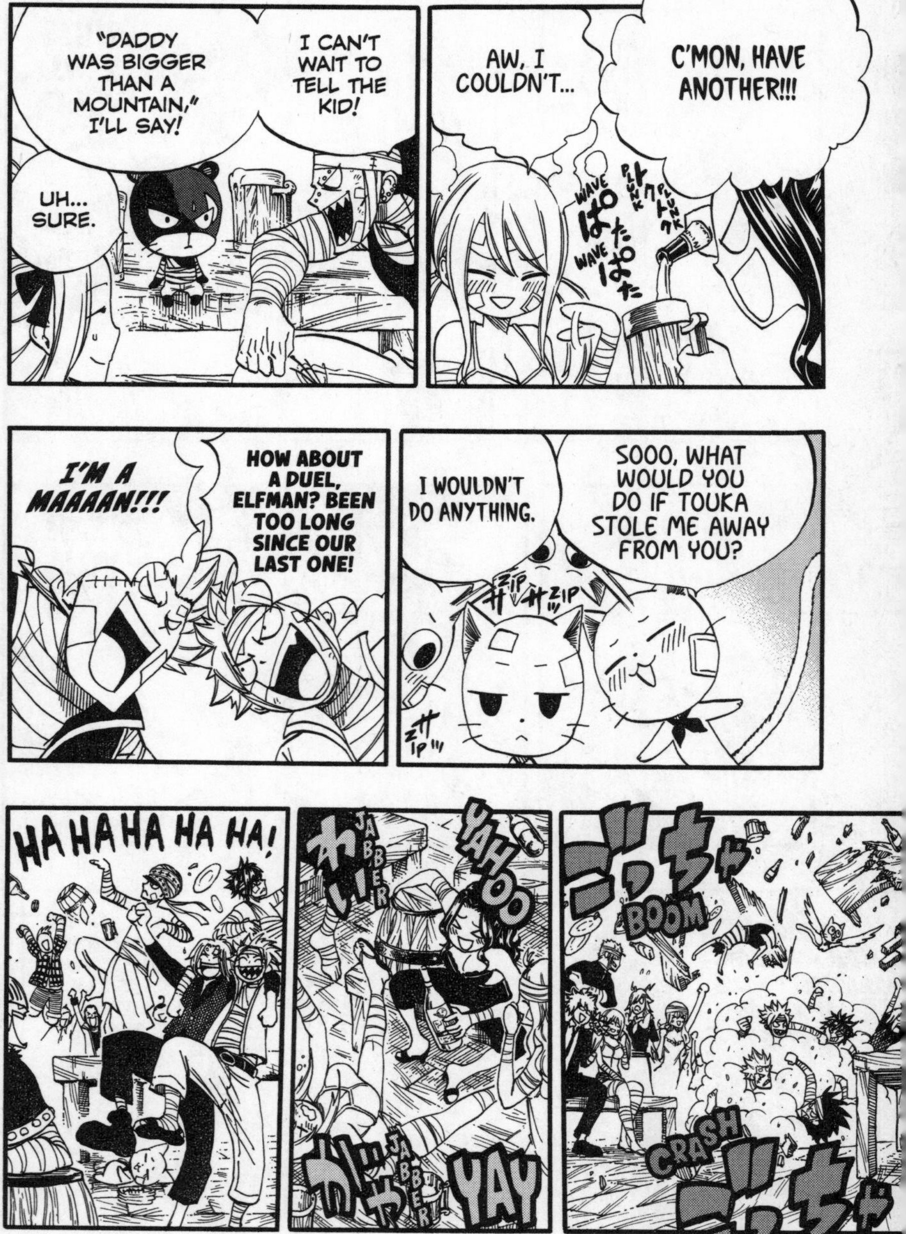
C'MON, HAVE ANOTHER!!!
AW, I COULDN'T...
PLUNK PLUNK
WAVE WAVE
ぱたぱた
I CAN'T WAIT TO TELL THE KID!
"DADDY WAS BIGGER THAN A MOUNTAIN," I'LL SAY!
UH... SURE.
SOOO, WHAT WOULD YOU DO IF TOUKA STOLE ME AWAY FROM YOU?
I WOULDN'T DO ANYTHING.
ZIP ZIP ZIP
HOW ABOUT A DUEL, ELFMAN? BEEN TOO LONG SINCE OUR LAST ONE!
I'M A MAAAAN!!!
ごっちゃ
BOOM
CRASH
ごっちゃ
YAHOO
JABBER
JABBER
YAY
HA HA HA HA HA HA!

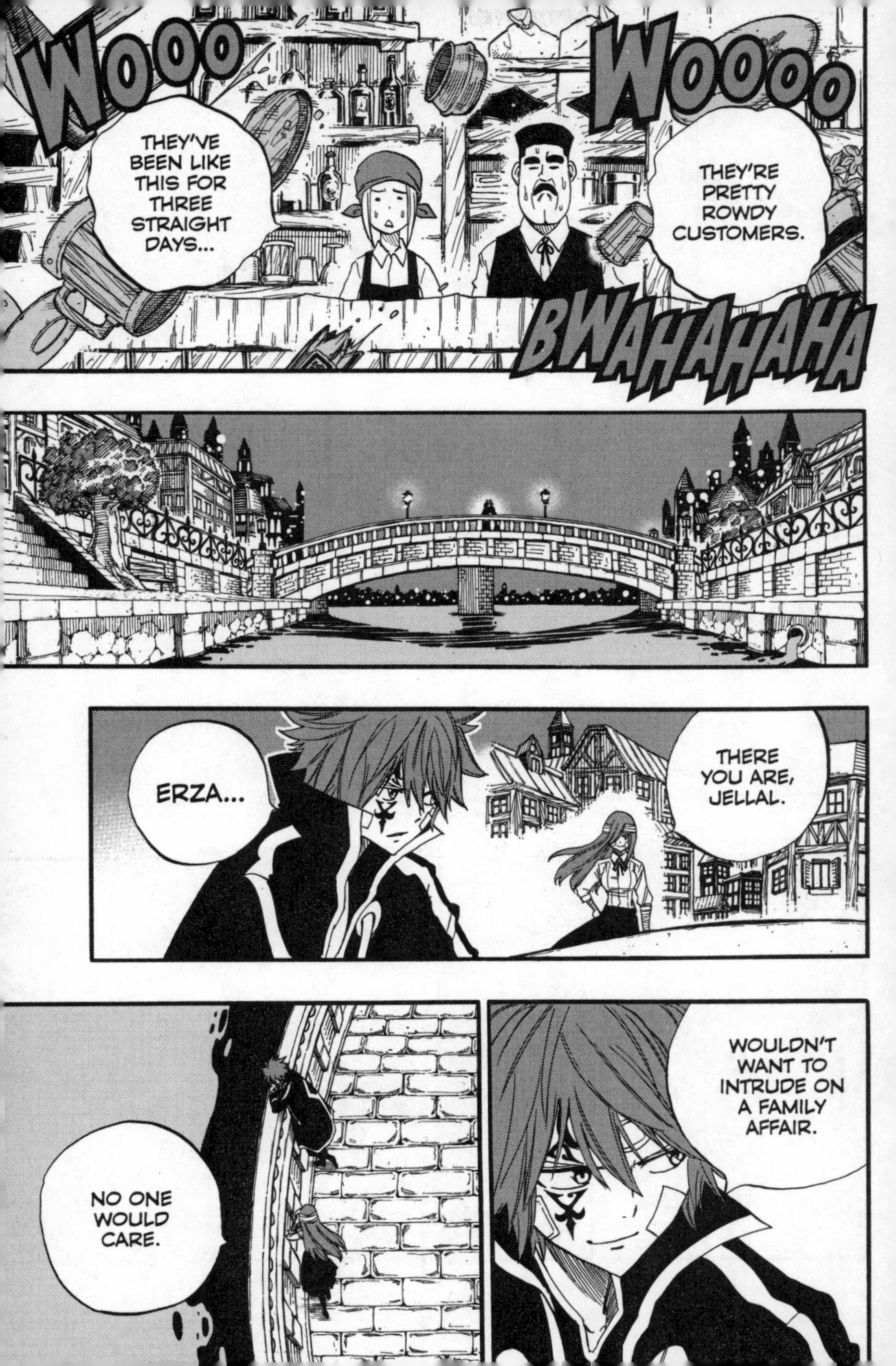
WOOOO
THEY'RE PRETTY ROWDY CUSTOMERS.
WOOO
THEY'VE BEEN LIKE THIS FOR THREE STRAIGHT DAYS...
BWAHAHAHA
THERE YOU ARE, JELLAL.
ERZA...
WOULDN'T WANT TO INTRUDE ON A FAMILY AFFAIR.
NO ONE WOULD CARE.

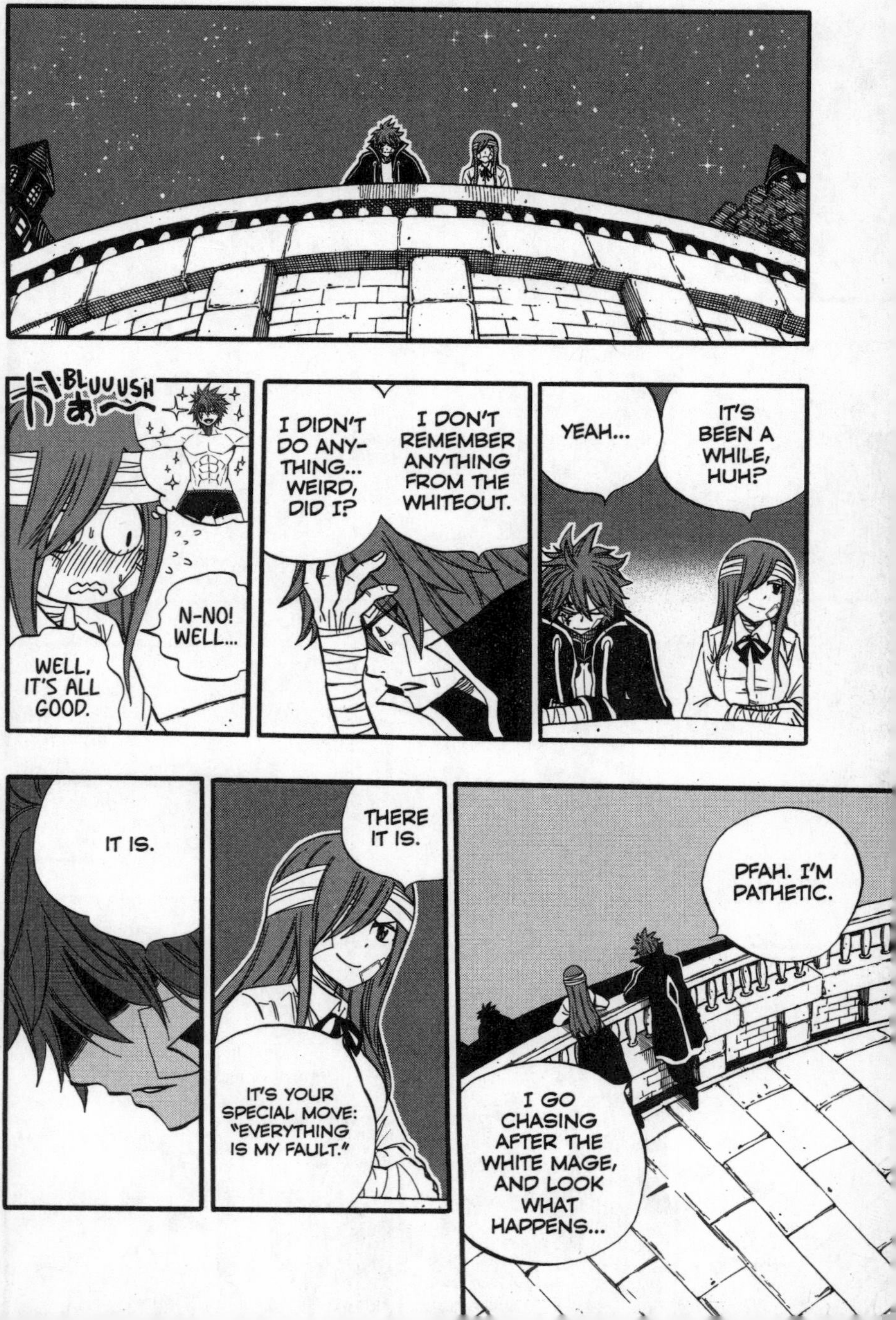
IT'S BEEN A WHILE, HUH?
YEAH...
I DON'T REMEMBER ANYTHING FROM THE WHITEOUT.
I DIDN'T DO ANY-THING... WEIRD, DID I?
BLUUUSH
N-NO! WELL...
WELL, IT'S ALL GOOD.
PFAH. I'M PATHETIC.
I GO CHASING AFTER THE WHITE MAGE, AND LOOK WHAT HAPPENS...
THERE IT IS.
IT'S YOUR SPECIAL MOVE: "EVERYTHING IS MY FAULT."
IT IS.

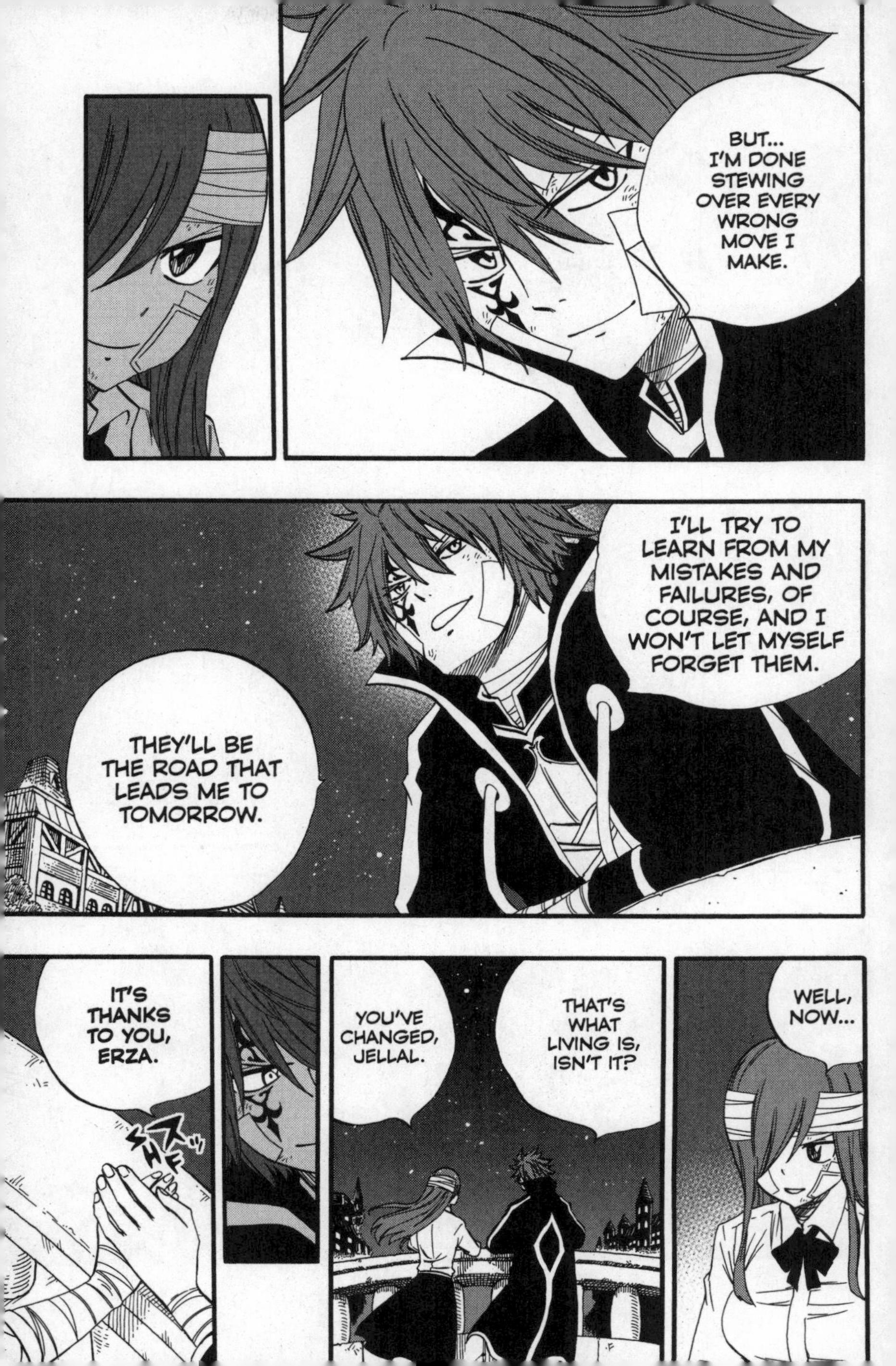
BUT... I'M DONE STEWING OVER EVERY WRONG MOVE I MAKE.
I'LL TRY TO LEARN FROM MY MISTAKES AND FAILURES, OF COURSE, AND I WON'T LET MYSELF FORGET THEM.
THEY'LL BE THE ROAD THAT LEADS ME TO TOMORROW.
WELL, NOW...
THAT'S WHAT LIVING IS, ISN'T IT?
YOU'VE CHANGED, JELLAL.
IT'S THANKS TO YOU, ERZA.
SHF

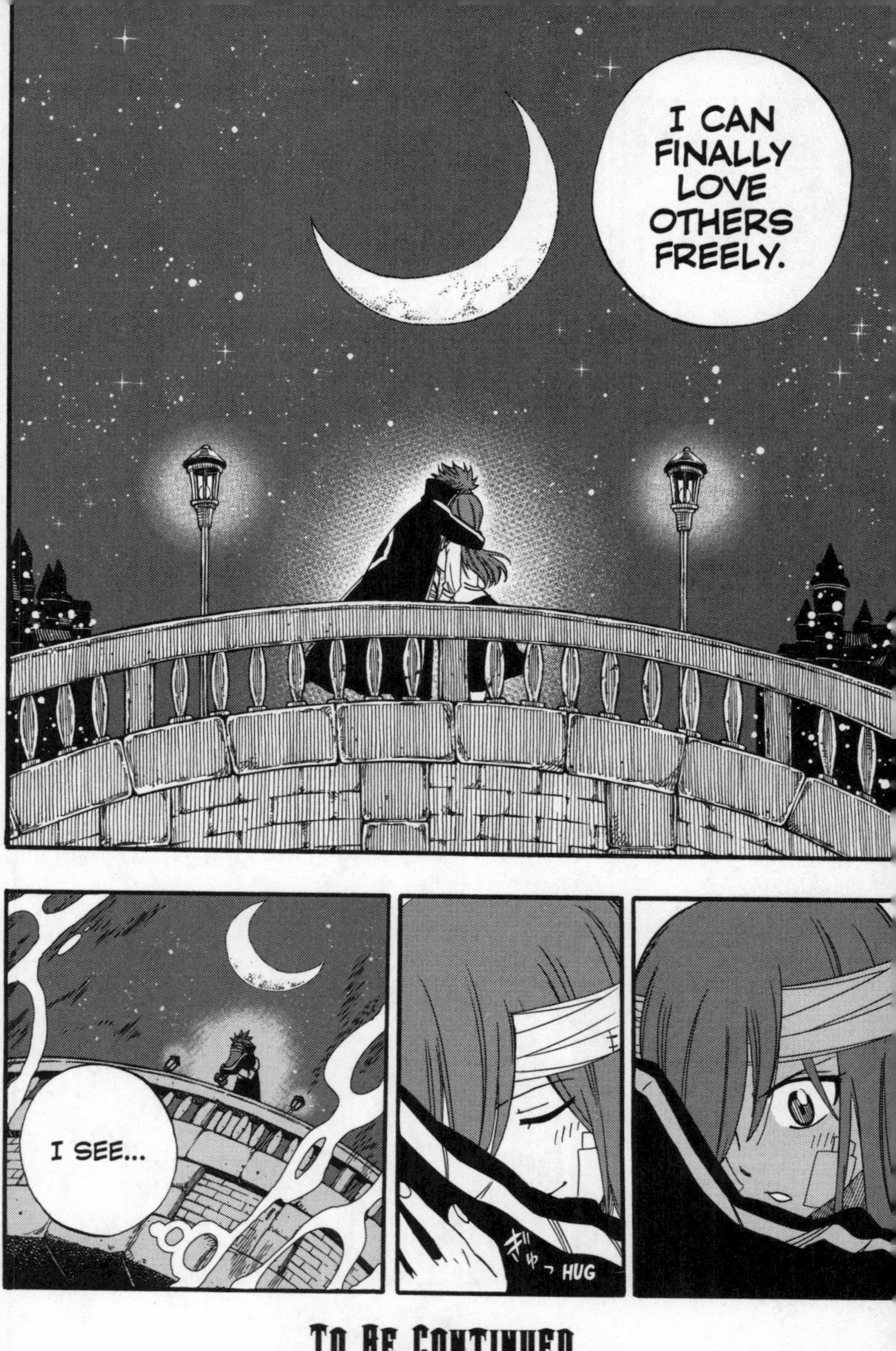
I CAN FINALLY LOVE OTHERS FREELY.
ぎゅっ HUG
I SEE...

TO BE CONTINUED

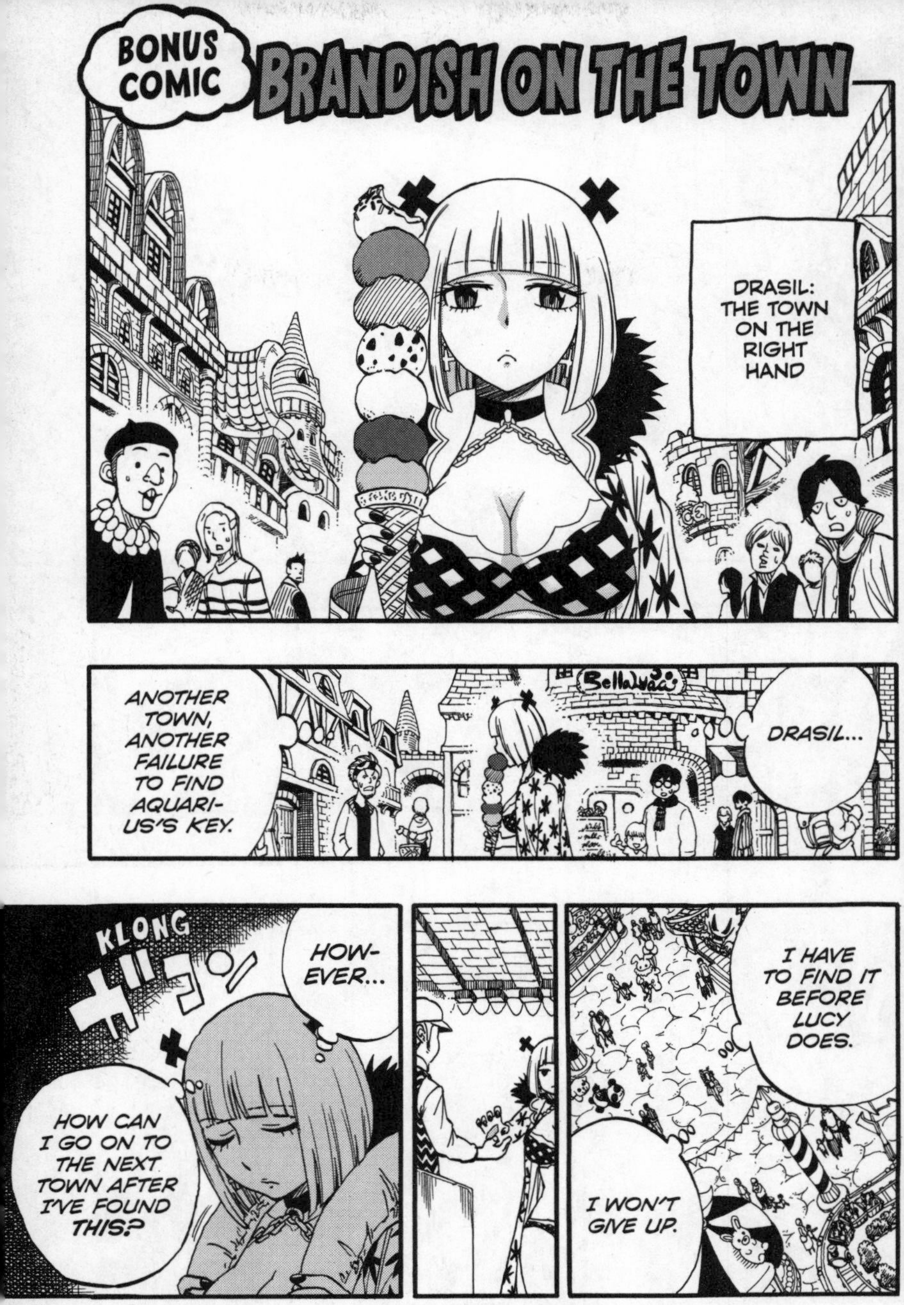
BONUS COMIC
BRANDISH ON THE TOWN
DRASIL: THE TOWN ON THE RIGHT HAND
DRASIL...
ANOTHER TOWN, ANOTHER FAILURE TO FIND AQUARI-US'S KEY.
I HAVE TO FIND IT BEFORE LUCY DOES.
I WON'T GIVE UP.
HOW-EVER...
KLONG
HOW CAN I GO ON TO THE NEXT TOWN AFTER I'VE FOUND THIS?

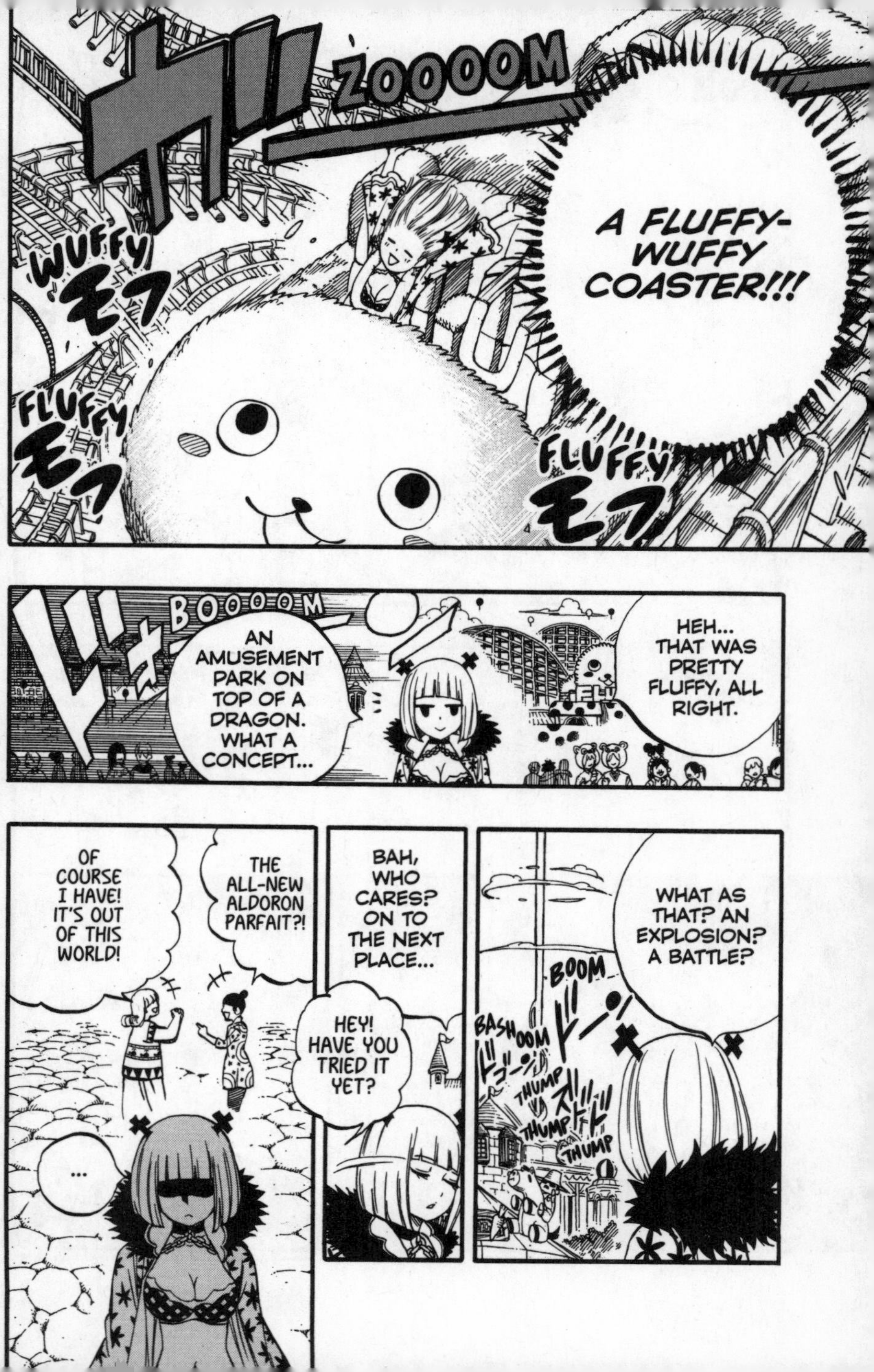
ZOOOOM
A FLUFFY-WUFFY COASTER!!!
WUFFY
FLUFFY
FLUFFY
HEH... THAT WAS PRETTY FLUFFY, ALL RIGHT.
BOOOOOM
AN AMUSEMENT PARK ON TOP OF A DRAGON. WHAT A CONCEPT...
WHAT AS THAT? AN EXPLOSION? A BATTLE?
BOOM
BASHOOM
THUMP
THUMP
THUMP
BAH, WHO CARES? ON TO THE NEXT PLACE...
HEY! HAVE YOU TRIED IT YET?
THE ALL-NEW ALDORON PARFAIT?!
OF COURSE I HAVE! IT'S OUT OF THIS WORLD!
...

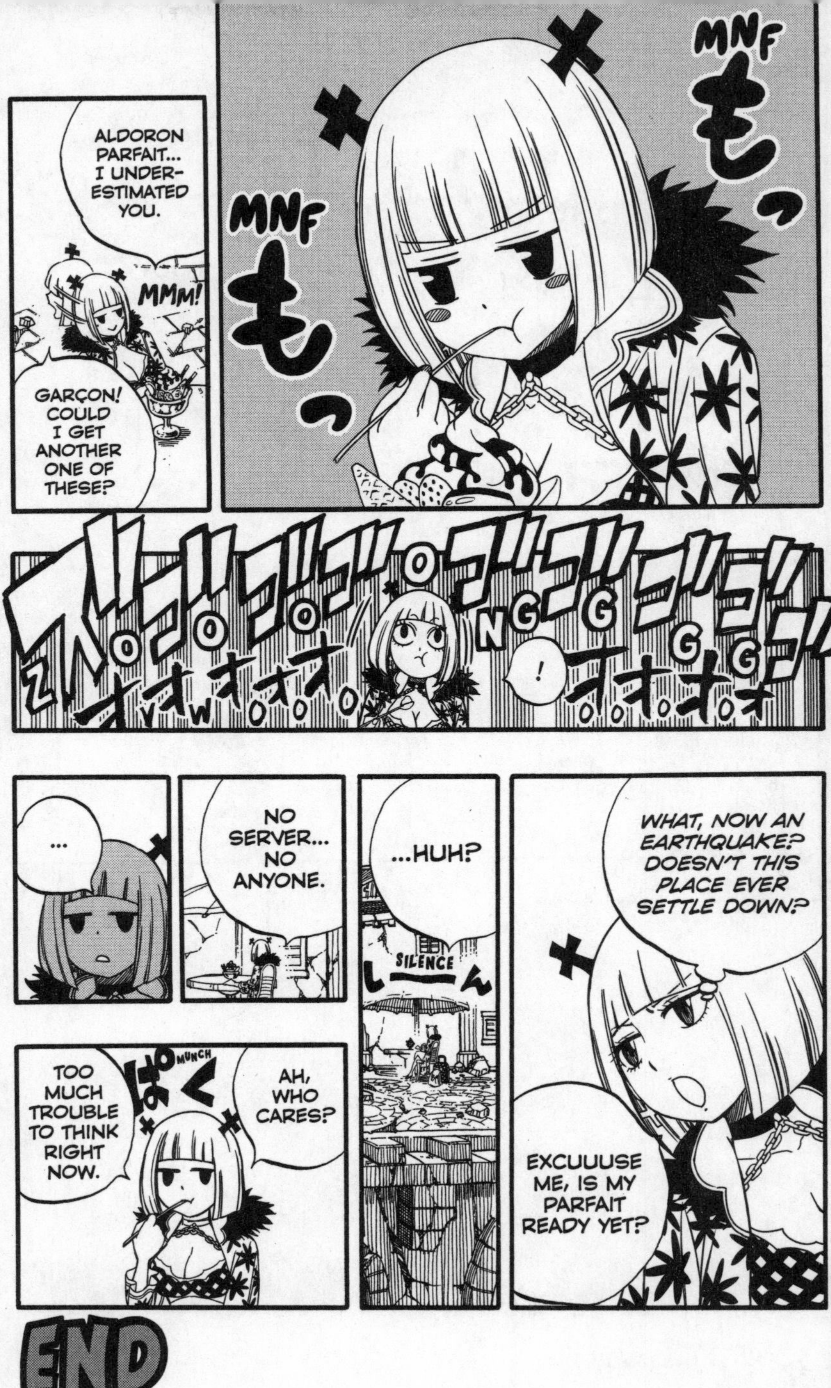
MNF
MNF
ALDORON PARFAIT... I UNDER-ESTIMATED YOU.
MMM!
GARÇON! COULD I GET ANOTHER ONE OF THESE?
!
WHAT, NOW AN EARTHQUAKE? DOESN'T THIS PLACE EVER SETTLE DOWN?
EXCUUUSE ME, IS MY PARFAIT READY YET?
...HUH?
SILENCE
NO SERVER... NO ANYONE.
...
AH, WHO CARES?
MUNCH
TOO MUCH TROUBLE TO THINK RIGHT NOW.
END

DE ART RETURNS

(IBARAKI PREFECTURE KAE SHIBATA)

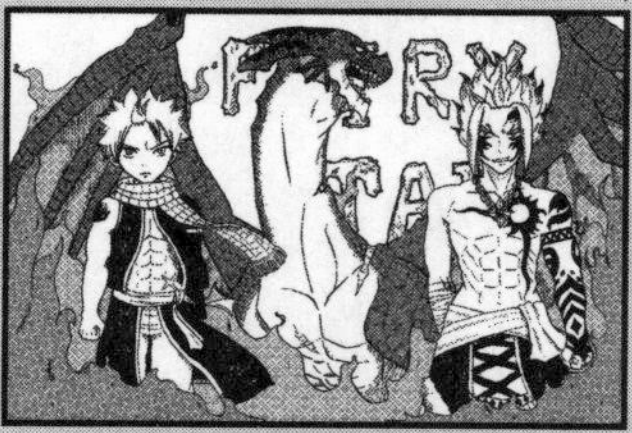

▲ SO COOL! GREAT WORK! WHEN WILL THEY FINALLY FACE EACH OTHER?!

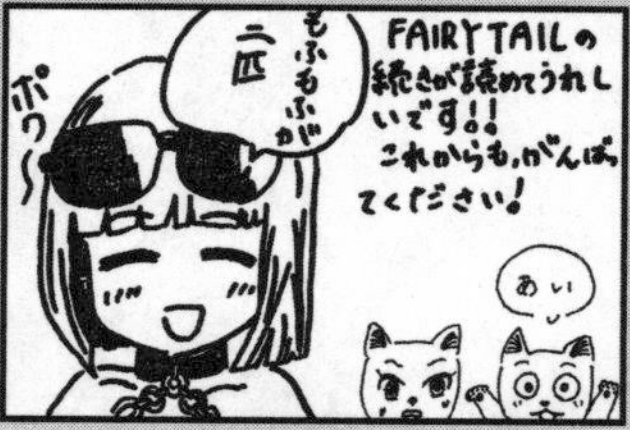

もふもふが二匹
ポワ~
FAIRYTAILの続きが読めてうれしいです!! これからも、がんばってください!
あい

▲ GREAT EXPRESSION! I'LL KEEP GIVING IT ALL I'VE GOT!

(HYOGO PREFECTURE WAFFLE)

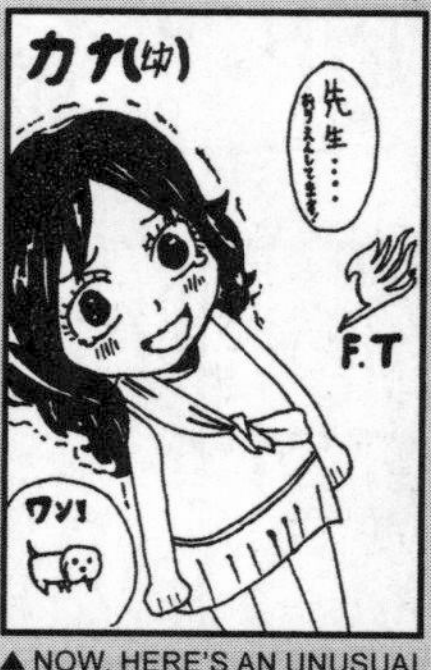

カナ(幼)
F.T
ワン!

▲ NOW, HERE'S AN UNUSUAL TAKE! HARD TO REMEMBER KANA MUST'VE LOOKED LIKE THIS ONCE... (GRIN)

(HOKKAIDO PREFECTURE ROUA)

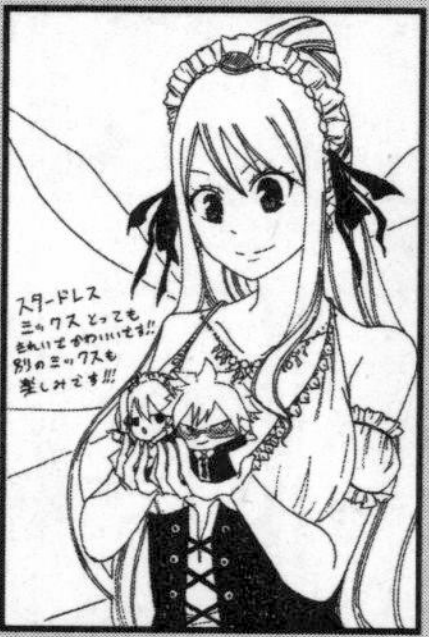

スタードレスミックスとってもきれいでかわいいです!! 別のミックスも楽しみです!

▲ TERRIFIC! THE DETAIL ON THE STAR DRESS LOOKS GREAT!

(GIFU PREFECTURE MISAKI KAMURA)

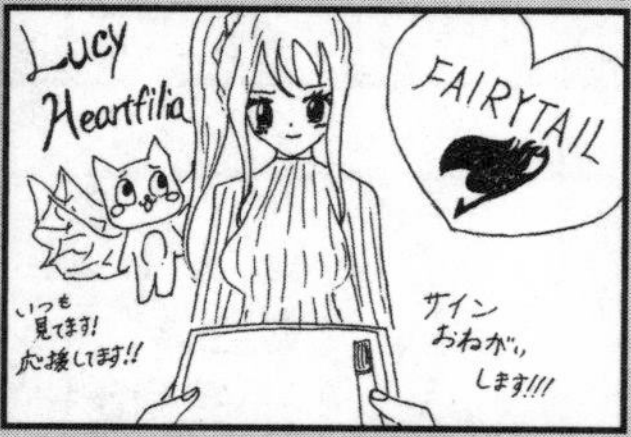

Lucy Heartfilia
FAIRYTAIL
いつも見てます! 応援してます!!
サインおねがいします!!!

▲ YOU CAN JUST SEE HAPPY GOING, "I'M BLUSHIN', HERE!"

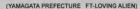

FAIRY TAIL 100 YEARS QUEST GUILD

(YAMAGATA PREFECTURE FT-LOVING ALIEN)

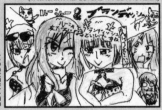

▼ I CAN FEEL THE LOVE! THINK THEY CAN EVER BE FRIENDS??

(MIYAGI PREFECTURE KOUROU KAZEHA)

With My Partner!

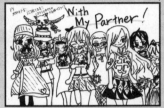

▲ THANKS FOR DRAWING SO MANY CHARACTERS!

(FUKUSHIMA PREFECTURE HIROSHI YAMAZAKI)

I love FAIRY TAIL

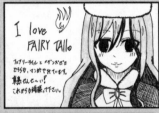

▼ I CAN FEEL JUVIA WATCHING OVER ME. THAT FIRES ME UP!

(IBARAKI PREFECTURE AMINO PROPANE-GAS)

ルーシー ハート・フィリア
(LUCY HEART FIRIA)
ハッピー
(HAPPY)

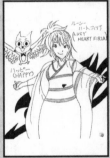

▲ OOH, A NEW DRESS FOR LUCY? I LIKE THE JAPANESE FLAVOR!

FAIL CORNER • • • • • • • • • • • • • • •

(TOKUSHIMA PREFECTURE TOSHIHIRO MIKI)

モスコイテイルで
スモス
ゴッワス

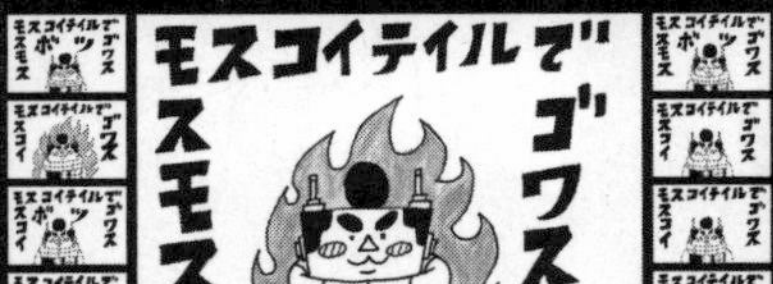

▲ I WAS LIKE, "HOW MANY OF THESE DID THEY SEND?!" I'M GOING TO BE SEEING THIS IN MY DREAMS! (LOL)

HERE'S OUR FOURTH BATCH OF FAN DRAWINGS! ENJOY!

EDITOR'S NOTE: DRAWING SUBMISSIONS LIMITED TO JAPAN.

TRANSLATION NOTES

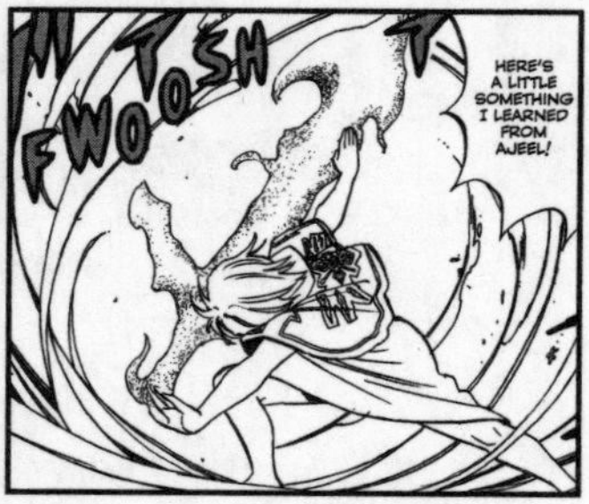
FWOOSH
HERE'S A LITTLE SOMETHING I LEARNED FROM AJEEL!

A Little Something I Learned From Ajeel, page 9

In the Japanese, Max describes his move as *"Ajeel jikiden." Jikiden* means "direct transmission" and often refers to a teacher's most profound or central teachings, which are conveyed directly from the teacher to their chosen successor. Strictly speaking, the Japanese is a noun phrase, but as it isn't the proper name of a technique, we decided it was best to translate as an entire sentence.

Namu, page 170

Namu comes from *namu amida butsu* ("In the name of the Buddha Amida") and is the standard funerary invocation in Japan. Madmole has a very Buddhist appearance (notice, for example, his extremely long earlobes, a sign of wisdom in much East Asian iconography and often associated with the Buddha), so we decided to retain the Japanese expression, rather than translating it as something like "rest in peace."

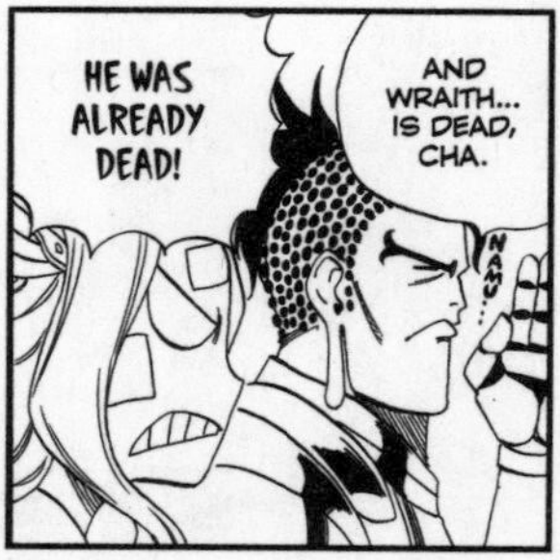
AND WRAITH... IS DEAD, CHA.
NAMU...
HE WAS ALREADY DEAD!

FAIRY TAIL
100 YEARS QUEST

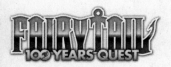

A Kodansha Comics Trade Paperback Original
FAIRY TAIL: 100 Years Quest 7 copyright © 2020 Hiro Mashima/Atsuo Ueda
English translation copyright © 2021 Hiro Mashima/Atsuo Ueda

Published in the United States by Kodansha Comics, an imprint of
Kodansha USA Publishing, LLC, New York.

Publication rights for this English edition arranged through
Kodansha Ltd., Tokyo.

First published in Japan in 2020 by Kodansha Ltd., Tokyo.

ISBN 978-1-64651-152-5

Original cover design by Hisao Ogawa (Blue in Green)

Printed in the United States of America.

www.kodanshacomics.com

9 8 7 6 5 4 3 2 1
Translation: Kevin Steinbach
Lettering: Phil Christie
Editing: David Yoo
Kodansha Comics edition cover design by Phil Balsman

Publisher: Kiichiro Sugawara

Director of publishing services: Ben Applegate
Associate director of operations: Stephen Pakula
Publishing services associate managing editor: Madison Salters
Assistant production manager: Emi Lotto, Angela Zurlo